WILD RICE
and the
OJIBWAY PEOPLE

The author tries his wild rice knocking technique with Mary McGeshick's ricing sticks as Mary and her husband, George, look on, at the McGeshick's rice camp on the Michigan/Wisconsin border, September 1986.

WILD RICE
and the
OJIBWAY PEOPLE

THOMAS VENNUM, JR.

MINNESOTA HISTORICAL SOCIETY PRESS
ST. PAUL • 1988

MINNESOTA HISTORICAL SOCIETY PRESS
ST. PAUL 55101

Manufactured in the United States of America

10 9 8 7 6 5 4 3 2 1

International Standard Book Number
0-87351-225-1 Cloth
0-87351-226-X Paper

**Library of Congress
Cataloging-in-Publication Data**

Vennum, Thomas.
Wild rice and the Ojibway people / Thomas Vennum, Jr.
p. cm.
Bibliography: p.
Includes index.
ISBN 0-87351-225-1. ISBN 0-87351-226-X (pbk.)
1. Chippewa Indians—Food. 2. Chippewa Indians—Ethnobotany. 3. Indians of North America—Lake States—Food. 4. Indians of North America—Lake States—Ethnobotany. 5. Wild rice—Lake States. I. Title.
E99.C6V46 1988 87-38333
306′.34—dc19 CIP

Contents

Preface

IN 1964 on Lake Totogatic northwest of Seeley, Wisconsin, I first harvested wild rice with Fred Morgan, a Minneapolis photographer who had moved to Hayward, Wisconsin, and begun to document the culture of nearby Lac Court Oreilles Reservation. The events of that day are still vivid. Having purchased ricing licenses for one dollar each, we embarked in Fred's canoe about midmorning. Other ricers on the lake—all of them local Ojibway like Frances Mike (see cover)—had long since started harvesting. I felt a certain embarrassment at our late intrusion; inept at working the rice sticks to knock the grain into our boat, I sat back to take in the sights and sounds. The crisp early autumn day, with clear, deep blue sky and sugar maples beginning to turn color, was reflected from the lake. With children back at school and summer residents and tourists gone, a certain quiet had settled. There was little talk on the lake. The only perceptible sounds were the quiet rustle of rice falling into canoes and the occasional honk of wild geese flying south.

As a child I had spent summers on Madeline Island in Lake Superior, and I had played pool and roller-skated in Bayfield, Wisconsin, with friends from Red Cliff Reservation, but this was my first experience with a traditional Ojibway activity. That day's wild rice harvest piqued my general curiosity about Indian culture, ultimately leading me to pursue the riches of American Indian tribal music, my principal field of study.

I also became interested in wild rice—its rich history, its significant role in Ojibway life, and the problems Indian people have faced in maintaining this resource. A native Minnesotan, I was familiar with the grain. Served as an occasional luxury at the family dinner table, it was represented as a treat, replacing potatoes on special occasions. Before that day on Lake Totogatic I knew nothing of wild rice culture. Little did I suspect that years later my companion Fred Morgan's sensitive photographic work would illustrate my own text.

My search for information led to no major studies before the beginnings of the twentieth century. With the end of intertribal warfare at the close of the nineteenth century, however, interest in American Indian culture intensified, as many thought that it would become extinct. Much of the work of the Smithsonian Institution's Bureau of American Ethnology was initiated to rescue Indian culture from oblivion. As a result of the bureau's documentation effort, the first major study of wild rice appeared in print. Albert E. Jenks's classic study, "The Wild Rice Gatherers of the Upper Lakes," was published in the *Nineteenth Annual Report of the Bureau of American Ethnology* (1900). In his model research project the gifted young scholar approached a topic unknown except to those living near lakes and rivers where wild rice grows.

Nearly a century has passed since Jenks's work. Wild rice, although still a luxury for the non-Indian epicure, is increasingly a commercial enterprise. Yet few outside Indian culture appreciate its place in native American tradition or understand the complexity of the growth, harvest, and processing of the crop. The only substantial contribution to the literature has been anthropologist Eva Lips's *Die Reisernte der Ojibwa-Indianer,* based on field work conducted with her husband, Julius, on Nett Lake Reservation in Minnesota in the summer and fall of 1947. Nearly all ethnologies on the Ojibway and other (mostly) Algonquian peoples mention wild rice to some extent, but its role in Indian culture has received minimal attention.

In any case, the Jenks and Lips publications are generally inaccessible, and both need updating. *Die Reisernte* has never been translated, is little known, and out of print. The study is missing, for instance, from the bibliography of the *Northeast* volume of the *Handbook of North American Indians* (1978), and Kathren J. Borgelt's Mankato State College thesis, "Wild Rice in the Cultural Landscape of Nett Lake Indian Reservation" (1970), makes no reference to it. Ruth Landes, in her 1957 review in the *American Anthropologist* (59: 1098), correctly criticized most of Lips's book as "a stale re-hash" of standard works in Ojibway ethnology. (The frequency with which I cite the field work portion of *Die Reisernte* makes it apparent my reservations are not so strong as Landes's.) Jenks's essay can be found, for the most part, only in libraries that have systematically collected the early publications of the now-defunct Bureau of American Ethnology. Jenks's primary sources are almost exclusively non-Indian, and Lips focused on only one of the many Ojibway bands who traditionally harvested wild rice.

This study compiles and synthesizes research on wild rice to date for those interested in Ojibway culture generally, for students of ethnobotany, ethnohistory, and Indian-white relations—and for those who have tasted wild rice and are curious to know more about it. I draw heavily but selectively on Jenks and Lips as well as their sources. Readers will not find here the nutritional tables and Indian population statistics that fill many of Jenks's pages. Neither does this study include the larger part of Lips's book clearly intended for Europeans—the long rehearsal of Minnesota history, fauna, and flora, for example. Since Lips's and Jenks's works, valuable manuscript material has surfaced, adding to the data. Even more important are the recent verbal recollections of traditional Ojibway elders, providing a long-needed Indian perspective. Elements of my eighteen years of field research have been integrated with material from these and other sources.

This book retains words such as *savages* and *squaw,* used in the source material. Although offensive to Indian people today, these words did not always have their present connotations. Where clearly derogatory, they comment on the social attitudes of the period; to delete them would be a disservice to historical accuracy. Also retained is much of the colloquial English spoken by the Ojibway in their oral histories and interviews. English was not their native tongue. It was imposed on some in boarding schools; many others learned "bad grammar" as much from working alongside immigrants in lumbercamps as from other rural Americans. The English some Ojibway speak is thus a variant of what might be considered standard English. In citing oral interview material, I have edited only judiciously, to clarify meaning or to remove redundancies and pauses. For ease in reading, typographic peculiarities of old sources, particularly the letter *s,* have been converted to modern style. The translations from Lips's German are my own; occasionally they have been edited, and the reader may wish to consult the original text.

In studying the culture of wild rice, I found myself investigating topics outside the normal purview of an ethnomusicologist. I enlisted friends to review my text and to suggest improvements and additional sources for investigation. In particular I thank James E. Meeker for his help with botanical questions; Barre Toelken and Christopher Vecsey for insights regarding the interpretation of Ojibway legend; Robert E. Bieder, Peter J. Hedberg, and Kathryn L. Tierney for assistance with legal questions and treaty rights; Forrest G. English for his experience with the economy of wild rice; Ives Goddard for linguistic help; John D. Nichols and Earl Nyholm for Ojibway spellings; Rayna Green for consideration of my final chapter; Edward Brown for research assistance; and Catherine S. Fowler and Nancy O. Lurie for general assistance. I owe special thanks to Tim E. Holzkamm, who made accessible to me much of his fine work in the study of Ojibway subsistence history and scrutinized the manuscript with his fine eye for detail, and to Ellen B. Green and Anne R. Kaplan for patient editorial assistance. My deepest gratitude goes to the many Ojibway who provided technical information and reminiscences of a time when rice camps presented an important social occasion. Particularly helpful were William Bineshi Baker, Sr., Mary and George McGeshick, Lawrence Mitchell, James Mustache, Sr., and Earl Nyholm.

THOMAS VENNUM, JR.

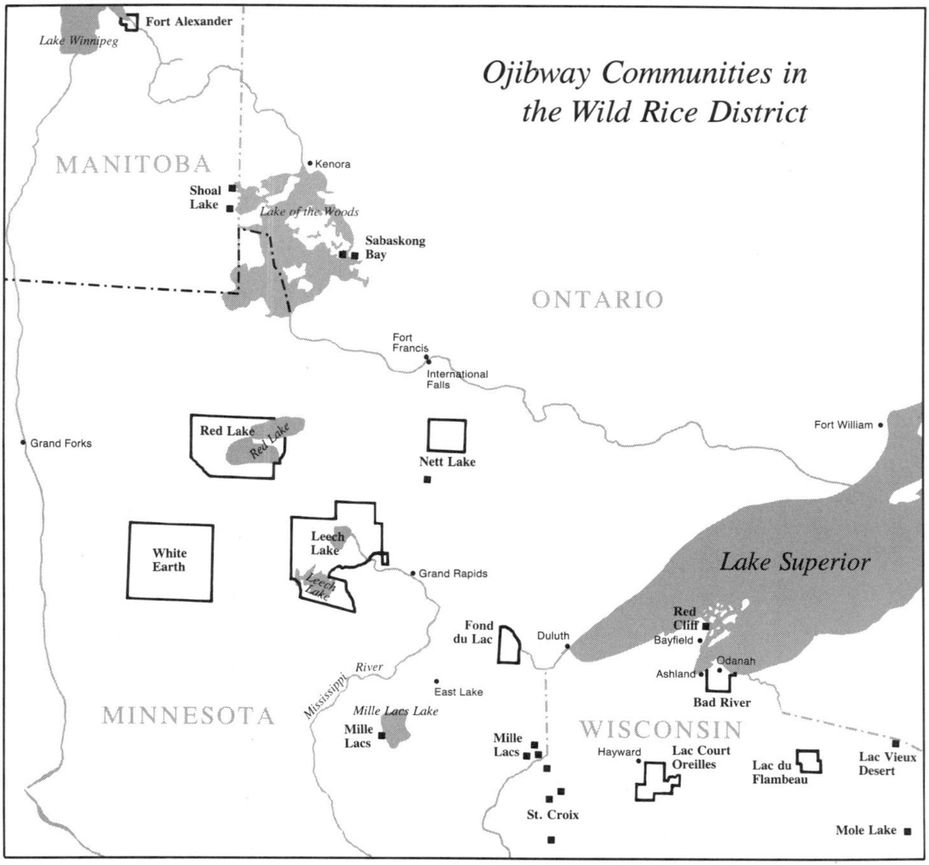

Ojibway Communities in the Wild Rice District
Fort Alexander
Lake Winnipeg
MANITOBA
Kenora
Shoal Lake
Lake of the Woods
Sabaskong Bay
ONTARIO
Fort Francis
International Falls
Fort William
Grand Forks
Red Lake
Red Lake
Nett Lake
White Earth
Leech Lake
Leech Lake
Grand Rapids
Lake Superior
Red Cliff
Bayfield
Fond du Lac
Duluth
Odanah
Ashland
Bad River
Mississippi River
East Lake
MINNESOTA
Mille Lacs Lake
Mille Lacs
Mille Lacs
WISCONSIN
Hayward
Lac Court Oreilles
Lac du Flambeau
Lac Vieux Desert
St. Croix
Mole Lake

Introduction

THE OJIBWAY (Ojibwa, Ojibwe, Chippewa) Indians, now living mostly on reservations in the upper midwestern United States and central Canada, face a social and economic dilemma. Wild rice, one of their most important natural resources, is no longer as accessible to them as it once was. The close of the fur trade, the surrender of large areas of the wild rice range in treaty cessions, and the confinement of Indian people on reservations have severely curtailed aboriginal subsistence patterns. At the same time, the dominant Euro-American society has imposed laws usurping traditional Indian control of the harvest of wild rice.

Of greater consequence is that wild rice plays a diminishing role in the Indian economy. Previously, the Ojibway counted on modest sales of wild rice to supplement their incomes. Because of destitution, however, the care and pride once taken in harvesting and processing wild rice have in many places given way to expedient shortcuts. The profit motive has led some individuals to ignore the ecological attention the Ojibway community traditionally accorded its rice fields. Yet competitive efforts have been in vain, for whites have learned to domesticate wild rice and mechanize its processing, and the product has become a marketable commodity. Ironically, the rapidly developing industry is almost totally out of Indian hands. Wild rice has even been appropriated as a symbol by the state of Minnesota, which proudly proclaims wild rice its official grain.

Wild rice, called *manoomin* in the Ojibway language,[1] once played a central role in tribal life. It was endowed with spiritual attributes, and its discovery was recounted in legends. It was used ceremonially as well as for food, and its harvest promoted social interaction in late summer each year. Consequently, many Ojibway view the commercial exploitation of this resource by non-Indians as an ultimate desecration. For greater understanding of their position, let us review the traditional place of wild rice in Indian culture and the changes in harvest technology and Indian attitude since wild rice has become a commodity.

Although the Ojibway have been the principal harvesters of wild rice for nearly three centuries, the food played a minimal role in their culture before contact with Europeans. In the mid-seventeenth century, the Ojibway lived in small dispersed bands at the east end of Lake Superior, mostly outside the natural range of wild rice. They would have known of wild rice only through trade with Indians to the west and south. According to early French sources, individual Ojibway bands were designated by totems or clans, a social system that survived relatively intact into the twentieth century. They spoke mutually intelligible dialects of an Algonquian language, today most closely related to Cree, Potawatomi, and Ottawa. Living on both sides of the outlet of Lake Superior, the bands, drawn by the great seasonal concentration of whitefish as well as opportunities for social interaction and religious ceremonies, congregated each summer at the great rapids of the St. Marys River.

The Ojibway found themselves in the position of middlemen in the fur trade with Europeans. They began to migrate along both shores of Lake Superior, acting as guides, interpreters, and trading partners with the French. Wherever the French established fur trading posts, the Ojibway concentrated their numbers enough to facilitate trade. In their westward movement they drove out other peoples—the Huron, Sauk, Fox, and, most important, the Dakota (Sioux)—in small skirmishes occurring well into the nineteenth century. Once established on the shores of Lake Superior, the Ojibway began to move inland, into northern Wisconsin and westward into northern Minnesota—directly into the wild rice habitat, where they established principal villages by the mid-eighteenth century. Following the Treaty of Utrecht (1713), the value of beaver fur escalated, stimulating further European expansion. For this reason, the Ojibway are today widely scattered over the area surrounding the western Great Lakes into Canada, with small populations as far west as North Dakota and Montana. They are mostly settled on reservations established in the nineteenth century to contain them and bring an end to intertribal warfare, thus to secure the area for white settlers in ceded territories.

With geographic dispersal, regional variations in Ojibway culture emerged, making it possible to speak of an Ojibway language, religion, economy, or political structure only in the broadest sense. Distinctly different patterns of living reflected Ojibway adaptation to the biophysical nature of the specific areas occupied. Generally speaking, those in the boreal forests north of Lake Superior were hunters and trappers; those in the coniferous-deciduous forests along the southern and western edges of the lake depended to a greater extent on fishing; those farther inland, principally the southwestern Ojibway, were wild rice gatherers. This generalization does not imply that varying subsistence patterns were exclusive of each other. For instance, all Ojibway fished to some extent, but fish played a greater role in areas where the resource was most plentiful. Furthermore, as ethnohistorian Leo G. Waisberg has argued, all these people practiced "switching," that is, short-term reliance on alternate food sources when others failed: "Peaks and troughs in animal population cycles, vegetational successions, high and low water levels, temperature and precipitation variations, either periodic or random: all affected the relative abundance of particular resources." Waisberg also stressed the social factors that aided in survival; through kinship ties and marriages, "initial matrilocality or extended 'visiting' accomplished the same objectives as 'switching.' "[2]

The southwestern Ojibway, who counted most on wild rice, practiced a diversified economy, moving seasonally to the locus of particular resources (fig. 1). Even after they settled on reservations, they remained seminomadic. Anthropologist Robert E. Ritzenthaler's field notes from Lac Court Oreilles Reservation, Wisconsin, in the early 1940s include a reconstruction by his informants of their traditional economic cycle, providing a good picture of the subsistence practice of Ojibway living in the wild rice habitat. From about November through February the Ojibway families tracked deer in their hunting grounds, often moving well south from Lac Court Oreilles, sometimes as far as the Eau Claire area. They supplemented their winter venison diet by trapping small animals and spearing fish through holes in the ice of lakes in central Wisconsin. During this time, they dried surplus venison and packed it into containers for early spring sustenance in the sugarbush. In March they moved north to Lake Chetac to tap maple trees for sugar; there they stayed until the end of April. In mid-April began the run of suckers, a freshwater relative of carp, which the Indians caught in traps they had made during the sugar harvest. At the end of April, fish were filleted, tied in bales, and taken north to the summer camps with the sugar. Some food already awaited the Indians' arrival at their Lac Court Oreilles summer village base—the caches—mostly potatoes and corn they had hidden the previous summer in holes lined with blue sweet grass or bark. During early summer (May, June), they planted corn, potatoes, and squash, and continued their trapping and spearing. Beginning in July, they stripped birch bark for canoes, wigwams, and containers, and gathered and dried ripe berries.[3]

In August the Lac Court Oreilles Ojibway moved to their rice camps for the harvest. These camps also had food caches. While waiting for the rice to ripen, the Indians continued to fish and trap. If they ran out of meat in the rice camps, they trapped muskrats and used the skins for moccasins and leggings. They also hunted ducks and dried that meat to store or carry when, in late October, they moved south to begin the cycle anew.

This, then, was the yearly subsistence pattern of the seminomadic people whose principal resource is the focus of this study. Wild rice was their staple, accompanying all other foods they ate. In lean times it was often the only item

Fig. 1. *Generalized Annual Work Cycle of the Southwestern Ojibway*
adapted from Leo G. Waisberg, "Ethnographic and Historical Outline," 130

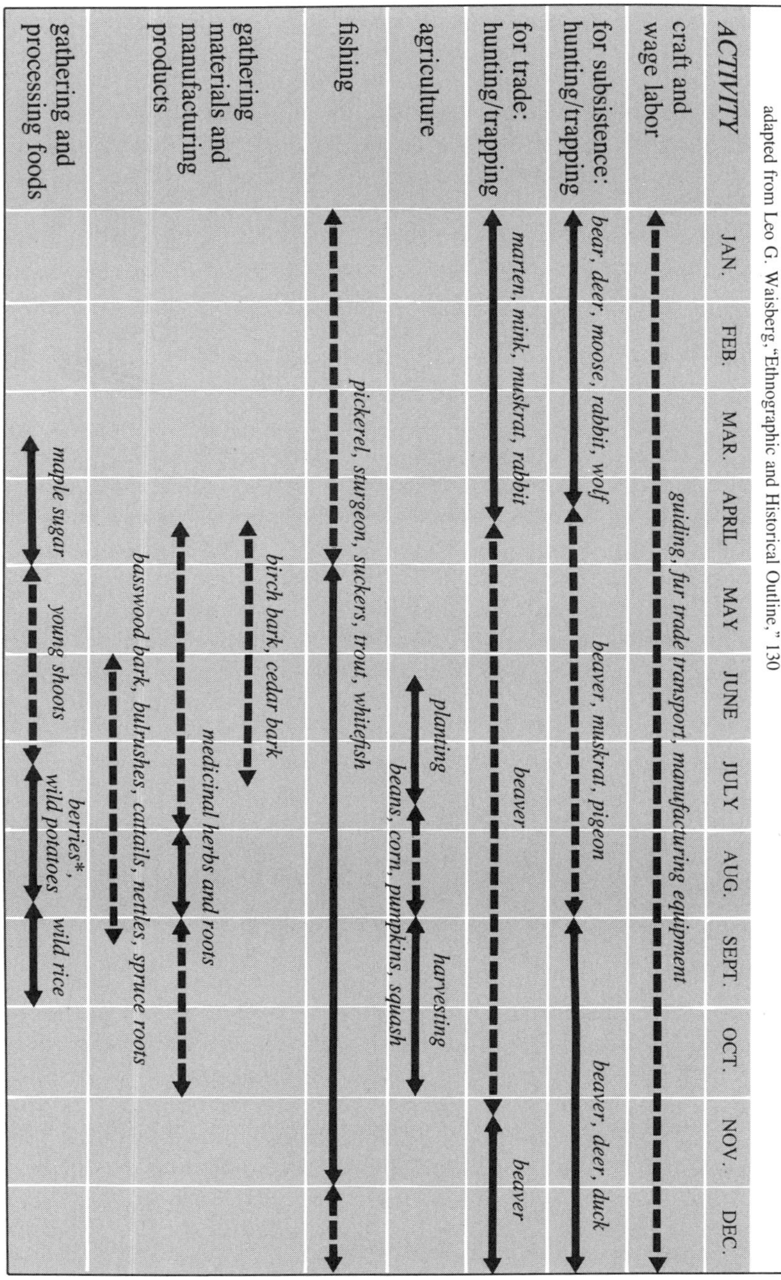

ACTIVITY
JAN.
FEB.
MAR.
APRIL
MAY
JUNE
JULY
AUG.
SEPT.
OCT.
NOV.
DEC.
craft and wage labor
guiding, fur trade transport, manufacturing equipment
for subsistence: hunting/trapping
bear, deer, moose, rabbit, wolf
beaver, muskrat, pigeon
beaver, deer, duck
for trade: hunting/trapping
marten, mink, muskrat, rabbit
beaver
beaver
agriculture
planting
harvesting
beans, corn, pumpkins, squash
fishing
pickerel, sturgeon, suckers, trout, whitefish
gathering materials and manufacturing products
birch bark, cedar bark
medicinal herbs and roots
basswood bark, bulrushes, cattails, nettles, spruce roots
gathering and processing foods
maple sugar
young shoots
berries*, wild potatoes
wild rice

▬▬ Intensive activity

▪▪▪▪ Occasional/intermittent activity

*wild strawberries, pincherries, raspberries, chokecherries, blueberries, gooseberries, cranberries

Note: Because seasons could vary by as much as a month across the lands of the Southwestern Ojibway, items on each line are arrayed in alphabetical order.

they had. Wild rice was also one resource that induced the Ojibway to move west and south of Lake Superior; the rice lakes were areas they were willing to fight to retain.

The Ojibway were neither the only ones nor the first to harvest this valuable crop, however; before Ojibway occupation of the wild rice range, its principal harvesters were Siouan and non-Ojibway Algonquian peoples. Each of these groups had a diversified economy and therefore depended upon wild rice for food and trade to differing degrees. François de Crépieul in his 1672 report on La Baye des Puans (now Green Bay) told of Indians dependent upon wild rice but upon fish and wildfowl as well: "[P]erceiving that Ducks, Teal, and other birds of that kind dive into the water in quest of the grains of wild oats [rice] to be found there toward the Autumn season, they stretch nets for them with such skill that, without counting the fish, they sometimes catch in one night as many as a hundred wild fowl." Such early sources are not always specific about the tribal peoples they describe. And Green Bay, like other protected areas on the Great Lakes abounding in food supplies, was an important trading center for many tribes before European contact. The people de Crépieul observed may have been Winnebago (Siouan speakers who adopted many aspects of Woodlands culture), but they could just as well have been Fox, Potawatomi, or Menominee – all Algonquian peoples.[4]

Many Indian bands in North America were known in native tongues by their principal economic activity (the fish-eaters) or location (those who inhabit the thick forest). Before the Ojibway, the Menominee at Green Bay were probably the most intensive wild rice harvesters, and they were called "wild rice people" (*manoominiig*) by the Ojibway and most other tribes as well as by the French. The Menominee, however, were not the only ones to harvest rice. The pervasiveness of words for wild rice among Algonquian groups, including those along the eastern seaboard, suggests that many of them knew some species of this food.[5]

The origin and exact meaning of the Ojibway name for wild rice, *manoomin,* is uncertain at best. The popular interpretation of the word as "good berry" or "good seed" may reflect the deeper meaning of wild rice in Indian culture or recognize its nutritional properties, but linguistic evidence does not support this folk etymology. Many, like Jenks, have interpreted the word *manoomin* to be a compound of *mano-,* identified as the element *mino-* (or *minw-*), meaning "good, right, well" – the opposite of *maazhi-,* or "bad, evil" – and *-min,* an element with reference to berries, seeds, nuts, grain, and the like. The problem linguistically is not with the final syllable; indeed, *-min* is the suffix for a large variety of botanical names in Ojibway. *Mano-* simply cannot be equated with *mino-,* since the vowel difference is unexplained and, according to linguists, unmotivated. Furthermore, in at least one Algonquian language,

Mesquakie, it is impossible to make nouns out of the equivalent of *mino-* (or *minw-*), and in the cognate Cree word for wild rice, *anoomin* or *athoomin,* the *m* is lacking altogether, though it is present in the Cree element for good, *minw-* (or *mithw-*).[6]

The word is probably a very old one, with cognates in many languages of the Algonquian family. Linguist Frank Siebert, Jr., has reconstructed a proto-Algonquian word, *maθo·mina,* meaning "perhaps originally 'any stiff grass bearing edible grain.' " Siebert found a cognate for *manoomin* in Powhatan, the language spoken in the area of colonial Jamestown at the beginning of the seventeenth century. Captain John Smith wrote about a grain similar to the species familiar to the Ojibway: "Mattoume groweth as our bents do in meddows. The seede is not much unlike to rie, though much smaller. this they use for a dainty bread buttered with deare suet."[7] (Similarly, in the Great Lakes region the French likened wild rice to rye, and the Ojibway pulverized wild rice to make a sort of bread and customarily flavored rice with animal fat.)

Other Algonquian variants given by Siebert are Penobscot *malóminal,* meaning "lyme grass," and Abenaki *mar8men,* which, in the Jesuit Joseph Aubery's manuscript Abenaki-French dictionary (1715), is *avoine sauvage,* meaning wild oats. The first mention of an Algonquian term for wild rice in the *Jesuit Relations and Allied Documents* series is a cognate describing the ancestors of today's Menominee. Gabriel Dreuillettes in 1658 listed the "Names of Many Recently-Discovered Nations" in the region explored by Pierre Esprit, sieur de Radisson, and Médard Chouart, sieur de Groseilliers: "The second Nation is composed of the Noukek, Ouinipegouek, and Malouminek. . . . They reap, without sowing it, a kind of rye which grows wild in their meadows, and is considered superior to Indian corn." Radisson confirmed the name in a manuscript written in English, presumably for Charles II, whose patronage the explorer sought. During his fourth voyage (around 1661), Radisson encountered "an ancient witty man" living with his large family in a "cottage. . . . They weare of a nation called Malhonmines; that is, the nation of Oats, graine y^t is much in y^t countrey."[8]

English-speaking explorers by the early nineteenth century called the grain "wild rice" or "Indian rice" because its aquatic habitat suggested a relationship to the Asiatic white rice with which they were more familiar. The first Europeans in the area, the French, were struck more with its resemblance to tares, the troublesome weed mentioned in the Bible and a bane to French wheat farmers, who called it "folle avoine" (literally, fool oats or wild oats). Throughout the *Jesuit Relations* wild rice is referred to as oats or rye; as late as 1900 some Canadians still called it "la folle avoine." Various other designations included "riz sauvage," "riz Canadien," "water oats," and "water rice."

Eventually, as the French lost the territory to English speakers, the term wild rice predominated.[9]

Many Indian settlements and bands in wild rice country had names derived from the edible grass seed, and many American towns, rivers, and lakes also bore these designations in English, even after the plant disappeared from their locales. The Dakota equivalent of the Ojibway *manoomin* is *psin;* in 1700 Pierre Charles Le Sueur mentioned the eastern Siouan *Psinoumaniton* (village of wild rice harvesters) and in the west *Psinchaton* (village of red wild rice). Jean Baptiste Franquelin's 1699 map of New France shows the latter on the east bank of the Mississippi at its confluence with another river; to the south is the village *Psinoünaton* on the shore of a lake, represented as the headwaters of a river flowing into the Mississippi (see Chapter 1, fig. 5). Ojibway historian William W. Warren subdivided Ojibway groups according to the sections of land they occupied, indicating that they were named for either their principal vocations or their principal foods. Those along the shores of Lake Superior were called "Men of the Great Water"; the people inland were "Those who sit on the borders." The latter group included the Mun-o-min-ik-a-sheenh-ug (Rice makers) living on the wild rice lakes of the St. Croix River area.[10]

Father Louis André in 1673 called what is now the Menominee River the "Folle Avoine," and Johann G. Kohl, the German cartographer, wrote in 1860 that French-Canadians used that name for the interior land south of Lake Superior, saying, for example, "Je veux hiverner à la folle avoine" (I want to winter at the wild oats). Zebulon M. Pike recounted meeting two Indians on November 27, 1805, "who informed me they were two men of a band who resided on Lake Superior, called the Fols Avoins, but spoke the language of the Chipeway." Possibly they were Menominee, but they may have represented any band of Algonquian speakers, including Potawatomi, who were also rice harvesters. Many non-Ojibway spoke the Ojibway language, which had become the Indian *lingua franca* of the fur trade. On December 6 Pike used "Fols Avoins" and "Chipeways" interchangeably.[11]

The Ojibway did not harvest wild rice until they moved westward. The southwestern Ojibway moved inland from the south shore of Lake Superior. Equipped with weapons obtained from the French, they forced the Fox, who joined forces with the Sauk, from the wild rice district. The northern Ojibway, called Saulteaux (for the rapids on the St. Marys River), settled in the Rainy Lake region. They integrated more peacefully with Algonquian-speaking peoples such as the Cree, already in the region. Father Claude Jean Allouez's journal (1666–67) described a hunting people called the "Kilistinouc" (Cree): "They are much more nomadic than any of the other nations, having no fixed abode, no fields, no villages; and living wholly on game and a small quantity of oats which they gather in marshy places." When Alexander Henry (the elder) visited the Cree they greeted him with "the usual presents of wild rice and dried meat, and accompanied them with the usual formalities."[12]

Although the French reached Lake Nipigon in 1660 and the upper Mississippi headwaters area sometime between 1672 and 1680, the expedition of Christophe Dufrost de la Jémeraye in 1731 provided the first documentation of contact with Rainy River Indians. Shortly thereafter the explorer Pierre Gaultier de Varennes, sieur de la Vérendrye, observed that Ojibway speakers from the east occupied the area around Lake Superior. Inland on the Rainy River and Lake of the Woods were the Monsoni, Sturgeon Cree, and Cree. The Assiniboin Indians may have shared the area with them or operated there only as trading partners. A mid-eighteenth-century French manuscript enumerates peoples living along the boundary area: from Grand Portage to Lake Saganaga were the "Bear Grease" Indians, from Saganaga to Fort St. Pierre were three bands of Monsoni, and on Lake of the Woods were the people of Sturgeon Bay. The manuscript noted that all were Saulteaux speakers (northern Ojibway) and that north and northwest of Lake of the Woods were Indians speaking some variety of Cree. While the Ojibway seem to have mixed peaceably with these people, skirmishes (often over access to lakes and rivers bearing wild rice) with the eastern Dakota continued until the late nineteenth century.[13]

For the eastern Dakota wild rice was a staple. Around 1661 Pierre Radisson visited the "Nation of the beefe" (buffalo), clearly the Dakota, and was happy to receive provisions including wild rice: "Those men each had 2 wives, loadened of Oats, corne that grows in that countrey, of a small quantity of Indian Corne, wth other grains, & it was to present to us, wch we received as a great favour & token of friendshippe." Allouez wrote in his journal of the "Nadouesiouek," an Ojibway name for Dakota, specifically noting their talents in cooking wild rice: "They cultivate fields, sowing therein not Indian corn, but only tobacco; while Providence has furnished them a kind of marsh rye which they go and harvest toward the close of Summer in certain small Lakes that are covered with it. So well do they know how to prepare it that it is highly appetizing and very nutritious." Father Jacques Marquette about 1670 contrasted the Dakota with the Algonquian and Huron peoples: "[T]hey chiefly adore the Calumet, and say not a word at their feasts. . . . They have the wild oats, use little Canoes, and keep their word inviolate."[14]

Reports of Dakota dependence on wild rice continued into the eighteenth and nineteenth centuries. In the late 1760s Jonathan Carver wrote that they had no bread but used wild rice as a substitute; Zebulon Pike, during his exploration in 1805, was invited to a feast of wild rice and venison by Chief Wabasha, and two weeks later the explorer found Little Crow's village deserted, "all the Indians having gone out to the lands to gather fols avoin." George Catlin in the

1830s sketched a Dakota rice harvest and described how the women gathered the crop, using eleven canoes they had purchased from the Ojibway; in the illustration, one boat carries ricers and two duck hunters with guns. Henry Rowe Schoolcraft in the mid-nineteenth century reported three large divisions of Mdewakanton Dakota living in villages on both sides of the St. Peter's (now the Minnesota) River six miles from its mouth; nearby was a large, flat expanse of marshes where the people of the three villages riced in the autumn. Albert Jenks, basing his figures partly on place names incorporating the syllable *psin,* estimated that five thousand to seven thousand Dakota were rice harvesters when the Ojibway controlled the area east of the Mississippi.[15]

Much strife between the Ojibway and Dakota was over hunting territory, particularly the habitat of the Virginia deer, but the zone also included much of the wild rice range. Access to wild rice stands was important; as the product became an exchange commodity in the fur trade, both Ojibway and Dakota entered into production beyond their own needs. On Carver's various maps, for instance, the area between the Red Cedar and Chippewa rivers is marked: "This is call'd the Road of War between the Chipeways and Naudowessie" (fig. 2). Repeatedly, the Ojibway and Dakota risked attack by continuing to collect rice near each other—especially dangerous because each side knew well the locations of the wild rice stands. Pike wrote to a General Wilkinson from the St. Peter's River on September 23, 1805, that the nearby Dakota had just collected their ricers to march against the Ojibway in retaliation for recent attacks. Warren told of the four-acre island in Prairie Rice Lake (now Red Cedar Lake in Barron County, Wisconsin), where Ojibway ricers camped to secure themselves against nearby Dakota villages. Jenks wrote of the Chippewa and Red Cedar rivers: "Almost every bend . . . has been the scene of an Indian battle, and each of these streams has borne a name synonymous with 'Wild-rice river.' " Echoing Warren, he wrote of those "most fearless of the Ojibwa" ricing each year at Red Cedar Lake "notwithstanding that they lost lives from the sudden attacks of the Dakota almost yearly." John P. Williamson, a missionary among the Dakota, wrote Jenks that the Indians formerly carried the freshly harvested rice home with them in sacks. Jenks surmised, probably correctly, that it was simply too risky for them to remain long enough to process the rice at the lakeside.[16]

The St. Croix area was particularly unsettled. Eliza Morrison, an Ojibway mixed-blood, had been told of the danger in the contested area where her grandmother had lived: "The St. Croix river was well supplied with game, fish, ducks, and rice, and they fought for that country." For this reason her grandmother rarely went downriver. Instead, she once took her children upstream as far as the mouth of the Brule River to escape the Dakota. In August 1830, Medicine Bottle led eighteen Dakota against the Ojibway at the very

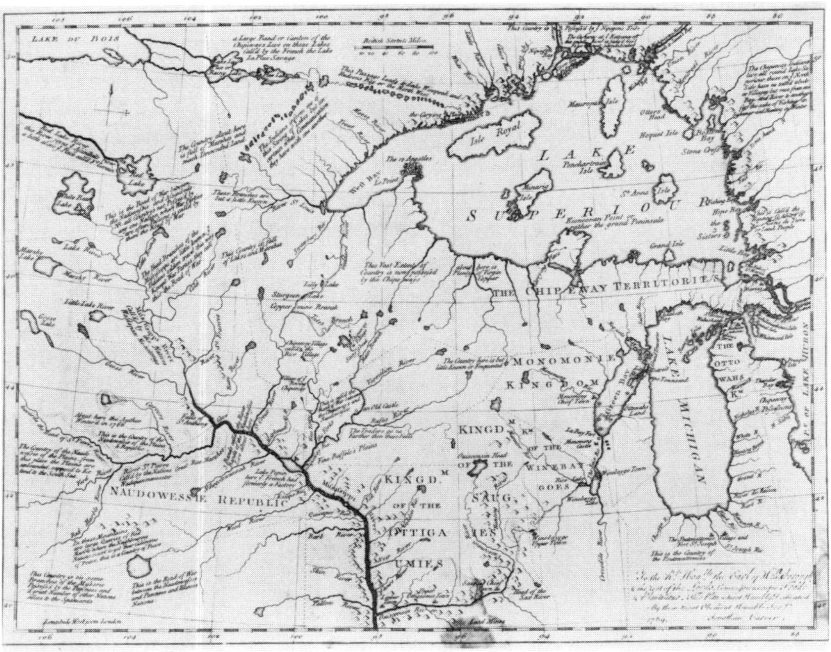

*Fig. 2. Jonathan Carver's 1769 map encompassing most of the wild rice district and showing the general location (*counterclockwise*) of the Chipeway (Ojibway), Assiniboils (Assiniboin), Naudowessie (Dakota), Ottigaumies (Fox), Saugies (Sac), Wineybagoes (Winnebago), Monomonie (Menominee), and Ottowahs (Ottawa). All of these people, to varying degrees, harvested or at least traded for rice.*

time that Little Crow was negotiating a treaty at Prairie du Chien. A month later Little Crow's people experienced a rice failure, but they were afraid to go very far up the St. Croix to rice elsewhere. Five years later Indian agent Lawrence Taliaferro found the Dakota starving on the river because their rice beds had been unproductive.[17]

After intertribal warfare in the rice district drew to a close, Ojibway people continued ricing as they had for more than two centuries. The last fifty years have seen enormous changes not only in the technology of wild rice harvest but also in its traditional role in Indian life. Furthermore, the economics of wild rice harvesting has changed drastically with the advent of paddy-grown rice and the mechanical means of harvesting and processing it. Such changes portend political consequences as well. Current review of Indian treaty rights raises the potential for litigation regarding control of the crop and its harvest. John W. Powell's 1900 prediction, that "Should this natural product come into the general use to which it seems adapted, it will add another to the many debts of Caucasian to Indian," is being rapidly fulfilled.[18]

CHAPTER 1

The Plant

The wild oat, whose name they bear because it is found in their country, is a sort of grass, which grows naturally in the small Rivers with muddy bottoms, and in Swampy Places. It greatly resembles the wild oats that Grow amid our wheat. The ears grow upon hollow stems, jointed at Intervals; they emerge from the Water about the month of June, and continue growing until they rise About two feet above it. The grain is not larger than That of our oats, but it is twice as long, and The meal therefrom is much more abundant. The Savages Gather and prepare it for food. . . . In The month of September.

—Father Jacques Marquette, May 7, 1673[1]

CLASSIFICATION

WILD RICE, technically not a rice and since the era of paddy production mostly not wild, is the only cereal native to North America with well-documented food uses. Unlike wheat, oats, barley, and other Old World cereals, wild rice has not been improved scientifically by selection and breeding for commercial production until recent times. The plant that grows in natural stands of North America today is essentially the same one first encountered by Europeans.

Wild rice is a grass belonging to the family Gramineae, the genus *Zizania,* and the species *aquatica* (or *palustris*). One can easily distinguish *Zizania aquatica* from *Oryza sativa,* or common white rice, the Asian staple. Although both are distantly related rice grasses, the latter is a cultivated species, planted by hand for thousands of years. Still, some wild forms of *Oryza* exist; for food and trade South American Indians have harvested it, like wild rice, by beating its ripe kernels into boats. The presence of wild rice in Asia, however, and the fact that carp on both continents feed on the plant have led to speculation about Asian origins for wild rice.[2]

Species of wild rice other than *Zizania aquatica* have been found in the New World, and there has been some confusion about them in the past. *Zizania texana* is an endangered species growing in Texas. *Zizaniopsis miliacea,* an American grass sometimes called "prolific rice," was common in the brackish waters of the South and reportedly grew in shallow water in Ohio and Wisconsin as well as in the bayous, ditches, and swamps of Louisiana. The botanical distinctions of these species is in the location of male and female flowers on the fruit head: on all *Zizania* species the female flowers tightly surround the top of the one-to-two-foot panicle, while its male flowers are found separately on lower branches; on *miliacea,* the two genders intermix on the fruit head.[3]

Early European explorers, having never seen wild rice, likened it almost immediately to the pesky Old World weed *Lolium temulentum,* commonly called "fool's oats." In the Bible, Matthew (13:25–30) called this injurious plant "tares." In wet years, wheat kernels will not sprout, but *Lolium* will, making it a nuisance. The botanist Linnaeus (Carl von Linné) in 1753, with a dried specimen of wild rice from Virginia as well as data from colleagues abroad, was able to discern what the plant had in common with *Lolium:* both were wild grasses whose seeds could remain dormant for long periods without losing their germinating capacity, and both needed water. Linnaeus chose the Biblical (Greek) plural *zizania* for wild rice, adding its Latin species name *aquatica* to distinguish it as a plant growing in water (though rooted in soil).[4]

The root system of wild rice initially depends on the developing seed (caryopsis) for anchorage in alluvial mud deposits in lakes and rivers. Because of this, the absence of wild rice in Europe has been attributed to the sand and lime composition of the continent's waterbeds. The plant can neither anchor itself in sand nor derive nourishment from sand alone, and lime is simply too dense for its roots. Once established, the old root systems in a wild rice bed become extremely thick and interwoven enough to support the weight of someone walking upon them. If gas forms underneath, large sections of the root mass may dislodge and float to the surface, without apparent harm to the plant.[5]

Genetic differences in wild rice plants combine with environmental variables such as light, water levels, and the makeup of the water and alluvial soil to account for differences in yield and the size and quality of kernels from one wild rice stand to the next. Plant taxonomists recognize two strains of wild rice: the tall, wide-leafed *Z. aquatica aquatica,* which tends to flourish in the southern and western parts of the wild rice range and produces thin, pointed seeds averaging two centimeters in length, and its relative, *Z. aquatica an-*

gustifolia of the northern areas, with narrower leaves and shorter, thicker kernels. There are intermediate strains, and both the northern and southern varieties may be found in the same bed. For example, Lips observed that the kernels of Nett Lake (northern) wild rice sometimes reached the length of those of southern rice. *Z. angustifolia* is more common in water with a total alkalinity of fewer than fifty parts per million (ppm), and *aquatica* prefers the harder water of the southern areas.[6]

Water quality is also a factor in growth. Wild rice is dependent on the circulation of mineral-rich water and does not tolerate chemical pollutants. Tests in Minnesota have shown the plant grows within the alkalinity range found in the state (5–250 ppm), but that it is adversely affected by sulfates and will not grow at all in water with a sulfate content of 50 ppm. It grows best in carbonate waters with a total alkalinity exceeding 40 ppm.[7]

GERMINATION AND GROWTH

Wild rice stalks remaining from the previous season die down below the water surface, and new growth appears to be generated in the same spot, thus the mistaken impression that a perennial root is the source of each year's plant. An annual, wild rice requires reseeding each year. The seed is heavy and, lacking natural buoyancy, it sinks immediately, heavy end down, settling on the bottom near its parent plant. (For this reason, wild rice spreads very slowly; the enlargement of a bed is gradual and downstream from its point of origin.) Its barbed awn anchors the seed firmly in the soft, muddy bottom. Wild rice seed has a tough outer coat and an imbalance of growth-regulatory hormones that may keep it dormant for several years. About half the seeds sprout each year.

Aeration of the muddy alluvial bottom through any means of stirring the soil, such as the roiling of fall and spring flooding, improves the growing medium. As the bed is thus naturally "cultivated," nutrients from upstream sediment are added. Some turbulence occurs naturally, through wave action or when bottom ice breaks up in the spring and floats to the already melted surface, effecting an upheaval of the old plants—roots, mud, and all. As the ice mass melts, the plants resettle on the bottom. However it occurs, disturbance of the growing medium promotes healthy growth. A bush pilot in Manitoba once sighted a moose feeding on aquatic vegetation and buzzed him with his plane. The startled animal fled through the shallow water with much churning and splashing. Flying over the same area the following year, the pilot discerned a clear strip of green wild rice growth, marking exactly the path of the frightened moose.[8]

Germination of the wild rice seed begins with snowmelt and spring runoff from mid- to late April. Given an increase in sunlight, longer days, and gradual warming of the water temperature to about forty degrees Fahrenheit, the seed sprouts and quickly establishes whitish, straight roots. As the plant develops, long ribbonlike leaves form under water. These take about a month to grow long enough – from one to five feet – to reach the surface of the water. Near the end of May, when the seed's energy is spent, the plant becomes totally dependent on its leaves to receive the sunlight needed for growth. Low light levels at this stage reduce crop yield. By late June newly formed leaves spread on the water's surface in the so-called floating stage (fig. 1), which lasts until they are two to three feet long. Ten days later the plant forms its aerial leaves.

During the first part of July the stalk emerges; a few inches above water, it begins to form fruit primordia, which eventually become blossoms – an important development because they determine the number of seeds the plant will bear. At this point the rice field resembles a grassy meadow. Catherine P. Traill, a traveler in Canada in about 1836, was struck with the beauty of this growth: "seen from a distance, they [the rice beds] look like low green islands on the lakes . . . when the rice is in flower, it has a beautiful appearance with its broad grassy leaves and light waving spikes, garnished with pale yellow green blossoms, delicately shaded with reddish purple, from beneath which fall three elegant straw-coloured anthers, which move with every breath of air or slightest motion of the waters."[9]

The stalk is thick and spongy, up to an inch in diameter and, like bamboo, hollow and divided by nodes. At these nodes the tillers and leaves emerge. The plant continues growing to as much as eight feet above the water. By mid-July a shoot, or spikelet, which will bear the fruit head, emerges from the center of each stalk and reaches up to four feet above the highest leaf. By August each stalk terminates in a pyramid-shaped panicle; its lower branches are spreading and staminate (male), the upper ones erect and pistillate (female), maturing from the tops down and requiring about a week to unfold from their protective coverings (fig. 2). Paul Buffalo from Leech Lake described this stage: "We begin to see the heads. How beautiful. . . . The wild rice will start to load up. . . . And when it's treated right, the water and the weather treat it right, wild rice forms up into a head, a good crop if it's right." At the upper end the few dozen female blossoms begin to bloom; a few days later, the male blossoms open from numerous tender side branches.[10]

Some Ojibway believe that the staminate flowers, which die and fall to the water, add nutrients to the mud. Speculated Buffalo: "[W]hy does that blossom fall back in the lake at blossom time? Does it help the necessary requirement of the bed? Does that blossom scatter into the water to give the strength to that rice? I wonder. . . . Nature does that, so that blossom skims off, drifts away

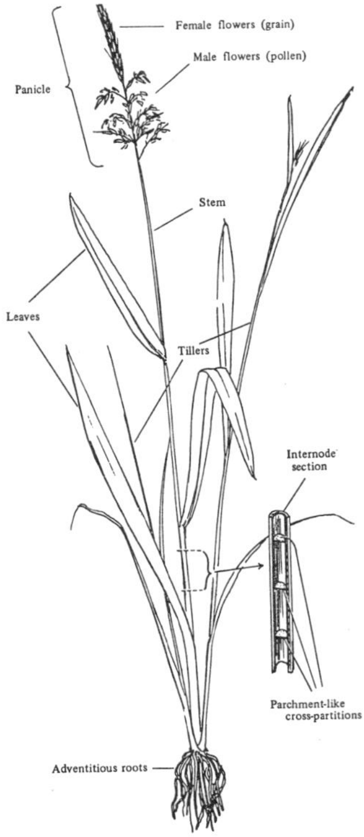

FIG. 1. Wild rice in both the emergent and floating-leaf stages (July) shares its habitat with the white water lily.

FIG. 2. Wild rice plant before pollination, after which the male flowers die and fall off, leaving the kernels to develop and ripen along the top of the panicle

at times. Where does it go? Maybe some fertilize to the rice. . . . That's requirement to get rice back. So the rice continues, grows, grows."[11]

Wild rice is primarily wind pollinated, a process that ensures genetic diversity through outcrossing. In addition, the plant has some capacity for self-pollination. The location of the flowers of *Zizania aquatica* results in an unusual means of fertilization. Whereas the pollen of corn *falls* to make contact with the plant's stigma, the lightweight, small pollen of wild rice *rises* when released. Breezes, birds feeding on wild rice worms, and insects—particularly bees—all assist pollination.

Each seed is covered by a persistent palea (upper bract) and an awned lemma (lower bract). Following pollination, the fruit head turns a purplish-red and the seeds begin to build up white starch content. At this point the rice is in its "milk state." After about two weeks all the seeds mature fully to the "dead ripe stage." Because the fruit stalk is brittle, if the rice is not harvested, each grain eventually disarticulates itself from the plant in a process called "shattering out." The grains fall into the water, sinking to the bottom to begin the cycle anew. As the grains on any given panicle ripen at different times, experienced Ojibway harvesters return periodically to the same beds for successive gatherings of rice that would otherwise shatter out.[12]

Several factors determine the rate of maturation, the size of the fruit, and its quality. Wild rice ripens earlier in shallow lakes that depend on streams for circulation; in colder, springfed lakes, it ripens later. Water levels are a principal determinant, but opinion varies as to the ideal depth for maturation. Fur trader William Johnston in 1833 felt the best rice was found in one foot of water above which stalks reached only three to four feet: "where there is more water and on the marjin [*sic*] of rivers, it is generally of a poor quality." Jenks's figures indicate great variety in the length of mature plants: wild rice will grow in water from one to twelve feet deep, with mature stalks reaching from two to twelve feet above the surface but averaging five to eight feet, their thickness dependent upon the water depth and soil fertility. The most productive lakes, like Nett Lake, are rarely deeper than four to five feet throughout. Sandy Lake (Minnesota) Ojibway customarily went south to Rice Lake each September for their harvest. About 1820 James D. Doty, secretary and recorder on an expedition into what later became Minnesota Territory, reported that this three-by-five-mile lake, not over five feet deep, was almost entirely covered with wild rice.

Wild rice ripens over a ten-to-fourteen-day period, beginning with the topmost grains and moving gradually down the panicle. Small-grained rice with shorter straw growing in shallow water is usually the first to mature; tall rice with more grain per panicle and rice growing in deep water ripens later. In Minnesota the ripening period begins around August 18 and lasts until about September 12, the greatest amount maturing about September 5. Most harvesting occurs between August 25 and September 12; farther north, it begins earlier. La Vérendrye, for example, in 1736 found the Cree and Monsoni Indians ricing on August 11.[13]

Weather affects ripening; clear, warm days hasten maturation. According to Paul Buffalo, "wherever there's lily pads you see the wild rice leaving [shattering out] there. It matures quicker. The reflection of the sun and the heat matures that rice faster." Each stand ripens at the same time every year relative to other stands. In the Kakagon sloughs on Bad River Reservation in Wisconsin, for example, upriver rice always ripens before the stands closer to Lake Superior, which are affected by its cold water.[14]

Because the stages of wild rice maturation parallel somewhat those of cultivated rice (*Oryza sativa*), Lips reviewed the growth of white rice to explain differences in harvesting the two crops. When cultivated rice is in its milk state (when squeezing its kernel produces a thick, milky juice), the stand is mostly still green though the lowest leaves may already be turning color. The next stage, which Lips called "yellow ripe," is reached when the entire stand turns yellow. In "full ripe" state, the beds look dead; the kernels are hard and fall out easily. This is followed by the "dead ripe" stage, when the seed and all straw parts of the plant are easily broken with pressure. Cultivated rice must be harvested before it reaches this state or the kernels will shatter out and be lost. Between the yellow- and full-ripe stages, said Lips, is an intermediate one, when food build-up in the kernel has ceased. This is the optimum time for harvesting white rice by cutting the stalks of the plants still bearing their seeds.[15]

While cultivators of domesticated rice in this way prevent kernels from falling out before the dead-ripe state, this is exactly the point at which wild rice harvesters begin their work. Noted Red Laker William Dudley: "Rice doesn't mature all at once. The good Lord made it that way. When it matures, you have to be there right away or it will blow away." As many plants as possible should reach the condition in which, as Schoolcraft put it, the "capsule is in a fit state to part with the grain, by agitation." Harvest activity is thus concentrated over a relatively short period. If it began earlier, repeated visits of boats would damage the plants before the kernels matured. Said Paul Buffalo: "A good crop if it's right, hit it just right. At places that head of wild rice will go someplace, I think it'll go nine, eight inches . . . and it'll hang over by the water. The heads get so loaded it bows back its head. It's nice stuff."[16]

Kernel size and number vary. The glumes (husks) of the fertile female flower average an inch or less, but the barbed awn may extend it by nearly the same length. The glumes contain thin cylindrical kernels, ranging in length from one-half to one inch. When ripe, they are of a characteristic dark slate color due to a thin pellicle, which, when scratched, reveals the greenish-white contents. Schoolcraft cautioned European friends accustomed to white rice to expect something different from this New World product: "This pellicle adheres tightly, and is left on the grain, and is consequently of a dark color when served up."[17]

Wild rice kernels collected from eighty-five sources in Minnesota in the early 1940s measured from 6 to 20 millimeters (mm) from the base of the spikelet to the base of the awn, with an average length of 13.6 mm. Kernels longer than 15 millimeters were called "giant wild rice" by those selling it for seed; those shorter than 10 millimeters were called "bird" or "river rice." Counting the kernels per head, researchers found from 15 to 212 per panicle. Generally, the shorter rice with narrow leaves bore fruit heads producing fewer kernels (under 50), but were larger in size and easiest to harvest into boats. This characterizes Nett Lake wild rice, which, Dan Raincloud (born about 1903) of Red Lake claimed, had the largest kernels in Minnesota; compared to it, he said, "some lakes, just half of that. Little bitty rice."[18]

The vastness of a natural rice stand never failed to impress newcomers to the area, who often compared it to large cultivated fields of corn, oats, or rye (fig. 3). Albert B. Reagan, superintendent and special disbursing agent at Nett Lake from 1909 to 1914, described it as resembling "a great barley field," and Eva Lips, as late as 1947, wrote of the same beds: "If one has not seen them himself, one can scarcely imagine adequately the size of the rice fields. They stretch as far as the eye can see." William Warren reported that Red Cedar Lake, eight miles long and one-fourth mile wide, was almost completely covered with rice, and today the Sokaogon (Mole Lake) Ojibway continue to harvest from Rice Lake, where 320 acres of dense crop make it one of the most productive in Wisconsin. The appearance of such a lake, when full of rice obscuring the shoreline, could prove deceiving. "It might, perhaps, be called a *marais* [marsh]," said James Doty in 1820, describing Rice Lake.[19]

Stands along rivers were equally impressive. George W. Featherstonhaugh

Fig. 3. Minnesota rice field, about 1910

estimated the wild rice on the Fox River in 1847 at two miles wide and five miles long. On an 1857 expedition Henry Youle Hind wondered at the large number of game animals and wildfowl attracted to the region, "Some distance from the [Winnipeg] river the extensive rice grounds cover many thousand acres, and continue for miles on either bank."[20]

Early observers in the rice district made note of the surrounding wilderness, thus leaving ecological records of the area in its pristine state. Describing portages leading to Leech Lake in 1858, Lutheran missionary Ottomar Cloeter wrote: "From Swamp Lake on . . . the entire region becomes one vast swamp; the woods consist only of cedars and larch trees, which are known to grow only in very low places; and it is very difficult to find a place to camp." David D. Owen in his geological survey of 1852 paid particular attention to flora along the Big Fork River: "The clay-beds still show themselves in the river banks; and the bottom lands begin to bear rich meadows. The rice plant is also frequently seen in the margins of the stream. Back of the meadows are low, rounded hills, some of them covered with grass, and others with cypress and small poplar. Since leaving 'Big Fork Falls,' the principal timber has been oak, birch, aspen, poplar, fir, cypress, and a few large white and yellow pines. . . . The river, which, up to this point has been growing narrower for a long distance is not over ten or fifteen yards in width, at the last granitic exposure. It now becomes wide, and is filled with the rice plant."[21]

Even on the biggest rivers and lakes wild rice established itself in quieter, more sheltered places (fig. 4). Some Winnebago Indians at the end of the nineteenth century harvested large quantities of rice from the sloughs on both sides of the Mississippi at La Crosse, Wisconsin. When explorer Stephen H. Long arrived at Lake of the Woods in August 1823, the Ojibway were harvesting rice "in the coves and recesses of the lake [where] it is abundant."[22]

ENEMIES

Despite the vastness of its natural stands, wild rice is a relatively delicate plant. Subject to attack or damage from the elements or the intrusions of humans, the crop can easily fail or be destroyed at any stage of growth. Already noted is its intolerance for pollution and reliance on slowly circulating, well-balanced, mineral-rich water. Proper water level is above all the crucial factor for a successful yield; irregular levels, usually too high, are responsible more than anything else for its failure.

If the water is too high in the spring, seedlings may fail to grow due to lack

FIG. 4. Ricers dwarfed by rice field, Red Lake Reservation, about 1970

of light. Because the wild rice plant anchors in soft mud with only a few short spongy roots at its base, a sudden rise in water level—above six inches in June during the floating leaf stage—will uproot it. Even when the water level rises gradually, if too high it reduces available sunlight. The plant either is unable to reach the surface and so drowns or is forced to expend its energy elongating and becomes incapable of producing seed. If water is high until late in the season and then recedes, the tops of the plant become too heavy and fall over into the water, often breaking the stem.

According to historical reports, high water levels frequently deprived the Ojibway of food supplies and affected their ability to trade. Fur trader John D. Cameron in 1825 wrote: "From the great rise of the water we may bid adieu to Rice for this year—and to [fur] Returns for next spring." In 1857 water level precipitated a rice failure on the Winnipeg River and also led to a scarcity of fish according to explorer Hind: "In general, the Winnipeg teems with fish, among which are sturgeon, pike, two kinds of white fish, perch, suckers, &c., affording a bountiful supply to the Indians who hunt and live on or near the lower portion of this majestic river. The extraordinary height of its waters during the summer of 1857 had so extended the feeding grounds of the fish, that they were with difficulty caught in sufficient numbers to provide the Indians with their staple food." Invariably this sort of crisis disrupted settlement, inducing entire bands of Ojibway to relocate simply to find alternate food sources. A rice failure at Fond du Lac (now Minnesota) in 1783 forced the people to move to the prairies west of the Mississippi for the winter in pursuit of buffalo. Annual reports of the Commissioner of Indian Affairs from about 1850 show that rice failures were particularly widespread for the period called "the starvation years." In 1849 the Pillager band of more than one thousand members at Leech Lake moved west to hunt buffalo. In that year and again in 1850 most of the Sandy Lake Ojibway spent the winter on ceded land near Crow Wing and Fort Gaines (later Fort Ripley), "hunting and begging for a living" because of a rice failure. Similarly rice failures, combined with a rabbit distemper epizootic, brought hunger to the Nett Lake Ojibway, thirteen of whom starved to death.[23]

With vagaries of weather and other environmental factors, stands of wild rice in any given area naturally have had irregular annual yields (Table A). Some researchers have concluded that in any four-year period a given stand might provide one bumper crop, two mediocre-to-fair crops, and one near or complete failure. Furthermore, with variances in rainfall in the rice district, one community might experience a rice failure in the same season that another had a plentiful harvest. In 1867, while the Ojibway on the upper Mississippi experienced a rice failure, the Lake Superior bands harvested double that of the previous year. Data collected over the years from several lakes in Minnesota show that rice fails completely when the water level is twelve inches or more above normal from May 15 to July 1. Water six inches above normal causes about half the crop to fail.[24]

From long experience the Ojibway know what water levels will do to the wild rice crop, and they are able to predict outcome throughout the growing period. On August 20, 1803, Michel Curot, trader in charge of the Yellow River post of the XY Company in the St. Croix Valley during the season of 1803–04, opened a letter that declared there would be no rice that year. Ojibway associates confirmed his prediction of a turbulent winter for trader and Indian alike. When asked about the prospects for 1947, Kee-way-keenee-kichik at Nett Lake told Lips there would be no bumper crop because some mud had recently risen from the bottom of the lake. This indicated that pockets of air had formed between the clay subfloor of the lake and the mud where the roots should anchor. A canoe paddle easily pushed through the mud layer to the clay—ordinarily four feet deep—indicated the presence of these open places. Traditionalists, however, have used natural observation together with

TABLE A

*Good and Bad Rice Years, Lac la Pluie District**

1814–15 - good	1828–29 - bad	1846–47 - good
1817–18 - good	1829–30 - good	1847–48 - bad
1822–23 - bad	1830–31 - bad	1848–49 - bad
1823–24 - good	1831–32 - good	1849–50 - bad
1824–25 - bad	1833–34 - good	1850–51 - bad
1825–26 - bad	1837–38 - good	1851–52 - bad
1826–27 - good	1842–43 - bad	1852–53 - bad
1827–28 - good	1843–44 - bad	

Source: compiled by Victor Lytwyn from Hudson's Bay Company Archives, Winnipeg
*for years with adequate documentation

spiritual explanation to interpret the cause of crop loss. When asked why he thought the wild rice would fail, Kee-way-keenee-ki-chik told Lips that opinion was divided between those who blamed the high water level and others who believed a menstruating woman had bathed in the lake, causing the spirits to curse it for a year.[25]

The only diseases to which natural stands of wild rice are susceptible are certain fungi (Jenks listed four varieties) that attack the stalks or kernels. The most common of these is ergot, a fungus of the genus *Claviceps,* also known to attack grasses such as rye, replacing the seed with its own dark, club-shaped body. Ergot works through its mycelium, which invades the tissue and surface of the young ovary to form a sclerotium. The fungus releases its spores to attack the plant as the sclerotium, which remains dormant during the winter months, germinates in the spring. The Indians call wild rice so afflicted "frozen rice."[26]

Aquatic plant growth next to or amidst wild rice can be harmful or beneficial. Except in tidal areas pickerelweed (*Pontederia cordata*) is a particularly fierce competitor; one of the first plants to appear each year, it gets a head start on wild rice, cattails, and sedges. Recently, purple loosestrife (*Lythrum salicaria*), a European exotic, has become a nuisance. On the other hand, an adjacent zone of protective vegetation along the shore can save young wild rice plants from water currents that might otherwise dislodge them. Examples known in Minnesota are coontail (*Ceratophyllum demersum*), bladderwort (*Utricularia macrorhiza*), and bushy pondweed (*Najus flexilis*) which, like wild rice, attracts wildfowl. Cattails and other competitive perennials are sometimes drowned by high water levels in summer—a technique deliberately applied by paddy rice growers after harvest to eliminate them.[27]

Wild rice, with its heavy seeds, competes successfully with other plants in locations where surface currents carry away their light, buoyant seeds. In landlocked or stagnant waters, however, wild rice loses out. This also occurs when water levels recede. In 1922 Harry D. Ayer at Mille Lacs Lake, Minnesota, wrote: "The lake has been so low the last few years that the shores in many places—otherwise fine sandy beaches—are growing up to weeds and willows and many thousands of pike died last summer from the shallowness and hot weather." Although at that time the lake was full of rice, it was too shallow for canoes to enter for harvesting. On Big Rice Lake, three miles south of Remer, was one of the best wild rice stands in Minnesota. Formerly producing in excess of 100,000 pounds annually, it became choked with weeds because of receding water levels in the 1930s.[28]

The natural roiling of the growing medium in the spring buries the root systems of perennial competitors as it aerates the soil. Wild rice root systems require more dissolved oxygen than such major competitors as water lilies and cattails; thus, a harvest of plenty is usually followed by slender returns as the thick stalk masses and former root systems take up to a year to decay before the bottom soil is sufficiently loose for aeration.

More often attacked by creatures than choked out by plants, wild rice has numerous predators. Muskrats, generally fond of rushes, have been known to chew off its stems at the waterline, and carp, especially fond of the plant, can destroy the roots of an entire bed. Cattle and horses from pastures abutting wild rice lakes are often tempted by the green stalks and will wade in or even swim out to feed on them. They may easily become bloated on the plant, however, and can even die from overconsumption; nevertheless, L. A. Paddock at Grass Lake, Illinois, wrote Jenks that he had "known farmers to gather the [green] stalks to take the place of hay."[29]

Insects have at times reached plague proportions. In *Narrative of the Canadian Red River,* Henry Hind cited Sir John Richardson's report that in 1847 "multitudes of caterpillars spread like locusts over the neighbourhood of Rainy River. They travelled in a straight line, crawling over houses, across rivers, and into large fires kindled to arrest them. . . . They destroyed the *Folle avoine* (wild rice) on Rainy Lake, but left untouched some wheat that was just coming into ear." Another natural enemy is the rice worm (*Apamea apamiformis*), about one-fourth inch long. It feeds on the grain and can ruin rice stands near shore, and its bite is an annoyance to harvesters. The water weevil eats the leaves of the plant, while its larvae work into the root system. Other minor pests are the rice stalk borers, midges, leaf miners, and maggots.[30]

Birds have been both a blessing and a bane to the Indians, for wildfowl, in competition for seed, are easily captured while feeding. In 1669 and 1670 Father Allouez, traveling the upper Fox and Wolf rivers and Grand Lake (then

Butte des Morts), remarked on the "Bustards, Ducks, Swans, and Geese . . . in great number on all these Lakes and Rivers, – the wild oats, on which they live, attracting them thither." The Fox and Mascouten Indians, he noted, could trap fifty of these birds in a night by setting snares for them at the mouth of the Fox River.[31]

Netting was only one means of catching rice-feeding wildfowl. Anthropologist Gardner P. Stickney noted that: "The rice not only served as a decoy, but also as a blind, the Indian easily concealing himself in its thick masses and sometimes being able to kill the birds with a club." Wildfowl became easy targets when they overfed on rice and became sluggish in flight. As a boy around 1910, William Bineshi Baker, Sr., of Lac Court Oreilles Reservation in Wisconsin picked off "rice birds" with a slingshot. *Manoominikeshiinyag* in the Ojibway language, they were probably Virginia rails, which nest among stalks of rice and other aquatic grasses. Once Indians had guns, they hunted such wildfowl from canoes. In fact in former times, when collecting rice was mostly women's work, Ojibway men kept just as busy "harvesting" ducks. Non-Indian rod-and-gun clubs still deliberately sow wild rice seed to encourage the migrating birds to stop in their game preserves, for blue-winged teal, wood ducks, mallards, and other puddle ducks are all rice eaters.[32]

Most ducks did not adversely affect the crop but simply "cleaned up" after the Indian harvest. As Jenks observed, ducks were really no more than gleaners, eating the kernels that the Indians had missed. Other birds, however, often consumed the crop before the Indians could get to it. Particularly in its milk state, wild rice is attacked by flocks of migrating blackbirds, red-winged blackbirds, grackles, and ricebirds (also called reedbirds or bobolinks – *Dolichonyx oryzivorus*). Among other birds consuming the ripe seeds are rails, pigeons, quails, herons, cedar waxwings, and woodpeckers.[33]

Throughout the world, people have devised scarecrows to prevent bird damage to crops. In the cultivated rice fields of Java, for example, special watchtowers were erected on bamboo poles for people to perch on and drive away the rice finks, and in North America Mandan women, posted on similar scaffolds overlooking the cornfields, did handwork when not scaring off birds. The Ojibway were just as adept at driving off their chief competitors for wild rice. William Baker's great uncle, Henry Baker, lame and thus unable to participate actively in the harvest, chose to frighten away blackbirds through an ingeniously devised scarecrow. He erected a pole in the midst of the rice bed, mounted a cowbell on top, and attached a string reaching to shore. Whenever birds threatened the crop, he simply pulled the string to ring the bell and drive them away.[34]

Beyond bird, animal, and insect damage, wild rice is also subject to the elements and has sometimes been lost to windstorms, hail, frost, heavy rain, or flooding. In the *Annual Report of the Commissioner of Indian Affairs* for 1870, J. H. Knight described the plight of the Lake Superior bands: "The past year has been one of unusual severity, hardship, and sorrow to the Indians committed to my supervision. Owing to the heavy cold rains of the summer and fall of 1869 the rice was destroyed, and has not reappeared in the quantities heretofore found."[35]

Storms in the early stage of rice growth can knock plants over so they cannot straighten up; when kernels are dead ripe, storms can shell out an entire crop. In 1899 nearly all the rice was lost to a storm at Vermilion Lake; in 1941 unusual windstorms on Star Lake (Otter Tail County, Minnesota) wiped out a good portion of its eight hundred acres of wild rice. Jonathan Carver in the eighteenth century found large quantities of wild rice between Lake Huron and Lake Erie but was informed that none of it ever matured; the plants simply blossomed, withered, and died. Carver blamed the northwest wind, which, in this body of water, was far stronger than in the interior, where rice flourished. Superintendent of Indian Affairs Thomas L. McKenney at Fond du Lac in 1823 told of how he sowed wheat for chicken feed later than usual because of a flash flood, "which swept over all this place last spring, and carried away every thing that could be floated. . . . This same freshet . . . destroyed the wild rice—and this makes our visit with the supplies we have brought with us, so opportune."[36]

Such potential calamities explain why the Ojibway gave thanks for a normal course of weather while waiting for rice to reach the dead ripe state. Paul Buffalo explained: "Storms, hails, different things that might destroy. That's why we act. We fear, yet we're not sure of this crop until we receive it in our hands. And life, it gives us strength. Beware! Anything could happen between now and then, that we are 'bout ready to receive it from the great natural. We should say thanks."[37]

Even clear weather, if too hot and dry, can affect the rice. Spikelets on the fruit head might not set flower, and fewer than half of them may mature, the others producing only lightweight rice. To salvage the good rice for processing, one would have to remove sterile grains through flotation.[38]

Of all adversaries of wild rice none continues to have more potential for harm than humans. As non-Indians realized that profits could be made from the sale of rice, they began to compete with the Ojibway, without the centuries-old knowledge of how rice grows or of proper harvesting techniques. Their ignorance led to abuses by some Indian people who emulated white methods. For example, traditional Ojibway waited for permission from their rice chiefs to go out in their canoes to collect rice, but before laws were passed against injurious practices, whites began to harvest rice before it had matured. Their broad boats broke the rice stalks, leaving the fields a shambles and preventing successive collecting. Furthermore, such premature harvest knocked into the lake grain insufficiently ripe to germinate and reseed. Traditional Ojibway were angry, as is evident in recent remarks by one Mille Lacs Lake resident: "And [the old-time Ojibway] harvested his own wild rice, and he kept it to last all year round. . . . They don't keep the wild rice now like they did before. There's lot of inexperienced white men that go wild ricing, and they break the stock, and the rice doesn't get a chance to grow back again the next year."[39]

One of the most devastating acts hastening the general decline of natural wild rice stands was the construction of dams, as early as the mid-nineteenth century, which raised the levels in the backwaters and drowned the rice. The Ojibway took their own steps to combat this threat. In an 1855 report, D. B. Herriman, Indian agent at the Chippewa Agency, told how a few years earlier a lumber company had put a dam across the Rum River, the outlet of Mille Lacs Lake: "The maintenance of this dam, by flooding, or raising the water in these small lakes, destroys from two-thirds to the whole of the crop. The Indians have frequently raised the gates and let the water off. I cannot blame them; the dam is on their own land . . . and the Indians mainly depend upon this crop for a subsistence."[40]

Problems with dams at Mille Lacs continued well into the twentieth century, apparently due to ill-advised moves on the part of the state of Minnesota. Fred Jones (born about 1908) remembered that when he served on the Mille Lacs tribal executive council "They put the dam in 'cause the state had already signed the orders, they could go ahead and put it in for the tribe . . . they dammed this up, and they raised the water. We didn't have no rice in this lake for a number of years. Then they [not] only knock out this one, they knocked out two other lakes beside it, clear down to Onamia. See, that Onamia Lake used to be full of rice, you know. I used to rice in there always."[41]

Raising the water levels with dams wreaked havoc wherever there was wild rice. Pelican Lake once had better, longer rice than nearby Nett Lake, but after a dam was put in (apparently to increase the supply of pike for sport fishing) the rice disappeared. Lake of the Woods had a bumper crop in 1977, but the Lake of the Woods Water Control Board raised the water two feet the following year, causing a complete rice failure. Only fifteen thousand pounds were harvested in all, and that from nearby rivers somewhat protected by water-control structures.[42]

While man-made dikes caused much destruction, there is some evidence that the removal or prevention of the obstructions of nature's dam-builder, the beaver, may also have affected wild rice stands. The plant thrives on slow currents such as those downstream from beaver dams. Wide-scale slaughter of the animal for its pelt probably resulted in the breakup of old damsites, altering the course of many waterways in the wild rice range, and causing an increase in water flow, which rice stands cannot tolerate.

HABITAT

"The Wisconsin, where we crossed it, was very shallow, full of sand bars and small islands, and at that low stage of the water, not more than forty rods in width," noted Caleb Atwater, who was sent by the United States government to negotiate for mineral rights with upper Mississippi River Indians about 1830. "Its average depth was not more than three feet, perhaps even less. The numerous little islands and sand bars, in height only a foot or two above the surface of the water, far as I could see the stream, above and below where we crossed it, presented to view wild rice in bloom. That plant, grows on the islands and sand bars, and in the water near them, to the height of three or four feet; and when in full bloom reminds one of our cultivated fields at home."[43]

The general topography of the wild rice habitat is a consequence of glacial activity beginning about 7000 B.C. As glaciers receded, they left behind countless small hollows and crevices that make up the many lakes, streams, and flats that collect alluvial deposits providing the ideal growing medium for wild rice. Anthropologist George I. Quimby discussed the formation of the area: "The Upper Great Lakes region is a product of the Ice Age. The drainage patterns, land forms, and soils are all results of glaciation. The advancing glaciers of the Ice Age covered all of the Upper Great Lakes region, grinding down rock masses, gouging out basins, and pulverizing stone into sand and soil."[44]

While some lakes created by the ponding of meltwaters from the glacial retreat were landlocked, many others were connected by streams and rivers, forming long chains of waterways that ultimately drained into principal North American rivers like the Mississippi. Some of the smaller lakes are no more than occasional widenings of rivers; where they are sufficiently shallow and contain a rich, muddy bottom of sand, soil, gravel, and other alluvial detritus, and where the water current is not too strong, they become ideal hosts for wild rice. Consequently, many of the most productive stands are in areas around the headwaters of major rivers such as the St. Croix and Red Cedar in Wisconsin, or the source rivers of Nett and Pelican lakes in Minnesota and Lake of the Woods in Ontario.

These river systems typically support a rich aquatic plant life, including wild rice. Recent palynological research suggests that wild rice was growing in about 500 B.C. A study of Gramineae pollen at Rice Lake, Minnesota, revealed that fossil pollen coincided "with the increase of bogs and muskeg in the study area" and concluded that wild rice was present at the beginning of the cooler, wetter climate of the Laurel period. Archaeological evidence indicates the occupation of the general area of wild rice habitat as early as 7000 B.C. and suggests the existence of watercraft needed to harvest it. Early Indians camped on the shores of glacial Lake Agassiz, which stretched from what is now central Manitoba to the Rainy River area; there was also human occupation of the northwestern shores of Lake Superior. Evidence of settlements of the period has been found on what were probably islands created by the retreat of glaciers; we may assume the occupants possessed boats of some sort. Because the vast network of waterways throughout the upper Great Lakes area served as a highway system, Indian people invariably established their villages alongside lakes, rivers, or, for security, on islands. This ensured their constant contact with aquatic plants and probably led to an early knowledge of their food value. The discovery of wild rice, then, must have been early indeed.[45]

Until very recently, wild rice itself had not been found in archaeological excavations. Pointing out that wild rice seeds survive nearly intact after burning and that metal kettles for parching and boiling were not available before European contact, archaeologists assumed that rice was not an important food until historic times. Other explanations counter this view: although seeds might survive burning in refuse pits, they would disintegrate after prolonged exposure to moisture; fire drying and smoke drying on racks were used to process the kernels before metal kettles were available for parching; and rice was easily boiled for consumption in birch-bark vessels. Furthermore, until recently Indian people processed rice in camps by the lakeside. Because of fluctuating water levels, these sites were disturbance areas subject to flooding. With the introduction of flotation-recovery techniques, archaeologists have found increasing evidence of Indian knowledge and use of wild rice as early as the Late Archaic-Early Woodland period.[46]

The riverine network provided Indian people direct access to rice stands. Even if principal settlements lacked nearby rice lakes, they were accessible by water with minimal need for overland portage of boats and equipment. Residents of Lac Court Oreilles, the first major inland village of the Lake Superior Ojibway, were still harvesting rice at the upper waters of the Red Cedar, Chippewa, and St. Croix rivers at the time of Jenks's study.[47]

Explorers, missionaries, and traders have provided an almost uniform picture of wild rice country. They were at once struck with the beauty of the region, the sudden changes in topography, the occasionally formidable difficulties in traversing it, and the great abundance of an unusual New World plant. Typical of many who recorded fairly detailed descriptions of canoe voyages through this wilderness was Joseph Nicollet, who was investigating the hydrographical characteristics of the Mississippi headwaters. In 1836, upon entering Laura Lake from the Little Boy River, Nicollet wrote: "We penetrated right into a wild rice paddy that we crossed as freely as if there were no rice there. . . . The horizon cleared, widened, and we arrived in the middle of a huge expanse of water and rice bordered by the series of hills we just left. These have expanded and widened to encompass a circular surface of practically five square miles, beautiful to behold. Take away the vegetation covering the water, and this surface becomes a first rate lake for these parts, bordered at the foot of the hills with tamarack. . . . Between this lake and the canal we had just left, the river is barely one mile long. When we arrive half the lake is indeed without rice. At 5:05 we left the lake. I estimate the chord we followed to be four miles long and the diameter five. We entered a river that continues to wind through wild rice following a northwestern course."[48]

All chroniclers mention the winding course suddenly encountered when the waterway turned into rice fields. Rice will not grow in a landlocked, stagnant pool, nor can it tolerate fast-moving water. Nett Lake, for example, contains ideal currents for promoting the growth of wild rice, with seven small streams quietly moving fresh water into it; the lake empties to the Nett Lake River, which in turn joins the Little Fork. The customary nature of a channel through a rice bed is undular, providing two advantages: it tends to slow the current without losing the freshness of the water, and the curves along the waterway collect the alluvial materials necessary for healthy growth of the rice plants. Thus wrote Stephen Long in 1823: "Having passed this lake [Little Vermilion] which is only 3½ miles long, we entered the river de la Croix [Loon]. This a small stream exceedingly crooked, its folds almost doubling upon one another. Its general courses only were attempted. Wild rice and Reed grass are abundant along its shores." Cloeter, some twenty-five years later, reported on the area between Leech Lake and Pokegama: "[T]he river winds about in endless curves between reeds 10 feet high, and far and wide there is nothing but bottomless swamp. Before one comes into Shallowdust Lake (also a large rice lake), the sinuosity becomes so horribly tiresome that, if one does not want to ride back and forth in the same spot for half a day, one must decide upon an unusual portage which is nothing less than enviable."[49]

This characteristic of channels through rice beds is explained in a Wisconsin Indian legend about the creation of the Fox River by a gigantic snake, who once spent the night in the marshes between the Wisconsin River and Lake Winnebago sleeping off his evening meal. When he awoke the next day, he found that dew had settled on his back. He shook the water off, creating a chain of small lakes, before slithering away to Lake Winnebago.[50]

Although the wild rice beds had distinct channels, travelers often found the growth thick enough to cause problems in navigation. In 1767 Jonathan Carver remarked on the gentleness of the Fox River's current, adding: "In some places it is with difficulty that canoes can pass, through the obstructions they meet with from the rice stalks, which are very large and thick." Early in September 1832 the thickness of the rice at one stretch forced Colonel Charles Whittlesey and his party to push rather than paddle their boat for two miles on the Fox River. In about 1850 John J. Bigsby, traveling on the Canadian border, said: "Wild rice grows so abundantly and fine on the south shore of Lake Lacroix that we sometimes could hardly push our canoes through it." Three years earlier Featherstonhaugh pulled his canoe through the thick rice on the Fox River near Fort Winnebago by grabbing onto the rice stalks.[51]

Other rivers offered similar obstacles. The Reverend Sherman Hall, having described the Chippewa River's narrow channel following a "very crooked" course lined with wild rice, compared it with the Flambeau River, which served as the outlet of a chain of lakes in what is now Wisconsin: "Near its mouth it resembles the Chippeway very much, except it is not so large. Farther up it becomes wider, passing through swamps and marshes, and has but little current. Its channel at this season is full of wild rice and weeds, which very much obstruct the passage of canoes. Its course is extremely crooked."[52]

Rice beds, like the poppy fields of Oz, were often so vast that travelers expressed their quandary at finding a way to traverse them. Father Marquette, searching on the Fox River in 1673 for a waterway to the Mississippi, was provided two Miami Indian guides and told to head west/southwest: "But the road is broken by so many swamps and small lakes that it is easy to lose one's way, especially as the River leading thither is so full of wild oats that it is difficult to find the Channel." Marquette's party was forced to portage some 2,700 paces, the Miami helping them carry the canoes.[53]

Where wild rice grew really thickly, travelers had to cut the stalks to get through the field. Such was the condition of Red Cedar Lake, visited by William Warren in the fall of 1850: "The lake being miry-bottomed, and shallow, is almost entirely covered with wild rice, and so thick and luxuriant does it grow, that the Indians are often obliged to cut passage ways through it for their bark canoes."[54]

The contour as well as the width and depth of a riverbed affects the speed of the current. Slowly moving streams are hospitable to the growth of wild rice, while wider, deeper, and swifter currents of major rivers with less undulating courses are not, except perhaps in their backwaters or peripheral sloughs. Jenks demonstrated the relationship of topography to wild rice using the Fox River as an example. For the first 104 miles, to Lake Winnebago, its currents are relatively slow, as the river falls gradually, only forty feet; the stretch is filled with wild rice. Leaving Lake Winnebago on its way to Green Bay, the river falls rapidly—170 feet in just 37½ miles, with little rice to be found. Thus the headwater areas of rivers and their upper courses generally bear the richest rice growths.[55]

In the great chain of waterways, wild rice usually grew best at the lower ends of smaller lakes or where the river emptied into a large body of water, in low, marshy areas or estuaries surrounding the river's mouth. Warren Upham in his *Catalogue of the Flora of Minnesota* pointed out the near absence of wild rice from lakes without outlets: "It seems to select, by preference, the lower terminations of these expansions, which generally debouch by a narrowed outlet and considerable fall, constituting rapids." David Owen in 1852 reported the Red Lake River leaving Papushkwa Lake as only fifteen feet wide and choked with "rushes and reed grass," eventually expanding into small lakes filled with wild rice. Henry Hind remarked on the United States-Canadian boundary waters in 1857: "Instead of following the course of the Great Winnipeg, after arriving at the Otter Falls, I passed down the Pennawa River into Bonnet Lake, in order to avoid the dangerous 'Seven Portages,' and save several miles of route. Near the entrance of the Pennawa into Bonnet Lake, the little river winds through an immense marshy area covered with wild rice, and I succeeded in collecting a considerable quantity as the voyageurs paddled through its light and yielding stalks with undiminished speed."[56]

The rich stand of rice at the mouth of the Menominee River at Green Bay attracted waterfowl and probably led to the settlement of the ancestors of today's Menominee Indians, whom French travelers named *folles avoines*. Marquette, having left St. Ignace (in what is now Michigan), on May 13, 1673, arrived in Green Bay on June 7. As his journey continued, "We left this bay to enter the river [the lower Fox] that discharges into it; it is very beautiful at its Mouth, and flows gently; it is full Of bustards, Ducks, Teal, and other birds, attracted thither by the wild oats, of which they are very fond." Half a century later, Pierre François Xavier de Charlevoix surmised the derivation of the name of the local Indians from their principal staple: "After we had advanced five or six leagues, we found ourselves abreast of a little island [Chambers Island?], which lies near the western side of the bay, and which concealed from our view, the mouth of a river, on which stands the village of the Malhomines Indians, called by our French *Folles Avoines* or Wild Oat Indians, probably from their living chiefly on this sort of grain."[57]

JENKS'S DISTRICT

At one time wild rice appears to have grown naturally over a fairly large portion of North America—from the Atlantic Ocean to the Rocky Mountains and from the Gulf of Mexico nearly to Hudson Bay, according to Jenks. Lacking data for some areas, he provided a map showing wild rice in more than half the states in the country and in two provinces of Canada, where it extended roughly to the fiftieth parallel. States with Indian production of wild rice included Florida, where it was harvested by the Seminole, and New York, by the Seneca. At the end of the nineteenth century, wild rice grew along the Potomac River at Washington, D.C., in the Chesapeake Bay, and on the Connecticut River at Essex.[58]

Normally a fresh-water plant, wild rice grew along the Atlantic shore only because streams and estuaries there diluted the salinity of the ocean water. Wild rice found an ideal growing medium in the mud flats and marshlands alternately submerged and exposed by tidal action, as long as fresh water reduced the salt water's effect. After tests at the turn of the century, Carl S. Scofield concluded that "when water is appreciably salty to the taste it is too salty for the successful growth of the plant."

Jenks's correspondents provided widely scattered proof of the ubiquitous inland range of the plant: C. W. Mathews, a botanist at the State College of Kentucky at Lexington, had a specimen in his herbarium collected from a lake in the "barrens" of western Kentucky; in Florida, wild rice was abundant in deep ponds of Columbia and Suwannee counties; marshes and riverbanks bordering Lake Champlain and its tributaries had rich wild rice stands; and Potawatomi Chief Simon Pokagon wrote that his people had gathered much rice in the St. Joseph Valley of Michigan. Thus with confidence Jenks made the general statement that: "It grows abundantly in the brackish, almost stagnant, waters of the Atlantic and Gulf states, and along the sloughs of [the] Mississippi river from its headwaters as far south as the state of Mississippi."

Even at the time of Jenks's writing, the large wild rice habitat was shrinking rapidly. Pressures of population, the conversion of land to farming, industrial growth, and changes in water quality all hastened its decline except in its most concentrated natural setting, which Jenks came to define as the "wild rice district." Wild rice is now virtually absent from lower Michigan, for instance, where it grew in the Early Woodland period. Generally speaking, the perimeters of Jenks's district—the section of country in the United States which "bore wild rice so abundantly"—remain. The area's boundaries roughly encompass the upper two-thirds of Wisconsin and that portion of Minnesota lying east of the Mississippi. Echoing earlier views that this region was once a utopia for its native inhabitants, Jenks said that "no other section of the North American continent was so characteristically an Indian paradise so far as a spontaneous vegetal food is concerned, as was this territory in Wisconsin and Minnesota."[59]

Accepting Jenks's findings, anthropologist A. L. Kroeber also attributed the Indian population density of the region—his "Wisconsin or Wild-Rice

Area"—to this staple. Its importance, wrote Kroeber, "must be due to a cultural patterning as well as unusual abundance; but it clearly was a subsistence influence of the first order." Eva Lips explained the increase in Ojibway population resulting from this staple: "The fact that the Ojibway in the course of two centuries, full of stormy history (in which other tribes suffered gruesome reductions or disappeared completely from the stage of existence) have observedly increased their numbers considerably must be attributed to their close connection to the presence of the secured subsistence basis which the wild rice district afforded them."[60]

While aware of Canadian data, Jenks concentrated his study on the United States; consequently, his map of the district did not include the Winnipeg drainage system extending to the Laurentian upland region. If anything, the perimeters of the wild rice district today must shift generally northward into Ontario and Manitoba to take into account the many seeding efforts and large-scale Ojibway production of rice in Canada.[61]

Boundary lines for the wild rice district can only be approximate. Even within the district there are some areas where the grain grew little or not at all. While the headwaters of the Mississippi were rich in rice stands, the immense marshes west of them were not. The area described on Carver's 1769 map as "The Country about here is full of Marshes and much Drownded Land" (see Introduction, fig. 2) was decisive in determining native settlements. For example, about 1898 the Bois Fort Ojibway were scattered in sixteen bands at Nett, Pelican, and Vermilion lakes and northward into Canada. Their population distribution was determined in part by the excellent prospects of annual rice harvests from those lakes. They had deliberately not moved farther west because the marshes, or muskegs, there were too acidic to bear rice.[62]

Redefining the district northward eliminates areas of southern Minnesota where rice once was harvested, principally by the Dakota. Jenks estimated that between five thousand and six thousand Dakota gathered wild rice, placing them mostly east of the Mississippi despite evidence that the habitat extended south and west as well. Carver's map shows "Great Rice Marshes" just south of the St. Peter's River where it joins the Mississippi, definitely Dakota country at the time. In the early nineteenth century Zebulon Pike discerned the Woodlands characteristics of the culture of the Minowa Kantong—the only Dakota band he knew to be using canoes. These people inhabited the area from Prairie du Chien to thirty-five miles up the Minnesota River; although they raised some corn and beans, they were equally dependent upon wild rice. Pike wrote: "[A]lthough I was with them in September or October, I never saw one kettle of either [corn or beans], they always using wild oats for bread." Other eastern Dakota depended upon a mixed Plains/Woodlands economy including wild rice. Joseph Nicollet in June 1838 depicted "The White Bluff [White

Rock]," a bluff near Ottawa and "The beautiful prairie which it overlooks: formerly the rendezvous of all the villages of the Sisseton when they left for the buffalo hunts or when they went to gather wild rice in the beautiful lakes which are in the area." In August he attended a feast at the village of Chief Sleepy Eye and was treated to boiled rice before the evening performance of the Grizzly Bear Dance by Crow Man.[63]

Most Dakota used wild rice to supplement the customary diet of buffalo meat and cultivated corn, as is evident in reports such as Radisson's in 1661 (see page 8). The Dakota taste for wild rice persisted despite their removal in 1851 from the district. Jenks cited correspondence from a missionary to the Dakota: "Even after that [1851] a considerable number would visit the rice fields every fall to gather what they could 'til 1862, when the Minnesota massacre occurred, and they were removed to the Minnesota river. A few stragglers remaining in Minnesota [about 1899] still gather some." And in the twentieth century, Dakota Indians from North and South Dakota attended powwows on the White Earth Reservation in Minnesota each year, bringing beaded moccasins to trade for wild rice.[64]

As late as the mid-nineteenth century the rice district included tribes farther south than the Dakota. Wild rice formed part of the diet of Indians in Nebraska, such as the Omaha, Ponca, and, after removal, the Winnebago, who found it in the lakes of the Sand Hills area. John D. Hunter, a captive of the nomadic Osage Indians in the early part of the nineteenth century, told how they collected wild rice from the swamps after the buffalo had trampled it. About 1840 the Potawatomi at Grass Lake, Illinois, harvested from the two thousand acres of wild rice on that lake.[65]

The natural habitat of wild rice shrank as settlers poured into former wilderness areas to establish homesteads and rice harvesters ceded territory to be converted to farmland. Ecological changes within Jenks's rice district continue to diminish or increase the growth of wild rice in particular areas. As Gardner Stickney pointed out, "it does not grow in all of those [lakes and streams] which seem fitted for it." In three adjacent lakes with seemingly identical ecosystems and topologies, wild rice may thrive in one and be absent from the others. Ojibway elders today speak about changes in the traditional rice lakes. At one time Mud Lake (White Earth Reservation) had a good crop, but, according to William Morrell (born about 1886), most people in his day preferred to harvest in Goose Lake: "It's part of Mud Lake back in the south of the lake there is good ricing there but it is just spots in the lake where you can get rice." Similarly, James Mustache, Sr., (born about 1903) of Lac Court Oreilles noted declines and increases in rice production on Lake Pakweiwong near Seeley, Wisconsin, where his family riced earlier in the century: "used to be a good rice bed there, it's coming out pretty good again now." Some incursions of civilization have created new rice stands or enhanced the capacity of older ones to thrive. On the Eau Pleine flowage in Wisconsin is a big lake created by a dam, apparently slowing the current enough for a good wild rice bed.[66]

IN NOMENCLATURE

Universally, North American Indian toponymy designated localities by some geographical peculiarity (the place where there is a cleft in the hills), by association with certain abundant flora or fauna (Deer River, [Musk]Rat Portage), or role in the Indian economy (Sugar Point, named for the maple trees on Leech Lake; Sucker Bay, for the profusion of the species of fish caught there). At one time, there were within the district numerous Indian place names related to wild rice and its harvest. Franquelin's 1699 map shows what is now the Red Cedar River as "Malominican ou Riviere Bacuille." *Malominican,* using the older Ojibway *l* in place of *n,* means "the place of much wild rice" or "where much rice grows," formerly true on this river (fig. 5). By the time of Warren's study the river was called "Menominee." Place names of some localities today bear a vestigial reference to wild rice even where natural stands have long since vanished, as on the lake adjacent to the city of Rice Lake, Wisconsin. One can only speculate on the location of the "Chipeway Village call'd the Rice Village," on Jonathan Carver's map (1769) north of what he designated the "Village of ye Roving Chipeway." (Lake Chetac seems the likely candidate.)[67]

Beyond common designations like Rice Lake or Rice River are distinctions in nomenclature, such as Upper and Lower Rice or Big and Little Rice lakes. Some places had alternate names associated with wild rice. Rice Lake north of Mille Lacs was also known as Mallard Lake, no doubt because the rice there attracted migrating ducks. By the twentieth century most Indian names had been abbreviated in English translation. Mud Lake at White Earth (by 1887 called Ripple Lake) in Ojibway was *bepashkojiishkiwagaag-zaaga'igan,* translated by the Reverend Joseph A. Gilfillan as "Thick-mud but smooth as it were shorn lake," an obvious reference to the superb growing medium of its bottom. Lawrence Mitchell (born 1920) of White Earth qualified it further, saying the name means mud that is pure, deposited in layers over time.[68]

The term for the wild rice plant also was incorporated into nomenclature. John Tanner related how a war party of Ojibway starting out from Leech Lake stopped at "Gah-menomonie gah-wun-zhe-gaw-wie see-bee, (the river of the wild rice straw)." They had scattered for hunting and trapping when a large party of Dakota arrived. Surrounding topography also played a part in place

FIG. 5. Detail from Franquelin's 1699 map of the area now Wisconsin, showing the "Malominican, ou Riviere Bacuille." Maps made as late as the mid-eighteenth century generally designate the Chippewa River "Malaminican."

names. Warren referred to Prairie Rice Lake (today Red Cedar Lake), a direct translation of its Ojibway name Mush-ko-da-mun-o-min-e-kan; the French called it Lac la Folle. The lake was so full of wild rice that Warren estimated it could feed two thousand people. Its unusual prairie setting was due to fires that had destroyed most of the timber around it.[69]

Jenks's final chapter, "Influence of Wild Rice on Geographic Nomenclature," was meticulous in cataloging more than 160 place names related to wild rice. While arguing a case for retaining Indian place names for historic and scientific study, Jenks cautioned that some terms, not Indian in origin, may be translations from the French language and others may simply represent people such as Henry M. Rice, for whom Rice County, Minnesota, was named. Still other places have been renamed over the years; for example, Manomah Isle in Green Bay, so-called in 1848, is now Chambers Island.

With many maps dating as far back as the seventeenth century, Jenks assembled a long and comprehensive list of place names including the word *rice* in whatever language—Algonquian, Dakota, French, or English—to show the imprint of the plant on the land where it grew. Through time, variant spellings and pronunciations of the original Indian names have produced a wide variety of corruptions. The frequently used Algonquian *manoominiig* (wild rice people), for instance, has appeared variously as Nenamonee, Menominee, Malomine, Nonomonies, Manannah, Manohtin, Gaunenoway, and Monomina. Jenks began with sections of the country designated in early references as "folle avoine country," generally used by Canadians to mean land south of them, by fur traders to mean inland from Lake Superior, and by the North West Company to refer to one of its four departments, specifically the one whose jurisdiction covered the country drained by the St. Croix River. Jenks went on to counties, townships, cities, stations, and finally—his most extensive list—rivers, lakes, and ponds. His final paragraph: "After a cursory comparative study it is believed that more geographic names have been derived from wild rice in this relatively small section of North America than from any other natural vegetal product throughout the entire continent."[70]

CHAPTER 2

As Food

Wild rice is the most nutritive single food which the Indians of North America consumed. The Indian diet of this grain, combined with maple sugar and with bison, deer, and other meats, was probably richer than that of the average American family of to-day.
—Albert E. Jenks, 1900[1]

NUTRITION

JENKS'S ASSESSMENT of the high nutritional value of wild rice is incontestable. Extremely rich in carbohydrates, it converts easily to energy in the body; low in fat, it also contains protein essential to growth. Easily digested, it is rich in thiamin, riboflavin, and vitamin B. In the traditional Indian diet, wild rice was more nutritious on the whole than any other naturally available vegetable, grain, animal, or fruit source. Even the cultivated cereals introduced to North America (oats, barley, wheat, and rye) rank below wild rice in over-all nutritional value (Table B).

Recognition of the food properties of wild rice, however, led Jenks to speculations that have been challenged as more data became available. For instance, Jenks devoted several pages to a consideration of precontact population density within the boundaries of his wild rice district. He was convinced that "the section of country in the United States which grew wild rice so abundantly sustained an Indian population equal to all the other country known as the Northwest territory, viz, all those States lying between the Ohio and Mississippi rivers and Lakes Superior and Huron."[2]

While his population figures may be correct for those *living* in the rice district shortly after contact, they neither represent the number of people subsisting principally on wild rice nor present an accurate picture of the percentage of active harvesters. Some tribes may only have traded for rice; their presence

TABLE B

Nutritional Value of Wild Rice Compared to Other Grains
(per 100 units; dashes denote lack of data)

	Wild Rice (raw)	White Rice (raw)	Oat Flour (whole grain)	Corn Meal (whole grain)
Moisture (g)	7.6	10.6	12.2	10.0
Food energy (calories)	360	370	365	364
Protein (g)	10.5	6.9	11.7	9.0
Fat (g)	1.0	0.7	4.2	4.0
Carbohydrate, total (g)	79.4	81.2	70.2	75.9
Crude fiber (g)	1.4	1.0	–	–
Total dietary fiber (g)	5.7	1.6	10.9	–
Ash (g)	1.5	0.6	1.7	1.1
Calcium (mg)	21	13	53	5
Iron (mg)	1.93	3.70	4.94	4.04
Magnesium (mg)	177	33	125	167
Phosphorus (mg)	433	116	368	43
Sodium (mg)	46	4	2	45
Potassium (mg)	427	68	368	276
Zinc (mg)	5.96	1.09	2.78	1.97
Copper (mg)	0.52	0.15	0.45	0.20
Ascorbic acid (mg)	0	0	0	0
Thiamin (mg)	.115	.49	.39	.40
Riboflavin (mg)	.262	.13	.057	.12
Niacin (mg)	6.733	4.63	2.00	2.09
Pantothenic acid (mg)	2.488	0.88	2.507	2.74
Vitamin B6 (mg)	.391	.15	.16	.27
Folacin (mcg)	109	43	25	27
Vitamin A value	19	–	–	148*

Source: United States Department of Agriculture Human Nutrition Information Service, December 1986

*yellow corn meal

N.B. The relatively low mineral content of white rice results from polishing in processing.

in the rice district was temporary, often sporadic, and due principally to determinants other than the presence of wild rice. Particularly effecting population movement was the establishment of French trading posts, which became the lodestones for Indian settlement. Pressure from aggressive tribes to the east was also a factor. In fact, Iroquois warfare helps explain the sparseness of the Indian population in the Ohio Valley at the time of European contact, although Jenks used this idea in developing the argument that the nutritional value of wild rice drew people from other areas to its natural habitat.[3]

Another factor was the role of gardening in the Ojibway diet, only now beginning to receive attention. Until recently, a relatively simplistic assumption has been held concerning the Ojibway annual economic cycle. Some ethnohistorians, in recognizing a fairly differentiated summer and winter subsistence pattern, have failed to see it as part of an integrated system and to appreciate the role of wild rice *throughout* the year.[4]

Associating certain foods exclusively with certain seasons distorts the picture. Earlier observers tended to underestimate the amount of food dried and stored for year-round use, remaining oblivious to Indian strategies to integrate fresh and preserved foodstuffs in times of poor harvest, rice failure, game loss, and the like. Contributing to the impression that the Ojibway lived on one staple at a time was the perception that they tended to indulge in a given staple during or after its harvest. Considerable quantities of wild rice, for example, were consumed when it was in abundance in early autumn. Jenks described a three-week period following ricing at Lac Court Oreilles in 1899: "I was daily, almost constantly, in their houses, wigwams, war-dance [Drum Dance] circle, and Midé society lodge, and did not witness a meal in which wild rice was not consumed. In fact, during the eight days covered by their dances, when I saw them eat three or four times daily, wild rice, cooked in a manner similar to oatmeal, and eaten alone, was their entire diet nearly every meal. At times also the rice was used to thicken venison and dog stew."[5]

This concurred with a report to Jenks by the Nett Lake government farmer Stephen Gheen that in the fall Ojibway there ate wild rice three times daily. Paul Buffalo, however, attributed such consumption of wild rice to younger people, saying that formerly the "old-timers" were careful not to overindulge: "That's the only thing they had lots of times they eat. In order to get full they eat too much of it. When we eat too much of it, when you cook it, there's a reaction on it. Too much wild rice, something you got to eat, balance that diet with some other. It goes good with meat, and it's better satisfaction to your taste." James Mustache, Sr., who gave up ricing, counted on his son to bring him about twenty pounds, about all he used in a year: "I didn't want any more, I don't cook much at a time. Too rich."[6]

The almost exclusive subsistence on wild rice upon harvest does reflect somewhat the traditional eating patterns of precontact Indian people, who took advantage of what was abundant at the time. As Lawrence Mitchell of White Earth put it, "We ate rice year around, they were really frugal with it, except for during ricing, there's where we could really gorge on it!" To Jenks's general query about when Indians ate wild rice, Potawatomi Chief Pokagon responded simply, "Indians eat when hungry." It was common among Indian people to have food available at all times for anyone to eat at will. For example, although much of the berry crop was dried and stored for later use, a good portion was eaten during picking. Like wild rice at harvest, maple sugar became the principal staple in the spring camps. Wrote Alexander Henry: "Sugar-making continued till the twelfth of May. On the mountain, we eat nothing but our sugar, during the whole period. Each man consumed a pound a day, desired no other food, and was visibly nourished by it."[7]

The Ojibway economic pattern was far more complex than has previously been assumed. Essentially, the Indians aimed at a diversified subsistence base, so that if one staple failed, they had others to fall back on. As examples of such diversification, Tim E. Holzkamm cited the increased planting of crops in the United States-Canadian boundary waters area in 1826, when high water portended certain rice failure. Conversely, Leech Lakers, whose three hundred garden acres were destroyed by drought in 1864, were sustained through the winter by the large wild rice crop that year. Holzkamm stressed how cautiously the Ojibway pursued a differentiated economy: "When environmental conditions threatened particular resources . . . the Ojibway tended to withhold provisions from commercial sales and retain them in caches for subsistence use. . . . Only highly valued trade goods or liquor could induce them to trade these caches."[8]

That wild rice played a key role in their over-all strategy is evident. According to Holzkamm, "Fur trade records and other accounts are quite uniform in linking a shortage of stored provisions among the Ojibway with prospects of poor returns. The failure of the wild rice harvest is frequently mentioned in this regard. . . . The ethnohistoric documentation suggests that the Ojibway evaluated the subsistence use of cereal products as being more important than commercial trade in these products." The ecological effects of wild rice on the fur trade are also apparent. The Lac la Pluie district report for 1822–23 noted that when the rice failed, the Ojibway abandoned their fall and winter hunts. During that year no martens were caught, the water was too high in the fall to get muskrats, and, lacking provisions, the Ojibway could not hunt anyway.[9]

Reliance on carbohydrate-rich foods like wild rice and corn to sustain them through hunting crises was an integral part of Ojibway subsistence. Corn crops were essential during the so-called starvation years of 1848 to 1851, when the snowshoe hare population gave out, bison were driven west by Red River hunters, and both rice and fish harvests failed. While the skins of small game like lynx, fox, and otter were valuable in the fur trade, the food value of the meat was minimal. Holzkamm saw a direct relationship between the adoption of horticulture and the depletion of traditional meat resources, such as beaver and bear. He argued that, given the mid-nineteenth century beaver pandemic from which there was no recovery until about 1864 and the lack of any increase in bear returns, *something* had to replace these energy resources. Although the snowshoe hare's habitat extended as far south as Leech Lake, extreme fluctuation in numbers made that animal unreliable for subsistence. Furthermore, exclusive reliance on the low-fat, high-protein rabbit for subsistence could lead to protein poisoning, or nephritis, a kidney inflammation sometimes called "rabbit starvation." Because the Hudson's Bay Company returns for this period indicate no increase in the harvest of animals such as beaver or bear with higher fat content, Holzkamm concluded that the Ojibway survived on corn and wild rice reserves.[10]

Victims of warfare also relied on wild rice to sustain them through recovery. Alexander Henry in 1775 arrived at the remains of what had been a large Ojibway village on "Lake Sagunac" (probably Namakan) before it was destroyed by the Dakota: "I found only three lodges, filled with poor, dirty and almost naked inhabitants, of whom I bought fish and wild rice, which latter they had in great abundance." That this was in July is remarkable. These Ojibway must have cached a great deal of rice from the previous year.[11]

Before the influx of white settlers, wild rice was unquestionably the principal staple of Indian diet in Jenks's rice district; because the number of plant foods used by the Ojibway was one of the lowest for Great Lakes tribes, wild rice assumed even greater importance to them. When other grains were introduced from the Old World, the Ojibway invariably used their staple *manoomin* as a referent: thus barley was wild rice with a tail; oats were horse rice. Because of children's general fondness for wild rice, they were sometimes nicknamed in reference to another of its admirers: *waawaabiganoojiinh* (mouse).[12]

Foods other than wild rice may have been equally important at times, but more often than not they were combined with rice in a stew or gruel or served with rice as a side dish. Added to a soup, wild rice was used to wean babies at about ten months of age. John Mink, noted medicine man at Lac Court Oreilles in the 1940s, recalled his change in diet during infancy: "I remember the taste of my mother's milk. It tasted rich and good like bear fat and I remember crying for the breast. When I was able to eat wild rice and venison and blueberries, I stopped nursing." Except when unavailable, then, rice was as pervasive as bread is today. As Lips stressed, whatever their former subsistence basis, tribes migrating to the western Great Lakes region made wild rice their basic foodstuff. She also forwarded the possibility (overlooked by others) that, under pressure to provide traders with furs from animals whose meat was distasteful, Indians increasingly relied on wild rice; the flesh of fox, lynx, marten, and muskrat was surely discarded, for an Indian would eat these animals *only* in times of dire necessity.[13]

In some places within the rice district, however, the consumption of wild rice was comparatively minimal, particularly where European gardening took hold, such as along parts of the south shore of Lake Superior. Sherman Hall in 1831 wrote frequently of Indian "gardens" at La Pointe, on present-day Madeline Island in Wisconsin. Pondering subsistence possibilities in carrying out his missionary work among the Ojibway, he concluded: "[W]e shall be able to raise a large part of the provisions for a small family at this place, after a year or two. Garden vegetables grow here very well. Potatoes can be raised in large quantities. Corn grows here, though it is not long. Oats, barley and peas which have been cultivated by Mr. Warren have succeeded well." Only rarely did Hall mention wild rice—once in the context of a funeral, another time when he was inland, at Lac du Flambeau. Possibly there were rice failures in the area, for in a journal entry dated September 6, 1831, he lamented that the La Pointe Indians seemed to be without food and thus uninterested in discussing religion. Hall felt compelled to give them a few quarts of corn from his own provisions.[14]

Thomas McKenney's 1826 *Tour to the Lakes* is also instructive about the south shore diet. Curiously, wild rice was not mentioned among the staples of the settlements he visited. His journey was in midsummer, when rice supplies might have been depleted, for he took careful note that "The wild rice does not grow on the lake, but far beyond, between it and the Mississippi; it abounds on the Fox river." He said the Indians ate small swan's potatoes—starchy tubers collected in wet ground in midsummer, peeled, and dried for preservation. Six years later Lieutenant James Allen echoed McKenney's observations in a report on Henry Schoolcraft's 1832 expedition: "The Indians of this [La Pointe] department, *excepting those about Lake Superior,* subsist chiefly on wild rice and game, such as deer, bears, &c, and generally also supply their particular trader with these articles of provisions."[15]

J. J. Ducatel, who visited Madeline Island during the annuity payments in August 1835, found standard provisions essentially the same—the only winter food other than game and fish "a few potatoes and a very little corn." He allowed that some wild rice was stored and whortleberries were dried as "the only summer gifts that are hoarded . . . not as a delicacy, but for nourishment," although he mentioned only smoked game, animal lard, and fish as contents of the caches. In 1855 another visitor to Madeline Island, Johann Kohl, frequently discussed Indian foods but almost never mentioned wild rice. When he attended a La Pointe Grand Medicine feast to initiate a child into the society, "at sunset a huge kettle, full of steaming maize broth, was dragged in and placed in the centre of the hut." Almost anywhere else in the rice district, such soups contained wild rice, not corn, as the base. Given the proximity of the Kakagon rice sloughs directly adjoining Lake Superior's shore, just south of Madeline Island, the seemingly minor role wild rice played in the diet of these people is surprising.[16]

Red Lake, Minnesota, was another Ojibway settlement where the consumption of wild rice was minimal. Several factors made corn rather than rice the principal staple there. The rice crop was apparently sporadic and not found in the same places each year. Elders at Red Lake still remember having to travel to Leech Lake for the rice harvest. A large corn harvest enabled fifty outside families to be accommodated at Red Lake through the winter of 1842. Their move there presumably was prompted by rice failures in their own communities, and their acceptance at Red Lake was probably an act of reciprocity.[17]

PREPARATION

Where wild rice was the main staple, it was traditionally prepared by boiling in water or broth. (The recipes for wild rice dishes in connoisseur cookbooks of the twentieth century are totally outside Indian tradition.) Before metal kettles were available, dried grain and hot water were mixed together in bark pails suspended above a fire. (A birch-bark vessel does not burn so long as it contains liquid.) Most cooking traditionally was done outdoors; once the Indians had semipermanent homes and manufactured kitchen equipment, however, they moved this activity indoors. There was a transitional period when older and newer ways of cooking coexisted, said William Baker: "Well, in my days too, they would cook on a stove, but my grandma used to cook outside in the fireplace—just a regular rack, three or four pails hanging there, boy, just like you were making syrup."[18]

Before cooking, the processed rice was washed several times, sometimes with a small amount of soda (once the Indians had it) added to the first rinsing. This removed dust or dirt particles accumulated during storage and floated off bits of chaff left from winnowing; it most certainly was *not* to remove the smoky flavor imparted to the rice through parching, as Huron H. Smith asserted. When clean, the rice was simmered with water or broth until it absorbed the moisture.[19]

Cooking time depended on the condition of the rice and the desired consistency of the final dish. Freshly harvested green rice cooked in ten minutes or even when boiling water was poured over it. Parched rice required half an hour, and fire-cured black rice took twice as long. Completely processed rice and old rice taken from storage might require overnight soaking. Albert Reagan, who prepared wild rice for breakfast, recommended soaking: "[T]ake a cupful of the rice and pour a cupful of boiling water on it at bedtime and then cover it over so as to keep the steam in and let it set till morning, then put it on the stove and evaporate the remaining water. It is then puffed-rice, and is delicious with sugar and cream." Whether Reagan learned this method from the Indians or came upon it himself through experimentation is not known. Nor is it evident whether the Ojibway followed the practice of the Dakota of Titoha village, who "put some to rot in the water, and when they return in the spring they find it delicious, although it has the worst kind of an odor."[20]

Paul Buffalo cautioned against eating green rice: "It doesn't agree with your body . . . you're too anxious. You get pale, you see, it's got to be right before it's good . . . but in milk [state] it's tender. It's just like veal, you eat veal, too much milk. It goes through you. So some of that I've seen at times. This other epidemic, it hits old people harder. . . . So the green rice, it build up, it swells up in your stomach, and there's a reaction. It makes you drink water."[21]

An admonishment against eating green rice was couched in a story recorded by Mille Lacs Ojibway Fred Jones during interviews for the University of South Dakota Indian Research Project. Jones said he learned this story from his grandfather. Seemingly set in medieval times, it may have come from French or Scandinavian loggers, as the Ojibway learned many tales in the lumber camps and retold them as Indian legends. This particular story, versions of which have been collected elsewhere in North America, was one of Jones's narratives of a string of traditional tales involving Wenabozhoo (variously Wenaposo, Nanabojo, Nanabush, and so forth), the Ojibway culture hero. It concerns a game between the hero, a young soldier, and a king who turns out to be the devil. The hero has two dogs, Cast Iron and Steel, who fetch food for him. The action occurs in a town where the king's palace is guarded by soldiers. The hero cuts off the heads of a monster and puts their tongues in a sack, saving the town as well as the king's daughter, whom he marries. Wild rice comes into this otherwise European pageant when the king provides a bed and supper for the hero's dogs: "Oh, he gave them some green rice there, you know, that's how the wild rice came in nice and green, and oh, that was good . . . [the hero] told the guys, 'Just before I eat any place, I've got to give my dogs something to eat first.' So he called the dogs in . . . the dog wouldn't take some, the other one wouldn't take some. 'No, the dogs won't eat, so I can't eat.' Finally, you know, he got this green rice then, dogs, they sniffed it, you know, and they put their tongue out and they took it back, so they tasted it. So finally the old king told him he would have to put his dogs out. The dogs tasted the rice and it's all right for him to eat. So the dogs ate, and so he put the dogs out, and he had the rice." The young soldier sleeps, awakens with a stomachache, goes outside, and vomits worms and insects. There is no further mention of wild rice in the story.[22]

Because the wild rice makes the hero sick, this story might be interpreted thus: A traditional Ojibway would probably not feed his dogs before himself. Here, the dogs seem to serve as poison detectors for the young soldier, much like a Roman emperor's food-tasters. Their initial refusal to touch the green rice and final, albeit reluctant, sampling should be noted as a warning unheeded by the hero.[23]

This episode may represent an allegorical admonition against ingesting wild rice of any inedible condition. Eating raw rice was apparently a problem with the children hanging around camp as rice was processed. Maude Kegg (born 1904) of Mille Lacs told how, as a child, she became violently sick from eating *manzaan,* the fine, broken rice that spills out with the chaff during winnowing: "I'm always eating that rice. Then a lady, Dookisin was her name, says: 'Don't eat it. Don't do that! You'll get bloated.' So then I steal and eat a great big handful of that rice. And that night I really get sick."[24]

Fred Jones's tale, then, describes the consequences of eating "green rice"—rice that has not been processed. The vomited insects and worms may be understood as dirt and detritus removed in the drying stage or destroyed, like rice worms, through parching. Despite his dogs' warnings against eating unprocessed green rice, the hero foolishly accepted the king's (devil's) unclean food offerings with predictable results.

COOKING

The proportion of liquid to grain and the cooking time determined the consistency of the final product. For unsticky, nonglutinous (fluffy) rice, the rule of thumb was to use about twice as much liquid as grain. Some Indians preferred wild rice in the form of a gruel, requiring more liquid. In his journal, trader John McLoughlin substantiated the fairly large amounts of liquid added to rice: "One quart of the Grain boild in two Gallons of any kind of Broth or in the same quantity of water with an ounce of Grease till it comes to consistence of porridge or rather thinner is in General as much as any man will eat in a day."[25]

This way of cooking applied to fully ripe wild rice, but the Ojibway often collected some green rice and considered it a real treat. Because the kernels were immature and not as large and the moisture content was proportionally higher than that of ripe rice, green rice did not cook to as high a volume as regular wild rice. At Lac la Pluie in 1823 McLoughlin described the difference: "Their [*sic*] is an other Way of preparing oats [wild rice], it is collectd in the same way as the other but before it is Ripe, and then dried in a Kettle stirring it about continually until it leaves the chaff. then van'd as the other this is called Roasted Oats and it requires at least three pints of this to answer to two of the other."[26]

Cooked wild rice was frequently eaten alone or steamed and used as dressing—before the treaty era with fish, duck, or venison, later with government-provided salt pork or hamburger. Once prepared, rice was eaten in short order, as it did not keep well unrefrigerated. As Paul Buffalo described, "[I]t begins to turn into lime and eats itself away, right out from the hulls."[27]

Wild rice was also used throughout the year to thicken broths including venison, bear, fish, and wildfowl. William Baker likened the final dish to a soup, with endless variation possible. After cooking the meat, the Indians added rice to the broth, then "you add your bacon, or your carrots, or macaroni, or whatever you want to put there." The antiquity of using wild rice as the basis for such soups is reflected in a traditional legend about the discovery of rice by Wenabozhoo (see p. 61–62).[28]

Gardner Stickney mentioned rice being "Cooked into a paste . . . [and] used as a substitute for bread"—a possible reference to a sort of wild rice flour noted in early sources. Marquette asserted that, when not boiled, rice was pounded to flour; trader and interpreter John Long in 1791 noted that to nourish and strengthen their children, women gave them wild rice and oats, "which being cleansed from the husk, and pounded between two stones, are boiled in water with maple sugar." A kind of wild rice bread was made at White Earth in the 1920s by mixing flour with ground rice called *manoomin daabishkoo bakwezhigan*. William Baker, probably referring to the small, powdery rice left from winnowing, said something similar was used in soups: "[T]hey call it the powder, *manzaan* . . . sorta put in soup, cook some venison, some bones, make a soup out of bones, and they take the bones out and put that [*manzaan*] in there, a piece of salt pork. Boy, that's a good meal." This was probably the dark powder sometimes referred to as "head-rice."[29]

The most common Indian wild rice dish was a combination of rice with other ingredients in a stew. At powwows today, especially around harvest time, food stands still offer a thick venison-rice stew or soup, as much a statement of local Woodlands "Indianness" as fry bread is of general Indian identity.

Traditional Ojibway stews included almost anything—"one promiscuous *chowder*," said Ducatel in 1835 of a dish of meat, fish, and vegetables he saw boiled together at La Pointe. James W. Biddle spoke fondly of another Indian stew, "an object of early love" remembered from Green Bay around 1816:

"The Indian women used to make a favorite dish of wild rice, corn and fish, boiled together, and called *Tassimanonny.*" In the same manner, the Ojibway boiled dried wild potatoes with meat for a winter stew. Paul Buffalo recalled: "Many of them would thresh rice here, go from one another camp to another. Help pound out the housing [hull], the rice, you know. Some was down the river, catching fish, setting nets. Catching bullheads, cooking the big bullhead stew, and fish stew. Then take their stew about, north, take a stew of that and then put it in the wild rice, with a little salt pork, pork balls, you know. Oh, you got something there. And a few potatoes with it, wild, and fried salt pork."[30]

A wide variety of small game animals were used in wild rice stews. William Baker's family prepared meals of four to five squirrels, cleaned, skinned, and cooked with wild rice. Just as often they might "mix [rice] up with everything, woodchuck, porcupine. It all depends on the size of the family, they cook according to that."[31]

To make such a stew with duck—the favorite meal on the first day of the harvest—Nett Lake Ojibway simply cut a cleaned bird into pieces, cooked it in water, then added rice enough to produce a thick porridge. A similar Ojibway wild rice-wildfowl dish was described by Doty in a letter to Lewis Cass, then governor of Michigan Territory, as "one of their highest epicurean dishes . . . they accasionally [*sic*] take a partridge, pick off the feathers, and without any farther [*sic*] dressing except pounding it to the consistency of jelly, throw it into the rice, and boil it in that condition." Lawrence Mitchell remembered how his mother and grandmother cooked at their camp at Big Rice Lake after the first rice was gathered: "This is where the first feast, you know, with duck, mallards, or most times I remember it was the mudhens, they were nice and fat, really delicious dish. . . . They'd boil their duck, and then when it's just about done, then they would add the rice. And once in awhile they'd put other stuff in there, like potatoes and leftover bread and things like that. I remember my grandmother had one of those cast-iron kettles for parching the rice." Such stews were fairly common throughout much of the North American woodlands east of the Mississippi. Outside the wild rice district, some other available grain or vegetable such as corn served as a base for stew.[32]

The only seasonings that the Ojibway and other Woodlands rice gatherers traditionally used with wild rice were maple sugar, berries, and animal fat—any or all of which might be added during cooking. For example, when the Cree at Whitedog Reserve, Ontario, decided to destroy an old man known to practice sorcery: "[T]hey fixed up nice dishes of good things to eat and put bad medicine in them to poison him . . . and there was one dish there it had indian rice and blue berries and maple sugar and that was what he ate."[33]

The acceptance of such European condiments as salt, pepper, and butter to season wild rice has been recent, and many older Ojibway still eschew them. Precontact Indian people had their own way of cooking: deer tallow mixed with bear grease was an effective shortening, and ashes were used in place of soda for baking bread. The absence of salt, a comparatively recent introduction, was often remarked upon in early sources; for example, an explorer at Lake of the Woods in 1857 found rice cooked with blueberries a welcome relief from foods seasoned with salt. Minnesota Ojibway began to acquire a taste for salt only in the mid-nineteenth century. The government's 1847 "Salt Treaty" with the Pillager band at Leech Lake, for instance, included the stipulation that they receive five barrels of salt annually for five years. Perhaps to commemorate this treaty, the Indians composed a song: "Let them despise us; we [who] live here, beyond the belt of timber, have salt," an apparent taunt at other Ojibway not so fortunate.[34]

Father Frederic R. Baraga, in answering inquiries about Indian food practices, replied that the inland Indians rarely used salt, butter, milk, or cheese, but that they liked salt and butter when they could get it. At the time of Frances Densmore's field work (about 1910), many older Ojibway had not acquired a taste for salt; at Lac Court Oreilles in 1941, Waboos said her mother would not touch any food with salt in it. (James Doty's somewhat sensational assertion that northern Wisconsin Ojibway used rabbit excrement to season rice for partridge stew seems as questionable as his claim that they ate skunk which, when prepared for a meal, made it "impossible to approach the lodge except to the windward.")[35]

Maple sugar was certainly preferred. The Ojibway and other Indians such as the Menominee often ate rice seasoned only with maple sugar. Berries of almost any variety—blueberries, chokecherries, Juneberries—might also sweeten the dish. They were customarily left on birch-bark mats, pieces of cloth, or rooftops to dry in the sun for two to three days. Since sun-dried berries were usually put into storage, they were available year-round. They could be steeped or added to broth during cooking.[36]

Using animal fat to season wild rice is an old custom that still continues—possibly obviating the need for salt. Missionary Claude Dablon in 1671 called rice mixed with buffalo fat, "the most delicate dish of this country," an opinion echoed by Marquette: "Cooked in This fashion, The wild oats have almost as delicate a taste as rice has when no better seasoning is added." Bear fat with wild rice was to have been part of the last supper of a hapless English captive of the Potawatomi. Preparing to execute a fur trader named Ramsay, they "brought him to the war-kettle to make his death-feast; which consisted of dog, tyger-cat, and bear's grease, mixed with wild oats, of which he was compelled to eat." Ramsay supposedly made an escape by intoxicating his captors with rum and cutting their throats.[37]

Grease of some sort continues to flavor Ojibway cooking. Rendered salt pork, for instance, is put on potatoes with salt; boiled milkweed shoots and ferntops are seasoned with grease of any sort. Lips observed people at Nett Lake steaming rice with a piece of fat the size of an egg for five minutes before slowly adding boiling water and a little salt. At Ojibway powwows today, where cooked wild rice is sold at stands, concessioners invariably provide coffee cans of bacon drippings to smear on the hot rice.[38]

The only alternative to boiling rice was roasting until it exploded like popcorn: "When it is desired to parch it, the rice is placed in pots over a slow fire until the grain bursts and shows the white, mealy centre. Without further preparation it is often used by hunters and fishermen when out on expeditions."[39]

Popped rice was a favorite of children, who made their own on hot stones. Ojibway author Ignatia Broker listed popped rice among the treats that were part of the traditional naming-ceremony feast in her great-grandmother's time: "There would be much food, for it was after the ricing time when food was stored and buried. Acorns were roasted. Hazel nuts were ground and mixed with dried berries to make small cakes. Ma-no-min, the precious wild rice, was popped and mixed with . . . maple sugar." Newton H. Winchell asserted that the first rice gathered was popped, a small amount at a time over a slow fire, the grains nearly doubling in size as they burst. Popped rice must be what Schoolcraft had in mind when he said: "It is also sometimes roasted and eaten dry." At White Earth in the 1920s, popping rice was not much different from preparing popcorn today: "They'd take a fry-pan and maybe put just a little bit of lard or grease in the pan, just a little bit, and then they'd hold it over the fire, but they were very careful, they'd keep shaking it, so that it pops even. That was real good." Also fried in a greased pan was *manzaan,* the fine bits of rice left over from winnowing. George McGeshick of Mole Lake ate it raw, simply adding water and sugar.[40]

"AN EXCELLENT ARTICLE"

Whether the wild rice the early Europeans sampled was boiled or popped, their reactions to this unusual New World food item were positive, and even the earliest sources expressed delight at its discovery. Upon his first taste of wild rice, Zebulon Pike asked Chief Wabasha to have four bowlfuls delivered to his men. Despite the considerable labor in gathering and finishing wild rice, wrote J. P. Bardwell at Cass Lake in 1849, it was "an excellent article of food, preferable I think to our Southern rice." And Colonel Whittlesey extolled it on several counts: "With wild rice, sugar, and the fat of animals, well mixed they make excellent rations, which will sustain life longer than any preparation known to white men. A packer will carry on his back enough to last him forty days. He needs only a tin cupin [*sic*] which to warm water, with which it makes a rich soup."[41]

Missionaries, from Jacques Marquette through Frederic Baraga and Chrysostom Verwyst, invariably shared the diet of their Indian converts. At the head of Lake Tracy (now Superior) in 1666–67, Father Allouez first tasted wild rice prepared by the "Nadouesiouek" (Dakota), who had not as yet been driven from the area: "They cultivate fields, sowing therein not Indian corn, but only tobacco; while Providence has furnished them a kind of marsh rye which they go and harvest toward the close of Summer in certain small Lakes that are covered with it. So well do they know how to prepare it that it is highly appetizing and very nutritious." Marquette in 1673, noting that the grain was twice the size of oats, remarked that "The meal therefrom is much more abundant."[42]

In particular, Father Louis Hennepin in his journeys through the western Great Lakes made repeated reference to wild rice, a "Corn . . . somewhat like our Oats, but much better." For winter fishing on Lake Huron, his party broke holes in the ice to sink nets for salmon, which "made our *Indian* Wheat go down the better, which was our ordinary Diet." From his captivity at Milles Lacs Lake he remembered wild rice as the best meal provided. The Indians "gave us some wild Oats to eat. . . . in great Dishes made of Birch-trees; and the Savage Women season'd them with *Bluez* [blueberries]. This is a sort of Black Grain, which they dry in the Sun in the Summer, and are as good as Corrans [currants]." On August 14, 1680, Hennepin was invited to a great feast attended by 120 men from the villages of the Issati (Santee Dakota), at which Ouasicoude brought him "some dry'd Flesh and wild Oats in a dish of Bark, which he set before me upon a Bull's Hide, whiten'd, and garnish'd with Porcupine Skins on the one side, and curl'd Wooll on the other." Ouasicoude later sent Hennepin off with a map and provided him with bushels of wild rice for subsistence: "We have already observ'd, that these Oats are better and more wholsome than Rice." A steady diet of even the best of foods wearied the Franciscan: "Many a melancholy Day did I pass amongst these Savages. *Aquipaguetin,* who adopted me, gave me nothing to eat but a few wild Oats five or six times a Week, and the Roes of dry'd Fish. All this Trash the Women boil'd up in an Earthen Pot."[43]

At the end of the nineteenth century the Franciscan missionary Verwyst, whose abiding interest in Ojibway culture led him to a lengthy compilation of Indian place names and publication of a practical grammar of their language, had grown quite fond of the wild rice harvested by the Bad River Ojibway from the Kakagon sloughs. He said, "[W]ild rice is very palatable, and the writer and his dusky spiritual children prefer it to the rice of commerce, although it does not look quite so nice." Joseph Gilfillan, the Episcopal missionary at White Earth, noted simply, "Most people like it better than white rice. I do."[44]

Wild rice became an early staple of traders living in semipermanent posts, and they depended on it as much as their Indian customers did. Wrote Henry Schoolcraft to Lewis Cass in 1831: "The articles which are purchased of the northern Indians in addition to furs & skins, are wild rice, ready made canoes, or canoe-bark, gum & wattap, and maple sugar. The proportion which the rice & sugar bears to the general stock of subsistence for the clerk & his men, cannot be stated, It is, however, so much as to be always relied upon by the trader, & when the rice crop fails, as it did in 1830, scenes of suffering ensue." Employees of the fur companies also depended on traditional Indian food supplies. Eliza Morrison, whose father and father-in-law both had worked for the American Fur Company, recounted: "The company headquarters was at La Pointe, but they would send men and goods a great way off to the north and the west. . . . They had to depend on the Indians for their meat, wild rice, and other food. If there was a severe winter and deep snow, they and the Indians would likely go hungry before spring."[45]

This reliance on wild rice is nowhere more evident than in the journal entries of traders such as François Malhiot, whose outpost was in northern Wisconsin. A French Canadian, Malhiot had been transferred in the summer of 1804 by the North West Company from its Upper Red River Department to take charge of the Lac du Flambeau fur post. Malhiot's matter-of-fact, frequent references to wild rice attested to its pervasiveness. In the course of deploring excessive drinking, he wrote on September 16: "The Savages overwhelm us; we cannot set our nets, and we constantly eat our rice with water only. A fine and good dish! dogs would get thin on it." Ten days later, he complained that the Indians depleted his food supplies: "The Savages pester me and my provisions are disappearing like straw in the fire. . . . We hardly have time to put a kettle of rice on the fire before 50 of these dogs are around us asking for some even before it is boiled." After another two weeks, he expressed relief that the Indians had departed for their winter quarters: "We shall therefore begin fishing again and have some fish to season our rice. It is time, for my stomach was getting weak." Malhiot made it evident that wild rice had entered the realm of metaphor in repeating how Little Cadotte depicted the stinginess of a trader named Lalancette. Cadotte advised the Ojibway: "Do not trade with him; he knew you were starving and he did not deign to bring you a single grain of rice; he is a hog; he makes a god of his belly."[46]

Implicit in Malhiot's complaints was the recognition that a steady diet of wild rice alone was insufficient. When David Thompson arrived at the North West Company fort at what is now Cass Lake, he found "Mr. Sayer and his Men had passed the whole winter on wild rice and maple sugar, which keeps them alive, but poor in flesh." William Johnston's 1833 letters on the fur trade noted that voyageurs frequently ate wild rice: "but it is not found so strengthening and the men commonly fail in strength from the to[o] constant use of it." The deficiency was corrected by adding meat to the rice.[47]

By the beginning of the nineteenth century, many whites living in the rice district had come to prefer wild rice to the commercial variety. In November 1819 Robert Stuart sent Lewis Cass a small parcel of wild rice from Mackinac, with an apology for not sending more because supplies were exhausted. Caleb Atwater in about 1830 discovered wild rice to have "a sweet taste like our oats." Whites owning property adjoining rice fields allowed the Ojibway to camp there during the harvest in exchange for some of this table delicacy. Because it is so easily digested, hospitals in the twentieth century have served wild rice to patients with stomach disorders.[48]

Given that wild rice is affected by regional variations in climate and ecology, it is not surprising that individual Ojibway preferred rice from particular areas. Lips was constantly told by Nett Lakers that *theirs* was recognized as the best rice—thus the frequent requests from others to join their harvest. Lawrence Mitchell likewise insisted that rice from Big Rice Lake at White Earth was the finest, which helped explain the presence of guest ricers from as far away as Wisconsin Ojibway and Menominee reservations: "Big Rice Lake had real fine rice, whereas these other lakes have this heavy rice, big grain. The finer rice, the smaller grain, that might be the reason why a lot of them went out there, because you go around Mille Lacs or Nett Lake, they got the big grain rice, and [Big] Rice Lake has probably the finest grain rice there is. Flat Lake on the White Earth Reservation has a little heavier. It takes longer to cook, and then it doesn't seem to have the flavor the other rice has. Seems like the bigger the grain, the less flavor it has."[49]

Sister M. Inez Hilger found one Lac Court Oreilles woman in 1934 traveling a hundred miles west to rice in Aitkin County, Minnesota, claiming the kernels there were smaller and better-tasting than those in her own community. Paul Buffalo praised not only the vast quantity but the taste of the wild rice from Mud Lake, where his family harvested. He attributed its excellence to the water quality of the lake, which had a good outlet and an inlet of fresh water and circulated freely: "He's got a lot of rice off of this lake. Because, there's a good filter in this Mud Lake right here . . . it was one of the richest flavor, richest tasting and good flavor. . . . You can't hardly get enough of it, when you eat it." Almost any Ojibway today who keeps rice in the pantry knows where it came from and, in many instances, who processed it. On one day in the late summer of 1985, William Baker showed the author a plastic bag of rice finished by Rosebud Boulley at Odanah, Wisconsin, one hundred miles north of Baker's house, and James Mustache produced a bag he thought was harvested at Long Lake, thirty miles south of his residence in Hayward, Wisconsin. Ojibway connoisseurs can distinguish between the taste of lake and river rice. Such familiarity with the taste of natural wild rice caused the Ojibway to reject the cultivated paddy rice first developed by whites in the 1960s, not only for cultural reasons but also because of its flavor. George McGeshick compared differences in wild rice taste with those in venison: "Same with a deer; if you get a tame deer, if you feed it, tastes different."[50]

How much rice would suffice an Indian for a meal? One of the earliest reports is that of Pierre Radisson, who in 1661–62 noticed: "for each man a handfull of that they putt in the pott, that swells so much that it can suffice a man." Jenks said a coffee cup full of wild rice, when cooked, would produce a full dinner for two, an amount that jibes with William Baker's use of about half a cup of rice when cooking for himself. A resident of Bad River Reservation once wrote to Stickney on the salutary effects of such food: "Fill the stomach real full and then lay down. It keeps from hunger. Not strongly nutritious, it produces great rest and sleep to men, while women work."[51]

The decreasing amount of wild rice in today's Ojibway diet is sometimes cited as contributing to Indian health problems, particularly tuberculosis. Many older Ojibway tend to blame illnesses on the shift in Indian diet from traditional food sources to a reliance on items obtained in white grocery stores. William Dudley at Red Lake lamented: "The food we eat now is different from what they ate years ago, which would make them more hardier people." Josephine Clark, from Pine Point, said: "Well, long time ago people didn't get sick like they do now, you know. Sometimes I blame the food we eat now. Maybe it's the food that does it. . . . See, the Indians all had their own land. They had [wild] potatoes, they had rice, they had maple sugar, they had deer meat, they had ducks—all these wild stuff, you know, they eat. They never bought anything from canned stuff. And they fixed their own food their own way."[52]

"FAT AND DELICIOUS"

As early as the eighteenth century, both Indian and white connoisseurs of wildfowl found that rice-fed ducks were more delicious than fish-eaters. Jonathan Carver observed that "the sweetness and nutritious quality of it attracts an infinite number of wild fowl of every kind, which flock from distant climes to enjoy this rare repast; and by it become inexpressibly fat and delicious." In particular, the geese, ducks, and teal caught on Lake Winnebago, he said, were "remarkably good and extremely fat, and are much better flavoured than those that are found near the sea." Furthermore, the rice stalks offered good duck blinds. In the next century, Whittlesey recollected that the Fox River rice bed "serves to shelter [the Indian hunter] in his insidious designs against the wild ducks, who congregate among it, and lay claim to what they wish to eat."[53]

Jenks noted that the waterfowl, far from damaging the wild rice crop, "were really gleaners, and picked up and preserved in most delicious form the grain which otherwise the Indian would have lost entirely. Heavy waterfowl could not do very great damage to the standing plant, and while the grain was standing the Indian must gather his harvest. When the kernels shelled out into the water they were loss to the Indian, but gain to the fowl, which picked them up by diving to the bottom."[54]

Wildfowl feeding on rice often became so bloated and sluggish that they were easily dispatched with a canoe paddle. Rice rails in particular were easy to catch. M. Catesby in the early eighteenth century observed that in Virginia the "Soree" (rail) became so fat eating "Wild Oats" that the local Indians were able to "catch Abundance by running them down." After feeding on wild rice, wrote Elisha J. Lewis in 1863, "they are particularly tender, rich, juicy, and delicate, and do not cloy the stomach by quantity or pall the appetite by daily indulgence." Thus storekeeper Harry Ayer in 1920 wrote a Chicago friend in hopes he would visit Mille Lacs "when the ducks are ripe." At White Earth Gilfillan waxed eloquent in 1876: "The Indians look forward to rice-gathering as a very happy time, as they then have not only an abundance of rice, but by a happy combination of circumstances, the ducks go in great numbers to gather wild rice at the same time that they do. So *they meet,* around the smoking board and elsewhere. The ducks are old and very dear friends of the Indians, their families having been on intimate and visiting terms for I know not how many centuries past . . . and the pleasure of meeting, on one side at least, is rapturous. Often the ducks get so fat with eating rice that they cannot rise to fly, and are therefore obliged to receive their friends who come to call upon them, sitting; but the pleasure of the interview is not at all diminished by this apparent want of courtesy on their part, the cause of it being well understood on both sides, and excused."[55]

Paul Buffalo compared Leech Lake mallards favorably with those from the Red River, which fed on bugs, giving them a "muddy, boggy, musky" flavor. Lawrence Mitchell told how White Earth ricers took time off from harvesting to catch fat rice-feeding rails: "At that time there was nobody in a hurry, and this is when all the hunting took place, you know, the duck hunting and the rice hens. They're little, what they call rails, they get nice and fat. Usually they ran a boat right into the lake shore where weeds are thick, and then they would back off from it and then these birds would gather in that clearing. They used to shoot them with a little bow and arrow or sling shot. I don't remember ever shooting them with a shotgun. They gather there just about the time the rice is getting ripe, they nest right along the, oh different lake, not really necessarily [a] rice lake, but they'd nest right close to that area, and then when the rice is getting ripe they've had their little ones, they're learning how to fly, and they go into these rice fields, and they're very noisy birds, but they are good eating, and once again we get into this thing of patience, where the Indian was patient in plucking the feathers and getting the little bird ready to eat."[56]

CHAPTER 3

In Legend and Ceremony

In dreams we have learned how everything given us is to be used; how the rice is harvested and the animals hunted. So that we would learn all the crafts, once a pair of humans was taken from the earth and brought to a place where they learned everything that the Indians know, even how you follow the [dictates] of dreams and honor the spirits. The two thought they had been gone for eight days, but it was actually eight years.
—Bill Johnson, Nett Lake, 1947[1]

WERE WILD RICE merely a staple in the Ojibway diet, one might ask why it might not be replaced with foodstuffs easier to harvest and process. Traditional Ojibway life elevates rice above being food simply for consumption or barter. Stories and legends, reinforced by the ceremonial use of *manoomin* and taboos and proscriptions against eating it at certain times, show the centrality of wild rice to Ojibway culture. These factors together suggest that wild rice, at least in the past, approached the status of a sacred food.

In ritual use the Ojibway people have accorded wild rice a vitality beyond its nutritional value. Even today, though the beliefs behind such customs may be obscure to many Ojibway, the practices of leaving wild rice at a grave and refraining from the harvest while menstruating or mourning persist. No less important is the place wild rice held in traditional legends recalled by elders, but not regularly recited today. In these stories, wild rice is a crucial element in the realm of the supernaturals and in their interactions with animals and humans; these legends explain the origin of wild rice and recount its discovery by a culture hero. Allegory and symbolism often shroud the deeper meanings of tales in Ojibway culture; because of this, some writers have ventured so far as to assign wild rice the role of a "mystique."[2]

To be sure, wild rice is a topic of everyday Ojibway conversation. Nearly everyone recollects bountiful or poor yields, accidents on the lake while ricing, or games, dances, and courtships set at the rice harvest. Maude Kegg related taking advantage of the adults' preoccupation with processing rice near Mille Lacs Lake to sample the contents of her uncle's snuffbox: "I admire the looks of that thing, the little birchbark box. It must have been a snuffbox that I had, then I peek at my aunt parching rice, take a pinch, put it in my mouth, and go playing around outside, spitting around." Predictably, she became dizzy and sick from her experiment.[3]

Ricing serves the Ojibway as a marker of time. Anecdotes from previous seasons are incorporated into the joking and teasing that characterize group banter when all are in good spirits and waiting for the rice to ripen. People recall upset boats with occupants forced to swim to shore, or someone who cheated an unwitting rice buyer with a sack of oats topped with a layer of wild rice, or those who customarily brought so much lunch they scarcely had time for harvesting.

Certain historical events recalled as happening during harvest are related again in that context. John Tanner spoke of an early nineteenth-century epidemic that occurred when he was ricing with a group of Indians. Ethnohistorian Calvin Martin, who recently analyzed Tanner's description, concluded that the disease was probably tularemia, which resembles pneumonia in its symptoms. The responsible microorganism thrives in a water/mud medium—exactly where wild rice plants grow. Nett Lakers tell of a time (probably in the early or mid-nineteenth century) when their people, while knocking rice, noticed near the shore of an island a place in the water muddied as if by some animal. On inspection they discovered several Dakota warriors hidden in the reeds, many of whom they overpowered and scalped right in the water. Meanwhile, the Dakota, knowing all adults would be on the lake ricing, had already begun to slaughter the Ojibway children in the village.[4]

More serious forms of verbal narrative, reserved for special people to tell at certain times of year, have given *manoomin* an exalted place in the activities of the supernaturals. These are the stories and legends explaining the origins of wild rice, how the Indian people came by it, and how, magically, the grain sustained the spirits of old as it does today the *anishinaabeg* (original people, the Ojibway name for themselves). Some of these were told at harvest time, and many Ojibway still remember hearing rice tales in camp. The more powerful tales, however, were more likely narrated by grandmothers to grandchildren over the long evenings of the winter months; there was a taboo against telling legends in summertime for fear of snakes. Such legends have disappeared except from the memories of the oldest generation.[5]

Almost universally, American Indian cultures have passed down stories attributing the discovery of important tribal staples to the supernaturals, who in turn gave them to the Indians. The Shasta Indians of California, for example, depended greatly on both salmon and grass seed for nourishment. Each year the predominance of one staple over the other was explained in their traditional belief system as a result of a wager between Thunder and Dove. All winter Thunder bet on the salmon, Dove, on the grass seed. If there was thunder before the dove cooed in spring, Thunder lost and the people received salmon in profusion. If the sounds of the dove came first, the Shasta had grass seed in abundance, while fishing was poor.[6]

Wild rice harvesters had similar legends. In their earlier history, when the Menominee were organized along totemic lines, they believed rice was the property of the Bear and Sturgeon clans. Big Thunder (Wishkĭ′no) visited the Bear phratry, offering maize and fire in exchange for rice. The Menominee story of this event shows how much like humans the supernaturals behave, and how, allegorically, the natural elements—wind and rain—have to be propitiated to protect the harvest: "When the wild rice was ripe in the fall, the eagles, all decorated with feathers, had their canoes and rice sticks ready. After they had gathered four canoe loads, a thunderstorm came. It destroyed all of the grain which had not been gathered, and spoiled the beautiful feathers on the heads of the eagles. Then Wishkĭ′no [head of the Big Thunder phratry] said to Shekatcheke′nau [the first Indian and head of the Bear phratry], 'It won't do for you to give me the wild rice, for wherever I go there is thunder, and wind, and rain. I will give it all back to you, and you'd better control it always.' So after that when rice harvest came Shekatcheke′nau called all of his people together, and they made a feast, and smoked, and asked the Great Spirit to give them fair weather during the harvest. Since then there has always been a fine, stormless harvest season." The Michigan Potawatomi told a similar story with the Bear phratry offering corn and fire in return for wild rice.[7]

Ultimately, however, members of ricing tribes believed that wild rice was the gift of their culture hero, from whom they derived all beneficial items and learned the crafts and techniques needed to survive and flourish. Thus, for the Menominee, Manabush was the giver of rice (through Bear, whom he created for the task) as well as of fish and maple sugar, their other principal staples. Ojibway belief attributed to Manabush's counterpart, Wenabozhoo, the gift of wild rice, as well as the creation of the earth and establishment of the medicine lodge. For the eastern Dakota it was Wahkeenyan who brought wild rice, the tomahawk, and the spear.[8]

The Ojibway incorporated into the cycle of Wenabozhoo stories their most deeply held religious beliefs, ethical codes of conduct, and explanations for natural phenomena. Anthropologist Christopher Vecsey described the central meaning of their creation myth as the alleviation of hunger: "The folklore, like religion, reflected the need for food and the means of obtaining it." Thus when

Jenks remarked that the wild rice mentioned in Algonquian folktales was usually just a natural product, he failed to appreciate that the tales contain symbolism and that they encode certain Indian precepts. Even Henry Schoolcraft recognized that Indian belief set the origin of wild rice apart from the rest of creation, although Schoolcraft placed it in a less-than-significant category: "They say the Great Spirit did not make the wild-rice, it came by chance. All things else the Great Spirit made." In any case, the Wenabozhoo legends make it clear that wild rice was, above all, a food especially intended for the Indian people.[9]

Wenabozhoo's discovery of wild rice is recounted in legends with wide circulation. Jenks collected this version of the tale at Lac Court Oreilles in 1899. The story begins when Wenabozhoo's grandmother tells him that to prove his manhood and become accustomed to hardships he should embark on a long journey without food. "Many days he wandered, and finally came to a beautiful lake full of wild rice, the first ever seen. But he did not know that the grain was good to eat; he liked it for its beauty. He went into the forest and got the bark from a large pine tree. From this bark he made a canoe with which to gather the grain. After the canoe was made, he went to Noko′mis [grandmother] and they both came and gathered the rice, and sowed it in another lake." Wenabozhoo again departs on his fasting journey. He encounters some bushes that speak, telling him that they are edible, whereupon he digs up their roots and eats them. This causes him to become so sick that he is forced to lie there three days. When he resumes his journey, other plants speak to him too, but he assiduously avoids them.[10]

"At last he was passing along the river, and saw little bunches of straw growing up in the water. They spoke to him and said: 'Wenibojo′, sometimes they eat us.' So he picked some of it and ate it, and said: 'Oh, but you are good! What do they call you?' 'They call us mano′mĭn,' the grass answered. Wenibojo′ waded out into the water up to his breast and beat off the grain, and ate and ate, but this time he was not sick." Thus sated, he remembers having sown this very plant with his grandmother, so he returns home.

A familiarity with the Ojibway puberty fast helps explain this legend. Customarily, a young boy was sent without food to fast in the woods until such time as, faint from weakness, he received a dream or vision in which some tutelary spirit appeared to make a covenant. Often the boy received a special dream song with instructions from the spirit to encode the experience in some design on his clothing or drum. The exact meaning of the song or the symbol was known only to its owner; it was for use whenever he needed assistance from his supernatural guardian.[11]

As Wenabozhoo embarks on his puberty fast, wild rice appears as his vision; because each vision is personal and unique, the grain he encounters is "the first ever seen." Remember that he does not as yet know its value as a food, but simply admires its beauty. He returns to tell his grandmother of his discovery, just as an Ojibway youth on a vision quest returns to inform his parents of his success in dreaming. Wenabozhoo and his grandmother then sow wild rice seed from the lake of its origin into another lake. This corresponds with a widely held Ojibway belief that rice, once discovered (given by Wenabozhoo to the Indians), was deliberately but spiritually sown from its original source into other bodies of water. Lac Court Oreilles Ojibway, for instance, told Jenks that wild rice was first found on the Red River of the North (about 1660, by Jenks's calculations). Red River rice was then sown at Snake River, Minnesota, then Shell Lake, and farther east into Wisconsin, from one Indian community to the next.[12]

Continuing his journey, Wenabozhoo is tempted by bushes to eat their roots, much like Alice is enticed by the foods in Wonderland. He falls ill for three days as a consequence of violating the taboo against eating during a vision quest. Having learned his lesson, he avoids other tempting plants, until he sees wild rice growing in a river and succumbs to eating it, discovers its name, and recalls that he already has sown some for its beauty. Despite breaking his fast, he does not become sick.[13]

Several lessons are implicit. Despite violating the proscriptions against eating during his fast, Wenabozhoo enjoys the grain without suffering the disastrous consequences that befell him earlier. By tempting fate, he provides the Indians with one of their most important staples. Wild rice is consequently a very special gift, with medicinal as well as nutritional values—a belief reflected in the Ojibway use of wild rice as a food to promote recovery from sickness as well as for ceremonial feasts.

As a trickster Wenabozhoo constantly violates Ojibway taboos, but in doing so he brings progress to the human condition, or, as anthropologist Laura Makarius put it, "acquir[es] magical power for the group." Throughout the legends, he acts contrary to traditional Ojibway wisdom and comportment. His very birth is abnormal—perhaps a foreboding of his later antics. In various stories, among other things, he commits incest with his sister, obliges his grandmother to relieve herself in his presence, and enters a menstrual lodge to find a wife. Through his violation of this last taboo, Wenabozhoo "hunts abundant game," obtaining hunting magic for the Ojibway.[14]

Beyond the discovery legend, wild rice is the focus of several Wenabozhoo stories in which the principal characters are waterfowl. Throughout the cycle of Wenabozhoo legends, birds, like all sky beings, are generally helpful to the culture hero, providing him with knowledge.[15] This tendency is demonstrated in the story of Wenabozhoo and Mallard, one of the many "bungling host" stories found among North American tribes. Wenabozhoo is a trickster figure par excellence, typically portrayed as a bungler, whose humanlike foibles leave him outwitted or embarrassed by others. In one version, Wenabozhoo visits Mallard, becomes hungry, and, observing no food about, wonders what there is to eat. Mallard tells the woman of the house to hang up the kettle. He paints his head completely green, alights on the cross-pole suspending the kettle, and begins to utter the sounds "kwish, kwish, kwish" and say "ho, ho, ho, old woman! keep it stirring." Thereupon Wenabozhoo hears the sound of rice boiling. When it is boiled, Mallard descends and says, "Now, therefore, shall you eat. What you do not eat, then to your children [the Indians] may you take."[16]

Sometime later, faced with a guest and caught without food himself, Wenabozhoo attempts the same trick. Telling his wife to hang up the kettle, he paints his head green and jumps up, making "kwish, kwish" noises. "Finally he was perched over the place where hung their kettle, he could be heard uttering: *'kwish, kwish, kwish, kwish!'* " Wenabozhoo produces only "a miserable droplet of dung," which whirls about in the kettle. His embarrassed wife washes out the kettle, whereupon the visitor paints himself green. "[T]hen began the sound of the Mallard, who then was alighting upon their cross-pole. So thereupon he began muttering, and forthwith some rice came pouring out [of his anus]. When their kettle began to fill, then down he alighted." Mallard then tells Wenabozhoo that his children will have plenty to eat. (This author interprets painting the body green as the transformation into green, or ripe, rice and the "kwish" sounds as those made during harvest.)

Albert Reagan in the 1910s collected the story "Manabozho [Wenabozhoo] goes Visiting," which has themes clearly related to those above. On his journey, the hero comes to a distant village of his people. Duck-Bill invites him home, but his wife has nothing to feed the guest: " 'Get things ready,' commanded Duck-Bill. 'I'll get you something to cook.' Then the men continued to tell more stories for a considerable time. As the [cooking] stones began to show a white heat, Duck-Bill began to flap his wings. In a few minutes he flew off over the country to a rice field and soon returned with his mouth full of rice. This rice he put in the cooking tray and it soon swelled till it had filled the whole vessel. His wife then threw in the heated stones and in due time a feast of wild rice was set out before them and they had all that they wished to eat." On the following day Wenabozhoo reciprocates, and *his* wife is without food for her guest. Attempting the same solution, Wenabozhoo changes himself into a large clumsy duck and flies off to find wild rice. On his return, he loses his balance, falls, and injures himself badly, but manages to stagger to the cooking tray to spit out the rice he has gathered. Instead and unexpectedly, out flows sour mud, quickly filling the tray. Wenabozhoo has mistakenly turned himself into a mud-diver. The horrible odor of the mud causes his wife to throw it out, whereupon Duck-Bill gets rice for them. Once it is cooked

Duck-Bill refuses to eat it, saying, "No. . . . This is for hungry people. My people have plenty to eat."[17]

The collectors of this tale noted that in three other versions of the story wild rice is produced from bird droppings. This theme is also found in a story Jenks heard at Lac Court Oreilles. Here rice is ranked with venison in importance in the Ojibway diet: "One evening he [Wenabozhoo] returned from hunting, but he had no game. As he came toward his fire he saw a duck sitting on the edge of his kettle of boiling water. After the duck flew away [Wenabozhoo] looked into the kettle and found wild rice floating upon the water, but he did not know what it was. He ate his supper from the kettle, and it was the best soup that he had ever tasted. So he followed in the direction which the duck had taken, and came to a lake full of mano′min. He saw all kinds of duck[s], and geese, and mud hens, and all other water birds eating the grain. After that, when [Wenabozhoo] did not kill a deer, he knew where to find food to eat."[18]

A literal interpretation of these stories is somewhat problematic. Bird droppings scarcely resemble wild rice kernels, cooked or uncooked; furthermore, because rice seed, unlike some others, is easily digested by birds, little of it comes through in their excrement—one reason birds play a minimal role, if any, in spreading wild rice. Still, these tales reflect the fact that rice increases greatly in volume when cooked and is exceptionally nourishing. Also implicit is the Ojibway knowledge that rice-fed mallards are better to eat than mud-divers.[19]

Comparison of this bungling host tale with versions of the story collected from the Menominee, neighbors of the Ojibway to the east, helps elucidate the structural meaning of the episode. In the Menominee tale Mallard is replaced by Red Squirrel, who produces wild rice, not by defecating but by slicing open his testicle, from whence pour the rice kernels. He closes the wound and the rice ceases to flow, whereupon he opens the other testicle to let out grease—a typical flavoring for wild rice. When Manabus, the Menominee culture hero, tries the same trick, he produces only blood, prompting him to say, "My wife has spoiled this; she is having her sickness."[20]

These stories clearly impart to wild rice (the food) a magical quality, placing it vividly in opposition to menstrual blood, semen, fecal matter, and the like—the realm of Wenabozhoo, the bungler. Instead of producing wild rice, the culture hero draws only blood or spits out sour mud. As Makarius observed, "All things impure fall under his rule. No wonder his comportment is foul, obscene, vulgar."[21]

By contrast, Mallard (or Red Squirrel), in defecating (or spilling semen) to produce wild rice, demonstrates the power to perform magic or "to make medicine" (*manidoowaadizi*). To accomplish this, one must maintain a proper harmony with the spiritual or supernatural world. Wenabozhoo may have *dis-*

covered wild rice, but his arrogance leads him to "try the trick" of producing it, with disastrous results.

The capacity of wild rice to enlarge upon cooking and to provide a nourishing meal is the focus of several other stories. In the course of Delia Oshogay's narrative of "Wenabozhoo in the Whale and His Fight with an Ogre," collected by anthropologist Ernestine Friedl at Lac Court Oreilles in the early 1940s, the trickster spends the night at the home of an old woman. As she prepares a meal for him, he notices that her kettles are no larger than small apples. She puts a single kernel of corn in one kettle and one of rice in another, causing Wenabozhoo to wonder how he will be fed sufficiently. But each time he eats a kernel from the kettles with a wooden spoon, another kernel is left. "When he was real full, the kettle was empty." A contemporaneous version collected by Robert Ritzenthaler on the same reservation identifies the hero as Bebókowe, the hunchback, who lives with his sister. The two wonder whether they are the only people on earth, and the hero decides to make a journey and find himself a wife. He, too, encounters an old woman who prepares him a meal consisting of a few grains of wild rice cooked with dried blueberries in a kettle only one inch in diameter. The old woman, reading Bebókowe's mind, says, "I suppose you thought there was just one mouthful there."[22]

The same tale is told with a different hero – the First-Born Son – who, in pursuit of his wife, arrives at the home of a grandmother and is fed dried blueberries mixed with grease. After sleeping he eats again the next morning, departs, and by evening comes to the house of another grandmother. She boils him one grain of rice in a tiny kettle and hands it to him as he thinks, " 'I shall not get enough to eat, such a small bit is my grandmother feeding me.' Then into his hand he poured the rice, ever so full was his hand, (and continued so) till he was sated with food." Seemingly related but without conclusion is a Lac du Flambeau story in which two sisters come to a hut above the clouds. The old woman within puts a tiny kettle on the fire and asks, "What shall we give these people to eat?" She puts in some wild rice, such a small amount that one sister, Matchikwewis, questions whether that is all they are being fed, to which her sister replies, "It's better than nothing."[23]

Along with Wenabozhoo legends are stories explaining the discovery of wild rice and its propagation. Although the ability to spread rice by deliberate seeding is today well recognized by Indian people, their ancient belief was that this was always accomplished by supernaturals. The Menominee Chief Nio′pet, for example, told Jenks that his people did not need to sow rice, for it would follow them wherever they went. Shawano Lake, south of their present reservation, never had wild rice until they moved there, and when the Menominee were banned from Lake Winnebago, the rice there nearly disappeared. The Ojibway expressed similar views. Bill Johnson at Nett Lake in

1947 repeated what he had learned from his grandfather, that wild rice was created for the *anishinaabeg:* "Man has never planted the rice; it had been put in [Nett] lake and other lakes and rivers, when the land was formed for the Indians. Also, one cannot sow the rice; humans can't do that. Sometimes there's no rice, but when the *manidoog* [spirits] want it, it grows again."[24]

The Ojibway often localize stories to explain the presence or absence of wild rice in nearby lakes as the result of the deliberate activity of legendary figures. Ed Burnside (born 1896) attributed rice in Whitefish Lake (Ontario) to a boy named Spruce, later to become a great chief. Angered at being refused ricing privileges in Nett Lake, he destroyed all its rice, saving one bag for sowing elsewhere: "[T]hen he went to White Fish Lake, told those suckers [fish] go around the lake and plant that rice for him, and in three years time was White Fish Lake full of rice along the shore land. And this boy was big enough to notify all his relatives nearby to come and gather the rice in by this lake."[25]

How rice came to grow in Nett Lake is related in several tales of how the Ojibway discovered the lake and decided to settle there. In all of them, Spirit Island is intricately bound to the presence of rice. A half-acre island sometimes called "the heart of the lake," Spirit Island is surrounded by rice fields on all but the south side, where the water is too deep. The island is believed to be the home of a certain *memegwesi,* the principal supernatural provider for Nett Lakers. *Memegwesiwag* are a sort of Ojibway leprechaun, said to be three to four feet tall and covered with hair. Thought to live in the water, the creatures are invisible unless they come to the surface, whereupon they assume human form. Their boats are of stone and, said John Bisonette of Lac Court Oreilles, "Sometimes they just sit in the boat and travel through the water fast without paddling." Joe Littlepipe saw two of them out in their boat on Sand Lake, Wisconsin. At first he had mistaken them for tourists, but then they suddenly disappeared.[26]

Like all supernaturals, the *memegwesiwag* behave very much like the Indians in many of their activities; they, too, riced. Maude Kegg remembered her family encountering them at Boy River: "We were ricing there, sitting down towards evening; she [stepmother] was saying that they had seen *Memegwesiwag.* 'They knock rice there . . . [Boy River] too,' she says. 'We were knocking rice along there,' she says. 'Maybe there's someone over there,' her old man was saying, and they stop there and she puts down the [ricing sticks]. Sure enough, the sound of [the sticks] was coming toward them where they were sitting in the water. Later a boat suddenly appears, coming around the corner. There are two knockers and they sit there watching them. They want to see who they are, but as they blink their eyes, they disappeared from sight. He said, 'those *memegwesiwag* have hair on their faces.' "[27]

Because a *memegwesi* is believed to live on Spirit Island in Nett Lake, much reverence is accorded the place; ancient spiritual petroglyphs have been found there, and when the lake is agitated, small caverns along the island's shore give off a sound said to be the spirits "drumming." Lips collected several versions of the following story, both sacred (that is, privately owned) and secular—the so-called free tales anyone could tell. John Nett Lake's story of Spirit Island begins: "A long time ago hunters came over the hill and saw a wide green field. They thought it was grass, but it was rice. After awhile they noticed that there was water there, got their canoes and pushed off onto the lake. They came to the island we call *manidoo-miniss* today; but there were only rocks and no tree stood on it. On the island they saw an old man, clothed entirely in cloth strips which surrounded him like a net, but he disappeared in the rocks and they saw him no more." This was the *memegwesi* who ruled the island. The story goes on to tell how the Indians encounter the "hairy-faced ones," who plot to steal fish from the Indians but in return direct them to a fat caribou, which they quickly dispatch with their bows and arrows.[28]

In Ed Burnside's version, the Indians find the *memegwesi* walking on top of the water wearing something resembling a net. He banishes the Indians from his island, saying he does not wish to be disturbed, but he shows them where they may settle: "And you can go back and tell them people where you come from. They can come over here on the shore and have their wigwams, and you can harvest all this rice; that's my rice and you can have it as long as you can get ahold of [it]. Bring your canoes and get that rice. Tell the people to say something about God, to him before they eat that rice because that's going to be my rice."[29]

Another version of the discovery of Nett Lake, which Lips collected from Peter Smith, does not mention the *memegwesi.* (The "rock," which in the story turns out to be a turtle, however, may be interpreted as a vestigial reference to Spirit Island, as turtles often symbolize islands in Ojibway lore.) In any case, the discovery of wild rice led Indians to settle at Nett Lake: "In the old days the Ojibway used a path which led from Canada to our country. On the way, where they used to camp, lay a large waterfall. One day the hunters followed an animal through a thick pinewoods. They lost its track but found themselves suddenly on a hill unknown to them until then. . . . Before them lay open land like the prairie. They thought it was a meadow, but it was the lake completely covered with rice. When they went further to the place that's now called sugarbush, one man saw a round rock and jumped on it. But it was a large turtle sunning himself there. The rock began to move and the man fell in the water and saw the rice. He crawled out of the lake and told his companions about the rice. They all went back to their families and told the people what they'd seen. They held council and decided to move there."[30]

Author Dan Brogan provided another story of Nett Lake's discovery without naming a source. In this tale the Ojibway, after paddling through Vermilion and Pelican lakes, come upon some "half sea lion, half fish" beasts on an island; they chase the animals westward through the rice until the earth swallows them (catches them in its net). Brogan says the beasts represent the Dakota, driven west from the area by the Ojibway.[31]

The special place of wild rice in Ojibway legends helps explain its ceremonial use in real life. Throughout North America, Indian people always celebrated the harvest of their most important staples with thanksgiving feasts and religious rituals. Each staple—maize for the Mandan and Hidatsa, pine nuts for the northern Paiute, whitefish for the Klamath Indians—is accorded a status endowed with sacred properties. Taboos surround its use; it is woven into legends and song; it is incorporated into rites of passage.

The everyday use of wild rice both as a food and for its medicinal properties is distinct from Ojibway beliefs and practices that accord it more special powers. A mother unable to nurse her infant would give the baby wild rice boiled with meat or fish broth as a milk substitute. Such a gruel is simply an old and widely held native American health formula. As medicine, fine, broken rice (*manzaan*) was boiled, then strained to render its "juice," which was mixed with certain herbs gathered in the spring or late fall to produce a poultice. This salve was applied to relieve skin inflammations caused by nettles or poison ivy. Included in the *materia medica* of John Mink was a cure for gonorrhea that used the root of the wild rice plant in two ways: in a brew made from the root and store-bought goldenseal, or in a root decoction injected into the urethra with a syringe. There was nothing particularly magical about these cures. Acquaintance with such basic remedies was quite different from the belief that if a pregnant woman ate popped rice her baby would have difficulty breathing, that someone who tasted human blood and was thus in danger of turning into a cannibal could recover by drinking boiled rice broth, or that girls should abstain from all foods *except* wild rice during their puberty rites. These beliefs and practices derive from the spiritual significance of wild rice, not from its nutritional or medicinal qualities.[32]

The sacral nature of wild rice is reflected in the many attitudes concerning its growth, the size of the harvest, damage to the crop, and the like. Consider, for instance, ambivalent Ojibway beliefs about the propagation of wild rice. Lips found at Nett Lake that, although the people recognized themselves as responsible for reseeding the rice each year by knocking it into the water during harvest, the idea of sowing rice was inconceivable; its reappearance each year was attributed to the spirit controlling the lake. Charlie Day (Mayminobidonk) told her, "Any attempt to sow the rice like whites sow corn would curse the lake, and rice would never grow in it again." Lips said this belief was widely held by other Minnesota Ojibway, and that Nett Lakers broke into laughter trying to imagine humans spreading rice. They believed that Wenabozhoo would always provide them with rice and that, if the Great Spirit so desired, rice would always grow. Attendant was the fear that one might offend Mother Earth by attempting to sow what was naturally *given,* and that, as punishment, the spirits would destroy the plants.[33]

Such supernatural concepts help to explain how the abundance and disappearance of wild rice from a given area through crop failures or devastating storms have become incorporated into stories or legends. In Ed Burnside's quasi-historical story (see page 66) of how Nett Lake rice came to be seeded into Whitefish Lake, the young boy Spruce came from Grand Portage with his mother, presumably to rice at Nett Lake at the time when Black Stone was chief. (Since the chieftancy passed from him to White Feather, thence to Moses Day, this sets the story early in the nineteenth century.) Apparently there was opposition at Nett Lake to allowing the Grand Portage Ojibway to rice there. Burnside said: "And they [Spruce and his mother] were about two days behind time, and they got into Nett Lake. And they came in too late in the day to go out and pick rice. And most of the other chiefs let her out gathering rice for her son. And the old chief didn't like it, got mad and took the rice away from the old lady, and the old lady got sore, and then she started to cry." Thereupon her son told her they should return home; en route he would destroy all the Nett Lake rice. As they went, he knocked some rice into the basket where his mother kept her fish and fishnet.[34]

Spruce informed his mother that he possessed supernatural powers and asked her to smoke the pipe while he performed some magical songs; these caused a violent storm just before midnight. Hailstones the size of small pine cones destroyed the entire crop, leaving Nett Lake barren for eighty years and angering the other chiefs toward Black Stone. Meanwhile, Spruce and his mother fled via Lac la Croix to Grand Portage, and the three suckers in her basket kept the rice green. Upon Spruce's direction, the fish magically sowed Nett Lake rice into Whitefish Lake.

Traditionally, anything afflicting the wild rice crop was attributed to supernatural causes; only individuals with spiritual prescience could foretell disastrous events concerning the harvest. In the 1930s at Manitou Rapids Reserve in Ontario, the story was told of an eight-year-old boy with special powers who was ignored as too young to possess forecasting ability. No one listened when he said there would be no blueberries that summer. When the berries were ripe for picking, "a big rain hail came and knocked all the blue berries off and destroyed them and only then the indians believed Nah wi Gi shik and they moved back. Also he said there would be no rice and sure enough there wasn't."[35]

Such stories, with their admixture of historical fact, allegory, and human and supernatural interaction, have been an integral part of Ojibway oral lore. In addition to these tales were those mentioning wild rice in the context of feasts given by spirits, animals, or human beings. In the story of Hell-diver and Gabibonike (the spirit of winter), for example, Hell-diver volunteers to remain behind during the winter to tend to a whooping crane and a mallard, both with broken wings. To prepare a feast, he gets some wild rice, whereupon Gabibonike arrives. As Hell-diver stokes the fire, Gabibonike becomes too warm, "but he liked the wild rice and wanted to go on eating it." This causes him to begin losing his winter powers.[36]

Wild rice was the focus of many human celebrations, such as the first-fruits feasts common to traditional cultures. While these meals were partly thanksgiving festivals, they were also meant to ensure that the spirits would continue the bounty in future years. The Ojibway applied this precaution to animals as well as to wild rice; for instance, similar ceremony surrounded the killing of a bear. Its decapitated head was festooned with beads and ribbons and laid out on a mat together with its paws for four days before being cooked. Wild rice was among the offerings placed before it. Noted John Quaderers of Lac Court Oreilles: "People come to visit the bear and bring things for it like a bowl of wild rice or maple sugar or syrup or blueberries. . . . If this is done in the evening, the first person coming in the morning could eat the food on the mat. . . . People would talk to the bear while he was laid out."[37]

Once, when George James killed a bear and her cub on that reservation, Whiskey John Mustache, following tradition, was sent as a runner with tobacco to invite people to the feast. Served with the bear meat were wild rice, dumplings, maple sugar, macaroni, bread, cake, and tea. Those who had recently lost relatives ate first. Accordingly, John Mink "spoke about how those in mourning should be fed according to the old ways or the one who killed the bear wouldn't be able to kill any more meat and the wild rice would not ripen. He addressed the spirit of the bear and asked that she go back and tell the other bears how well she was treated. Bones and other remains were buried. The dogs were not allowed to have any meat or bones, nor were they tolerated near the food. All the meat was either eaten or given away. Whiskey John took the head and paws home where he laid them out on a mat and decorated them. They were kept several days and people came to visit."[38]

To partake of the first animals or fruits *without* going through some ceremonial propitiation was surely to invite trouble. Thus the Ojibway always made offerings to the Great Spirit before eating the first fish caught, the first blueberries of the season, or the first deer killed in the fall hunt. As Maude Kegg remembered from her youth at Mille Lacs: "In the spring when they finish off the sugar, they wouldn't take a bite of anything unless they first have the necessary feast. They give a feast, have a ceremony, and give thanks for the sugar. . . . It's like that too for wild rice. It's like that too when they first knock rice. They won't take a bite." Because Kegg's grandmother processed the rice, she also hosted the feast, offered tobacco, talked to the thunderbirds and the sun, and put tobacco out—all before the others were allowed to eat. Speeches and thanksgivings using wild rice to celebrate the first of the maple sugar harvest were noted by missionary Edmund F. Ely in a March 1841 diary entry as he traveled to Knife Lake (near Pokegama?): "A large Kettle of Rice was cooked & sugar mixed with it. Shagobe harangued the Company. I did not understand that he made any address to the *Great Spirit*—although he often spoke of His Mercies to them. He offered me a dish of Rice & sugar."[39]

Such feasting frequently took place in the dance halls that began to appear on reservations toward the end of the nineteenth century with the spread of the Drum Dance. Dan White (born about 1900) of Leech Lake recalled the spiritual purpose behind such communal dinners: "They had to go through a ceremony before they ate. . . . They wanted to put tobacco out and say a few ceremonial words and all that to the Great Spirit, for to share in that stuff, they were sharing their foods with the Spirit."[40]

While wild rice was served as a matter of course at these larger gatherings, it was just as often a part of special smaller family feasts, such as when a child was named or at curing ceremonies. For the naming feast, a child's parents customarily prepared venison and rice. In 1940 at Mille Lacs, the mother of a two-month-old child gave a naming feast to which she invited six elders. After the name was given, the child was passed around, kissed by each in turn, and told to have a long life; wild rice, boiled meat, cake, cookies, and coffee were served. In the early 1940s, following John Mink's treatment of a patient, wild rice and buns for everyone in attendance were placed on the blanket where the patient lay. On the same reservation a special curative ceremony, the Chief Dance, was used during rice harvest. Originally derived from war ceremonials, the dance developed into a ritual to cure sickness or protect veterans. Occasionally it was used at Lac Court Oreilles during the rice harvest to ensure a favorable crop or ward off inclement weather.[41]

Wild rice played an important role in Ojibway religious ceremonies, within both the older *midewiwin* (Grand Medicine Society) and the later Drum Dance, which evolved as the Ojibway version of the Grass Dance sometime after 1880. During these rites, rice was not only a feast food but also an offering. Ritual feasting during medicine ceremonies always included wild rice alone or as a basis for stew. White Earth medicine lodge ceremonial meals in the 1930s consisted primarily of wild rice, beef, and dogmeat. When Paul Buffalo was about nine years old and attending a government school, he once relished a meal being prepared for a medicine dance: "When it come to meal time, they had a big dish, old time dish pan, two handles, cooking, maple sugar and wild rice, great big stew, all thick and the raisins and everything they put in there, you know. Oh, it was big! . . . I was just set for that." His sister, however, wisely admonished him to keep his distance and not to expect to receive any of the consecrated meal.[42]

It was customary to purchase *midewiwin* membership or advancement with offerings or payments to one's preceptors. A typical array of gifts at White Earth in the 1930s consisted of four cotton blankets, three two-gallon pails, some cooking utensils, calico, groceries, and packages of wild rice. When Johann Kohl witnessed the induction of a small child into the medicine lodge at La Pointe in 1855, the priests offered to the father gifts tied to the cradleboard and meant to be held in trust for the child: packets of dried roots, shells, a thimble, and a small bag of wild rice. Similarly, wild rice was used to pay for Indian doctoring services. When a white doctor in Bayfield, Wisconsin, was unable to cure the eye trouble of Josie White's two-year-old in about 1924, she took the child to Tom Baker, an Indian: "Josie went and got a pint (whiskey) from Henry La Roche and some tobacco and wild rice. It cost her $30 by the time she was finished." Similar payments were made to Delia Oshogay: "She made lots of the same kind of [anticonsumptive] medicine for different people, for Georgy La Rouge after he grew up. She also made some for Louis Corbine's son. They paid her cash and garments, groceries, Indian rice and things like that."[43]

The conjunction of fall *midewiwin* rites and the ripening and harvest of wild rice was not accidental, for it was believed that the medicine ceremony helped the rice to mature. Furthermore, a primary *mide* goal was the attainment of a long, healthy life, and wild rice was believed to help one achieve it. Lips wrote: "The rice harvest of the Ojibway is not just an event with temporal boundaries of weeks – namely the weeks of the ripening of the harvest fruit and its processing and storage; it is the decisive event of the year, of the total economic life and with it, life itself."[44]

During Lips's field work, the leaders of the medicine lodge played a crucial role in blessing the first fruits of the wild rice harvest. Even the most "progressive" Nett Lake Indians, fearing public reaction, would not consider eating new rice without first taking part in a brief ceremony performed by one of the four *mide* priests who officiated at Grand Medicine ceremonies. In 1947 the blessing took place in William Bony's house. As soon as the first rice was cooked, the head of each family brought some to Bony's home in a small covered jar, pot, or can. The rice chief, Charlie Day, that year brought an additional pot for a sick man unable to come in person. The containers were covered to ward off errant evil spirits who might contaminate the rice before it was blessed. When Bony's house was filled with people, others gathered outside to await a repeat performance. Each family head put his pot on a low table and uncovered it, whereupon the medicine man performed the traditional Ojibway pipe ceremony, lighting the pipe and blowing smoke to the four cardinal directions, then passing it clockwise for all present to puff.[45]

A prayer given by an elder was recorded as follows: *Miigwetch manidoo miinawaa odisaabandamaang 'o manoomin gaa-bagidinamowambaneh anishinaabe ge-miijid* (Thank you spirit that again we come to see this rice that you must have offered to the Indian for him to eat). Implicit in this prayer was the notion that the Great Spirit gave wild rice to the Indian people as *their* food, whereas the whites were given other foods by their god. The Indians thus gave thanks for being allowed to live another year to eat once again of the rice. Lips stressed that this concept was founded in the *mide* belief that a long, healthy life is given by the spirits. The brief ceremony concluded after the medicine man took a small bit of rice to eat from each pot. Its owner did the same, then covered it again and took the consecrated rice home. Bony's house filled with the next group. Similar rituals were performed in Wisconsin. After the first rice was gathered, Louis Martin and his family at Rice Lake, for example, invited Alec Martin and his family to join them. After tobacco was passed around, a medicine man made a speech, and the company ate a meal of wild rice, bread, and tea.

The tradition of feasting on wild rice in the course of religious ceremonies was incorporated into the Drum Dance. Formerly, the Leech Lake event featured a large feast about one or two o'clock in the afternoon, including everything associated with Indian repast: "[T]he leader of the feast . . . takes the kettle and puts it down and those that wants to eat, they go get the dish of what they want to eat. Wild rice, blueberries, dried blueberries, wild rice, maple sugar and everything there. Real nature, oh, but they're living." An important subrite of the Drum Dance was the Dog Feast, a Woodlands borrowing of a northern Plains Indian warrior ceremony. Often the dog ceremonially killed for the occasion was stewed in rice, a practice observed on the White Earth Reservation in Minnesota and as far east as Lac Court Oreilles in Wisconsin.[46]

The fall Drum Dance at Mille Lacs, which by 1966 was the largest of the four seasonal dances, was held immediately after the wild rice harvest. As a gesture of thanksgiving, green rice was offered to the four winds and the Great Spirit in the course of the dance. Clearly this custom predates the Drum Dance. Ignatia Broker, in recounting her great-grandmother's history, remembered that some of the "first rice" was blown in the four cardinal directions "on the wind to be carried to the [Great Spirit]."[47]

While the religious beliefs behind such practices have sharply declined in the twentieth century, the general celebrating with song and dance that customarily took place at harvest continues on many reservations. Late August powwows coinciding with the harvest are often given names associated with the crop: at Ball Club on Leech Lake Reservation the powwow is called "Megwetch Manomin" (thanks for wild rice); at Bad River it is the "Manomen Celebration." Yet there is little to suggest the existence of a special genre of ricing songs reserved for the occasion. Lips's general unfamiliarity with Ojibway music led her to infer that dancing in the evenings during harvest represented a special "Harvest Dance," which she described at some length, lapsing into a rather romantic style. ("In the evening, when the powwow began, the dance hall lay like a large dark shadow in the rapidly sinking night. From afar already one heard the muffled drumming.") The details of her description make it clear that the evening gatherings, though coincidentally serving as an opportunity for the rice chief to make announcements concerning the harvest, were little more than social affairs.[48]

Because there were songs associated with the harvest of other Ojibway staples—Begging Dance songs to solicit maple sugar from workers in the sugarbush or sacred songs for success in hunting deer, for example—the scarce mention of songs connected with wild rice and its harvest is surprising. The earliest collectors of Ojibway song, such as Frederick R. Burton and Frances Densmore, failed to record any ricing songs per se, and it seems none have been collected since.[49]

There have been, however, occasional references to songs, both sacred and secular, somehow associated with wild rice. At Nett Lake burials, after a package of wild rice was thrown into the grave, mourners sang a song referring to how wild rice would help the deceased on the journey to the land of the dead. Sylvia Cloud of Odanah remembered a special song used when her father "danced" (hulled) the rice for their relations, and James Mustache recalled a song at Lac Court Oreilles performed when "one old fellow" trod the rice: "I don't remember that song anymore, but they got that slow beat; we'd pound on anything . . . you pound on two sticks, not loud, you know, but just so he'd hear the time."[50]

Songs also may have been performed to prevent storms from devastating the crop. Two of Stuart Berde's eighteen informants at Leech Lake remembered hearing some mention of "ricing medicine," which may have been connected with songs or have been used, together with song, to ensure a bountiful, safe harvest. Propitiating the spirits before the rice was harvested often involved singing with the drum. Paul Buffalo explained: "We're leaving for the journey . . . to look over the crop. Maybe take something that we need for sample, for taste, that's matured. . . . I pound the drum, thank the Great Spirit, make signs to the north and west and east and south. The Great Spirit has given directions, given the power, given these parts of the storms. It could come from either way, make a lot of damage in the area, which may destroy our crop, may hurt the feelings of the people, may hurt the life of the people. So that's why we are carefully, that's why we do these things in our Indian way." Although Sister Bernard M. Coleman asserted that in the rice camps "in each group there was one man, usually the head of the family, who owned a ricing drum," this author's exhaustive research into Ojibway drum types failed to unearth evidence of special ricing drums. Possibly someone belonging to the *midewiwin* brought a water drum, as songs performed with it at other times ensured good harvests and hunting. However, given the social atmosphere of the harvest, large, secular dance drums were probably the only type taken to the rice camps.[51]

Customarily, tobacco offerings were for thanksgiving and for protection. As Paul Buffalo warned, "You gotta remember before you pick rice, take that tobacco, put it in water. Water's a big thing, dangerous." At Vermilion Lake, one old woman put a pinch of tobacco into the fire before eating the first rice, a widespread practice observed at Lac Court Oreilles into the 1940s as a protection against windstorms. Storms could also be warded off by putting a piece of plug tobacco on a stump and invoking the assistance of thunderbirds. Canadian Ojibway at Sabaskong Bay take the first handful of rice harvested and, with tobacco, put it in the water while giving thanks.[52]

The underwater spirits who controlled the lakes and rivers were potentially dangerous and could not be neglected. In the sixteenth century, Indians in what later became Virginia were observed offering the spirits tobacco to calm rough waters and ensure success in fishing. In the seventeenth century, Jesuits noted that the Ojibway made sacrifices to the water spirits for the same purposes. If ignored, these spirits could not only devastate the crop with storms but also cause ricers on the lake to drown. Consequently, the evening before harvesters first embarked to knock rice, they held a special feast, during which tobacco was passed, the Great Spirit was asked for a successful harvest, and the water spirits were petitioned for safety. The Indian agent at Coucheeching Agency in Ontario wrote Jenks: "Before commencing to gather the rice they make a feast, and none are allowed to gather the grain till after it. They thank the Master of Life for the crop, asking him to keep off all storms while they are harvesting." According to James Mustache: "That's what they *used* to do. But they don't do it anymore. . . . I know, either my grandfather or some other would talk . . . to the Great Spirit, and also to the water spirits . . . asking them for a safe and bountiful harvest."[53]

The use of wild rice in funerary practices, its inclusion at memorial feasts, and proscriptions against eating it during periods of mourning are clear evidence that Ojibway people continue to associate wild rice with sacred matters. Among many cultures where the old ways of doing things are dying out, the last vestiges of tradition are usually found among the practices and beliefs surrounding death. This is one explanation for the persistence until recently, at least, of such Ojibway customs as non-Christian wakes to prepare the dead for the four-day journey to the land of souls, removing the body from a house through a window rather than a door to avoid spirits at the threshold, having a medicine man in addition to or instead of a Christian minister officiate at burials, and constructing small houses over graves.

The Ojibway people believe that the spirits of the dead must be fed not only during their journey to the afterlife but at regular intervals thereafter. Almost universally wild rice has been selected exclusively or included as one of several foods for this purpose. In his journal for 1833, Sherman Hall described a funeral for a young boy on the mainland opposite La Pointe: "After the body was put into the coffin, one of the Indians took a small piece of cloth in which some apparently hard substance was tied up in two separate parts, each about as big as a man's fist, and put it into the coffin. . . . After the coffin was nailed up, the clothes which the person had worn, and a pan of wild rice which was cooked, were placed upon the lid. . . . After the grave was dug, which was but a few rods distant, the coffin was carried out by the Indians and followed by the relatives and friends of the deceased. The clothes and the rice also were carried and placed by the side of the grave." In the same year at a Sandy Lake Indian cemetery, more than a hundred miles west of La Pointe, Edmund Ely encountered a memorial dinner in progress: "I forgot to mention Sabbath Evening, that I had seen a *feast* around the grave of an Indian—by his relatives—as I [was] walking toward the rise of ground on which some are interred, I observed a Circle around the head of a Grave—curiosity prompted me to go to them. I found several dishes of *Wild rice, Boiled* (smoking from the Kettle)—distributed to the Company."[54]

Reagan in 1924 mentioned that Nett Lake Ojibway threw a package of wild rice into the grave to provide sustenance for the deceased. Sister M. Inez Hilger reported that a Red Lake man was buried in 1930 wearing full ceremonial regalia, including moccasins and feather bonnet; with him were dried meat, berries, a frying pan, and wild rice. At Mille Lacs the deceased was dressed in new or clean clothes; two bags made from flour sacks or muslin, one containing tools, such as a jackknife, the other food, such as wild rice, were laid near the body during the wake and later interred with it. Nett Lake Indians in 1947 took the first rice of the new harvest, cooked it in a small pot, and hung it on the gravepost so the spirit of the rice would assist the deceased. Such practices are ancient; rice grains have been recovered as part of a mortuary offering in Michigan, dated by archaeologists at 400–600 B.C.[55]

Following burial, those closest to the departed observed a period of mourning—in some places six months, elsewhere a year—during which they displayed their mourning in a number of ways—by blackening the face, leaving hair unkempt, or, if a child died, carrying around a "death bundle" in its place. Food was regularly placed before the bundle to feed its spirit. Termination of the mourning period was traditionally accomplished through the ritual removal of mourning, usually within the context of some larger ceremony such as a Drum Dance. Special songs accompanied ritual cleansing, hair-parting, face-painting, and the like.[56]

The condition of bereavement was considered dangerous, with possible contaminating effects. Consequently, the Ojibway imposed restrictions on those who were in the mourning period during harvest. They were excluded from sugaring, fishing, hunting, and ricing unless they underwent a special taboo release that consisted of being spoon-fed some of the first food gathered. If the food was game, it had to be caught by someone not in mourning, after which the mourner gave a feast and was permitted to join the others in the harvest. In the words of one Lac Court Oreilles resident in the 1930s: "Whenever a man lost his wife or a woman her husband, in the old day, the person left behind could not gather nor eat anything like venison, fish, sirup, berries of any kind, nor wild rice, until a feast was given at which they were fed." To ignore this danger was to invite certain trouble. John Mustache, Sr., told how: "One time my wife and I went ricing. There was a good crop and we tied a lot. Mrs. Kingfisher came out to the fields, she was in mourning. Louis Corbine was there and he knew she was in mourning and told her not even to get into the boat until she had been fed rice [ritually], but she went out anyhow and knocked rice. The crop was ruined. They'd knock and [get] only shells, no grain. Even the rice that they had tied turned out to be empty. She ruined the whole crop."[57]

At Mille Lacs, explained Fred Jones, "There is a wrong way and a right way. . . . One group that was clean, they'd go out and they'd pick their day's picking, and maybe half a day, then they'd come home and then they [clean] it up, and thrash it out. Then they'd call all those that lost some relation, or relative through the year, and the last harvesting time, they'd get him in there and get them all together and then they'd treat him in this new . . . batch of rice. Then after they fed him and then they were free to go out and pick it. It wouldn't hurt the crop. But if they went right out, then they always hurt the crop in some way." It was, however, permissible for mourners to eat what was left from previous harvests. At Lac Court Oreilles a custom similar to that at Mille Lacs prevailed, with an individual rather than a group ritually feeding the mourners: "You gotta have the first rice, the new rice, that's what they got to be fed with, then they can go out. . . . They can eat the old stuff while they're in mourning, but they've got to have the fresh before they can eat it, they gotta be fed by one person."[58]

When a feast was held to remove the taboo, someone would speak on behalf of the mourner. Some of the forbidden food was put on a fork or spoon; it was motioned three times toward the mourner's mouth, then withdrawn. The spoon was offered to the four cardinal directions and up and down to the zenith and nadir, then inserted in the mouth of the mourner, who was then free to eat with the others. This ritual requirement extended to those who inadvertently had been victims of taboo violations. George Bisonette, paralyzed on one side because a woman in mourning had picked him up as a child, explained: "The bird in my body has paralysis of his left wing just like I have of my arm. He can't fly. . . . I can't eat rice or maple sugar or berries until someone first feeds it to me or unless we put tobacco into the fire. At home my Dad puts tobacco into the fire, but when we go out to a feast, someone has to hold a spoonful up to the four directions and then feed it to me, otherwise my paralysis will get worse." Bisonette suggested that a friend with stunted growth had probably not heeded this advice.[59]

Ritual feeding to ward off danger may have derived from earlier practices associated with warfare. Peter Grant described a special ceremony of the Saulteaux held about 1804 for a departing war party: "Smoking and singing were alternately repeated . . . for the first part of the night; we were then entertained with a feast consisting of wild rice, pounded meat, bear's fat and sugar, all mixed in a large kettle, which the *Michinawois* [chief's aide] himself distributed to the company, not, indeed, by their ordinary custom of giving each individual his share on a separate dish. In this particular occasion, the feast was too sacred to be polluted with either dishes, spoons or even the fingers of the profane. The Michinawois alone, as the immediate minister of the ceremony, could presume to handle it. He, therefore, cautiously took the kettle in one hand, while, with great solemnity, he crammed the other in the kettle, taking a small portion of the victuals between his fingers and forcing it in the mouths of the company as he went around the circle." This sort of early nineteenth-century communion before battle seems to have been intended as a shield against possible death and to have survived well into the twentieth century as a ritual cleansing of those in mourning.[60]

As recently as the 1960s, the Mille Lacs people collected rice for bereaved families, particularly those who had lost a child. Vivian J. Rohrl saw this as a continuation of the taboo against ricing by mourners. The parents could not go out until after a special feast; in addition, the great-aunts and great-uncles had to offer tobacco to the harvest spirits before the parents could rice. The fear behind these and similar social prohibitions was that, if divinely sanctioned restriction were violated, all natural products were in danger of being lost—through disease, worms, or, in the case of wild rice, through destruction by birds or storms. The same taboo applied to a menstruating woman, preventing her from *eating* any food in season. Explained James Mustache: "Not only the rice or sugar or berries or anything like that, you're not allowed to eat. You can eat the *old* stuff, but not the new. Same way with animals, fowls, and things like that that the Indian killed to eat. You can't eat any of that fresh stuff . . . not any of the fresh kill." During ricing the woman was forbidden to bathe in the lake for fear it would kill the crop; neither was she allowed on the water to rice. A substitute took her place with her ricing partner until she was over her period. As a precautionary measure, claimed William Baker, in his rice camp only those who had reached menopause were allowed to knock rice.[61]

After death and mourning, food offerings were left by the grave at regular intervals for years. The shallow wooden grave house had a small window at one end for inserting the food, sometimes with a ledge below for food placement (fig. 1). It is still customary at memorial feasts, before the guests eat, to prepare a plate of typically Indian food, almost always including wild rice, for the relatives to leave by the grave or somewhere in the woods for the spirit of the departed.

The place of wild rice in Ojibway legends, customs, and ceremonies clearly indicates the special nature of this staple. Although most of the stories have passed from circulation with the death of their narrators, the fact that they have been collected as recently as the 1940s bears witness to the tenacity of traditional explanations for phenomena unacceptable to modern science. Ironi-

FIG. 1. Grave houses, White Earth Reservation, 1972

cally, white people came to grow wild rice scientifically about the time these tales became extinct. Wild rice, discovered by Wenabozhoo for the benefit of the Indians, has become a marketable commodity on a scale so grand that it eclipses the Ojibway involvement in the harvest. Still, the belief that wild rice was a spiritual gift persists, as Ojibway people give thanks each year for its return, mark important events by feasting on it, and memorialize the departed with wild rice as an offering.

CHAPTER 4

Traditional Indian Harvest

There is in that country a certain plant, four feet or thereabout in height, which grows in marshy places. A little before it ears, the Savages go in their Canoes and bind the stalks of these plants in clusters, which they separate from one another by as much space as is needed for the passage of a Canoe when they return to gather the grain. Harvest time having come, they guide their canoes through the little alleys which they have opened across this grain-field, and bending down the clustered masses over their boats, strip them of their grain.

—Hierosme Lalemant, 1662–63[1]

WHEN RIPE, wild rice kernels are collected by beating them with sticks into boats. On shore, rice is processed for food in several stages. It is first dried in the sun, then parched either by smoke drying or scorching in kettles. The chaff is broken away from the seed by treading or threshing, then removed by being tossed in the air with large winnowing or fanning trays. The kernels left in the tray are then ready for cooking or storage. The entire activity is called "making rice" or "ricing" (*manoominikewin*) in the English and Ojibway language alike.[2]

By the middle of the twentieth century, substantial changes were evident in the technology of wild rice harvesting. The problem in reviewing these changes historically is compounded by wide geographic dispersal of the Ojibway. While general outlines of the methods described here apply to the Ojibway people as a whole, variations by region or band are inevitable. Given the paucity and unevenness of data, it is nearly impossible to identify the origin of particular practices with certainty. Some methods reflect the natural materials available to a band; for instance, throughout the woodlands, birch-bark pails were commonly used to carry freshly harvested wild rice to the camp for processing, while bands living on the edge of the prairies used rawhide parfleches. "Improvements" in ricing methods often spread from one group to the next through the kinship network and frequent interband visitation. It is often easier to suggest *why* changes in technology occurred, however, than to pinpoint when and where. For example, people probably began substituting cardboard for birch bark in making fanning trays after lumbering and paper companies decimated the large birches that had provided good-sized pieces of bark. (This was a factor as well in the decline of canoe building.) Finally, information from a single source—oral or written—must be judged against the corpus of data. There is overwhelming evidence, for example, that until fairly recently only women harvested wild rice, yet one Lac Court Oreilles resident in 1942 insisted that "in the old days . . . a woman harvesting was regarded with contempt."[3] The following summary of native technology stresses its broader outlines, taking into consideration the many variations and contradictions present in the literature and weighing these against Ojibway oral testimony.

BINDING

Binding together bundles of wild rice stalks a few weeks before harvest, when the fruit is in its milk state, was a widespread practice now abandoned but reported in nearly all the oldest sources. Of the several reasons for this activity, the principal one was to declare ownership. Jonathan Carver observed in 1767 an entire rice field marked off in different styles of binding: "About the latter end of September they return to the river, when each family having its separate allotment, and being able to distinguish their own property by the manner of fastening the sheaves, gather in the portion that belongs to them." At Lac Court Oreilles in 1899 entire families were camped near the rice fields several weeks before the harvest, so that the women could spend several days binding their rice. About 1910, when he was a boy, William Baker and his close relations were one of five to seven families customarily ricing at Lake Pakweiwong, Wisconsin, some ten miles north of their reservation. The two rice beds on the lake—one each at the far north and south ends—were allocated by family: "They divided it: 'You harvest that, and you harvest that'. . . . They marked it by tying the rice, and that's *yours.*"[4]

Ricing as a harvest activity in the fall to some degree paralleled sugar making in the spring. Each family had an indisputable share of the rice field as of the maple grove, and just as people distinguished their maple trees with the mark of an ax, they established family rice turf by tying the sheaves in midsummer with binding "trade-marks." Each woman thereby silently announced her intention: "The border of each tract was defined by stakes, but this action [binding] showed that the field was to be harvested that year." Each family was usually allocated from two to five long rows of the bed. One Lac Court Oreilles resident in 1940 remembered seeing "old man so'gi" in a slough near Birch Lake, marking off patches or strips of the rice bed for each family. He created a sort of fence by inserting sticks in the rice field, tying rags to the last or marker sticks at the edge of the bed. He then assigned each of his relatives a certain patch, and they would go out to bind it.[5]

Although binding wild rice was a fairly common practice, each woman had her own way of doing it: "each woman knew her own by some peculiarity of the twist." Community members easily recognized particular techniques of binding, so "property" was generally respected. As added insurance, some women dyed their bark twine, each with a different color. Noted George McGeshick, "You couldn't hardly tell from the tying part, but they just use the color."[6]

A bound field trespassed upon was cause for consternation in the rice camp, as was revealed in this incident at Lac Court Oreilles: "Once my wife's folks invited some relatives down from Old Post. They came down and tied rice. Late one old woman went out at night and knocked rice before old man Dandy gave permission. He told her that she hadn't done the right thing—that she couldn't see at night to stay on her own patch and told her not to do it again. She was very ashamed."[7]

Because one person working alone could tie and later harvest that rice, older Ojibway who lacked ricing partners also engaged in binding. This was their principal means of securing their own supply of rice, and others respected their rights: "When they done that, all the people thought this person that got that has to tie that rice in order to get it. I think he is entitled to it. Everybody went around it, they didn't bother it." Lawrence Conners at Nett Lake said: "When you tied it, it meant: 'this belongs to me.' " Not only the elderly, but also the sick, widowed, and poor without relatives were assured a share of the harvest through binding.[8]

Two or three weeks before harvest (about mid-August), women entered the rice fields, usually two to a boat, one poling and the other kneeling or sitting, to gather the tops of the stalks in large shocks for tying (fig. 1). Because the rice by this time had risen 4 to 5 feet above water, they used a special stick—3 to 3½ feet long, forced into a curve, and tied to hold its sickle shape—to pull down the stalks (fig. 2), which could then be easily grasped and tied with strips of bark or twine. Indian women who riced in the Kakagon sloughs, several miles from their village on Bad River Reservation, prepared Indian "string" by tearing the inner bark of cedar into long narrow strips, tying them together,

Fig. 1. Opposite, *Mary Razer (Papa'gine' [Grasshopper]) binding wild rice stalks with twine made from the inner bark of basswood, White Earth Reservation, June 1917*

Fig. 2. Opposite, *Waboos (Rabbit) tying rice on the Lac Court Oreilles River, Wisconsin, 1941; the binding stick rests in her lap.*

Fig. 3. Mary Razer preparing her binding string, about 1917. Strips of basswood bark are soaked in the lake to loosen the inner bark, which is then peeled off and hung up to dry. Later it is torn lengthwise into thin strips.

and rolling them into a large ball (fig. 3). More commonly, basswood bark (*wiigob*), sometimes softened for use as string by being pulled through the hole of a bear's pelvis, was selected. James Mustache of Lac Court Oreilles, however, remembered his grandmother unraveling burlap sacks for binding thread. Whatever the material, "A large round ball of 'bast,' the bark string with which they were to tie the bunches, was ready behind them in their canoes. This ball is often a foot in diameter and is made of strings of the green inner bark of basswood; it is so wound that it unwinds from the inside, like the modern binding twine. The string averages a quarter of an inch in width."[9]

The ball of bark twine rested in a tray, and its end passed conveniently through a small birch-bark ring sewn to the binder's garment at the shoulder, thence into her hand, to keep it free from tangling. This method of threading the string suggests imitation of the white practice with store twine. Jenks detailed the technique practiced at Lac Court Oreilles: "When the bunch is formed the woman reaches up to her shoulder and pulls over the bark string, which passes from the ball behind her through a loop on the back of her dress immediately below the shoulder. While holding the stalks with one hand, she lays the string down along the bunch for several inches, and, suddenly checking this movement, begins rapidly to wind the string around the stalks toward their tops. In this way she makes secure the lower end of the fastening by putting several wrappings of the string around it." This winding continued for about two feet, whereupon the woman bent the wound stalks into an inverted U-shape and tied it to the upright shaft formed by the bound stalks, leaving it to resemble a shepherd's crook. In securing it, she used a simple loop and single knot of bark string. With this technique, which Jenks estimated took about 8 to 12 feet of string per sheaf, about half of the rice kernels were securely bound, while those at the top were prevented from being jarred by the wind through the support of the upright bound stalks.[10]

Alfred G. Ellis described another method that omitted bark twine but accomplished the same purpose: "One mode is to go into this 'standing corn' with their canoes, and taking as many stalks as they can compass with their hands, give them a twist and kink, and then turn the bunches downward, leaving them to ripen on the stalks. This gives the party twisting the bunches, a kind of preemption to so much of the rice, which before was all common."[11]

In most places the binder alternately reached out of each side of the canoe, tying up bundles of rice. These tended to lean inward toward the boat and each other, forming a sort of canopy (fig. 4). Charlie Day remembered helping to bind rice (before 1900) with basswood bark at Nett Lake in late August after the rice had blossomed: "Sitting in the canoe, we tied the rice to arches over our heads, and during the harvest all rice would fall into the boat gliding be-

Fig. 4. Rows of wild rice, bound by Waboos, on the Lac Court Oreilles River, 1941; the passageway between the rows facilitates harvest once the rice is mature.

neath the arches." Bound in this fashion, the rows resembled the substructure of "long wigwams."[12]

To protect the ripening rice, women tried not to disturb the plants with their boats or their hands more than necessary. Roger Patterson, a government farmer at Bad River in 1848, watched women about August 15, "tying [the stalks] with bark strings into sheaves, taking care to draw them together gently, so as not to break the stems or roots." During binding some women harvested small quantities of rice in its milk state, pulling a closed hand over the fruit heads. This premature rice, which when parched had a much lighter color than ripe rice after parching, could be cooked and eaten in advance of the harvest.[13]

Beyond simply marking an area of the rice field as one's personal property were the practical advantages of binding wild rice. These can be summarized as follows:

1. Rice that is bound and wrapped cannot easily be eaten by birds or lost to the elements. Father Louis Hennepin specified wildfowl competition as the motivating factor for Dakota women near Lake Issati (Mille Lacs Lake) to bind their rice: "The Savage Women are oblig'd to tie several Stalks together with White Bark of Trees, to fright away the Ducks, Teals, or Swans, which otherwise wou'd spoil it before it be ripe." Traveler and author E. S. Seymour said

that to keep the rice from being eaten by blackbirds, the women "cover each bunch with a band made of the bark of the linden or basswood tree." At Mille Lacs Lake, some rice was thickly bound to provide comfortable perches for hawks that would prey on blackbirds. Such wrappings also offered protection from strong winds, heavy rain, and hailstones that could jar the kernels loose.[14]

2. In collecting bound wild rice, the harvester catches the twine at the bottom, cuts and unwinds it to remove the binding—*aaba'oodoon*—then shakes the bunch of stalks or knocks them with a ricing stick to release the fruit; in this way a much greater quantity of rice is diverted directly into the boat. Since virtually every stalk is bound and little falls in the lake, it is little wonder the Ojibway agree that more rice was harvested when binding was the practice.

Densmore stated that wild rice not bound was called "free rice" and was kept separate from the rest. Bound rice is said to ripen more evenly, to produce heavier kernels requiring a longer cooking time, and to have a slightly different flavor. William Baker estimated that each sheaf, untied, yielded as much as a pound of green rice. ("'See, while it's been tied, it grows in there, then it gets bigger. Keeps the blackbirds off it.")[15]

3. Binding creates convenient "streets" through the rice field, facilitating boat traffic. (Most craft in unbound sections make rather haphazard and unsystematic paths.) Harvesters obviously took advantage of Lalemant's "little alleys" and probably traversed them in somewhat the same order they were created. Two over-all patterns of streets between the bound sheaves prevailed in the rice fields. Binders could progress from end to end of the field, then return to make parallel sets of rows, continuing until the area was completely tied. This resulted either in straight rows, as in a garden, or, if the binders began at the outer limits of the rice bed, in large curves. The handsome uniformity of the neatly tied sheaves is apparent in photographs (see fig. 4).

While bound rice beds were convenient for the Indian harvesters, they proved troublesome for whites traveling in the area. Daniel Stanchfield, who investigated pioneer lumbering on the upper Mississippi River in 1847, noted: "When the exploring crew came to the Rice lakes, eight miles from Mille Lacs, the squaws had tied the rice together for threshing, and therefore the canoe could not pass through and had to be taken to the shore."[16]

4. Sometimes rice was bound in places too shallow for canoes. Near shore, the harvesters (presumably wading) tied the rice in bunches. When the grain was ripe, they spread mats directly on the water between the rows and knocked the kernels onto the mats for collection. Jenks described this practice among the Menominee; whether the Ojibway did so is questionable.[17]

Although the vast majority of ricers collected bound rice on the water, some reports indicate that sheaves of ripe wild rice—bound or not—were cut and brought to shore to remove the kernels. John Bigsby wrote that in about 1850 on East Lake (Rainy Lake chain), "The men cut off the green heads of the rice-plant, and let them fall into the canoe, while the women stowed them away." At Rice Lake, Ontario, "a curved sharp-edged paddle" was used to cut the stalks. While acknowledging that knocking rice was the more common practice, Ellis wrote that the hand-twisted bunches at Green Bay were cut with a knife and brought to shore. Lips questioned the likelihood of this, as it would have been difficult not to lose a substantial number of ripe kernels. At Moose-Ear River in Barron County, Wisconsin, stalks bearing immature rice were cut about two feet long, tied in bundles "about half as large as a sheaf of wheat," brought to camp, and laid in rows on a rack with heads facing one direction. After ripening in the sun, the stalks were raised at one end by a pole and beaten over a blanket with a stick, after which the rice was further dried.[18]

Some Ojibway regard cutting the stalks as a harmful method introduced by whites. William Morrell of Leech Lake complained: "They come in before the rice ripes, before it matures, and they just cut the heads off, off from the stalk of the rice and then it doesn't reseed itself. . . . The white man came, they go and just chop the heads off and what little bit left that don't mature, see. Kept the stalk from growing, it deadened the rice."[19]

With so many practical advantages to binding rice—particularly the assured increase in yield—Lips pondered the abandonment of the practice everywhere she investigated. Although some women were still binding rice in Wisconsin at the time of Jenks's field work (about 1898), at Rainy Lake on the Canadian border as late as 1904, and a few at Lac Court Oreilles in 1941, the practice had been given up elsewhere long before—at Sandy Lake in Aitkin County, Minnesota, for example, as early as 1820. Lawrence Mitchell of White Earth heard that his grandmother had bound rice, but he never saw it done.[20]

Lips's conjecture about the disappearance of binding seems plausible for some localities in northern Minnesota at least. In her opinion, the abandonment was related to a decrease in the number of harvesters. In the days when ricers streamed out into the fields at harvest time, binding was a precautionary measure, a form of crop insurance, and a hedge against competition, particularly if one wanted a large supply of rice. Lips postulated that the practice had originated as people devised any means they could to secure as much rice as possible. But by 1947 the economy reduced the pressure to acquire so much wild rice. Indian people followed other pursuits, such as working in sawmills, serving as fishing or hunting guides, and harvesting cranberries. Also, store-bought foodstuffs gradually replaced traditional ones as staples. As a result, suggested Lips, only a few people depended entirely on wild rice.[21]

Lips's speculations may be partially correct, but most Ojibway who remember the practice of binding attribute its decline to the breakdown of tradition, premature harvesting, and the incursion of whites. George McGeshick, who guessed that binding was abandoned on Pickerel Lake (Wisconsin) about 1915, suggested economic motives: as traders began to buy up rice, the number of harvesters *increased.* As some ricers violated the customary property rights indicated by binding and (mostly younger) Indians began to ignore community mechanisms for controlling the harvest, rice that stood bound and ready was an open invitation to theft—as John B. Moyle of the Minnesota Department of Conservation put it, "because of the ease with which the sheaved grain could be pilfered by less industrious harvesters." By 1941 Robert Ritzenthaler knew of only two women who tied rice at Lac Court Oreilles, where formerly *all* the crop had been bound. Generally, only those whose land was adjacent to rice fields tied rice. The theft problem is supported in recent statements by older Ojibway such as James Mustache, who reckoned binding disappeared from his community by the beginning of World War I: "There were some Indians who were grabby, those are the ones that, well, kinda spoiled some of this technique of ricing."[22]

Elders associate binding with the days when proper Indian harvesting methods held sway. An interview with John Clark at Mille Lacs elicited such responses as "a long time ago . . . it used to be tied up in big bundles all over the lake until it got all ripe, and then they picked it. It was better. Today they rice, everybody goes out and in one day the whole thing is ruined," or "there was too many white people, they would just go out and knock it into the boat, and they don't get as much rice as they could. They don't let it finish growing. They go out and [harvest] before the rice is ripe. Even the younger [Indian] people go out into the lake." William Baker attributed the general decline of rice stands to the disregard of the older, "proper" techniques: "[E]verybody was so greedy, they even went out there before the rice was ripe, knocked the dickens out of it, even pulled the stalks and all that stuff. That don't go. See, that's the reason why the rice harvest of today is lacking the fertility of what it had been years ago."[23]

Although binding has long been abandoned, vestiges of the practice seem to direct Ojibway choices of areas of open rice field to harvest. At Bad River in the early 1950s, noted Earl Nyholm, people respected the rights of those who had favorite ricing spots. In particular, urban Indians returning for the harvest avoided ricing in places where the locals harvested.[24]

KNOCKING

Because ripe wild rice is harvested by threshing the stalks to dislodge the kernels, in common parlance the activity is called "knocking." Until the twentieth century when whites introduced mechanical combines, knocking was the only way to gather wild rice. Almost all Ojibway continue to knock rice in the age-old way.

When ricing, the Ojibway dress warmly at first; by midday they may shed some clothes as harvest toil combines with the hot sun of late summer to warm them. In 1947 one Nett Lake woman insulated her end of the boat with hay. Ricers may wear long underwear, heavy pants, flannel shirts, and jackets, but they usually sacrifice comfort for mobility, since the arms must be unencumbered for collecting rice (fig. 5, 6a, 6b). Anthropologist Barbara D. Jackson depicted Leech Lakers in 1965 selecting costumes for the ricing season from rummage-sale articles: "Outfitting is often conducted in a spirit of mock elegance, with individuals choosing and modeling the worn and ill-fitting garments as though they were preparing for a fancy-dress ball."[25]

Some clothing is worn for protection against the rice that accumulates in the boat. High rubber boots or long, heavy socks into which the trousers can be tucked keep out the sharply pointed rice beards and prevent rice worms from biting the legs. Ricers are also careful not to inhale the slightly barbed beards. "You don't go around out there with your mouth open!" Women wear shawls or bandannas to keep the rice out of their hair and ears. Earl Nyholm recalled that ricers at Bad River in the early 1950s covered their laps with long pieces of canvas that extended the length of the boats to the polers. The canvas protected the ricers and later facilitated the removal of green rice from the boats. Bad River women knocking rice buttoned up their collars or tied something around their necks because, "When the rice starts to fly, it gets in the collar just like pickers, or stickers." They also wore straw hats; otherwise, the hot sun and its reflection from the water caused sunburn, especially on the nose. Today nearly everyone wears dark glasses, not only to cut down glare but also to keep the potentially dangerous beard from the eyes. Paul Buffalo justified his aversion to woolen clothing for ricing: "It's very dangerous to wear wool, 'cause all that rice being sticks. . . . You wear wool, you wear flannel—we used to have flannel underwear—then you could hardly get that off, see, but if you wear a straight jacket on the rice field harvesting . . . that beard . . . it'll drop off."[26]

Until wild rice is parched and its pointed beard sections are singed off, the ricers exercise caution. Buffalo told how the twelve- to fourteen-year-olds hauled rice: "They can work. They won't spill, don't spill that rice. Be careful how you handle that rice, so it don't get on your hands and clothes. So they all had baskets to dip it with." Lawrence Mitchell also noted: "It was really almost like a bullet sometimes, you know, the little grains of rice, they would bounce around, they would ricochet around, and it was dangerous, though if

FIG. 5. Gloves, cap, scarf, and lap robe protecting ricer from the barbed awns of the rice, about 1920. She rests her arms comfortably, having laced her ricing sticks under and over the canoe thwarts.

Fig. 6a, 6b. Wild ricing, presented in a pageant, probably at Itasca State Park, in the late 1930s. To keep the show colorful, organizers required the actors to wear ceremonial dress.

it got into a—especially some people didn't go out if they had a sore on their arm, or something, 'cause that [barb] could get in there."[27]

Except where rice grows near shore, it must be harvested by boat. Formerly, birch-bark or dugout canoes were used to collect rice. Later, as the art of canoe building declined, wooden boats replaced them, and, more recently, canvas, aluminum, and fiberglass canoes have been used (fig. 7). In the mid-nineteenth century the Ojibway used what Henry Schoolcraft described as a "moderate-sized hunting-canoe."[28]

FIG. 7. A wooden skiff and birch-bark canoe en route to the rice fields about 1920, being pushed with forked ricing poles. The use of both types of craft suggests a transitional period.

Special canoes were made for the harvest. Edwin T. Adney's and Howard I. Chapelle's *The Bark Canoes and Skin Boats of North America* shows numerous Ojibway craft, two specifically called "rice harvesting canoes." In 1841, Georges A. Belcourt wrote the bishop of Quebec that he had arrived at Wabassimong (on the Winnipeg River) on July 4 and found only a few families present, most "having returned to the forests in order to gather birch bark with which to make the canoes that were to serve them in harvesting the wild rice." Charles A. Eastman, a Santee Dakota, recalled from his boyhood in the 1860s that men and women were busy making canoes before the harvest, "for nearly every member of the family must be provided with one for this occasion."[29]

Whether such ricing canoes were bigger or smaller than other Ojibway craft is moot. One Jenks respondent reported that "about August 15th the Squaws using small Canoes go out along the River" to bind rice, and the fur trader Peter Pond, about 1775, used *small* to describe the harvesting boat: "But Just in the Caneu the Wild Oats was so thick that the Indians Could Scarse Git one of thare Small Canues into it to Geather it." On the other hand, the dimensions given by Adney and Chapelle were relatively large: a 3-fathom, 7-thwart ricing canoe from Lac Court Oreilles was 18 feet, 10 inches long, with a 39½-

inch beam, and the "long nose" variety from Long Lake, Ontario, was 16 feet in length. At Vermilion Lake a birch-bark canoe made especially for the harvest in August 1939 by a 75-year-old resident was 14 feet, 2 inches long; the stern-to-prow opening measured 12 feet, 2 inches and was 3 feet, 2 inches at its greatest width; the craft was 18 inches deep.[30]

Birch-bark canoes were still being used for ricing in some places until about 1940. *Indians at Work,* a publication of the Office of Indian Affairs, includes a photo of one in 1937, probably in the rice fields of the Cass Lake area, and a 1938 photo shows a birch-bark canoe under construction just before the harvest. As large birch trees became scarcer, the art of building bark canoes declined. In 1942 at Lac Court Oreilles, Bob Pine was the only one who still knew how to make such canoes, which he customarily sold for seventy dollars.[31]

The narrow, flat-bottomed boats of pine planks that eventually replaced the birch-bark canoe were far easier to construct; they could also be purchased ready-made from whites. The early ones, modeled somewhat after the canoe, were pointed at each end (fig. 8). Later models with square sterns (fig. 9, 10) were designed for ricing partners who did not switch assignments on the water. These skiffs differed from the canoe or pointed wooden boat, having only one seat (for the knocker) and considerably more room for rice as well as for the poler to shift his or her feet, making that task less tiring. A single wooden brace in the middle sufficed to hold the sides intact. Earlier models were of narrow cedar strips nailed together and caulked with pipe lead or roofing tar. Similar boats are made today of plywood, painted perhaps a dark green. By law, after 1939 in Minnesota, boats like these could not exceed 16 feet in length or 3 feet in width. White Earth boats from the 1920s were estimated at from 12 feet to 14 feet long, 32 inches at their widest, and 10 inches deep; Nett Lake boats in 1947 averaged 11 feet, 6 inches. The preference today for aluminum canoes is not so much a return to the past as a practical advantage; they are lighter than wooden boats and do not require constant patching.[32]

The ecological advantage of canoes and wooden ricing boats is that their smooth, flat bottoms and low displacement do not harm the roots of the rice plants, and the pointed ends of the craft bend the stalks only momentarily. The wooden boat's only disadvantage, it seems, is its greater weight. Like the canoe, the wooden boat was used for hunting and setting fishnets as well as for ricing. Similar skiffs have long been used along the eastern seaboard by non-Indian railbird hunters in the wild rice marshes along the Pawtuxet, Delaware, and Connecticut rivers. Today, even when rice fields are far away enough to warrant motor transportation, the Ojibway bring canoes or wooden ricing boats, too. To reach the sloughs at Bad River, inaccessible by road, ricers em-

FIG. 8. A flat-bottomed, double-ended, wooden ricing skiff with forked pole, paddle, ricing sticks, and whisk broom about 1941, Lac Court Oreilles

bark at a landing about two miles upstream. Canoes or ricing skiffs are laid across outboard motorboats for the journey downstream. Once in the rice fields, the motorboats are left unattended to drift until their owners are ready to return to the landing.

Ricing craft must be clean and waterproof, so some attention is given to removing detritus from the previous year's harvest and to testing boats for leaks before harvest. For additional cleanliness, perhaps, and to facilitate the removal of rice from the craft, some Menominee once lined their canoes with blankets; Ojibway do the same, using blankets, canvas, or mats.[33]

Respect for cleanliness extends beyond the boat. In one Leech Laker's opinion: "We have to have respect on everything we eat. . . . We put on clean clothes. Picking fruit, we got to be cleaned; picking wild rice we got to be cleaned. Have our boats clean—brand new boats, some of them. . . . Then they put the good clean clothes on, them clean clothes protects. . . . you're

FIG. 9. Double-ended boat, modeled after a canoe, about 1910; the wild rice in front of the poler suggests that the two harvesters have changed assignments in order to fill the other end of the boat.

FIG. 10. George McGeshick's homemade plywood square-sterned ricing boat, September 1986

clean, you feel better, keep your rice clean." Although most ricing boats that Lips saw were immaculate, a few had been neglected by their owners until the last minute. Even on the opening day of the 1947 harvest, people were repairing boats, exchanging canoes, looking for substitutes, and, once on the water, throwing out plant remains from the previous season.[34]

The only tools required for harvesting wild rice are those to propel the craft and to knock the ripe kernels into it. Harvesters may use canoe paddles to traverse deep or open water, but a long pole, forked at one end, is almost always used to push the boat when they arrive at the rice beds. On long trips both ricers might paddle, but if the water is not too deep and the person in the bow uses a paddle, the pole makes an effective rudder.[35]

Traditionally, the Ojibway used a straight pole about 10 feet to 12 feet long with either a natural fork or a carved one attached at one end (fig. 11). The

FIG. 11. Natural forks that appear to have been inserted in the ends of hollowed or split ricing poles, then held in place with nails

fork gripped the soft, muddy bottom without harming the root bed. In fact, to protect the roots, those controlling the harvest in early times forbade the use of poles without forks; even with forks, polers must push carefully into the mud or against the stalks so as not to break them or disturb the root system. In places where the rice was not thick enough for the poler to get a grip on the bottom, she resorted to a paddle to move the boat.[36]

After World War II, collapsible zinc or aluminum forks were manufactured as attachments for straight poles; as a pole was pushed, the fork opened to a V-shape, giving purchase against the mud; a wire spring collapsed it when the pressure was released. Some Ojibway men eschew these "duck-billed" appendages because they catch easily in the weeds; the men prefer to make their own by cutting a natural fork from a tree and nailing or lashing it with wire to the end of a straight pole. For strength, the fork, 15 inches or more in length, is usually carved of hardwood such as ash, maple, or hickory; the pole is cut from balsam for suppleness. Fred K. Blessing's sketch of an 18-inch fork suggests the short section of tree limb beneath the fork was gouged out to accept the shaft of the pole for lashing, probably in a manner similar to that used to support hooks on the stakes that suspend a dance drum off the ground. Because many articles in Indian culture serve multiple uses, a ricing pole might be used for a clothesline the rest of the year.[37]

A ricer needs much practice to push a boat properly through the rice fields, as Stuart Berde explained: "The poler must keep the boat in a steady pattern, while gliding toward the rice. He pushes his pole through the water in a climbing motion, constantly compensating for his last stroke. To keep the boat in a straight line, he places his pole directly in back of the boat, leaning to neither side. A good poler pushes his boat straight through the water and, if necessary, can turn the boat 180 degrees with 2 strokes." There are other ways to propel ricing craft: a ricer can work alone, grabbing at stalks to pull the boat forward, and in shallow water someone may disembark to pull the boat along. Shuniah Goneb remembered wearing snowshoes at Sabaskong Bay "to help plough a canoe through shallow stands near shore."[38]

While the poler maneuvers the boat, the partner collects the rice in the manner Carver described two centuries ago, "by placing their canoes close to the bunches of rice, in such position as to receive the grain when it falls, and then beat it out, with pieces of wood formed for that purpose." Men have traditionally carved these wooden ricing sticks, or "knockers" (*bawa'iganaakoon*), from light wood, such as white cedar (fig. 12). Every harvester owns a pair, and in all of the families Lips knew at Nett Lake the men carved them, although single women sometimes made their own. The smooth, round sticks vary in length from 2 feet to 3½ feet. A 26-inch pair of cedar knockers was purchased by the author at Cass Lake in 1970 for two dollars. The longest ricing sticks he has seen were 42-inch Menominee-made knockers in the collection of the American Museum of Natural History in New York City. Certainly larger than Ellis's description—"as thick as a man's finger"—ricing sticks average about 1¼ inches at the butt end, tapering gradually to a blunt point.[39]

Lightweight wood is essential (fig. 13); heavy sticks would soon tire a ricer's arms. (The author's sticks together weigh 5.6 ounces.) Sometimes knockers are made lighter and easier to grasp by carving hourglass indentations near the thick ends. Lawrence Mitchell indicated the considerable skill required for making ricing sticks: "Probably take all day for somebody. They were really perfectionists on carving them, so the handle, so that they made them for the individual size of the hand. They were quite plain . . . they wanted them smooth." Blessing illustrated a 28-inch example of the indented type, probably from Leech Lake, slightly more elaborate than most, with a decorative round bulb carved at its butt end. Good ricing sticks feel as light as cork and are scarcely noticeable in the hand.[40]

The basic technique for knocking wild rice is simple: the ricer holds one stick in each hand and as the poler moves the boat forward, the harvester reaches to the right with the stick and pulls as many stalks as she (or he) can

Fig. 12. Alice White Cadotte knocking rice at Lac Court Oreilles, about 1941. She cradles several stalks with one stick, preparing to flail them with the other.

cradle over the side of the boat. She then knocks the stalks with the stick in her left hand in a glancing stroke aimed at the bottom of the boat (fig. 14 and cover illustration). The stalks must be at a proper angle to the gunwale and the blow with the stick must be correctly aimed; otherwise the straw may break, ruling out a second harvesting. The Bureau of Indian Affairs agent at White Earth in the 1960s described: "You don't want to pound it. All you want to do is brush it. That's the only way to only get the purple [ripe seeds]. You

Fig. 13. Two pairs of ricers in the Kakagon sloughs, Bad River Reservation, 1971; boats run parallel courses about eight feet apart. Kenneth Roundwind (foreground) *poles while Russell Corbine knocks.*

want to slice it like you're shaving off a stick." When dead ripe, the rice virtually explodes its kernels into the boat at one stroke. To be certain she has all the rice off the stalks, a ricer may knock the sheaves a second or even third time. Then, reversing the procedure, she reaches out the left side with the hand that just threshed, pulls over the stalks, knocks with the stick in her right hand, and continues harvesting in this fashion from alternate sides of the boat. Shortly the bottom of the boat is covered with wild rice; two hours of knocking ripe rice might bring it a foot deep. Norma Smith, a Mole Lake Ojibway, said: "We can plan on a good crop when we see the rice pile up in little peaks on the bottom of the boat. Soon it will turn into a thick green carpet with the long beards standing straight up. After only a couple of trips across the lake and back, the rice is close to the top of the boat and it is time to go in and sack up." In this way Woodlands women with boats gather food not much differently from their Apache counterparts of the Southwest, who incline conical baskets under stalks of grass and hit the grass to release edible seeds into their receptacles.[41]

In the days when rice was bound, the long rows of bound stalks determined the path for the canoes. Perhaps through force of habit, older ricers continue to traverse rice fields systematically in parallel courses about four feet apart, turning to reenter the bed when they reach open water (fig. 15). Mary and

FIG. 14. Minnesota ricers in square-sterned skiff, about 1938. With proper technique, a large number of rice stalks can be pulled simultaneously over the gunwale for flailing.

George McGeshick said they consider this the most productive procedure. By using paths or "tracks" created the previous day, they can harvest the same amount of rice again. In their opinion, the helter-skelter approach of most ricers today results in much lost rice. George pointed out that on Sand Lake, Wisconsin, in two hours and only four trips—twice over and back again—he and his wife collected about two hundred pounds: "That rice was falling so good, it would just pour in." At Bear River, Manitoba, apparently in reharvesting, a ricer used the course of a previous canoe: "The canoe makes row marks; the next canoe had to follow up behind. We're not supposed to criss-cross. After four days when we passed over, there was as much rice."[42]

Like fishermen moving to spots where others seem to be getting strikes, knowledgeable Ojibway ricers keep an eye on experienced harvesters or follow the crowd, assuming they have found the best (ripest) places for knocking. Paul Buffalo remembered his mother's directions from early in the twentieth

FIG. 15. Craft on parallel courses near a Minnesota landing, about 1939, a transitional period as indicated by tent on shore, access by road, and the car towing a trailer.

century at Leech Lake: " 'You go there.' She laid down that rice, and she says to me, 'Do you see anybody on the lake?' 'Yeah.' 'Then go further.' She knows that old-timer ricing there . . . 'You go there, wherever there [are] two or three boats'. . . . So you follow the gang, go get rice. But if you run off, run alone, you just run here and there, you just working for nothing. Let's stay where it's full." If other ricers did not indicate the ripe sections, the birds might be informative: "Sometime I see nature tell us. . . . the birds, ducks are going through that rice that's ripe, good to eat, but they won't stay where it's green. So I used to kinda flock, chase them around. But if you chase them too much, they'll lead you out of that rice field!"[43]

Wind direction may also be a factor, as Lawrence Mitchell explained: "Sometimes you don't go against the way it's bent . . . you go sideways. . . . let us say, it's bent to the west, well you either go north and south, you don't go into it. Other times maybe a breeze or wind, you know, will turn it the other way, so they criss-cross, mostly according to how the wind was blowing."[44]

Although there is generally no preplanned course, ricers try to stay out of each other's way as they search for ripe patches. They take into account the position of the sun, which ripens the rice. At Mole Lake, noted Norma Smith: "We watch to see what side of the lake the others have chosen so as not to cross their paths while picking. . . . As our boat glides on the water we pause to see where the rice looks the darkest to determine where it is the ripest. That is where we will pick first. Then one partner readies for the first swipe at the tall stalks. How good to hear the first rice hit the apron."[45]

At the end of the rice field or when the knocker's end of the boat is full and low in the water, harvesters may exchange implements and assignments and head back to land, filling the other end of the boat en route to distribute the weight more evenly. Once ashore, they empty the rice from the boat. Formerly, they transported the rice to drying areas, either in winnowing trays or large pails called *makakoon,* cut from birch bark or sometimes elm bark (*aniib*) and folded and sewn into trapazoidal containers. Varying in size, *makakoon* were as deep as eighteen inches and held as much as forty pounds. The same bark pails could also be used to carry parched rice to the treading pits and to store processed rice for the winter. Today, freshly harvested rice, sold before processing, is usually packed directly from the boat into gunny or flour sacks and taken to a buyer to be weighed. Depending on the time of day and rice conditions, ricers may either return with the emptied boat to make another pass or postpone activity until the following day.

Older sources provide surprisingly little detail of ricing techniques; with few exceptions, only cursory attention has been given to harvest tradition. Knockers are invariably called "sticks"—scarcely an adequate description. Some faulty observations have been accepted *prima facie* and repeated by later writers. This is especially true of knocking, as few of those who describe it probably ever witnessed it firsthand.[46]

One source of confusion is James Smillie's engraving "Gathering Wild Rice" (fig. 16). Several peculiarities in the work signal caution in deducing ethnographic information from it even though Schoolcraft's accompanying text supports the details shown. *Three* harvesters in a small canoe would be crowded, unlikely, and contrary to sources from as early as the seventeenth century; bending stalks "in handfulls over the sides of the canoe" with the left hand to "beat out the grain with paddles," would be uncommonly violent. Nonetheless, Schoolcraft's Plate 4 has often been reproduced without comment in wild rice studies, and his description of the technology appears unchallenged.[47]

FIG. 16. Engraving made from Seth Eastman's fanciful depiction of women harvesting wild rice, published in Henry Schoolcraft's Historical and Statistical Information

Reports concerning the assignment of tasks, the division of labor by sex, and the techniques involved in harvesting wild rice—where people sat or stood in the canoe, the direction they faced, how they worked as a team—have varied over the years. Today, the poler most commonly stands at the stern, while the knocker sits either in the bow (facing the poler, see fig. 9) or near the middle toward the back, facing forward (see fig. 15). Apparently this has not always been so; Densmore's 1910 photograph of two boats entering the rice fields from open water on White Earth Reservation shows two women per boat, both facing forward (fig. 17), with the poler of each boat standing in the bow. Lawrence Mitchell recalled this method practiced at White Earth in the late 1920s, but said ricing is no longer done that way. He could not justify the poler in the bow: "Why it is, I can't really say. For one thing, the person poling from the back, it gives the person that's knocking the rice, I'd say, the first chance at the rice before it's knocked down [by the boat]. You see, the poling would knock some of it down. Maybe that's why they switched over." Joseph Gilfillan, on the same reservation in 1876, described ricers as two per canoe, seated, with one paddling in the stern. Still, the practice depicted in Dens-

FIG. 17. Women poling into the rice fields at White Earth, about 1910

more's photograph is confirmed in responses from Jenks's correspondents at both Fond du Lac and Rat Portage (Kenora), Ontario, and by missionary Cloeter's mid-nineteenth century report of the Swamp Lake method: "Two persons sail in a birch canoe among the rice in places where it is the thickest. The person in front paddles slowly forward, while the person behind thrashes the rice kernels into the canoe."[48]

Although bound rice also can be knocked, more customarily it was shaken into the boat—an old practice described by Father Marquette, Alexander Henry, Zebulon Pike, and others. One simply cut or untied the knot, unwrapped the binding, bent the heads over the gunwale, and shook (or beat) the kernels loose. These seeds are said to have been black due to their ripeness and nearly four times as heavy as green, untied rice. Paul Buffalo noted that older Leech Lakers who bound rice alone also harvested it by themselves: "He goes out, and then he goes forward with his boat. He unties them knots. Then all he's got to do is shake it with his hand, shake them. All the rice falls in the boat, and it don't take him long for just maybe a boatful. . . . So he comes in at that day, he ties enough of that so he could take care, he maybe, he may have two, three places where he tied. And he gets all well matured rice on the two, three places. Very, very good rice. . . . He never hurt the greens [unripe rice] any."[49]

Even unbound rice, when ripe, was often simply shaken into a boat. Dan White recalled Leech Lakers who harvested without ricing sticks: "I used to take them out there in the rice field. I seen these women just gather this rice. The heads lean toward the canoe there. And, well, they shook the rice right into the boat, and they didn't hit it there or nothing. Nowadays people go out and rice, they just murder the rice."[50]

How much rice is harvested? Each blow glanced at the dead-ripe fruit heads delivers about one-fourth pint into the boat's bottom. It takes about five minutes to harvest a pound. Two light blows with the stick should release the rice from the stalks; if it does not come loose in two blows, it is probably insufficiently ripe. Berde likened the sound of ricing to a steady waltz tempo, in that the ricer adopted an even three-beat motion per side (REACH and pull over, thresh, thresh, REACH and pull over, thresh, thresh). According to Paul Buffalo, the characteristic swishing sound of ripe wild rice being knocked is noticeably absent with immature rice: "The beaten, when you're in the green rice they sound different. The beaters sound nice when you're in the finish part. You don't have to hit it heavy. But the rice comes better. You can hear the sound of it in your boat. You can hear the sound of the beaters. How nice they sound." Buffalo also said that rice knocked into aluminum canoes did not have as nice a sound. Otherwise, aluminum canoes were acceptable, "providing your tools don't turn too short or go right under," which could easily capsize the boat.[51]

Estimates of yield vary. According to Charles E. Chambliss, when the bottom of the boat is covered and fairly full, the harvester has from 75 to 100 pounds of rice. Mole Lakers estimate that a good day's yield is about 150 pounds per boat. None of this is clean wild rice, however, since bits of stalk and the beard and chaff of the rice make up a good percentage of the weight. People not adept at knocking rice usually end up with much "trash," including stems, leaves, immature kernels, rice worms, and dirt. William H. Keating in 1823 guessed that harvesters easily collected 20 to 30 bushels a day; he did not say whether that was green or finished rice. Since there has never been an official weight for a bushel of wild rice, it is difficult to determine how much this might have been. Peter Big Bear of White Earth told Sister Bernard Coleman that 200 pounds of rice in about 1900 was "a good day's work." Recent Canadian estimates have been as high as 700 pounds a day per boat. Since natural rice stands yield only about 100 pounds an acre when harvested by hand, ricers would have had to cover an enormous amount of ground to achieve such returns. Still, in good years, bumper crops can be enormous; in 1972 the harvest from Lake of the Woods alone exceeded a million pounds.[52]

Since rice ripens gradually over a ten-day period, ricers customarily traverse the same areas every few days to collect what was not ripe on previous trips. James Mustache's family "worked" a rice bed at Lake Pakweiwong in this fashion. Four long rows of bound rice were untied and shaken into the canoe, producing about two full loads. The family spent two days processing, then returned to knock the same territory ("'not hard, just gentle then"), harvesting nearly two more canoes of green rice. They waited about three days and returned again. Mustache recalled a total harvest time of about six days. William Baker, whose family riced on the same lake, carried the process a step farther in asserting that, finally, the stalks were stripped bare: "They don't get it all, but they wait a few days and the old squaw woman, they take their hands and they probably got a glove on, moccasin glove, get ahold of that, push it off with their hands instead of using that club; they get more rice that way, they get it all clean." In other places, if the weather was favorable, the harvest could last as long as two to three weeks – the period noted by Gilfillan at White Earth in 1876. According to his estimates, each canoe collected a flour sack full of rice per day, a family gathering as much as ten sacks during the three-week harvest.[53]

Estimates of the percentage of ripe crop gathered vary. Lips observed at Nett Lake in 1947 that only about two-thirds of available rice was collected, a figure conforming to contemporaneous estimates at Cass Lake. Harvests half a century earlier suggest an even lower percentage, probably reflecting less emphasis on rice as a cash crop. During the 1898 harvest and again the following year only 50 percent of the crop at Bad River and slightly more than 40 percent at Fond du Lac was gathered; according to Jenks's observation, the Lac Court Oreilles Ojibway could have harvested a much greater amount both years. An earlier report indicated an even smaller percentage collected, prompting David Owen to remark on "the waste of breadstuff . . . from the indolence and improvidence of the Indians." On a geological survey in about 1852, Owen noted that on Cass Lake, about half a mile above the mouth of the Turtle River, "[W]e entered another lake, three-fourths of a mile long, and four hundred yards wide. Above this, the channel of the river winds through rice-fields, amounting in all to several hundred acres. Of all this, the produce of scarcely an acre is gathered by the Indians."[54]

While today there is no strict division of labor by age or gender, in past years the preponderance of harvesters was female, and for good reason: the men were busy hunting ducks and catching fish. Traditionally, in fact, with the exception of husking, *all* stages of rice harvesting and processing were performed by women, with some assistance from children. At the turn of the century Gilfillan noted at Rice Lake on the White Earth Reservation that of some six hundred to seven hundred Indians camped there, only five or six men – Christian converts – were harvesting. Schoolcraft, who included wild rice harvesting under the rubric "Distinctive Phases of the Hunter State," made clear "the labor of gathering it is a care of the females." Women not necessarily from the same families combined forces and divided the fruits of their labors according to prearrangement. This prompted those outside Indian culture and unaccustomed to Indian division of labor to compare the Indian woman's role with that of women in white society. Thus said missionaries Lucy M. and William Lewis in an 1844 letter describing the Leech Lake Pillagers: "The women are perfect slaves to the men, and are capable of enduring the greatest labor. . . . They cut all the wood and carry it to the lodge on their backs, do the fishing make the sugar gather the rice cultivate the corn & potatoes, everything that is called labor and the men nothing at all."[55]

Statements suggesting that the wild rice harvest was a man's obligation should be carefully assessed. For example, François Malhiot's journal entry for September 10, 1804: "L'Outarde [Wild Goose] started yesterday with his young men to gather wild rice at lac de la Truite [Trout Lake, now Vilas County, Wisconsin] where his village is," should be taken to mean that the band went to establish its rice camps, and not that the men were the harvesters. There have been, however, reports of men harvesting rice exclusively – at Rat Portage, for instance. Although he may not have been an eyewitness, Keating in his *Narrative* asserted that wild rice was harvested by two men with poles in each canoe. While the boat rested, one pulled the stalks over the edge while "the other thrashes it until all the grain is separated from the stem." Working as a team they did this on each side, then poled the canoe forward to stop again for another batch. W. Vernon Kinietz properly challenged Keating's account as contrary to other reports such as Gilfillan's firsthand description of the few Christian men ricing at White Earth. Whereas at that time the sight of grown men ricing was still a rarity, young boys often harvested with women, such as at Moose-Ear River in 1892, or at Leech Lake, where Dan White fondly remembered his grandmother as his favorite ricing partner. In these instances the boys poled the boats.[56]

Whatever the traditional division of labor by gender, men have increasingly become involved in all stages of ricing. George McGeshick associated the days of women as sole harvesters with the time of the rice camps, when the entire extended family moved to the rice fields; men began to harvest once wild rice became a commercial enterprise. Because teamwork is essential to a good harvest, the division of labor is now based more on experience than gender. As Berde pointed out, "a knocker cannot get the rice into the boat unless the poler is adept; and an excellent poler with a poor knocker is equally disadvantaged." The best ricing partners usually come from the same family, working together to combine income. In the twentieth century, husband-and-wife teams – the husband poling and the wife knocking – and two-man teams, such as at Cass Lake in 1947, have become common. Surmising that men began to take over in the 1930s, James Mustache said: "Never see any women now. The only team that you see now is Jim and his wife; that's the only team that I know of, that man and wife together, but most is two guys."[57]

Ojibway men may pick the same male ricing partners year after year for the same camaraderie that white hunters and fishermen find in seasonal excursions with companions they may not otherwise see. James Mustache, for example, riced with either Jim or Bill Barber: "Each party had their own. Myself, I did mostly knocking, when I used to go out with Bill. . . . We'd exchange, you know, I'd pole and he'd knock. Maybe you'd take a turn, maybe go ashore, maybe have a lunch."[58]

DRYING

Wild rice fresh from the lake must be dried almost immediately, to avoid mildew from moisture naturally contained in the kernel and water from the bottom of the boat. Keeping green rice even with precautions is risky, for once it begins to get moldy, it cannot be further processed. When more rice has been collected than can be dried immediately, however, it may be preserved in its green state for up to a week by keeping it wet. This measure is also used to prevent it from turning into black rice—unprocessed rice that after a week takes on a black color. Called *chi-manoomin,* it is virtually worthless. (Sometimes a few black heads can be seen clinging to stalks harvested earlier.) To prevent black rice, harvesters moisten any rice to be kept more than three days before processing—often the practice of guest ricers. Apparently Indians sometimes kept green rice this way in holes in the sand at the lakeshore. Lalemant, in the *Jesuit Relations* of 1662–63, wrote of the Ottawa harvest, "as often as a Canoe is full, they go and empty it on the shore into a ditch dug at the water's edge." More recently, rice has been stored for up to a week in barrels of fresh water.[59]

William Baker complained of the waste when people did not process rice properly: "They get that rice and then just set it aside, well, just shortening up, I call it. It gets black, just like you set a piece of meat and you let it there too long, it's going to spoil." He was particularly critical of white dealers who, he felt, had no real understanding of how rice should be treated and were interested only in profit. Recalling the last time he riced at Lake Totogatic with Sam Frogg (1964), he said, "There was a man right there ready to buy the rice right as soon as it come right off the lake. And what happened? They keep that rice, just like they do in Minnesota today, turns black. . . . [Wisconsin Ojibway] don't let it lay around like *chimookomaan* [white man] does today."[60]

The rice is unloaded from the boats and carried to the campsite (or wherever

FIG. 18. Emptying large winnowing trays, used to carry rice from boats to the camp for drying, about 1910

it will be processed) in bark trays, pails, sacks, or squares of canvas (fig. 18). Formerly, some women used a pack frame with a tumpline supported across the chest or top of the head. According to Lawrence Mitchell: "[Y]ou had to go through the marsh and then through the swamp and up to the campground. It was quite a trek. . . . It wasn't until later that these sacks came in, they used to have just squares of, oh, light canvas, and they'd put the rice in there, tie the corners together and carry it like that. Pack-sack like that, and one of the old ladies used to get part of it on their head, you know, and carry . . . on their backs. . . . usually a couple of trips. Usually you just kept on knocking rice all day [while others packed it back to camp]."[61]

Freshly harvested rice continues to ripen, but it must have air, sun, and sometimes the heat of a fire to rid it of moisture before roasting. Paul Buffalo stressed the importance of drying green rice soon after collection: "Wild rice has got to be cured. When you come in you should scatter it out, so that it'll surface to the top of the grain, then you are able to cure that, heat it. By heating it you kill the reaction." This initial drying is now done out-of-doors by spread-

FIG. 19. Mrs. Brown and her cat, near rice drying on canvas, Nett Lake, September 1970

ing the rice with a rake in a four-inch layer on canvas or blankets (fig. 19); formerly rice was dried on woven mats, animal skins, layers of coarse swamp grass or sheets of birch bark sewn together (called *apakwaanag),* commonly used in covering wigwams (fig. 20). According to John Tanner, these were "large enough to afford a partial covering for three men." Ojibway living on the fringes of the prairie sometimes adopted aspects of Plains Indian material culture and dried wild rice on buffalo robes, just as they carried rice from the lake in parfleches. Whatever the ground cover, it is laid out to get the most exposure to light and air—formerly near the wigwams in the rice camp, today in the yard (fig. 21). Still, the Ojibway avoid placing the covers in the direct sunlight to prevent the heat of the midday sun from beginning to cook the rice.[62]

While spread out, the rice is picked over to remove trash and pieces of stalk and leaves that have fallen into the boat (fig. 22), as well as dirt, pebbles, weeds, rice worms, and the like. Constantly turning the rice during cleaning helps the drying process. Some Ojibway fan their rice after drying to bring chaff to the surface for removal. Lips, who estimated drying time at about four hours, disputed as overgeneralized Jenks's assertion that at Fond du Lac drying took twenty-four hours. Hers is a minority opinion, however, for both Frances Densmore and Lawrence Mitchell said it took a day for rice to dry thoroughly, even when occasionally stirred. Some Ojibway let it go even longer, processing only small amounts as quickly as possible for immediate use. The Ojibway much prefer such freshly dried rice, which can be distinguished by its color from unfinished rice.[63]

The other and probably older method—drying while simultaneously curing freshly harvested wild rice—is to fire dry it on a scaffold. When not used for drying fish or preserving meat, such wooden scaffolds often served as sun shields. Sometimes they were even converted into summer sleeping platforms, the smoke from a smoldering fire beneath keeping the mosquitoes away. Blueberries were dried on such racks earlier in the season; the same scaffolds may have been used for the rice harvest.[64]

Just as it dries and hardens blueberries, smoke drying hardens and preserves wild rice; consequently, the product has sometimes been referred to as "hard rice." Greenish-black and much darker than parched rice (an alternative to dried rice, see page 118), hard rice took longer to cook, kept indefinitely, and, unlike parched rice, could be used as seed. Because this technique obviated the need for later roasting or parching, it required less labor; consequently, smoke drying was often employed when large amounts of rice were to be processed for sale or trade. Indian people today, however, seem to prefer parching. Traditional Ojibway at Nett Lake used smoke to dry rice *only* after they sun dried and parched enough for their own use, and Lac Court Oreilles

FIG. 20. Stirring wild rice on birch-bark mats with a parching paddle to hasten drying, Minnesota, about 1920

FIG. 21. Wild rice drying on a mat at Nett Lake, 1947. This rice would need frequent stirring; usually it is spread out in a three- to four-inch layer. Between the rice and the uncovered wigwam are two large makakoon; *the bark lashed to the side of the wigwam appears to serve as a sun shield.*

Fig. 22. Wild rice drying on birch-bark apakwaan, *probably borrowed from a wigwam, near Tower, Minnesota, about 1940. The covering is made from several sections of bark sewn together, with thin cedar strips lashed to the ends to prevent tearing. The man is filling a* nooshkaachinaagan, *probably to take to a woman parching rice nearby.*

Ojibway in 1899 declared their preference for parched rice, which brought the best price "and is considered far ahead of the other," despite the fact that they usually fire dried four times as much.[65]

The introduction of iron kettles during the fur trade era clearly marked a transition to a newer technique; almost all of the oldest sources mention fire drying. Marquette wrote that the Indians dried rice on a wooden grating in the smoke of a slow fire for several days "to clean it from the straw and remove it from a husk." Carver also mentioned smoke drying, followed by treading or rubbing to remove the husks. Once Indians had metal kettles, they parched as well as smoke dried their rice. On April 30, 1838, George Bonga at Leech Lake wrote the Reverend William T. Boutwell, "I have put 2 sacks Rice & 1 Corn aside for you[.] Scortch Rice [parched] I have none."[66]

Several sources suggest that both kinds of wild rice were used as rations for the fur trade. Near the St. Croix River, trader Michel Curot distinguished between the two in relating an argument he had with one of his men, Savoyard, on November 23, 1803: "I went into the storehouse and gave him two chopines of parched rice which he refused to take saying that of that rice The custom was to receive three chopines For two people [a married couple] for each Ration, Because it did not make as much as that that was not roasted." Curot held firm and the two eventually got into a brawl.[67]

Fire drying was accomplished on a flat rack raised on a scaffold several feet above a slow-burning fire. The scaffold, called *abwaajigan,* was constructed by driving forked stakes into the ground to form a rectangle. Cross-poles were strapped across them; slabs of cedar over the cross-poles formed the platform. To keep the kernels from falling through the spaces, mats woven of basswood or cedar bark, or possibly layers of hay, long marsh grass, or small willows were laid over them. One of Newton Winchell's illustrations shows six vertical, forked posts 3½ feet high forming a rectangle 18 feet long and 4 feet wide. William Keating, at Lake of the Woods in 1823, called this "a fine sieve made of reeds, secured in a square frame"; William Johnston a decade later said the scaffold was made by laying sticks crossways "but so near to each other, as not to allow the heads of the rice to fall through." Because such a drying rack was from 10 to 20 feet long, noted Johnston, it required two or three small fires for even heat distribution. An anonymous manuscript from Bear Lake (Wisconsin) contains a sketch of an *abwaajigan,* conforming in width and height roughly to Winchell's dimensions but from 30 to 50 feet long. Grass was laid over the crossbars, and two long poles held the grass in place (fig. 23). Jenks's correspondent from Rat Portage claimed the racks were 8 feet high, probably an exaggerated guess. Robert J. N. Pither, an Indian agent for twenty-five years, wrote Jenks that women "parch the first day's gathering in the manner Corn is popped. They use a kettle over a slow fire."[68]

FIG. 23. Drying rack near a rice lake at Lac Court Oreilles, 1899

The degree of heat and quantity of rice affected the time needed for drying. To confine and intensify the heat, a hedge of green cedar branches was piled up to enclose the scaffold at its base. In place of cedar boughs the Bear Lake rice rack was fenced with *wiigwaasapakwaaganag*, the sewn birch-bark strips used on wigwams, secured on the windward side only. This arrangement caused the smoke and heat to rise through the rice, piled four to five feet high on the rack. The fire was kept from blazing for about twelve hours. From time to time the rice on top was turned with paddles or shaken to hasten the curing process. Older sources – Marquette, for instance – said this took several days; more recent reports such as Stickney's claimed it was accomplished in one day.[69]

There is some disagreement about the relative merits of parching and fire drying rice. Stickney claimed parching destroyed some nutritive qualities of wild rice, but all of Lips's informants insisted the taste of wild rice suffered from fire drying. They resorted to the latter method only from necessity or to save labor, insisting that fire drying four-fifths of the harvest, such as Jenks reported at Lac Court Oreilles, would never be done at Nett Lake because the community was known for its special care in processing.[70]

PARCHING OR SCORCHING

When wild rice is not fire dried, parching or roasting the kernels is essential to preserve them for storage and render them edible. This process serves two main purposes: destroying the germ prevents the kernel from sprouting so that it can be kept indefinitely; hardening the kernel loosens the tight-fitting hull so it can be broken off and discarded. In addition, parching tends to scorch off the long, barbed end of the chaff and destroy detritus left after the initial cleaning. Like all originally wild species, *Zizania aquatica* is one of those plants having so-called bearded or awned fruits. (Its pericarp or fruitshell and testa or seedshell grow with each other to form the characteristic black covering of the kernel.) The awn is not part of the fruit and must be removed to get at the edible kernel. As it separates from the fruitshell in roasting, the awn takes on a golden, then brownish-yellow color, changing the kernel to a glossy dark brown or black.[71]

Although wild rice can be left unparched for a short time, the Ojibway almost universally prefer it parched as soon as possible after harvest: "Sometimes they leave the rice there for two days. Then the rice turns black. If they leave the rice for three days, they parch it quickly so it won't be coal black. That is Indian rice. If they dry and parch it immediately on taking from the lake, then the rice is green. It's very nice then; it is just put in hot water and soaked and it is real nice."[72]

When processing rice by hand, the Ojibway have used large cast-iron kettles for parching ever since they became available for trade (fig. 24). (Brass and copper kettles may also have been in use at one time, but by the 1980s they were rare.) What, then, did the Indians use before they had kettles? While some peoples – the Illinois Potawatomi, for instance – roasted rice on hot, flat stones, it seems probable that the Ojibway aboriginally used the scaffold method, effectively combining drying and parching. The only other possibility seems to be parching rice in a pit lined with stones heated by a fire in the depression. Author Dan Brogan observed "a few of the older Indians" at Nett Lake parching this way in 1955; most, however, used iron kettles. Lips saw kettle roasting as a fairly recent innovation, pointing out that the oldest sources, such as Marquette and Lalemant, omit all mention of parching rice in containers, describing only fire drying. Although there is evidence that some Algonquian tribes made pottery, she has dismissed the possibility that stoneware might have been used. The recent testimony of older Ojibway lends credence to Lips's assumption. Maude Kegg of Mille Lacs Reservation recalled how, when no kettle was available, her people resorted to the older method by collecting "iron rushes" (*biiwaabikwashkoonsan*) along the Mississippi River. The reed *Equisetum hymenale,* also used for scouring, is appar-

Fig. 24. Leech Lake woman parching rice in a large metal kettle near Federal Dam, Minnesota, about 1913

ently so fire resistant that it becomes red-hot without burning. The rushes were woven tightly together, making mats that no rice fell through. The mats were supported by a stick scaffolding that spanned the fireplace, and the rice was turned continuously until roasted brown.[73]

Once available, metal kettles became valued possessions, essential to a variety of food production processes. Such vessels were always kept scrupulously clean. The same kettle was often used to boil sap in the sugarbush, then buried in a hole for safekeeping until it was needed for parching wild rice in late summer. Called *okaadakik,* the cast-iron, short-legged caldron was an important item to bequeath to one's close relatives. As Maude Kegg remembered: "If someone has a legged kettle, she holds on to it always. When an old lady becomes elderly or perhaps is dying, she gives the kettle to her oldest daughter." When the daughter becomes old, she passes it on to *her* daughter.[74]

When the Ojibway roast or parch wild rice in an iron kettle or galvanized washtub (fig. 25), they prop the vessel up with rocks or logs over a slow-burning wood fire (poplar, birch, or tamarack). According to Dan White, "They had a certain way of keeping the fire so that they didn't have that fire blazing more than at any time, they seemed to control the fire just by adding

FIG. 25. Mrs. Field parching rice at Nett Lake, 1947

so much fuel into the fire, and they knew just how hot the fire was, and by that way they knew just about how long they could parch rice, and they parched the rice pretty evenly, even in the dark." The McGeshicks finish rice by using *two* tubs, one on each side of the fire, resting on a metal crossbar suspended over the middle of the fire by cinder blocks (fig. 26). George, who splits cedar for his fire and starts it with birch bark, said that old pine stumps were ideal for parching because their pitch content kept the fire going slowly without constantly requiring more wood. These stumps are hard to find today, and Indian insistence on reserving them in treaties permitting the clear-cutting of pine may have been as much for firewood as for the roots, which were split and used as thread for sewing bark.[75]

From a half-gallon to as much as a half-bushel of rice may be parched at a time. Although the Ojibway commonly call this step "scorching," the rice is constantly stirred with a special cedar paddle in a lifting motion, to keep it from burning. The paddle resembles a small, slender canoe paddle; a regular

FIG. 26. Mary and George McGeshick parching rice during rainy weather in an improvised tent at their rice camp on the Wisconsin/Michigan border, September 1986; note rice drying in the canoe.

canoe paddle can be used as well. (The McGeshicks use one of each.) Roasting time—usually from fifteen to twenty-five minutes for a small batch, about an hour for a peck—depends somewhat on the container: cast-iron kettles are slower than galvanized tubs, but they distribute heat more evenly. The drier the rice, the more easily and quickly it parches. In any case, the parcher must be skilled so the rice will not burn. Overparching in too hot a fire pulverizes the rice, resulting in a batch of *manzaan* (fine rice), so the hotter the fire, the faster the rice must be turned. A popping sound indicates too much heat; as

George McGeshick noted, "If it sounds like grasshoppers, the fire's too hot." Parchers test periodically for doneness by taking a kernel from the kettle and pinching it with a thumbnail; if the kernel breaks, scorching is complete.[76]

To begin the process, women carefully scoop off the top layer of rice spread to dry when it has reached a certain brittleness—usually after about two hours. They fill winnowing trays or pails and carry the sun-dried rice to the heated kettle. As the rice roasts, it steams and smokes a bit, spreading an appetizing aroma through the vicinity. Once parched, the rice is winnowed in fanning trays to rid it of as much loosened awn as possible as well as the considerable charcoal resulting from scorching the beards. It is then moved to a zinc tub, wooden barrel, or cardboard box, while the next batch is roasted.

At this point, several processing steps usually occur simultaneously. No one is idle. Lips's scene of Nett Lakers during the harvest of 1947 shows every individual in the village occupied in processing: "Everyone that belonged to the family, from the smallest child to the great-grandfather, began at once to busy himself with processing rice. Here no division of labor prevailed; whoever had two hands, pitched in, be it to turn over the drying kernels, to kindle the fire under the large iron kettle, to contribute the shallow bark trays, to pour rice from one tray to another, to carry the dried rice to be roasted, to bring the moccasins worn by the treader, to supply the paddles for stirring, or to watch over the duck soup in the cooking pot. In short, the community was transformed into a swarming anthill, where each individual had to undertake appropriate and exactly determined assignments, which nevertheless were in no way bound by conventions of age or sex. . . . A family member would squat on a box or chair next to the kettle hanging over the fire—usually the mother, but also the men took part in this work, mostly standing, and began to stir with the paddle. A strong aroma as if from roasting coffee now spread itself over the whole village. . . . One woman, busy fanning, is seen engulfed in a thick dust cloud. She tosses the contents of the shallow tray in the air and brings up the tray against the falling kernels so that they fall on it with considerable force and facilitate the loosening of the awns. Most of them burst open and blow away; even the black inner skins which surround the kernel crack open, and all these parts whirling away in the wind generate the clouds which surround the winnower."[77]

Just as Lips described, collecting, cleaning, drying, parching, and winnowing wild rice were generally accomplished on the same day, particularly in the bigger rice camps. In small camps of fewer people, however, the harvesters had to set aside late afternoon and evening to parch the rice they knocked earlier. Dan White indicated that these activities often continued long after dark. The Leech Lake Ojibway used pitch-coated birch-bark torches for light, as they once did to shine deer or spear fish at night: "[W]e'd haul the rice up and spread it out and let it dry out by the sun as much as we could and then went right to work and parched the rice, before nightfall, before it got too late. . . . Some Indians used to still parch way into the night and use birchbark torches in order to see just how much it was burning the rice."[78]

Comparing the reports of Jenks's far-flung correspondents shows that drying and roasting procedures varied from one locality to another. In northern Wisconsin some rice apparently was kiln dried in the 1850s and 1860s, and at Bad River rice was said to have been cured but not parched in kettles. At Rat Portage, Ontario, rice was parched first and then fire dried on a scaffold supporting cedar slabs; a layer of grass was spread out on the slabs, then a layer of rice.[79]

Hand-parched rice has a slightly different appearance from rice that has been sun dried or processed mechanically for commercial purposes. Because the parched kernels swell to burst the hulls, they tend to be larger and lighter in color. Many of them look slightly "popped," giving them what Jenks described as "a peculiar translucent crystalline appearance."[80]

HULLING

After parching, wild rice is hulled to remove the close-fitting chaff from the kernel. (This jacket with pointed beard gives rice at this stage a resemblance to oats.) Because of the nature of the job, hulling has always been assigned to men. Lips is probably correct in questioning Jenks's assertion that formerly this was women's work, except for very small quantities; the traditional method of breaking the chaff—whether through flailing, churning, or treading—involves strenuous labor. Thus it is scarcely surprising that automated hulling machines were among the first laborsaving devices in mechanized wild rice processing. Nevertheless, old-timers continue to insist that rice hulled in the traditional way tastes better.[81]

By far the most widespread method of hulling was to tread rice in a small pit dug in the earth (fig. 27). Excavations in Minnesota have unearthed small, clay-lined tramping pits, which archaeologists date to the Late Woodland period (A.D. 800–1600). According to Charles Eastman, Rainy Lake Ojibway even hulled rice in a "natural water-worn" hole in a rock, "filled half full with rice and covered with rawhide." In 1895 Jenks found depressions in the ground, the vestiges of hulling pits, on the west shore of Lake Koshkonong (Jefferson County, Wisconsin), which he estimated had not been used for half a century. And in the early twentieth century Albert Reagan noticed that pits at Nett Lake were "lined with cement or marl [clay] from the lake."[82]

An average treading pit measured about 18 inches deep and perhaps 2 to 3 feet in diameter. Traditionally, its sides were lined with wooden slats, and a

FIG. 27. A youth treading rice at Nett Lake, about 1947

FIG. 28. A treading pit at Lac Court Oreilles, September 1899. The support bars are embedded in the ground and lashed together.

block of wood was placed at the bottom. Such a pit was called a *bootaagan* (fig. 28). In postcontact years, a hole might be dug deep enough to accommodate a ready-made pork barrel, lard tub, keg, or metal pail, jutting perhaps 4 to 6 inches above the ground. A closed bag of rice was put in the pit, or the pit was lined with a skin, an old blanket, or some equally sturdy commercial bag. If a bag was used, it was usually made from a deerskin or mooseskin, wrapped and tied around the rice. This was an old practice; Marquette described skin bags containing rice trod upon "so long and so vigorously that The grain separates from the straw, and is very easily winnowed." If the pit was lined, the edges of the liner were gathered after the treading, and the rice and broken chaff were lifted out together. In the 1850s Henry Schoolcraft saw men treading rice in skin-lined pits at Rice Lake in Barron County, Wisconsin.[83]

Pits lined with slats and plugged at the bottom provide a firm, hard surface against which treaders compress the grain to break its chaff. (Some say keeping the rice warm facilitates the process.) For the side lining, handmade, half-inch-thick staves were overlapped in clapboard fashion (fig. 29). As Lawrence Mitchell joked, there was no need to make the staves smooth, as the action of hulling the first few batches acted like sandpaper. In fact, if the tub was ready-made, one deliberately roughened its inside with a wood chisel, producing a ribbed surface to help grind the hulls off the kernels. Maude Kegg said: "When

Fig. 29. Assembling a bootaagan *near a wigwam, about 1920. The boards appear to be fashioned from commercial shiplap.*

I used to help my uncle make a *bootaagan* . . . I held it for him. He cuts a log; then cuts it straight across. Then he points one end and carves some wooden pieces, pointing them so they'll fit well to make the *bootaagan* round. When he's through carving them, he digs a pit and puts grass in it. It's long grass that he puts in it. Then he puts in a willow strip bent into a circle to hold the grass there. Then he fits the boards together in it. I held them as I watched him. After he got done fitting in those things . . . the pieces of carved cedar, then he taps in the round piece of log. Then, it looks like a pail. He forms the boards into a circle and puts in the willow strips. It holds then and is round. No sand can get in there. We take care of it properly so it doesn't get wet; we cover it, perhaps with a birchbark roll, when it rains or at night when we aren't using it." Blessing measured a similar tramping pit of cedar slats at Inger (Leech Lake Reservation) in about 1952. While these wood-lined pits might be cylindrical, more often they were cone-shaped. (Winchell provided illustrated cross sections of each variety.) The Inger pit had a three-foot-diameter opening tapering to a small cedar disk at the bottom.[84]

Once ricing season was over, the disassembled hulling vessel was buried together with the knocking sticks and the parching kettle somewhere in the camp. Lawrence Mitchell told how ricing equipment was stored at White Earth: "All these things were put in a frame there, covered with bark, and we dug them out when we got back there again. They'd be just ground level, so that it doesn't get wet, you know, and sometimes even raised up a little bit with logs under there and things placed on top there so it don't get wet from the bottom."[85]

The job of treading rice was performed by an adult male (fig. 30) or divided among small boys taking turns. Mitchell, five years old when he began hulling rice, said that children were preferred because their lighter weight prevented excessive breakage. (The only time Jenks saw Ojibway women hulling rice, they were pounding it with pestles.) Sometimes, when children did the work, the rice was simply spread out on blankets. This was the experience of James Mustache, whose family also performed a preliminary treading *before* parching: "As kids, you know, we always walked on that rice ourselves. After we get it off the lake, that's what they'd do, and after it's dry then they start dancing on it." Then the rice was scorched, after which the children "danced" it again.[86]

For sanitary reasons, those hulling rice washed their feet and wore new or at least very clean moccasins, sometimes specially made of heavy cloth that came partway up the calves like leggings or that was sewn to the treader's pants cuffs (fig. 31). Equally effective was canvas wrapped around the feet; its slightly abrasive surface was useful in dehusking. Some today wear rubber boots or galoshes. In 1833 William Johnston described the Ojibway hulling rice in a hole large enough to hold half a bushel of rice and lined with an elkskin or mooseskin: "[T]he man or woman then put on mockesins and tread it out in the skin, which is easyly done, being dried to crispness." (The custom of treading rice barefoot reported at Vermilion and Rainy lakes appears to be exceptional.) Nett Lakers said that the moccasins must be sufficiently thin for the wearer to be able to feel the kernels through the soles. Also, precautions were taken to keep the treader from tracking dirt to the rice with his "Indian shoes"

FIG. 30. Jigging the rice with legs positioned as if doing the war dance, about 1938. Bootaagan *staves are overlapped to provide an abrasive inner surface for breaking the chaff.*

(fig. 32). Stressed William Dudley of Red Lake: "This they were very careful in the sanitation care. Where the jig hole is, there is a canvas spread so the jigger will not walk anywhere else, for he might bring in sand in the rice."[87]

Proper treading requires strength, suppleness, and endurance. Wrote Jenks: "Here, then, is the invention of the treadmill thrashing-machine. This is the power mostly employed in the thrashing of wild rice." To assist balance and help the treader control the amount of weight he applies to the rice, the Ojibway place a pole on one or both sides of the pit (see fig. 30, 32). Two poles may form a V shape, the open ends embedded in the ground, the tied ends angling up and away from the pit at about a sixty-degree incline; other arrangements include a tripod erected over the hole, or possibly a single pole propped over the middle of the pit. The forked pole used to push the canoe through the rice fields also can be converted to this purpose; one end rests on the ground, the other on a strong tree limb. For steadiness the treader grabs the pole(s) with both hands as if it were a railing.[88]

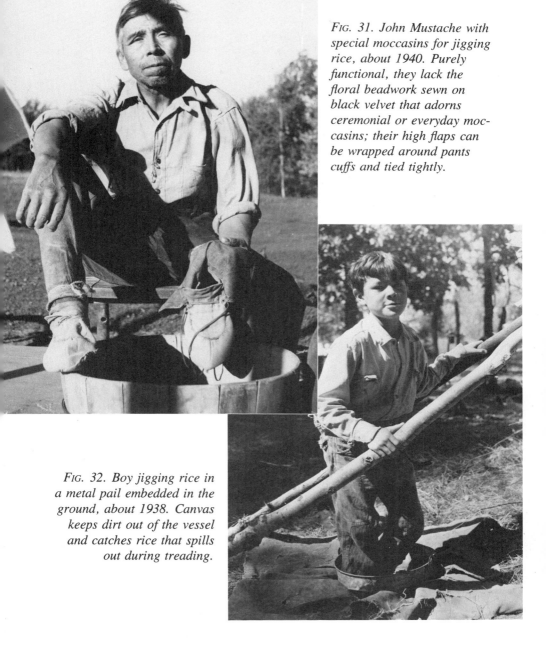

Fig. 31. John Mustache with special moccasins for jigging rice, about 1940. Purely functional, they lack the floral beadwork sewn on black velvet that adorns ceremonial or everyday moccasins; their high flaps can be wrapped around pants cuffs and tied tightly.

Fig. 32. Boy jigging rice in a metal pail embedded in the ground, about 1938. Canvas keeps dirt out of the vessel and catches rice that spills out during treading.

Stepping into the pit, the man tramps the rice in a circular motion, twisting his feet to force the grains into a small space against the staves of the pit lining; working vigorously with his feet, he cracks the chaff and breaks it from the kernel. Some call this "running in the rice." This motion—raising the knees alternately—gives the treader the appearance of performing the war dance (today, standard powwow dancing); consequently, treading is frequently referred to as "dancing the rice" or "jigging," and the *bootaagan* as a "dancing tub." In many places the Ojibway have sung to accompany the rice dancers. Although the jigger's knee motions resemble dancing, the action of his feet does not. Recently a young Ojibway was videotaped dancing the rice in a buckskin-lined pit to the accompaniment of powwow music from a cassette player. In a natural response, he used the toe-heel, toe-heel powwow step most familiar to him. An elder standing nearby remarked that the youth was incorrectly jigging the rice, but he had not the heart to tell him so because of the young man's sincere intentions. Dancing the rice was deemed colorful and intriguing enough to tourists to be included in the Itasca State Park pageant in 1937 (see fig. 6b).[89]

How much rice is threshed at one time seems a matter of personal preference, although the size of the pit dictates this to some extent. E. S. Seymour wrote that, after the pit was dug, about a bushel of rice was poured in and covered with a deerskin. Others have guessed that the skin and commercial bags contain about a gallon of grain. Lips estimated the hole was filled about a foot deep with rice. Whatever the amount, the process is continous, particularly as newly roasted rice constantly arrives. The treader needs about fifteen minutes to hull each batch.[90]

Lips depicted the exhausted state of men after treading. One broke into a sweat after only a few minutes of work; children stood by holding towels to wipe off his face and chest. She saw men lying panting on the ground after two hours of such exercise and doubted that they could have continued much longer. Lawrence Mitchell said that rice needed to be danced twice to remove the chaff completely. He estimated three-fourths of an hour for the first time, after which the rice was fanned in trays to remove chaff as well as detritus left from parching and put back into the pit for another forty-five minutes. George McGeshick preferred to hull five to seven pounds at a time, requiring only about twenty minutes for the first treading. He dehusked *all* of his rice partway on one day and on the next day gave it a second treading.[91]

While treading is by far the most common means of hulling, wild rice may also be churned or even flailed to accomplish the same end (fig. 33). Winchell illustrated a typical hulling pole, called *bootaaganaak:* 5½ feet long, it enlarged to 3 inches in diameter near the bottom. Densmore's photograph in *Chippewa Customs* of a rice pestle and a graining ladle for maple sugar shows them to be about equal in length. (Elsewhere she gave the average length as

FIG. 33. Hulling rice with pestles, about 1940

5½ feet.) A typical pestle would be carved from a 6-inch thick piece of poplar or other soft wood; the handle end was whittled to proper size, and the butt end was somewhat pointed so the stick could move up and down near the edges of the pit, where it caused the least breakage. Properly used, the sticks "were not heavily forced downward but allowed to drop of their own weight." Similar to these hulling implements was one at Fond du Lac in 1898, described to Jenks as "shaped like a handspike, being largest at the butt," used for pounding rice in a knee-deep hole. A year later at Lac Court Oreilles he saw both treading and churning—the churning in a barrel sunk almost entirely in the ground and nearly filled with rice, with one or two people pounding rice in mortar-and-pestle fashion or an individual using two churn sticks. Hulling with pestles at Lac Court Oreilles must have been discontinued within a decade or so of Jenks's field work, for both James Mustache and William Baker denied seeing dashers used for this purpose.[92]

The use of two pestles per person at Leech Lake is confirmed in Paul Buffalo's description: "There's poles made with the big heads on them. Already whittled down, green poles made of ash, then they get busy. There's this one old guy, go to the [sunken] pails, 'I'll take two of them,' you know. He's pounding that rice." Even a sizable group of people might hull rice together this way, according to Dan White: "And then the fun began when they was all ready to thrash. . . . They had these sticks, hardwood sticks, eight feet long or a little better . . . and they could be eight, nine, ten or maybe more, all get around that and they start poking their stick in there just a certain way." Janet Fontaine mentioned about eight men "poking the rice with sticks and circling the hole as if dancing." White's dimensions for the pit would certainly accommodate such large group activity: 3 feet across at the top, its cedar staves declining to a circle 1 foot in diameter at the bottom (which held a cone-shaped rock).[93]

The sequence of steps in removing the chaff varied by community and tribe; thorough hulling sometimes required repeated efforts. According to Densmore, several people were needed to hull rice; the sequence was parching, husking with long pestles, winnowing, and treading to remove the chaff. Sometimes the fine chaff (*manzaan*) was stored away with the broken rice and later cooked with it: "The chaff from this treading was usually kept and cooked similarly to the rice, having much the flavor of the rice, and being considered somewhat of a delicacy." Apparently this last treading was less strenuous and could be assigned to a woman. In Coleman's description the rice was "stamped out by foot" by a woman leaning on a pole after pestle-pounding and winnowing.[94]

In about 1663 the Ottawa Indians threshed rice in ditches by the lakeshore *before* they cured it. James Mustache has seen people use logs like rolling pins to break the chaff, and, on occasion, the Ojibway have rubbed or simply shaken off the hull into blankets or baskets. Ron Parisien of Bad River Reservation hulls his rice by hand. He simply takes as much parched rice as is needed for supper and cracks the hulls, like nuts, with his fingers. Possibly the most unusual method of hulling was described by Jenks's correspondent A. C. Stuntz, living in northern Wisconsin in the mid-nineteenth century. He asserted that a fresh or "green" deerskin was stretched out over coals and staked to the ground; the wild rice was poured onto it and trodden by a small boy.[95]

Whatever the hulling method, the rice and broken chaff were afterwards emptied in small amounts from the threshing tubs into shallow trays for winnowing.

WINNOWING

Once rice is hulled, the final step in finishing it is to remove the chaff. Although older sources have paid little attention to this activity, we can safely assume that hulled rice was cleaned of its chaff before being stored or cooked. Natural and human forces combine to accomplish this; although winnowing can be done manually, the Ojibway often invite the assistance of the wind to blow away the light residue of chaff by moving to high ground or rocky outcroppings beside a lake, where the wind is the strongest. They are careful to stand sideways to the breeze, so that the chaff does not blow into the face of the fanner—one reason some prefer a still day for winnowing. While parching wild rice can be accomplished in inclement weather under a tarp or plastic covering, winnowing requires a dry, sunny day. The process takes place in the open; the rice might otherwise become damp and stick to the tray or the chaff become too heavy to blow away.

To separate the broken husks from the kernels, the Ojibway either spread the mass on blankets or mats and fan by hand or, more typically, toss batches in a winnowing tray. With or without "nature's fanning mill," as Jenks called the wind, the processor generally uses some object to help blow the chaff off the kernels. The Lake of the Woods Ojibway whom Keating encountered in 1823 winnowed rice "by stirring it in wooden platters, exposed to a gentle wind," but more commonly a large birch-bark tray used for many other purposes during the rest of the year became the winnowing instrument in late summer. When the rice is spread out or agitated the chaff tends to rise to the top, where it is easily blown or fanned away. Or, as the rice is taken from the hulling pit, it is poured back and forth from one tray or dish to another or onto a blanket, so that the breeze carries off the paper-thin residue of chaff.[96]

For winnowing, the Ojibway use a tray called a *nooshkaachinaagan,* constructed similarly to the *makak,* or bark pail. (In English/Ojibway slang, these fanning trays are sometimes referred to as *gans.*) The tray is made of birch bark that is heated, cut, and folded, then sewn with basswood fiber. It has a protective strip of ash lashed around its rim. The only essential difference between the winnowing tray and the bark pail is shape; a shallow dish, wider at its oblong top than at its rectangular bottom, the tray is the reverse of the trapezoidal *makak.* Like bark pails, *nooshkaachinaaganan* are made in a variety of sizes. Those used for winnowing on several Minnesota and Wisconsin reservations measured from 3 to 6 inches in depth and from 12 by 17 inches to 16 by 24 inches at their tops. An average-sized tray in the author's collection was made in 1976 by Susan Anderson of Onigum (Leech Lake Reservation). Its bottom measures 9 by 13 inches and its top flares to 13 by 20 inches; its depth is about 4 inches throughout. Sturdy yet light, such bark trays are ideal for fanning.[97]

Before 1900, both Winchell and Jenks encountered considerably larger trays. The example Jenks saw in use at Lac Court Oreilles in 1899 was 2 by 3 feet at its top and 7 or 8 inches deep. Trays this large required bark from big birch trees, which was not always available. Sam Yankee (born 1906) told how Mille Lacs Ojibway had to go north to Tower, Minnesota, or to Vermilion

Lake to get bark. Such large trays – in fact the largest the Ojibway made – were used in winnowing to toss the rice in the air and to catch it again as well. In this way, wild rice was simultaneously cleaned and graded: the chaff was blown away and whatever broken, fine rice (*manzaan*) there was fell to some covering on the ground (fig. 34a, 34b), while the heavier, full kernels landed in the tray. Jenks witnessed one Wisconsin ricer working with about a peck of rice at a time, gradually emptying her load of its chaff. He described the ricer's work as she held the *nooshkaachinaagan* by its shorter sides: "The tray is lifted several inches and carried slightly outward. This upward and outward movement is checked quite suddenly, and the tray, while being drawn towards the body of the laborer, is let down again. The light chaff is thus spilled over the outer edge when the tray is at its highest point and just as it is suddenly jerked toward the laborer." This continuous movement was so rapid, noted Jenks, that it did not seem jerky. The chaff fell to the ground, was blown away by the wind, or was pushed off by the winnower as it collected on top of the kernels. Once the chaff was completely removed, the wild rice was ready for cooking or storage (fig. 35a, 35b).[98]

STORAGE

Rice that was not eaten during harvest was stored, principally for later consumption, but for trading or sale as well. A basic staple of Indian diet all year, wild rice was of crucial importance during the late winter; in the event of severe weather and scarce game, families might subsist solely on their rice supplies. Subsistence needs became a factor in the location of major Ojibway population centers. William Warren in 1852, while enumerating the natural resources of Leech Lake, wrote of the area's importance in providing "large quantities [of rice], of which the Indian women gather sufficient for the winter consumption of their families." A century later Leech Lake resident Josephine L. Clark remembered provident attention to staples: "[My stepfather] would make a lot of sugar. That would last all winter long; the sugar that they make, syrup, sugar cakes. When ricing time come, they go ricing. They'd save all the rice they make. Have rice all winter long, all summer."[99]

Indian attention to winter food supplies went beyond their own needs, for traders and missionaries had also learned to count on rice as a winter staple. Consequently, Indians were prepared to trade or sell from their provisions when the opportunity arose. Schoolcraft noted that, of the bags of rice the Ojibway set aside for their own winter use, "much of it is sold to the traders, to subsist their men, on their visits to the Indians." Profit motives as well as frugality are suggested by the fact that in 1775 Alexander Henry was able to

FIG. 34a. Winnowing rice, as chaff spills out into a pile, 1937

FIG. 34b. William Dudley winnowing, Red Lake Reservation, 1969

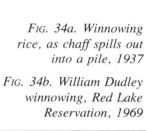

FIG. 35a, 35b. Parched wild rice (with most of the long, barbed awns singed off) and finished rice, completely hulled and winnowed

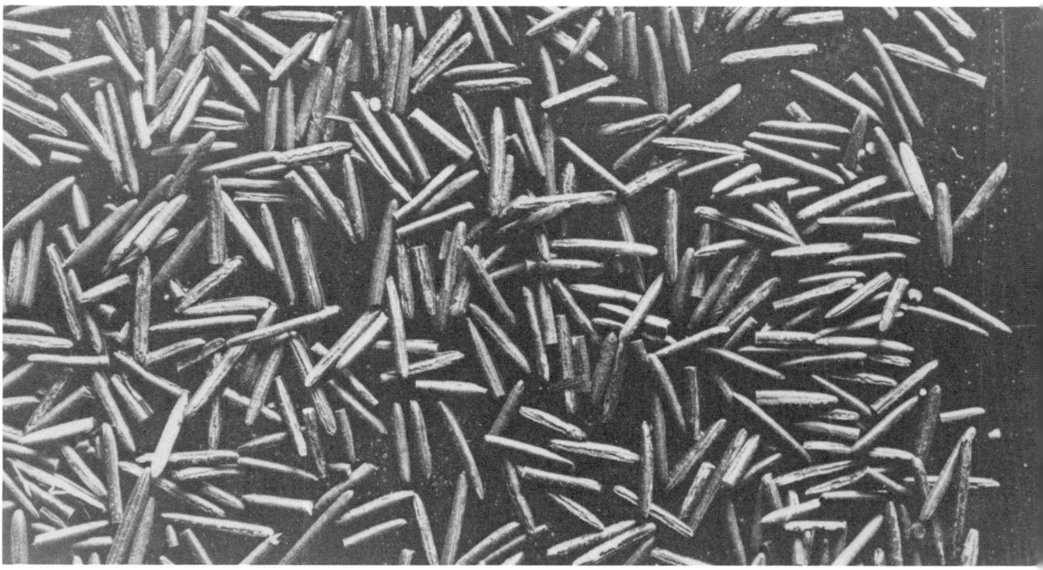

obtain rice from Indians as late as ten months after harvest. At Lake of the Woods in July, after bartering with Ojibway women all night, he was able to purchase a hundred bags of wild rice containing nearly a bushel apiece; on August 1, he bought even more rice on an island in the lake.[100]

Wild rice almost always accompanied canoe travelers. In the early nineteenth century John Tanner hired out as a guide to take American Fur Company traders into Indian country with $160 worth of goods: "We were furnished with no other food than wild rice at the rate of eighteen quarts per man, and instructed not to return until we should have exchanged for peltries all our goods." Already unhappy with the company over its claim on his muskrat skins, Tanner complained that he was forced to paddle by himself "a canoe heavily loaded with wild rice." A similar diet had been arranged for an earlier tour (shortly after the War of 1812), when Tanner was induced by Captain Tussenon at Rainy Lake to guide him and seventy men to the North West Company at the mouth of the Assiniboine River. In preparation for the journey, snowshoes were made and Indians were hired as hunters. In addition, said Tanner, "[A]s we had great quantities of wild rice, we were pretty well supplied with food." The lack of wild rice could pose a real food crisis to traders; on August 24, 1804, François Malhiot wrote: "We are threatened with a famine because the [Ojibway of the Chippewa River area] absolutely want to go on the war-path; consequently they will put the greater portion of their rice in caches, and we shall find ourselves with very little, which we shall have to purchase at its weight in gold."[101]

How much rice the Ojibway customarily stored is conjectural. Anthropologist George Quimby has suggested that, during the period from 1650 to 1760, about five bushels each of wild rice and corn was an adequate annual supply for a Sauk, Fox, or Miami Indian family, Algonquian neighbors of the Ojibway. Since little corn was available to the Ojibway, about ten bushels of rice per family probably would have sufficed for the winter.[102]

While Quimby's estimate may be accurate, there is evidence that by the nineteenth century less rice was saved for Indian use as more was traded or sold. A report to the secretary of war outlining the seasonal subsistence pattern of the Menominee at Green Bay in 1820 described them as living on sugar and fish in the spring, fish and game in summer, wild rice and corn in the fall, and fish and game again in winter. The report added that "those who are provident have some rice during the winter" as well, suggesting that rice supplies were generally depleted by early winter. According to James Doty, a family at Sandy Lake in about 1820 ordinarily processed only five sacks for its own use—scarcely enough for the winter—but a few harvesters finished as much as twenty-five sacks of wild rice, the excess presumably intended for exchange: "A few provident Indians save a little for the spring of the year to eat with their sugar, though generally by that time they have done curing it, the whole is disposed of for trinkets and ornaments."[103]

Paul Buffalo of Leech Lake provided some idea of an Ojibway family's rice needs early in the twentieth century, though his estimate seems excessive. For each of its six members his family customarily laid in eight flour sacks of wild rice, "to make it go around for the next season," and sold the remainder. Each 50-pound sack was filled with about 42 to 45 pounds, according to Buffalo, so that it could be sewn shut. This would average out to nearly a pound a day per individual.[104]

One critical distinction Lips made between hunting and gathering societies and harvesting peoples was the harvesters' inclination to transcend the immediate need to gratify hunger by preserving and storing the fruits of harvest for future needs. The earliest European travelers to North America made frequent mention of the Indian practice of putting preserved food into storage for winter use. Pierre Biard observed in 1616: "[T]hey will sometimes make some storehouses for the Winter, where they will keep smoked meat, roots, shelled acorns, peas, beans, or prunes bought from us. . . . They put these provisions in sacks, which they tie up in big pieces of bark; these they suspend from the interlacing branches of two or three trees so that neither rats nor other animals, nor the dampness of the ground, can injure them."[105]

Vestiges of such practices continued well into the twentieth century. In 1940 while visiting territory of the Mistassini (an Algonquian people) in Labrador, Lips saw platforms tied into the tops of trees as provision caches. Formerly, departing war parties ensured the survival of their families in their absence by this practice.[106]

The Ojibway traditionally stored provisions, including wild rice, underground in containers. Processed rice unexposed to moisture keeps indefinitely. The materials–skin or bark–and methods of packing ensured that the contents would stay dry.

A variety of animal skins have been used to hold wild rice. Jonathan Carver reported that the Indians kept rice in "skins of fawns or young buffalos taken off nearly whole for this purpose and sewed into a sort of sack, wherein they preserve it till the return of their harvest." (A fawnskin held about two bushels of rice.) Winchell added to the list of possibilities the skins of raccoons and duck feet (fig. 36). While such small containers were easily transported by a hunter, larger skins filled with wild rice held a war party's provisions; an individual away from central food depots for any length of time might also carry one. Fur trader Jean Baptiste Perrault related how once, while cutting wood at Fond du Lac in 1783, he was startled by an approaching Indian: "He came very nimbly, and had half a fawn-skin of wild rice. We now feared death or

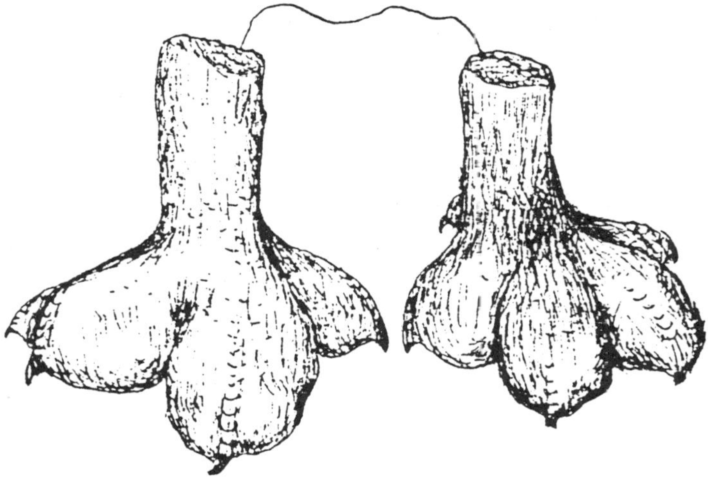

FIG. 36. Duck feet filled with rice, sketched by Herman Haupt, Jr., about 1897, for his unpublished ethnology of the Dakota and Ojibway Indians

some imminent danger. But it turned out to be the Indian who had formerly served as our guide."[107]

Fawnskins filled with processed wild rice served as measuring units in early Indian-white trade. At harvest time (September 5) in 1803, Michel Curot wrote: "About midday David came to meet us. Thinking he had returned from la folle avoine [ricing areas] I Asked him how many fawn-skins they had got." In early October he was forced to throw away about three fawnskins of rotten rice. In February 1804, he expressed concern for two of his men: "I am very Uneasy about Boisvert and Connor. It is now nineteen Days since they left for the fond du Lac, expecting that it would take Twelve Days To make The trip. They carried one fawn-skin of rice almost full for provisions to the fond du Lac."[108]

Perrault told about a trading adventure in about 1791 when his party arrived at La Pointe aux Chenes. They were met by Indians who, slightly intoxicated, insisted they disembark above the French fort. After the Indians unloaded the canoe: "They asked me the price of rum. I told them that it was 20 fawn skins per Keg. I gave them each a Roll of tobacco, and they went to their Lodges. A moment after they brought out 60 fawnskins Of wild rice which they placed in three rows, demanding three kegs of rum. I Delivered it On the spot, and they told me to build at that place; that they would be on my side. Then they went to drinking." Because the indulgence of the Indians lasted three days, the trader accomplished nothing more. His neighbors began to rue having cached their own supply of liquor rather than trading it in similar fashion; they were nearly out of rice and had not extended credit to the Indians.[109]

Maude Kegg remembered her grandmother at Mille Lacs using muskrat skins to store wild rice: "When she gets a muskrat in the trap, she washes him out carefully so he isn't bloody. Before the skin dries up, she puts green rice in it. When it's filled with a lot of rice, she sews it shut. After it's in, she hangs it up in the *wiigiwaam.* When that rice is put in hot water, it just swells right up."[110]

More common than skin were bark containers, either in the form of bags woven from the inner bark of cedar or *makakoon* of birch bark. (The Sauk and Fox Indians stored wild rice in painted rawhide parfleches, a part of Plains Indian material culture that they adopted after being driven from the woodlands; Ojibway living near the prairies likewise occasionally used parfleches.) Nett Lake Ojibway in 1947 insisted that rice kept its good taste only when stored in bark. They found burlap bags an acceptable substitute but felt that rice was easily ruined in the bowls or pots of the whites, and that cardboard boxes sufficed only if left uncovered, in which case the rice got dirty.[111]

Makakoon are mentioned in the earliest literature, the French calling them *caisses d'écorce.* Easily constructed and repaired, these ubiquitous, everyday items were used for tasks from cooking to carrying, often on a yoke; provided with lids, they were perfectly suited for storing things. They were often manufactured at the time of harvest—Josephine Robinson remembered that her mother, for instance, made them for storing blueberries. In addition to canning the fruit, she also dried blueberries for preservation in the older way, burying them 3 to 4 feet deep. While she sat by the fire, watching the berries dry, "she'd be making those great big muckok. . . . And when those berries get nice and dry that's where she'd pack them, in that birchbark muckok. She would sew it up and get it all filled up. It is amazing how many berries you can get in one of those things." Ed Burnside praised one craftsman near Lake Kabetogama, Minnesota, who was particularly skilled in making bark storage pails as well as canoes and flint knives: "He's a wonderful man, how he can do things, how he makes a good birch-bark basket for family rice." *Makakoon* holding dried meat were elevated on frames to prevent dogs and wild animals from getting at the food; cooked meat (such as bear or venison) in a *makak* was sealed with a layer of animal fat before the container was sewn shut and buried. These pantry vessels were noted by trader John Long in 1779 when he had to stretch his party's end-of-January diet: "We were reduced to a few fish and some wild rice, or *menomon* (which are kept in *muccucks,* or bark boxes), to support myself and seventeen men; the allowance to each being only a handful of rice and a small fish, about 2 lb. weight, which is boiled together and makes pleasant soup."[112]

Although bark containers were tailored in a large assortment of sizes according to their purpose, there seems to have been no standard size used for storing wild rice. In general, however, the larger variety was cached. Because they had to be completely waterproof, their seams were pitched with pine tar like those of a canoe. High, sandy ground was usually chosen for the cache as an additional precaution against flooding: "Those ancient people, those were the ones who left their rice at the rice camp, they only went for it as they needed it. . . . They dug holes, they hauled it. You can still see these holes, the land there is high and sandy, that is where they kept it, in those holes. They used dogs to haul it."[113]

When rice became wet it easily spoiled. This happened in 1833 to an Indian named Cotanse, a famous bear hunter at Sandy Lake. Edmund Ely wrote that the hunter arrived with his two brothers and son at the post looking pale and thin. Cotanse had cached all his rice provisions, but high water levels in the fall had spoiled his supply. The lack of early snow had caused the bears "to burrow" for the winter, leaving him only small game for subsistence. The Ojibway may have taken the same precautions with rice caches that they did with corn pits; at Red Lake they burned a fire in the pit for two to three days to rid it of moisture before layering braided corn with hay.[114]

While small *makakoon* are still made, mostly for sale to tourists, the gradual disappearance of large birch trees hastened the decline of the bark pail. Paul Buffalo lamented their passing: "They had big birch trees years ago. That's where they got that birch bark. Now you can't get much birch big enough to make baskets. They make little birdhouses out of little birch [for sale]. They'd patch [*makakoon*] up with pitch, you know. There was no flavor with pitch, there was no taste in that. They cooled it off with sticks, patch 'em just like they patch canoes."[115]

Also made in several sizes were woven cedar-bark bags; the inner bark of the basswood (*wiigob*) or elm bark was used when cedar was unavailable. The bags were filled with rice topped with a layer of hay and were sewn closed with a wide mesh of basswood fiber (fig. 37). Doubtless these were the "little rush bags" used by the Ojibway on Rainy River in 1841 to keep their rice for sale. As Georges Belcourt wrote: "[After hulling] they put it in little rush bags containing from three to four gallons each. It is thus that they sell it to the Company in exchange for little ends of tobacco, and especially for rum." Such bags required considerable skill to manufacture and were being made as recently as 1947 at Nett Lake by John Sasabis and his wife, Charlotte, who lived in a wigwam in the woods away from the settlement. They were known for their excellent craftsmanship in weaving, especially cedar-bark rice bags.[116]

Frances Densmore described the bag's mode of manufacture: strips of the inner bark of the cedar tree, perhaps a half-inch wide, were boiled until pli-

FIG. 37. Woven cedar-bark bag for keeping rice

able, then draped over a stick suspended at either end and woven closely into a seamless bag. As the weaver progressed, she shaped her work into a square or oblong form; when finished, she removed the stick, sewed down the corners, and tied off the strips at the upper edge, making a sturdy rim. Like the *makak,* the bag had no standard size; those made at Rat Portage at the beginning of the twentieth century held from three-fourths to one bushel of rice each. Schoolcraft described a similar rice storage bag, probably a substitute for the cedar-bark bag in the postcontact period: "It [the rice] is then put into coarse Mushkemoots [*mashkimodan*], a kind a bag, made of vegetable fibre or twine, with a woof of some similar material. Occasionally this filling material is composed of old cloth or blankets, pulled to pieces."[117]

Sometimes an unusual, seemingly whimsical version of the bark bag was woven to resemble a human form. One such bag was given in 1852 to Elizabeth Ellet, near the falls on the St. Croix River; she described it in *Summer Rambles in the West* as "a sack made by the Chippewas of braided strips of bark, in a shape rudely resembling a papoose, filled with wild rice which is one of the staples of the territory." Kinietz published a photograph of a Lac

Vieux Desert (Wisconsin) example in *Chippewa Village,* which he said was meant to resemble a man's suit with its arm, leg, and neck holes sewn shut to hold the wild rice kernels (fig. 38). Since cedar-bark shirts were once worn by Ojibway—the dead were formerly dressed in them for summer burial—their adoption in miniature as rice bags may have been a wry allusion to the earlier animal-skin containers.[118]

As much as one-third of the wild rice harvest was packed in containers and cached in a pit dug below the frost line, a custom widespread in North America. In New England, for instance, early captives of the Indians referred to the common custom of ground storage. Mary Rowlandson during her "Ninth Remove" in 1676 wrote: "When we were at this place, my master's maid came home; she had been gone three weeks into the Narragansett country to fetch corn where they had stored up some in the ground."[119]

In the North American interior, the painter George Catlin, on the upper Missouri River in the early 1830s, found the Mandan storing cob-dried maize, pemmican, and dried meat in pits 6 to 7 feet deep, "the insides of which are somewhat in the form of a jug, and tightly closed at the top. . . . packed tight around the sides, with prairie grass, and effectually preserved through the severest winters." The antiquity of this practice among Indians in the rice district is suggested by archaeological excavations such as at the Petaga Point site in east central Minnesota, where two possible storage pits dating from the Late Woodland period were unearthed. Such storehouses were crucial to early European travelers. In 1635 the Jesuit Paul Le Jeune wrote: "Frequently one has to fast, if he misses the caches that were made when descending; and, even if they are found, one does not fail to have a good appetite after indulging in them; for the ordinary food is only a little Indian corn coarsely broken between two stones, and sometimes taken whole in pure water; it is no great treat."[120]

Even the traders emulated Indian practice; recorded Malhiot on June 6, 1804, "I was lucky enough to get four sturgeon from the Savages today, which will, I hope, last me to la Pointe, where I left a sack of corn in a cache last autumn." Sometimes, however, traders arrived at their caches only to find them empty. Perrault, returning in about 1785 to Lake Superior from trading at Leech Lake, lamented: "The day after closing our trade, we set out to descend to our *cache;* for we had now but little meat; and we had got but two fawn-skins of wild rice from the Indians; a scanty supply to take us to the Fond du Lac. Having reached our *cache,* we found nothing; the large bear, the bear-skin, and the moose meat, having been eaten by carcajoux [wolverines] and foxes."[121]

The importance of caching wild rice becomes clear in light of the seasonal migrations of the Ojibway. Traditionally, when rice processing was complete, the harvest camp broke up and families departed to hunt game. The women

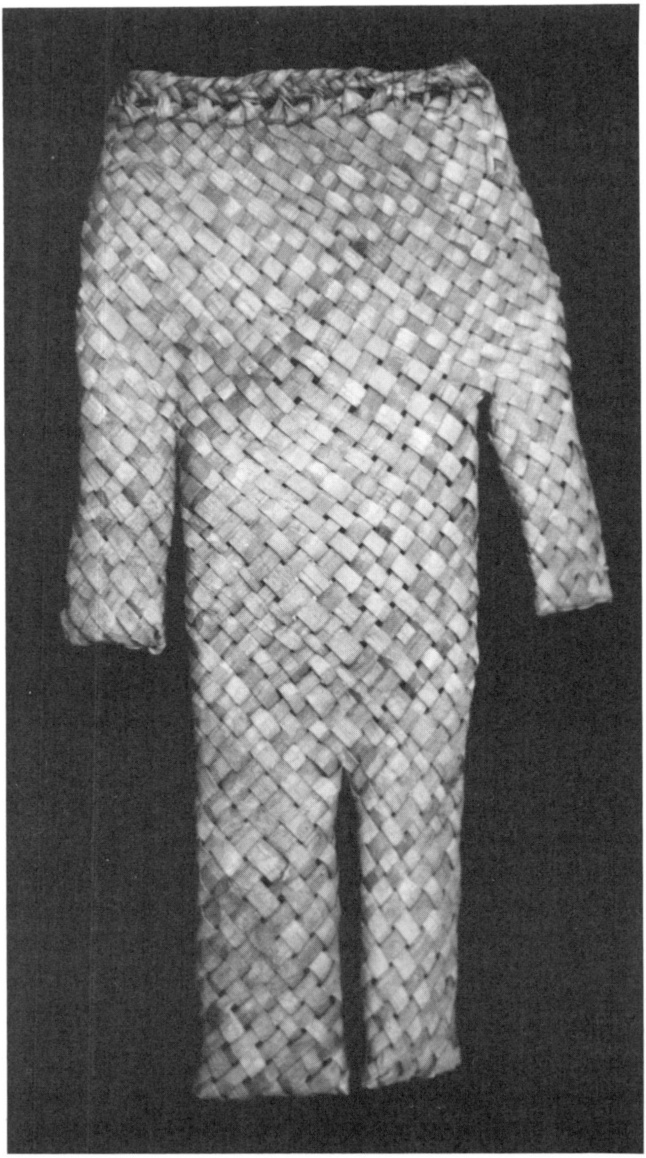

FIG. 38. Cedar-bark rice storage bag from Minnesota, 16½ inches high

of Lac Court Oreilles, for instance, dug cache pits near their home wigwams after ricing was finished and their garden vegetables were gathered. As soon as these were packed away in the ground, the Indians descended the Yellow River to the Chippewa Falls (Wisconsin) area to hunt, returning only after they had dried the meat from game they killed, tanned the hides, and made moccasins and snowshoes. Ultimately, the caches consisted of braided corn, wild rice in cedar-bark bags, and dried meat and fish wrapped in birch bark. Ed Burnside remembered from his youth at Leech Lake: "We used to live up there quite awhile, and then in the summer they come up to Pelican and Nett Lake, gathering wild rice pretty near this time of the year. Then my mother used to dry blueberries, for the winter, for all of us, you know. . . . You can keep them once they're dried up for a long time. Then they use them as they want to. And wild rice, then put that up for the wintertime. They dig the ground and put all the dried blueberries and wild rice in the big hole, and they bury it with dirt, and then whenever they want it in the wintertime, they dig it out and get it out as they want it, and then put it [dirt] back on."[122]

Because the Ojibway lived in territory contested by several tribes, their caches served mainly as hiding places from their enemies. Europeans, surprised that visible storehouses such as those in trees were left unguarded, were generally unaware of an unwritten law preventing Indians from stealing their neighbors' supplies. Still, as Jenks observed, the territory the Ojibway occupied was less than settled, so one took precautions: "It is a part of an Indian's code of morals not to steal from his friends, but it is equally a virtue to steal from an enemy. Inasmuch as tribes ordinarily steal from one another, the fall harvest of wild rice must be kept in a place of safety." Except in dire circumstances, for a person to rob a cache was considered the worst sort of thievery. Thus Pierre Biard in 1616 concluded there was no stealing among the Indians. Intrusions of whites on their caches were demoralizing to the Indians. In about 1821 the boundary waters Ojibway stopped gardening for a period after their food caches were destroyed by Hudson's Bay Company employees and settlers on the Red River.[123]

Someone intent on finding a cache needed only to probe the ground for soft spots: "The thief who wishes to find it, goes about with a sharp stick piercing the earth, until he strikes upon the hidden treasure." Deer, too, could become suspicious of soft places and invade a cache; to prevent their discovery, Indians sometimes felled saplings over the top of a pit. (Deer will not walk on dead limbs for fear of catching their feet.) Whether it was actually wolves, as the Ojibway avowed, or the Indians themselves who happened upon Michel Curot's wild rice cache in October 1803 is not known.[124]

Usually left intact until late winter or spring, a cache might be tapped earlier in emergencies. Tom Battise at Lac Court Oreilles recalled: "One fall a group of us were moving down to the hunting grounds and one boy who was very thin got very sick and they thought he was going to die. They all had to stop and camp and the parents dug up a cache of rice and a cache of maple sugar and brought that and some blankets and tobacco to my grandfather and asked him to try to cure their boy."[125]

In preparing a cache, Indians and fur traders alike removed the top layer of sod (keeping it intact) and, enlarging the hole below the frost line as they dug, carefully dumped the earth and debris in some nearby stream to float away the evidence. The cache was customarily lined with dry grass, hay, or twigs and hides, and its sod opening was replaced and concealed with forest debris to fool potential intruders. Another means of disguise was burning a fire over a cache after sealing it off. If woven cedar bags held the rice, the cache was lined with birch bark as a protection against moisture. At Red Lake in 1933 M. Inez Hilger watched a woman who wished to retrieve some stored potatoes open a cache. Located in a grove of maple trees, the cache—one of three she had filled with garden produce—was laid over with small trees, cornstalks, and dead leaves. The pit was 6 feet deep and 3 feet square, lined with 8 inches of hay on the sides and bottom. About 12 inches of hay lay on top of the potatoes and rutabagas. Another of her caches contained Mason jars with canned blueberries and gooseberries. This eighty-two-year-old gardener insisted that, surrounded by hay, such canned goods would not freeze. She added that she kept her winter provisions indoors: "Whatever I put in the caches stays there until the snow melts. That's the hardest time of all the year. Indians that don't provide for themselves in the fall often starve in the late winter." Among caches Hilger described was one at the end of Lake Pokegama (Wisconsin), containing two hundred pounds of wild rice in sacks. Another was a hay-lined pit at Lac Court Oreilles, 6 feet deep by 4 feet square, filled during the winter of 1934–35 with potatoes, dried corn, and maple sugar in *makakoon*. The provisions were covered with mats and rugs over which a layer of hay, then dirt, was placed to a level of 2 feet. Lawrence Mitchell, while visiting Inger in the late 1930s, was told of an island in the lake where rice had been buried for many years.[126]

Older Ojibway continued to store food underground well into the 1940s. Despite their living in semipermanent houses, people at Nett Lake preferred to cache rice in cedar-bark bags stacked carefully in a pit lined with dried grass. Otherwise, they would store it in gunny sacks in a blockhouse or specially built small wigwam (fig. 39). Most considered the alternative—cardboard cartons of rice—simply too bulky to keep in the house. Thomas J. Shingobe (born 1895) of Mille Lacs remembered: "In my times we usually had plenty of rice. It was nothing to walk into a [storage] tepee and there would be 15 or 20 flour

Fig. 39. Wild rice storage hut of birch bark and saplings, about 1910; the coverings were folded back to show its contents.

sacks full of rice. Stacked up. Finished wild rice. And there'd be still maybe 10 or 15 bags to be finished out there in the yard in big piles. It looked like little haystacks piled up and covered with birchbark."[127]

Increasingly, however, people stored their rice indoors. The Mitchell family at White Earth customarily kept rice in seamless canvas sacks on the second floor of their home, and the Bakers at Lac Court Oreilles piled rice sacks inside where it was cool and dry. (Noted William Baker proudly, "We had as high as ten, twelve sacks all winter long. That was nothing. Now we have two or three pounds.") He insisted that they did *not* use flour sacks because the material was too thin and said his family preferred hundred-pound grain sacks, such as those used for wheat or oats, estimating they processed from four to ten sacks a season. Thus from four hundred to a thousand pounds of rice lasted them through the winter.[128]

In the twentieth century, particularly as wild rice became a cash commodity, gunny sacks, flour sacks, and grain sacks displaced bark pails for hauling and storing grain (fig. 40). Paul Buffalo's description of the breakup of the Ojibway rice camp is fairly typical. To haul the sacks of processed rice that were stacked in the camp wigwam, his family customarily used a team of horses and a wagon for the four-mile trip from the west side of Mud Lake to their home. The wagon, which held about ten sacks, was carefully lined with hay, and the rice sacks were covered with canvas or birch bark to keep dampness from the rice. They made a second trip two days later, since those back at camp were still making a little rice, or "cleaning up." With a total of twenty-three sacks back home, his family began to sell the processed rice after storing enough for their own needs. Most older Ojibway estimated their families each brought home from ten to fifteen fifty-pound sacks of finished rice, sufficient to make it to the next ricing season, with enough left to sell for grocery money.[129]

However wild rice was kept, laying in a winter's supply was, until recently, a habitual concern in fall. Harry Ayer denied rumors that the Mille Lacs Ojibway faced a winter food crisis in 1933 by reporting to the Minnesota State Board of Control that nearly every adult male had killed a deer in the fall and that there had been "an abundance of rabbits" as well: "I understand that the camp was well supplied with food of their own obtaining when they entered the winter. Most of them had gardens supplying them in potatoes, beans, etc., and I know that many of them had a full supply of wild rice." Ayer often helped to ensure that Mille Lacs people had winter rations, such as when a dam built across the Rum River at its Mille Lacs Lake outlet raised havoc with the wild rice harvest: "It is a hardship on the Indians this season for the lake below the outlet is full of rice and hardly enough water to float canoes so it may be obtained. However there are several smaller lakes near here that they can reach

FIG. 40. Loading winnowed rice into commercial sacks for storage, about 1938

with a team [of horses] where they can get their winter's supply of rice and I am helping some of them that do not have teams to get to them with my car."[130]

When the Ojibway moved into the wild rice district, they quickly recognized the value of rice and adopted the technology of its former harvesters. Regional variations in the harvesting have probably always existed, and adaptations and innovations in technology have been continual. Still, from all reports, the basic techniques of knocking, drying, roasting, hulling, and winnowing have remained constant for three centuries. They enabled the Ojibway to feed themselves, except in times of crop failure, and to produce surplus enough to sustain nearly every non-Indian engaged in the fur trade. Furthermore, to last them through the winter, as a hedge against starvation, the Ojibway customarily cached or stored rice. We thus may question Harold Hickerson's claim that wild rice was never more than a seasonal staple because of the limited technology for production and storage.[131]

CHAPTER 5

The Camps

September 1, 1947, Nett Lake, Minnesota

Everyone was up and busy by 6:00 in the morning. After a breakfast of hot soup, warmly dressed people stood in pairs in front of their wigwams and frame houses. Each man carried two paddles and a pole; each woman her ricing sticks and an enamel or birch-bark drinking cup, to scoop a fresh drink from the lake later in the day. All were in a lively mood; groups shouted remarks at each other, amiably joking and teasing in Indian fashion. At about 7:25, old Mayminobidonk, the rice chief, lumbered slowly from his house to the rocks by the shore and, climbing the highest one, removed his cap. Cupping his hands together he shouted his long awaited permission: "He-wa-wa-wa. Giga-baa-bawa'aamin noongom naawakweg azhegiiweg." *(Listen. We will go out today and you return at noon.) As he climbed down from his post, he wandered towards his wife, preparing to join her in ricing. The others readied their boats on shore and waited for a rice committee member to pilot them to the fields they would work that day.*

—Eva Lips[1]

September 1983, Mole Lake, Wisconsin

At Mole Lake's Arrowhead Drive-In, cars and pickup trucks capped with boats, canoes, and sixteen-foot-long cedar poles with ends splayed in a V-shape crowd the parking lot. The cafe is busy. Teenagers battle videotronic space monsters, while lit-

tle children scamper from lap to lap. The older men and women are joking, laughing, and renewing old acquaintances. Some are from Milwaukee, some from Watersmeet, Michigan, eighty miles away. They are all Sokaogon [Ojibway], returning every year during the ricing season.

After finding a seat at a small table near the back, a young woman serves you a cup of strong, fresh, black coffee. "How about the special—venison-rice soup and fry bread?" she suggests. You hungrily agree and are then drawn to the conversation of a few men variously dressed in jeans or work clothes. "Maybe by Thursday Rice Lake will be ready," one says. "Well, I don't know. I was out there fishing last weekend, and a lot of that rice still hasn't filled out. . . . Maybe next week?" "Rice is falling pretty good over near Rhinelander." "Yaa, but that's that small river rice, and that's usually the first to get ripe. Rice Lake is always the last lake to open."

—Robert Gough[2]

IN 1919 a group of people living near Mille Lacs Lake sent a letter of complaint about their Ojibway neighbors to the United States Indian Service in Washington. The letter in turn was forwarded to C. V. Peel, special agent in charge at the White Earth Agency, with jurisdiction over the Mille Lacs band. Peel subsequently wrote to Harry Ayer at Vineland, knowing of his rapport with the Mille Lacs Ojibway and hoping he might use his influence to induce them to change their ways. Among other things, the original letter charged that the Mille Lacs Indians "refuse to cultivate the land on which they live; they refuse to accept employment from the neighboring whites at the regular going wages . . . they refuse to obey the state game and fish laws, taking fish and killing game whenever they feel so inclined and think they can get away with it; they do not establish permanent homes and try to cultivate the land or make substantial improvements thereon, but live in bark or canvas wigwams, tents, and rough board shanties; they scatter out over the country in the hunting season, the sugar making season, the rice season, and for berry picking and live practically in the same primitive state that their forefathers did years ago."[3]

Rather than comply with the request, Ayer did his best to defend the Indians' way of life. In reply he pointed out that many of the signators were not themselves without fault, some having illegally induced the Ojibway to sell them fish out of season, for example, and that some of the charges—refusal to raise crops—were groundless. Still, their letter expressed many of the attitudes of the majority culture in this country even today. A nation whose expansion was encouraged by the Jeffersonian ideal of permanently settled agriculturists tends to find the traditional economic cycle of its first inhabitants beyond comprehension and in direct opposition to more "civilized" ways of living.

The Ojibway pattern of using woodlands resources, developed over centuries, is deeply ingrained and will probably never be completely abandoned for Euro-American life styles, food preferences, and subsistence strategies. Although the mechanics of harvesting have changed, the Ojibway have continued to hunt, fish, trap, pick berries, make maple sugar, and gather wild rice, and the timing of these activities follows the seasons, not necessarily the legal statutes of the dominant society. Many of these pursuits have required the participation of the entire family, so the Ojibway traditionally moved en masse, often in bands, to locate and process food supplies.

The seasonal migrations required by the Ojibway economy proved a constant source of frustration to non-Indians. Particularly irritated were missionaries trying to establish schools for Indian children. No sooner had the Reverend Sherman Hall moved to La Pointe than he realized that his contacts with the Indians would be limited and sporadic. His journal entries, beginning in 1831, reflected a state of perpetual dismay. On November 27 he wrote: "The Indians are now all at their fishing ground, about three miles from us. At present we have but little intercourse with them." On December 27, with the Indians back from fall fishing, he had the opportunity to visit and offer medicine to two sick Ojibway, one with a "lung complaint," the other with "an affliction in the back and legs." Happy to be back at work among his "flock," Hall noted: "They always appear grateful for such acts of kindness and sympathy. Perhaps the Lord will make such opportunities the way for us to gain access to their hearts."[4]

The missionary's relief was short-lived, for by mid-February the Ojibway already had removed "to the other side of the Lake." They had settled about three miles away from La Pointe "in one compact village," probably somewhere near present-day Red Cliff Reservation. Their departure may have been made precisely to escape the Christian ministrations on the island, for on March 6 Hall found them "preparing for one of their heathenish [Grand Medicine] dances." That same day he complained that a sick man he had been trying to convert was "about to be removed from us as from instruction for the present, as the Indians are about to repair to their places of making sugar, and he must accompany them." Once again the traditional economic patterns had interrupted the missionary's efforts to convert his Ojibway charges. On March 11 he wrote: "Nearly all the people who reside here having gone to the sugar camp, we had no religious service in Indian to-day. We shall be deprived of all opportunity of communicating instruction for several weeks." Because families customarily took their children along, Hall was forced to cancel school until their return. His journal entries ended abruptly on this date, not to resume until two months later, when the Indians returned.

Hall was scarcely the first missionary to express frustration. Father Louis Hennepin complained a century earlier of the difficulties in converting the "savages," as they remained in their villages no longer than necessary for harvest, devoting the rest of the year to warfare and hunting. Missionaries continued these complaints into the twentieth century. Benno Watrin, for seventeen years a priest at Ponsford on White Earth Reservation, "was most distressed over how few Indians came to church regularly. Ricing and berry-picking kept them away." Beginning with the treaty era, annuity payments and alcohol simply compounded the missionaries' problems. Complained Cloeter in November 1858: "I am not in condition to say how we can make it possible to go to the Rabbit Lake Indians. They are not at home the whole year around. From gathering rice they go duck-hunting, and from there to the Payment of the yearly allowance and to drinking whiskey, from there to fishing and to the chase, from there into the sugar fields and again to fishing and thus throughout the year. According to their assertion this state will never be changed since the Indians will never suffer themselves to live like whites."[5]

Just as sugar making forced schools to close in the spring, the wild rice harvest disrupted the fall. Wrote Frederick Ayer in August 1839 from Lake Pokegama: "The Women and Children generally remain at home. They are about leaving to make Rice of which there is an abundant crop. Our school will be suspended until after the gathering of rice." The previous year Ayer had expressed hope that the school could remain open through the winter because of excellent prospects for a good harvest of corn and potatoes. The supply of wild rice in fact affected whether the children would even be around, for in the face of inadequate rations, the Ojibway might move their entire families (fig. 1). While the situation looked good at Pokegama, a rice failure the previous year made the outlook for schooling at Fond du Lac poor: "The Indians have been here but a small part of the time since being absent at LePointe & making Rice and elsewhere. . . . It is doubtful whether one Indian child attends school the coming winter as it will be impossible for any Indians to stay here, there being no game in this part *and but little Rice.*"[6]

Missionaries were often obliged to provide food as a means of keeping children in school. Postponing school opening until the rice harvest was complete, one schoolmaster in 1863 was busy purchasing food supplies for the Indian children: "I could not plant a garden last spring owing to my getting here so late, and so had to buy all the potatoes, corn, and rice needed for the support

FIG. 1. A family rice camp at Little Rice Lake near Tower, Minnesota, about 1940. The parents parch rice; their youngest child, in a cradleboard (tikinaagan), *rests against a tepee of birch poles covered with tar paper and blankets.*

of the scholars during the coming winter." Even when food was offered by the schools, Ojibway families were reluctant to leave children behind. Observed Hall: "When they go from place to place the whole family goes together. They are too poor to support their children at school while they are about on their hunts and for other purposes, without help."[7]

Whether or not poverty precluded schooling, the Ojibway needed their children to help procure food supplies. Truancy, a direct result of population movements, emerged as a contributing factor to the creation of Indian boarding schools in the twentieth century. Clearly, Ojibway families were inclined to let nothing stand in the way of traditional harvests. Harry Ayer, who brokered Indian crafts at Mille Lacs, once asked in early October whether Nellie Weaver-Bryan and her mother had anything to sell and was informed that "they have nothing at present to send over but will do so as soon as they can, they have just come back from rice making." After trying to get together an Indian baseball team in late summer to play a white team from Kimball, Minnesota, Ayer wrote its manager that "August is a bad time to keep the Indians together."[8]

Beginning with the establishment of reservations, which limited movement and encouraged the development of permanent villages, seasonal Ojibway migration changed considerably; with permanent houses and, eventually, vehicles that cut the time required to reach natural food sources, Ojibway people became vastly more settled than their ancestors. Nevertheless, the wild rice harvest of today clearly shows the vestiges of traditional practice, for there is still a large migration to gather food. Ojibway not only from the reservations but from Minneapolis, St. Paul, Milwaukee, Chicago, and Winnipeg meet and set up camp or move in with relatives to prepare for the harvest.

This continuity from precontact times to the more recent past can be seen in comparing the accounts of John Tanner, captive of Canadian Ojibway in the early nineteenth century, with those of Maude Kegg, an elder at Mille Lacs in the late twentieth century. Tanner told of his summer activities at Rainy Lake: "I remained in the village until the corn was planted; then we went to collect and dry the blue berries which grow in great quantities in that country. Afterwards to the rice swamps; then we returned to gather our corn. Thus we were busy all during the summer." Another year reflected the same pattern with the addition of some hunting, as ricing took Tanner to Lake of the Woods: "I spent the summer in the usual quiet manner, being occupied with hunting, and the employments about our cornfields, in gathering wild rice and fishing. When we were returning from the rice swamps, I stopped on one of the small islands in the route towards Rainy Lake, to hunt a bear with whose haunt I had long been acquainted."[9]

Maude Kegg's maternal grandmother belonged to the Pine family, and although its seasonal peregrinations were geographically more limited than Tanner's, they were nevertheless parallel. The Pines lived in a permanent house at Portage Lake a few miles northwest of Mille Lacs, where they kept a few farm animals and a garden. Their sugarbush, however, was on Mille Lacs Lake, where they also fished in late winter. After making sugar they returned to Portage Lake to plant their garden. In the summer they went to pick berries along the Mississippi River, returned to their garden, and in August moved to their rice camp at Little Rice Lake. Their mode of transportation involved walking, canoeing, or driving a team and a wagon.[10]

Some ethnohistorians have argued the existence of permanent year-round populations in the larger Ojibway villages long before the reservation period, pointing out that gardens, rice fields, sugarbushes, and fishing lakes were all adjacent to or near village sites. According to Harold Hickerson, the male population simply left these established centers periodically on war-party forays or hunting expeditions, returning to them for trade, counsel, and to replenish provisions: "The maintenance of corn fields partly fenced in one village, and family usufruct over sugar groves in at least three others, indicate some of the ways in which village lands were used by a permanent population. There is no reason to doubt . . . that ricing and fishing grounds in the various places were the common property of the villagers, and exploited heavily at the home villages and nearby sheltered lakes and streams. . . . The existence, then, of sugarbush, rice ponds and inlets, and in some places garden sites, indicates permanence of residence, and an orderliness to village life."[11]

While this theory is at least partly correct for some villages, it certainly does not apply to all. Hickerson ignored the practice of planting gardens, then leaving them, returning periodically to weed them or waiting until they bore fruit. Neither did he consider the pressures on the Ojibway to find other wild rice sources in years of failure. Although Lac du Flambeau would certainly qualify as a major Ojibway population center, Sherman Hall in October 1832 depicted it as a number of small villages. During his visit the entire area was being evacuated, as the Lac du Flambeau Ojibway collected at the post to descend en masse down the Chippewa River for their fall and winter hunting grounds on the lower part of the river. They left Lac du Flambeau virtually deserted until their return in March to make sugar.[12]

Luxuriant wild rice stands and richly stocked fisheries had always drawn congregations of otherwise scattered Ojibway bands. S. J. Dawson, civil engineer for the Red River expedition, filed a report in 1869 estimating the total population of the Canadian Ojibway at three thousand or more, most of it dispersed, with the only concentrations at Rainy River and Lake of the Woods: "They can, however, collect in summer in larger numbers than Indians usually do, from the fact that they have abundance of food. This is afforded by the wild rice of the country which they collect, and by the fish which literally swarm in the lakes and rivers. . . . I have seen as many as five or six hundred of them collected at one time, at the rapids on Rainy River, engaged in catching sturgeon, the flesh of which they preserve by drying it like Pemican and then pounding it up and putting it, with a due mixture of oil, into bags made of sturgeon's skin." Communal Ojibway fishing at rapids such as these harks back to the seventeenth century and earlier, before tribal identity emerged for these Algonquian speakers.[13]

Such periods of harvest activity served as important time markers. American Indians commonly assigned to most of their months, or "moons," names associated with some aspect of their traditional economy, as Jenks defined it, "after that natural product which, by its abundance or usefulness, or by other means, emphasizes itself for the time being above all other products." In the Ojibway language, June, July, and August have been called, respectively, the strawberry, raspberry, and blueberry moons, due to the successive periods of ripening. To be sure, there were regional variations in nomenclature. In some places April was called "snowshoe-breaking month," but in others, especially Minnesota, it was the "month of making maple sugar." Some harvests occurred earlier in the areas north and west of Lake Superior than in Wisconsin, a fact reflected in the names of the months. For example July, rather than August, was the blueberry month in the northern sector. Aboriginal names for some months changed because of contact with Euro-Americans. July, traditionally the raspberry moon, began to be called "moon of the shooting," as the Ojibway increasingly participated in Fourth of July celebrations.[14]

Almost without exception among harvesters, August or September was designated the month of making wild rice—in the Ojibway language *manoominike-giizis*. The persistence of such nomenclature among peoples who have long since given up harvesting wild rice is evidence of their former economic pursuits. Although only a few Winnebago still collected wild rice in the twentieth century, according to Paul Radin members of the Bear clan called September the month when rice was bound and the rice fields were traversed in canoes. Black Hills Dakota about 1895 still designated that month as the moon when one dries rice and October as the moon of dried rice.[15]

As the rice ripened and *manoominike-giizis* arrived, the Ojibway prepared to move to the place of harvest. Just as they set up camp among the maple trees in the spring when the sap began to flow, the Ojibway (and other harvesters) broke up their larger villages and moved in small groups to the edge of the rice beds on the shores of rivers and lakes. Such a move ensured proximity to the crop and the capacity to process rice, to prevent it from spoiling, as soon as it was unloaded from boats. The centuries-old tradition of setting up wild rice camps endowed this migration with a deep social dimension, one that led to communal bonding and a sense of identity. Dan White of Leech Lake expressed it simply: "We went and made a camp. Even when we didn't live very far from rice field. The reason why, I suppose, was the encampment was to be together with the rest of them, so they would be closer together."[16]

Except for communities like Nett Lake, where the village is directly on the lake bearing the crop, the Ojibway usually have traveled some distance to their rice fields. Before they had wagons or cars, they traveled as much as possible by water. George McGeshick's family, for example, riced on Pickerel Lake and on Mole Lake, their home, seven miles north. The rice ripened on Pickerel Lake first; when finished ricing there the McGeshicks moved by water as far north as Rolling Stone Lake, traversing only the last two miles on land.[17]

Canadians often had to cross the border to harvest. Lac la Croix and Seine River Ojibway, for example, riced at Vermilion River and Lake Kabetogama in northern Minnesota. When Indians acquired teams and wagons, they used these to get to the ricing areas. At Bad River in the early 1950s, those too poor to own vehicles loaded the gear into wooden wheelbarrows and pushed them down the gravel roads on the reservation to the principal boat landing. While today almost all Ojibway use cars or pickup trucks to transport themselves, their equipment, and, eventually, sacks of freshly harvested rice to their homes (fig. 2), many still camp by the rice fields. While this may have some practical advantages—Mole Lakers say they do so to get a good night's sleep and save on gas—there is little denial that being "one with nature" and close to the crop is also a determining factor, much as urban white game hunters enjoy an annual respite to "rough it" in the woods with their hunting companions.[18]

In fact, setting up camp is a favorite pastime of Indian people generally. The camaraderie and group identity of having a tent adjacent to the dance ring at a powwow is powerful today, even though participants might easily commute from home on the reservation or stay overnight with relatives. While most

FIG. 2. Bad River Ojibway trying out their ricing canoes at 7:00 A.M. at a landing on the Kakagon River, September 1971; two ricers have not yet met their partners. An outboard motorboat will tow all the craft some forty minutes downstream to the sloughs.

ricers at Bad River commute daily, leaving their boats at the main landing for the night, a few Odanah residents still camp on spots of high land near the Kakagon sloughs for the duration of the harvest. Formerly there was a special campsite on an island in the midst of the rice fields; today Bad River ricers may make arrangements to use the hunting shacks of white sportsmen from nearby Ashland on non-Indian land adjacent to the sloughs.

The decline of rice camps has been relatively recent and can be attributed to several factors beyond improved transportation. The general breakdown of family activities, addiction to television, the fact that knocking rice is now almost exclusively a male activity, and the abandonment of hand-finishing wild rice in favor of immediate sale to commercial processors all contribute. Still, the vast majority of older Ojibway, many with considerable nostalgia, remember participating in wild rice camps as youths. They regret that individual profit motives have eroded a formerly communal activity. Paul Buffalo lamented: "Everybody for himself nowadays, you know. . . . It's too cold and everybody is busy trying to make a dollar for their own pocket for a living, because that winter'll be here in a few days. . . . [Formerly] they worked together, they worked in groups. They moved their camp in here in groups. There was one bunch, one family . . . come on, we'll go to camp over there. Help one another."[19]

Although there is no mass exodus to camps in the ricing areas today, a spirit of excitement still develops as the community becomes aware that rice is ripening. One ricer at Bad River claims that, as harvest approaches, his knocking sticks begin talking to him from within the closet. Others check equipment, load boats and water jugs onto trucks, pack lunches, repair ricing poles, and fashion sticks to replace broken or missing ones. There may be a late-summer community powwow that enhances the generally festive air. In short, even without rice camps early fall is a favorite time of year, when relatives come from the cities or Ojibway from other reservations attend the dances. Still, according to those who remember, nothing today compares with the spirit prevailing when the people harvested from camps.

LAYOUT

Traditionally, a wild rice camp consisted of two to five or more extended families living in temporary wigwams (fig. 3). A lake with several rice camps might have fifteen to twenty families surrounding it. Since there was plenty of work in knocking or processing rice, everyone in a household, including grandparents and an occasional aunt or uncle, took part. Often families camped with other related families or neighbors with whom they shared com-

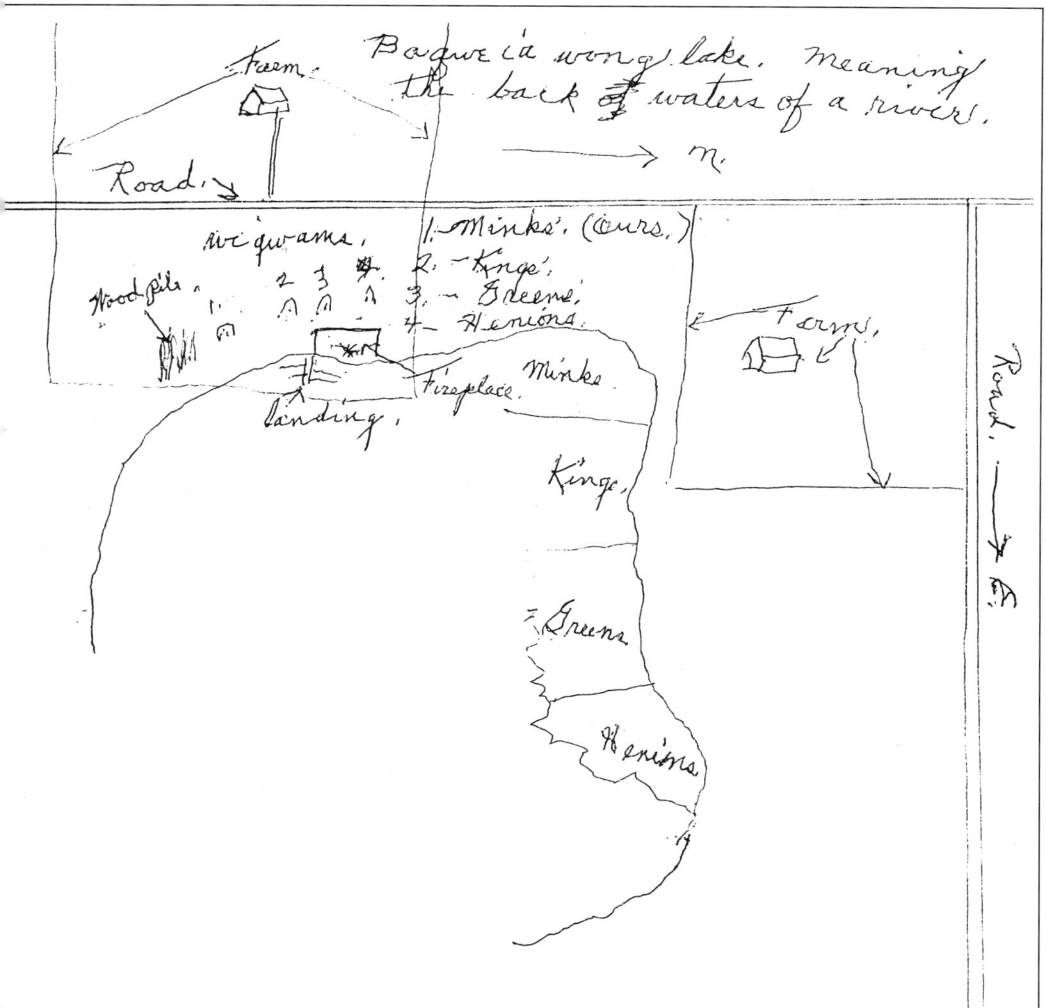

FIG. 3. James Mustache's reconstruction of the rice camp at Lake Pakweiwong, northwest of Seeley, Wisconsin, during his "growing years," about 1910 to 1916. The wigwam substructures were left standing all year; the woodpile was provided by the farmer who owned the property.

munal tasks. Such groups still are referred to by the part of the reservation they occupy or by their familial relationships. At Lac Court Oreilles, for example, there are the Round Lake, Whitefish Bay, and Barbertown groups, the latter so named because of the number of people named Barber; at White Earth in the late 1930s, people spoke of "the Le Duc community, the Island Lake group, the Brunette families." Each family set up its own housekeeping at the campsite; although social life and most of the wild rice processing were communal, such things as cooking were usually done separately.[20]

Each group returned yearly to the same site, as long as the rice held out. A community typically selected its ricing area as close to the permanent village as possible. Maude Kegg, born in August 1904 in her family's wild rice camp wigwam, identified the places where various Mille Lacs Ojibway traditionally riced: her own people from Portage Lake riced at Little Rice Lake near Bay Lake, a few miles northwest of Mille Lacs; the Indians living at Cove on the south shore of the lake riced to the southwest at the dam near Onamia; the Point Indians riced at Onamia Lake. Because Lake Pakweiwong in Wisconsin had such rich beds, it attracted a succession of families from Lac Court Oreilles ten miles to the south, among them the Baker, Strong, Cloud, Frogg, Mink, and Mustache families.[21]

To assure sufficient harvest, many families had alternate campsites near the first. Kegg's family also riced at Boy River and William Baker's family at Lake Totogatic; Josephine Clark's family of White Earth, who customarily camped with the Finedays, riced at Bass Lake where they lived and had a sugarbush and at Rice Lake, too. Those ricing away from their home lake traveled by water before they had horse teams and wagons. They brought back the finished rice by canoe.[22]

Camping gear as well as finished rice had to be transported over water. In the early 1940s on Hula Lake, Minnesota, canoes were tied together and loaded with food, dogs, children, and harvesting equipment in readiness for the rice camp (fig. 4). Of three camps on the lake, two were on the north side and one on the west. In one of these camps, one large wigwam and several smaller tents housed sixteen Ojibway ricers.[23]

Just as binding marked territory in the rice fields, campsites established the territory of families for several generations. Said Lawrence Mitchell: "It was pretty much the same place, Big Rice Lake, what we used to call the south end, *manoominikaaning*. They used to have, like landings. Each landing had a particular name, after a particular person, so ours was *wiinizisimaan* landing . . . something that we went back to every year. . . . Each one had their own particular place, their own way to get there." Such camps were easily recognized outside of ricing season by the skeletal substructures of wigwams. People could select new sites as long as they did not infringe on previously

FIG. 4. Canoes transporting equipment through the rice fields, Lake of the Woods, 1913

established campgrounds. The pattern described by anthropologist Ruth Landes for the boundary area in Canada was fairly common: "Residence loosely determines the frequenting of given spots. People usually did not go outside of their accustomed neighborhood. However, if they ventured further without intruding on others, they had a right to their findings. Some persons . . . know more locations than do others, and visit them."[24]

Not only were occupancy rights of campsites honored, but also sites were distributed to assure access to good ricing for all. In some ways this attitude paralleled the division of the sugarbush. Eliza Morrison described how her group of five or six families crossed with oxen or dog teams the nine miles of ice from La Pointe south to reach the sugarbush on the Kakagon mainland. Once they arrived, "We did not stay together. Every family had a sugarbush of its own, perhaps one half mile apart all over Bad River flats." When asked where his people had their sugar camps, William Morrell replied, "Well, they made it all at Leech Lake, Sugar Point, Hardwood, Otter Tail Point, and there's some down on Diamond Point, South Shore Point. . . . They had camps all around the lake."[25]

Particularly bountiful rice lakes could sustain many family camps. When William Warren visited Prairie Rice Lake in the fall of 1850, its two square miles of water were filled with wild rice; he counted fifty wigwams and estimated five hundred or more Ojibway camped there for the harvest. The separate campsites were spread out around where the rice was the thickest. Another lake accommodating many harvesters was Upper Rice Lake at the north end of White Earth Reservation. Missionary Joseph Gilfillan depicted six hundred to seven hundred people encamped at the turn of the twentieth century: "When the sun rises, hundreds of smokes appear from as many fires made outside their wigwams, where the women are cooking breakfast. Soon the breakfast is spread on the ground, and they recline around it; and a delicious breakfast it is, nice light biscuit, ducks deliciously cooked, with wild rice and tea." Other lakes were less congested. Maude Kegg remembered her family riced once at a lake near the Mississippi River, where there were only three wigwams – "not many Indians there" ricing. George McGeshick related that at Star Lake, Wisconsin, the location of families depended somewhat on the order of arrival. At the north end was room for three campsites; usually the first to arrive set up there because that was where the rice buyer parked. Later arrivals located toward the south end, close together or scattered, according to the condition of the ground, which had to be level. When families camped together, their tents might all face a communal cooking fire though each family had its own fire for parching wild rice. Frank Jackson's family and two or three others camped on one side of Little Flat Lake, at the south end of White Earth Reservation, apparently on or near property of his father's cousin. Counting only about eight boats harvesting wild rice, Jackson noted: "There was about four families that camped across the lake and then us. So we didn't hurt the rice a bit." Later they moved north to Big Rice Lake, a full day's trip. There the general inclination not to intrude on another's turf extended to knocking rice on the lake, even after the practice of binding was discontinued. Dan White explained: "[T]here'd be another bunch maybe ahead of them, so they would go to the next place."[26]

In times of want, particularly if the rice had failed, Ojibway with plentiful rice stands invited less fortunate residents of nearby reservations to take part in the harvest. About 1905, according to Dan Needham, Red Lake hosted outside families through the winter because of its abundant corn supply. In apparent reciprocity, Red Lakers were allowed to rice at Nett and Leech lakes because of the unpredictability of their own crop. Such exchange arrangements were once common; Dan White, who customarily riced at Leech, Long, and Rice lakes, and sometimes at White Earth, expressed little concern that guest ricers occasionally appeared on his people's lakes: "[W]e had plenty where we riced, you know, and we didn't have to go anywhere. We riced here. There was others that come in here and rice with us."[27]

How outsiders are welcomed by a given Ojibway community has varied with the local political structure of the time. The wild rice harvest was traditionally controlled by a designated rice chief, who together with his assistants maintained social order and regulated the number of outsiders permitted to share in the harvest.

SETTING UP

Originally, the Ojibway traveled to the rice fields on foot or, if possible, by water. Principal factors affecting the time of the move were the distance of the rice camp from the home village and whether or not the women would be binding rice before harvest. In any case, it was usually in August. Major Joseph Delafield in a journal entry dated August 9, 1823, reported that "a large band of Indians had lately left the fishery [at Chaudière Falls at the west end of Rainy Lake] for the wild rice grounds." Joseph Nicollet on August 31, 1836, between Lake Itasca and Lake Bemidji, spent half an hour with Ojibway "traveling in eight canoes from Lake Winnipac [Winnibigoshish] on their way to reap wild rice." Almost a century later, Harry Ayer wrote to W. F. Dickens, superintendent at White Earth, urging him to come the next week to find Mille Lacs people at home: "I am afraid many of them will leave for the rice gathering after that. I am sure they would be disappointed if you should not come."[28]

Families at Mille Lacs, such as the Boyds, Wadenas, Skinaways, and Shinodins, made their move on ponies they got from the Dakota in trade for Ojibway beaded pouches. Once at the campsite the horses were simply let out to pasture. Lawrence Mitchell pointed out that "you had to watch the horses, they used to like to eat that wild rice, you know, so there'd be a racket if the horses came through the village; they pretty much ran loose." With teams and wagons, the Indians usually could reach the rice camp in a day, but on some larger reservations the trip might take longer. Maggie Hanks Brown (born 1888) of White Earth said the journey to Rice Lake took two days, with an overnight camp near Naytahwaush, and Red Lakers took two days to reach Battle Lake, twelve miles south of Solway. Mitchell described the primitive condition in the 1920s of wagon roads leading to his family's camp: "Some places where a whole stretch supposed to be the road would be all maybe logs and brush, just to get across that bog or whatever it was, so it was a struggle to get out there."[29]

Because they would need space for the sacks of finished rice, the Indians loaded only essentials into the wagon for the trip out. They brought little food except perhaps maple sugar for seasoning and some flour and lard to make fry bread. Wild rice from the first day of harvest furnished the bulk of meals; wildfowl that the men hunted in the mornings, fish caught overnight in nets the women set, and venison, if the hunters were lucky, supplemented the wild rice. In addition to taking ricing equipment—parching kettles, knockers, and poles—a family might bring birch-bark rolls for wigwam roofing. A canoe might be put on the wagon, suspended by stakes extending from the bolster, about three feet from the bottom of the wagon box. With so many people in a group, some had to walk at least part of the way. The Mitchell family wagon was remembered fondly "with the dogs running along; the wagon would stop and we'd have lunch along the way, and take turns riding. Whoever was tired would ride, and sometimes even if a dog got tired, he'd ride, too."[30]

Ricing, more than any other activity, involved the *whole* family. According to the traditional division of labor, women were responsible for chopping wood, making sugar, gardening, cutting rushes, and weaving mats; men and women together made fishnets; but everyone in the family had a rice harvesting assignment. Shawahn Copenace of the Sabaskong Reserve in Ontario, for example, made camp each year at Ah ze ga koos ka (where many trees grow) with her husband, Kiwenze (the old man), seven grown children, and all her grandchildren. There was plenty of work for older and handicapped people as well. Women impaired by blindness were adept at knocking rice and would go out on the lake with their husband or partner who poled the boat; for example, at Nett Lake in 1947 Steve Benner and his wife returned to shore with a full load of rice much earlier than the others, and at Odanah today Irene Scott is reputed the most skillful knocker on the reservation. Blind men could jig the parched rice (fig. 5). Anyone left at home might be called to come to the campsite. Maggie Brown remembered a harvest unexpectedly so plentiful that they had to send for her cousin Eva.[31]

Upon arrival at the site, the Indians first prepared their lodges for occupancy. Well into the twentieth century the Ojibway almost always used wigwams in the rice camps (fig. 6). Even if they used tents during berry picking, they preferred the wigwam in both sugarbush and rice camp. In fact, the rice campsite was one of the last holdouts for this structure, recently used alongside tents or for storage. At Lac Court Oreilles as recently as the 1940s, when everyone lived in log or frame houses, an occasional wigwam could be found in the rice camps. When Sister M. Inez Hilger visited White Earth in the summer of 1938, she discovered on the shores of Rice Lake the frames of three wigwams used as storage depots for harvest equipment; two of them were filled with bark rolls and ricing gear, the third with a supply of firewood and washtubs, presumably for parching rice.[32]

The oldest type of wigwam was covered with elm bark for walls, then with birch-bark strips sewn into rolls for roofing; sometime later the Ojibway used blankets and canvas. The substructure was of saplings lashed with *wiigob;* although semipermanent, the wigwam could almost always use some repair work each year. In some communities the men (rice chiefs) inspecting the crop for ripeness would fix damaged wigwams before the ricers arrived. When

FIG. 5. White Earth man treading rice about 1925; dark glasses suggest that he is blind.

FIG. 6. Parching rice while more dries on birch bark, Nett Lake, about 1946; note use of both bark and metal vessels. Wigwams could be covered in rainy weather to allow parchers to continue making rice.

James Mustache was a boy about 1910, at Lake Pakweiwong, "The old fellows would go out first and they'd judge by the moon, and they'd judge by the birds too, you know, and they'd go out there and stay overnight and repair the skeletons on their wigwams. See, they'd move out there with some old poles, you know, and repair the skeletons of the wigwams and see how the rice is, probably about another week yet before they would [start ricing]." More commonly, though, wigwam repair was a woman's responsibility. Maude Kegg remembered: "She only has to tie up the frame and fasten it all around" before covering it with cattail mats and bark roofing. Frank Jackson told how members of his family set up a rice camp at Little Flat Lake; if a new structure was needed, they bent and tied ironwood saplings imbedded in the ground, put a small stove inside the wigwam, then covered it with birch bark and canvas. The same structure served a long time, perhaps requiring only the replacement of some poles every few years.[33]

Dispatching rice chiefs to inspect the crop before the arrival of campers was common. At Leech Lake, if the rice was ripe, messengers were sent back to inform the people: "The leaders moved first . . . and we all here got ready for it. We all moved. This first camp has messengers . . . getting ready to prepare to take care of the rice. They got racks they put up. They got camps. Working hard, getting ready. They get wood. During the building the camp ground, there's a man out there, one or two, always two from this camp, they send them out. Make one trip in all. Check it."[34]

Further inspections were made as the ricers moved onto the campsite. The women covering a wigwam might find a birch-bark roll needing repair or lengthening, in which case they sewed additional strips of bark on its end. Kettles had to be washed out and scratched clean, damaged paddles repaired, old ones shined with a stone, lost ones replaced, knockers carved, boat leaks caulked, and *makakoon* patched with pine pitch; the *bootaagan* had to be dug and lined, and the firewood cut into blocks by women, then split by men, and carried to a pile by children (fig. 7a, 7b). These activities consumed most of the first day. With the exception of the rice chief's inspection, no one attempted ricing until the following morning.

In the days of binding, some camps set up as much as several weeks before the harvest. If families moved out at that time, the women used the interval between binding and harvesting to weave cedar-bark storage bags or make birch-bark pails, while the men hunted and fished. Where the rice beds were near the village base, however, women simply bound rice in the fields by day and returned home without setting up camp.

Those inspecting the wild rice were always anxiously questioned, not only about its condition but also about the prospects for other food sources. Paul Buffalo had his eye on the total crop when he was a rice committee member: "We went up river, and up river we went all over Goose Lake. The birds and the ducks. Well, we might as well say that we were looking at the crop of the rice fields. We were looking at the crop of the ducks. Boy, there was plenty. Then we could bring the news back, 'The crop is wonderful . . . rice, everything is filled up. Ducks, young crop, bunches and bunches' and . . . 'How 'bout the meadows?' 'Deer!' In the evening we went there, one place there, and we seen two or three standing around an opening to blow the mosquitos out. Boy, they looked good. I think we are going to have a wonderful crop. Well, that's good news, see? And in the fall we expect something when it's harvesting time. Then we take rice, we take meat, whatever we can get there to eat. Boy, it's just like a warehouse to the local!" Close attention to the behavior of animals and birds enabled the rice chief and his assistants to make accurate

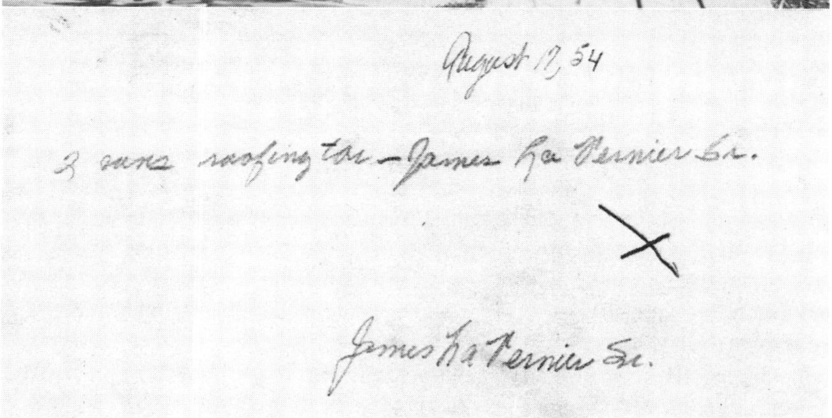

August 12, 54

3 cans roofing tar – James La Fernier Sr.

X

James La Fernier Sr.

FIG. 7a. Repairing a canoe with pine pitch, probably at a rice camp landing, Lake of the Woods, 1913

FIG. 7b. An order authorizing the Chippewa Post store at Odanah (Bad River Reservation) to charge to James La Fernier, Sr.'s, account supplies for patching leaks in wooden ricing boats. La Fernier had been an interpreter in Washington, D.C., for the Bad River band. Although bilingual, he was unable to write; Earl Nyholm prepared the order, and La Fernier signed with an X.

predictions. The comings and goings of wildfowl told much about the condition of the rice, and muskrats starting to build large nests indicated a cold winter.[35]

In earlier times, the Indians dared not go out on the lake before the rice chief formally granted permission. James Mustache told how the signal from the chief was eagerly awaited by the families encamped at Lake Pakweiwong: "One old fellow would take care of it, see. Every morning after the dew was out, he'd go out and he'd come back, 'Not ready.' Probably two or three mornings he'd go out there like that, and maybe there's one morning he'd be out there and the rice is ready, ready. He'd be out in the middle of the lake and he'd holler, 'a-HAUU!' Well, everybody's ready, everybody'd get in their canoes."[36]

Before the general harvest began in earnest, the people sent out one boat, usually carrying an elder, to collect the first rice of the season for religious purposes. When the elder returned with these first fruits, the community was eager to process and eat the food and get on with the harvest. Maude Kegg told what happened when rice from the first canoe arrived on shore: "Quickly they spread it out to dry. After noon, what they have there is dry and they parch it right away. They want to have *ozhaawashko-manoomin* (green rice) to eat. Sometimes they have a feast when they first get the rice. Then they are in a hurry. After my namesake (my uncle) finishes tramping the rice, his wife winnows it."[37]

Although Leech Lakers were also impatient to get out on the water, they took time beforehand to give thanks: "The first load of wild rice you come in, you so happy that you got all that. You hurry up and make it up. You expect to make good on the rice field. Nothing shall happen, no accident, no fires, no sickness. Great Spirit, harvesting time is here. You are ready for us to harvest this wild rice. You are ready to put aside the wild rice. Then every year that comes, and we see that he has given us a great gift."[38]

Once the harvest was underway, the camp members rose with the sun and ate before embarking on the water to begin knocking (fig. 8). Older children were left behind to care for those younger, though in the evening they might have a chance to go out on the lake. In some places there were one or two special camp watchers who cared for the small children. Also serving as camp cooks, the watchers prepared the fires, circling them with loose stones to keep them from blowing out. They readied food for the harvesters, who returned at noon when the rice chief signalled a halt: "When the harvesters come back there was warm supper ready. When they come back they pulled the canoes up. They are tired and hungry. Then take off their rice clothes again. So they each wash their hands, wash up, when they eat their supper, good warm supper." Everyone in camp, including children, hurried to shore with sacks and

Fig. 8. Meal in a rice camp at Long Lake, Wisconsin, 1941. Ojibway people traditionally used the ground, covered with a cloth, for a table; they do so today for special feasts.

pails to unload the boats, putting the rice that was not to be processed immediately into tubs and covering it with water.[39]

Whenever possible, the campsite was near a beach or some other accessible landing for convenience in handling the rice. Docks, however crudely constructed, facilitated unloading (fig. 9a). The topography of some lakes, however, made this impossible: "[W]here we camped, you know, we had to go to a swamp a long ways down to the lake. And we used to have to pack it out of there after my mother came in, and packed it up done" (fig. 9b).[40]

Sand was spread out over grassy areas to provide a good surface for drying. Once rice began to arrive from the lake, the Indians spent any spare time spreading it to dry or parching it. Dan White remembered that older teenagers helped with the rice processing, but he was excluded as too young. Still, he was able to pole ricing canoes for old women, in return for a share of their finished rice. He particularly enjoyed ricing with his grandmother.[41]

Finishing the rice was also a full-time activity. Maude Kegg said, "When we were living at *Gabekanaansing* [Portage Lake], all the old lady does is parch rice, and maybe a few of the knockers do too. We are always cleaning

FIG. 9a. Ricers preparing to unload their harvest at a log dock on Mille Lacs Lake, about 1920

FIG. 9b. Couple sacking up green rice at Nett Lake, 1947

FIG. 10a. Taking aim at wildfowl from a birch-bark canoe in the rice fields, Lake of the Woods, 1913

FIG. 10b. George Catlin's sketch of Dakota people harvesting rice near St. Anthony Falls.

rice. Sometimes it's after midnight when the elders go to sleep." As a small boy Frank Jackson often had to jig down rice until 10:00 P.M., and it was anything but a pleasant chore: "Itchy, though. Oh, it drives you crazy!"[42]

Non-Indians frequently commented on the preponderance of work done by women in camp. Frances Densmore, driving through wild rice country one afternoon, arrived at a camp consisting of three or four birch-bark tepees, sometimes used in place of wigwams. Typically, the men were at leisure while the women were busy: "The rice gatherers had returned from the fields, and the men were sitting on rush mats and smoking while the younger women stirred two parching kettles and an older woman tossed a winnowing tray. At a fire one woman was preparing the evening meal and at a distance another was seen chopping wood. Dogs and little children were running about." Densmore's is probably a reasonably accurate picture, but it should be pointed out that the men's work of laying in a supply of game meat was just as important as procuring and processing rice. While women knocked rice, men were busy catching wildfowl (fig. 10a, 10b), or men gathering rice might also hunt, as did Frank Jackson's father: "My dad, you know, he'd take a gun along and he would go pulling rice and shoot them ducks that'd get up in front of him."[43]

In fact, the wild rice harvest has served as the context for many Ojibway hunting stories. Once, when John Mink was ricing at Long Lake, some of the men decided to go out "fire hunting" (shining) for deer, taking along a small boy for luck; since the boy had received a dream before his vision quest, he was believed to have special hunting powers. As he successfully directed them to two deer, the hunters decided to give a feast for him: "They went back to camp the next day and cooked the deer and people brought maple sugar and wild rice and they ate and some of the hunters got up and told what this child had done."[44]

The older the source, the more stress on ricing as a woman's activity, especially since other months of the year were dedicated exclusively to hunting – the realm of men. As wild rice became increasingly central to the economy, more men began to take an active role (fig. 11). By the twentieth century nearly everyone was involved in some aspect of the harvest.[45]

HARVEST CONTROLS

Nearly every North American tribe had some mechanism for maintaining order during communal hunts and harvests. In some cases police were appointed to enforce rules. The Skidi Pawnee in Nebraska, for example, elected a head policeman to take charge of the attack on a buffalo herd. As part of the insignia designating his position, he carried a special wooden whip to beat any

Fig. 11. Processing wild rice in Ira Isham's yard, Nett Lake, September 1971, an example of the increased involvement of men in making rice; the only woman stands idle. The enormous parching caldron can accommodate much more rice than the earlier iron kettles or zinc washtubs.

restless hunter who tried to anticipate the assault. Pueblo peoples traditionally divided policing responsibility between summer and winter moieties (tribal subdivisions). At San Juan Pueblo, New Mexico, the head of the winter moiety society ruled the village during autumn and winter; hunting and trading expeditions—male activities—could not begin until he took over. Agricultural activities, mostly the work of women, were restricted to the period when the head of the summer moiety, who regulated summer religious events as well, was in charge.[46]

Tribes who harvested wild rice used similar controls. Directing the Menominee rice harvest, for instance, was among the responsibilities of the war chiefs, who were the main speakers at public ceremonies and were entrusted with tribal war medicines. Since tribal law was the principal focus of Lips's study, her Nett Lake data are particularly useful in detailing the structures for policing the traditional Ojibway harvest. The relative isolation of Nett Lake and proximity of the village to the rice fields no doubt accounted for that system's survival as late as 1947, when it no longer operated in most Ojibway communities.[47]

The governing principle of the wild rice harvest, said Lips, is that "what serves the rice is law; what harms the rice is illegal." The whole legal system of the rice camps was based on protecting the crop; its authority derived principally from public opinion. The entire band initially selected a rice chief and committee; through them the group expressed its common concerns, which ranged from contributions to the rice fund, observance of proper thanksgiving rituals, and attention to taboos, to meting out punishment, such as confiscating the boats of trespassers. Traditionalists consider this system of harvest control part of "the old [correct] way" of doing things.[48]

A review of the Ojibway concept of *chief* helps to clarify what this much-abused term meant in traditional society. Although in other aspects of ethnography Schoolcraft is sometimes in error, his definition of chiefs among the Ojibway and related peoples is accurate: "In the Algonquin tribes the chiefs are the mere exponents of public opinion . . . they express themselves with boldness, and frequently go in advance of, or concentrate the public voice, in a manner to elicit approbation." Typically, the Ojibway chief was one who provided good counsel, possessed powers of oratory, and exhibited courage, not only in warfare but also in matters of polity.[49]

Hereditary chieftainship per se operated to some extent among the Ojibway; if a chief was effective, public expectation was that the office would fall to his male successor. But should the chief's son lack qualifications for leadership, the people turned to another.[50]

The chief traditionally had one or more assistants acting in various capacities—as war chiefs, runners (messengers), spokesmen, or arbiters of justice. One such assistant was the chief's administrator (*oshkaabewis*), who among other things distributed gifts solicited from traders and merchants at the performance of the Begging Dance. Although by the reservation period their political powers had eroded, the positions of chief, speaker, and messenger survived at least nominally into the middle of the twentieth century. In the late nineteenth century, the emergence of Ojibway drum societies—with roles and functions derived to some degree from positions in the Grass Dance societies of Plains tribes—reinforced these latent official positions.[51]

Among Algonquian speakers, as was the case throughout much of native North America, chiefs, above all else, were the men most experienced in providing for their people. They were recognized and counted on particularly for hunting knowledge and skills. The so-called Ojibway headmen or principal men of a band were likewise the leaders of communal hunting expeditions, especially for deer.[52]

According to Lips, in 1898 the Bois Fort Ojibway, including the Nett Lake band, were dispersed in sixteen groups ranging from about twenty to seventy people, each under an individual chief. At the time, the Nett Lake chief was

John Johnson (Mah-jeesh-kong), son of Chief Four Fingers (Nee-on-in-gee-o-a-see), a local hero. In the nineteenth century, however, communal game hunts diminished in size and frequency, due in part to decreasing mobility and the geographic restrictions placed on the Ojibway by reservation boundaries. The last great hunting chief at Nett Lake was Tomahawk (Wa-baw-ga-may-gau), at the height of his power in the mid-nineteenth century. In Lips's view, the importance of wild rice as a food increased with the decline of hunting. This change in the economy was reflected in the rise to chieftainship of rice experts, such as the Tower band's Clothed in Feathers (Pe-dway-way-gwan).[53]

Unquestionably, political power operated differently in various Ojibway bands. Still, the Nett Lake political organization of 1947 probably resembled earlier systems and thus illustrated the role of the rice chief in a much older Ojibway society. The conservative nature of the community was extolled by one of Lips's informants, Frank Day, originally from Fond du Lac Reservation, who moved to Nett Lake so he could live as in the time "without bacon or salt."[54]

At Nett Lake the tribal chief (in the old sense of leader of the hunt or battle) held office for life, as did the medicine man; the rice chief, however, had to be reconfirmed each year. Because the rice chief was chosen from among experienced elders, and because he was viewed as the best ricer, as evidenced by his family's capacity to harvest large amounts of wild rice and finish it properly, he was rarely replaced. (Nett Lakers in 1947 could not remember this ever happening.) Next in importance to the band chief was the speaker, someone eloquent as well as bilingual, who could express, on behalf of the chief, his people's desires, particularly in dealing with whites. As the ink dried on treaties, this hereditary position became virtually obsolete. The last meaningful speaker at Nett Lake was Moses Day, the spokesman for John Johnson. Highly respected, Day was elevated to the rank of chief upon Johnson's death in 1923. Despite the Indian Reorganization Act of 1934, intended to render all Indian chiefs powerless, such men continued to act as the embodiment of the general will.

When Moses Day died, his son, Charlie, was made chief; although not elected, he was accepted since he possessed wisdom, experience, impartiality, and was a leading member of the medicine lodge. By 1947 he also functioned as rice chief. Born in about 1880, Charlie Day spoke no English but worked through an interpreter. Although in white law Day held no political power, he functioned in every way like a traditional chief.

Of abiding importance to Ojibway chiefs was the common good, a concern shared by the rice chief, who acted to obtain adequate food supplies for the community. In his capacity as experienced "hunter," knowledgeable in all aspects of the plant's habits, the rice chief knew how best to protect and divide the harvest fairly and to punish offenders of the public good.

To what extent would a chief intervene *pro bono publico* in the daily affairs of his people? In cases of minor theft, such as when someone stole a canoe, the chief expected the victim to get it back, good-naturedly or by force. If unable to accomplish its return, the victim was judged by the community as weak and therefore undeserving of outside help. A different mechanism operated when the common good of the band was threatened or violated. Many regulations sought to prevent ricing offenses of this kind: harvesting in restricted areas, secretly, or before rice was ripe. If the offender was found incorrigible, the chief warned him or banned him from the community. Should he return from exile, it was the chief's duty to kill him.[55]

Because chiefs were often medicine men and because annual religious ceremonials were connected with the crop, there has been confusion about the legal role of medicine men in regard to the harvest. Albert Reagan at Nett Lake described harvest preparations in late August, about 1915: "The Indians then have a secret ceremony and much powwowing. Then the chief medicine men give permission for them to go out and gather rice." Reagan's general impression is probably correct, but the permission to harvest came from the rice chief, not the medicine man.[56]

Beyond blessing the first rice the medicine man's responsibilities during harvest were minimal. With spiritual power and recourse to "secrets," the medicine man was as much feared as revered; because of this power, however, an Ojibway facing the greatest need—particularly when suspecting some supernatural force as affecting the course of things—went not to the chief but to the medicine man. Lips cited the "quiet power" of persuasion of John Nett Lake, head priest of the *midewiwin* and principal religious figure at Nett Lake in 1947. When Ed Tanner found half his rice stolen, he went to John Nett Lake instead of Charlie Day. Working quietly, John Nett Lake determined the culprit and, without saying a word, got him to return the full amount of rice, replacing what he had already used by borrowing from others. The thief reacted out of fear, knowing the medicine man had the power to inflict sickness such as "crooked mouth" through a stroke, or to kill him through sorcery. In contrast, the rice chief functioned more openly, his jurisdiction was voiced publicly, and his powers were clearly limited.[57]

Although they may not use the term *rice chief,* nearly all older Ojibway remember someone in their community responsible for the rice, making periodic inspection for ripeness and granting permission to begin harvesting. A typically casual depiction of such a man was given by Frank Jackson of White Earth: "There used to be an old man used to live there at Little Flat [Lake]. He used to go around looking at the rice, and when it [became ripe], then he'd come in, well, he said, 'You can go right out there.' " Or an Ojibway might recall "that old fellow that took care of the rice, that went out and checked it—the word would get around that maybe one or two days nobody would rice, and they respected that." According to William Baker, several people were responsible for the rice stands in the Lac Court Oreilles area, where they were called "guardsmen"; their principal function was to prevent people from harvesting early, and they had an intimate knowledge of the sequence in which stands ripened: "They used to have a man, he used to be on horseback or a team of ponies, he'd go look at the rice, all over these lakes, and watch it, and sample it. Alright, and he knows that this one [stand] is going to be ripe, because they got rice now in over to Clam Lake." Baker named as guardsmen George Weber at Ghost Lake near Hertel, Wisconsin, some forty miles west of Lac Court Oreilles, and Pete Cloud on the reservation. Respected elders, guardsmen usually were prominent in other community affairs. Pete Cloud, for instance, belonged to two drum societies.[58]

Ruth Landes viewed the function of rice chiefs along the Canadian border about 1930 as averting open competition between bands. In setting harvesting hours and controlling the number of participants, the chiefs were rarely challenged despite their lack of legal power: "The [rice] leader has no executive authority, and anyone can flout him, but no one does. A flouter finds it more fruitful to migrate to another rice bed."[59]

Lips saw the rice chief as equivalent to and commanding the same respect as the peace chief of former times—the man elected to head the band in periods of relative calm, during cessation of warfare, principally with the Dakota. With a rice committee or council, the chief assumed full responsibility for every aspect of the harvest, including accepting blame for such errors in judgment as false estimates of harvest yields or improper instructions to ricers.

When Charlie Day assumed his father's position at Nett Lake, he was recognized not only as the outstanding man in all Indian affairs but also as the leading authority on wild rice. Lips compared Day's general functions as a tribal chief in the traditional sense with his specific duties at the time of year he served as rice chief. To keep the reservation running smoothly, he acted as arbiter in all disputes, gave advice on marriage and child rearing, assumed authority in minor legal matters such as petty theft, smuggling liquor onto the reservation, and altercations between his people and visitors. Punishment ranged from reprimands to fines of money or rice, or, in extreme incidents, expulsion from the reservation. As chief of the Nett Lake band, Charlie Day ensured the orderly course of community life—as Lips put it, the "guaranty of peace from within and without."[60]

Day's duties as rice chief were more specific. He oversaw the selection of ricing committee members each May, when he sent out runners inviting all adults to the community dance hall. The committee, elected anew each year, consisted of from six to eight men and their alternates. (Women were eligible, but no one at Nett Lake could remember one having been on the committee.) The assistants made up a rice council that informed the chief, advising him of the condition of the rice beds and instructing harvesters on which fields were open; the council was empowered to put certain fields off limits without prior notice if there was damage to plants or they had not ripened according to expectation. With the rice chief, the council informed state authorities of the date for the start of the harvest. During harvest they policed the rice fields, principally to see that people did not knock rice beyond the time limits. As punishment for offenses against the crop they fined harvesters a portion of their rice; they could impound a repeat offender's canoe and prohibit that person from further involvement in the harvest.

Such punishments were meted out impartially for the common good and were imposed regardless of the offender. In 1946 a close relation of John Nett Lake secretly harvested before the official opening. As a result, his canoe and rice were confiscated and he was excluded from ricing for three weeks. (At Mille Lacs Lake, boats of such offenders were tipped over, dumping occupants, rice, and all into the water; some canoes were even destroyed.)

At regular intervals throughout the harvest, the rice chief and his committee assembled the community for public announcements. At these meetings they imparted information about open and closed rice beds, the sequence of collection, weather conditions affecting harvest, and the like. The rice chief at Hula Lake was an old man who lived the rest of the year on an island in Burntside Lake; the numbers ricing at Hula Lake apparently were small enough for him to operate without a committee: "When the weather was windy or rainy the chief would not let his people go for rice because canoes might tip over, and also because the rice will not fall off when the stalks are wet. . . . The chief also prevents undue waste in harvesting by dividing the lake into four parts. For a few days the Indians harvest in one section, then for a few days in another, until each part is covered in an orderly manner." Another reason for requiring ricers to stay ashore during periods of rain and wind was possible damage to the crop, according to Josephine Clark: "When it rains they don't rice. When it's windy, they don't go out. They were told when to go, how to do it, you know. I know that's the way I was trained too."[61]

Such controls were necessary because of the irregular ripening of wild rice beds. On the opening day at Nett Lake in 1947, committee member Robert Strong announced that, although the full sequence of fields could not yet be determined, five were already ripe. Accordingly, the harvesters divided into five groups, each piloted by a committee member to a ricing area.[62]

Putting unripe beds off limits was crucial at the beginning of the harvest;

gradually, all the rice ripened and the entire lake was considered open, with no further need to designate areas. Due to annual fluctuations in yield, however, the rice chief might put large sections of the fields off limits in a given year. This occurred in 1946 at Nett Lake. When the number of rice beds increased in 1947, Charlie Day restricted only two thin stands—one in the bay behind Fisher's Island and one in Swampy Bay. That year Nett Lakers began to harvest five stands near Mallard Bay and Poplar Creek at 8:00 A.M. The second day committee pilots led ricers to the same places and to new ones. As on the first day, ricers returned at noon, but since the crop was ripening quickly, they were permitted back on the lake in the afternoon as well, with a strictly enforced curfew of 6:00 P.M. Permission to begin was usually signalled by a shout—by Day, from a perch on some rocks, or the rice chief at Lake Pakweiwong, Wisconsin, from his boat in the middle of the lake. At Nett Lake the signal to return at noon was, likewise, Day's shout. All craft immediately headed for shore.

Another important function of the rice chief was to determine how many boats to allow on the lake and, after considering his own people's needs, how many guest ricers. Once he announced that the harvest would begin on September 1, 1947, Charlie Day made known his impression that some people had too many canoes. To assure a fair distribution of the crop, he asked that the boats be registered in advance; every man or woman wishing to harvest had to appear before the committee and report the names of each ricer and partner, as well as the number of canoes for each family. Every able-bodied pair had the right to register, provided conditions permitted and any younger partner was at least fifteen years old. A family with many small children might be allowed only one boat. Lips, who witnessed the registration, observed that it was not without controversy and that Day settled many disputes. One woman trying to register two canoes was unwilling to provide the names of the crew for the second boat; consequently, she was refused permission. In preliminary discussions, the rice chief and committee helped find partners for widows or elders living alone or partners whose spouses were sick. Once paired off, the couples agreed to split their daily harvest.[63]

After the number of local boats was tallied, the question of guest ricers was addressed. In 1947, following the Nett Lake registration, committee member Jimmy Drift announced that, provisionally, the only guests allowed would be six canoes from Vermilion Lake's Black Bay, because their rice beds had been put off limits by the state that year. Nett Lake is regarded as the common property of all the Bois Fort Ojibway, even those scattered north through Koochiching County and into Canada. Bois Fort Ojibway, including Vermilion Lakers, are thus looked on as neighbors, and the groups help each other in times of need. Canadian Ojibway often riced at Nett Lake; in 1947, however, they were at first excluded, though later in the harvest three of their canoes were permitted. Eva and Julius Lips were granted special permission to rice because they would donate all their harvest to the rice fund. Charlie Day assigned them a canoe and gave them "the freedom of the lake."

If a bountiful harvest was expected, a large number of guest ricers might be invited. It was customary for each outside group to delegate its own rice chief responsible for maintaining discipline among his people. These chiefs were subordinate in power to the local rice chief but worked together with him for the general good. Guest harvesters were subject to regulations applying to the host community. By and large, guests still are well behaved and welcomed. Most of them are close relations, and ricing time offers an occasion for social intercourse and the exchange of news about marriages, deaths, and births. Formerly, guests were invited, not as individuals, but as community representatives. The Nett Lake rice chief, for instance, gave permission to, say, twelve canoes from International Falls and eight from Pelican Lake. These bands then selected individuals to harvest rice. Apparently Nett Lake had a reputation on other Ojibway reservations as self-protective and fairly strict with outsiders. Fred Jones said he was usually free to rice everywhere *but* at Nett Lake: "And Nett Lake, this is a set up, they set up their own [system]. They allow some other Indians to come in there through their councilling . . . that time I was down there they had a rule that they went by, and that Indian that riced there had to finish this rice right there, which was a good deal. They wanted to see him come out of there with finished rice."[64]

One reason guest ricers were required to process their rice before leaving Nett Lake was that they had to donate a portion of it to the rice fund, in a sense paying a rice tax. This rice fund was a sort of community chest, and each boat was required to donate a predetermined amount of its daily harvest, guest ricers providing twice that amount. The rice chief safeguarded the fund and distributed portions of it to the needy, just as a Pueblo town chief kept large jars of seed corn buried in front of his fireplace from which to dispense to the poor. Proceeds from any sale of rice from the fund were used in ways that would benefit the general community.[65]

A rice chief's duties began in late spring with the breakup of ice on the lakes. He watched the crop at every stage, determining where the plants would come up and which areas would be harvested first. As large chunks of frozen mud containing rice seed rose to the surface, the rice chief watched wind and water currents carefully to see where the seeds would sink. If high water levels threatened to carry them off and prevent germination, he entered into negotiations with other Ojibway bands to apply for guest ricing privileges. Throughout the growing period, the rice chief made periodic inspections of the crop—about a month before the harvest and at least every two days during it. Because this effort deprived him of time when he, too, could be harvesting, the rice chief at Nett Lake, for example, was allotted a special canoe and two harvesters of his choice for compensation.[66]

Watching the weather, the rice chief hoped for a warm spring and a temperate summer free of heat waves that could dry out the upper part of the plant stems and leave them vulnerable to wind damage. About ten days before the 1947 harvest, an extreme hot spell followed by a severe thunderstorm and an unusually cold day at Nett Lake caused general alarm that the crop might be hurt. Charlie Day reassured his people that they had needed the rain to cool off the lake.[67]

Rice chiefs everywhere observed all signs of nature to predict the rate of maturation. One sign that rice was ready was the changing color of leaves on young birch trees growing on ridges; another was the ripening of chokecherries in the woods. Throughout this period, speculation mounted about how many boats and how many guest ricers would be allowed to harvest.[68]

Most sources other than Lips pay little attention to the rice chief's repeated inspections of the crop and the strict adherence to his dictates. Lips assumed that regulations still followed in the isolated traditional community represented by Nett Lake formerly had been even more vigorously enforced both there and elsewhere. Anthropologist Alanson Skinner enumerated much the same responsibilities for Menominee police as those of the Ojibway rice chief and his committee—inspecting rice for ripeness, guarding beds against trespassers, announcing opening of the rice fields, permitting people to begin harvesting only after the proper ceremonies, and prohibiting mourners and menstruating women from the harvest. Because the Menominee were rice harvesters before the Ojibway moved into the district, this evidence suggests that the Ojibway may have adopted the Menominee system.[69]

Ojibway rice committee members could deputize others if necessary. Paul Buffalo provided good information on rice councils and their functions from personal experience. He was appointed at Leech Lake in 1940 and 1941 to a six- or seven-man rice council; despite his parents' vast knowledge about wild rice, he was surprised to be chosen and attributed his selection partly to being bilingual, to his lack of timidity in confronting wrongdoers, and to a capacity to admit his own mistakes. When asked how old one should be to serve on a rice committee, Buffalo said that eighteen was too young, as youths were prone to be "disturbed by strangers, by temptations"; twenty-one- to twenty-six-year-olds were acceptable ("they get solid in mind"); but thirty-year-olds were even better. Still: "[Y]ou gotta have couple old help, experienced directors, then your experience with wild rice . . . you gotta balance. See, that's what we talked about. That's going to help. You know the law, bylaws, rules and regulations. You read up. Then experience come in, then that helps you, see."[70]

Buffalo explained the committee interrogation process: "They have a council. The council of the local areas of the rice field discuss, and know the guy's very capable, very active, and they got a treaty there, I guess. [The candidate] understands the rice, the nature of the rice . . . 'Have you been working the rice?' The background. 'Could you take interest in the wild rice to reserve our rice fields? You'll accept?' He's appointed. So each reservation, each council appoints their men." Committee members could also appoint assistants. "On that rice committee, when I was appointed, you have the right to deputize anybody; you appoint, and the people that's interested in wild rice will gladly work with you. That's the way it worked. 'How many do you want in this area with you?' 'I want a couple of good men. They got to be a little older than I am.' "

In policing the harvest, committee members were often sent onto the lake to stop abuses reported by other ricers or observed from shore. In such a capacity, said Buffalo, he considered himself one of the rice chief's scouts, always on the lookout for transgression and ready to paddle out to apprehend the violator. He described one incident when he was sent out to confront people harvesting on a restricted lake. Pulling alongside the boat, Buffalo had the following exchange:

" 'I'm sent out here to visit you people by my group of Indians that's on the board of committee directors, so I want to ask you a question. Did you know that this lake is closed?'

" 'I thought the rice was ripe.'

" 'No, they're not harvesting this lake.'

" 'Well, I don't care if they want, I'm here to get rice.'

" 'Very well, how about the other ones, why should they sit back and wait for the waters [when] you guys are out here ricing?' Well, because they like to play . . . games. The rice is ripe, this is right. Then he showed me the rice. They laughed at him.

" 'Yeh,' he says, 'I think you have control there unless it's the message is sent out all over. And when they all go, we'll all go.' That's the way we had it at that date.

" 'So it's closed today, 'cause if you want to continue ricing, I'm afraid we're gonna have trouble because they are watching me right now talking to you. They got eyes all around the lake, they're looking. They see me out here, so I'm message to you both, that they didn't open, the committee, the groups, the chiefs. It's not ready. So I ask you, will you cooperate with the Indians?' Just make it up. Get right out of the field, you can see that farewell, but if they sneak out again, they catch them out there again, then one or two boats goes out there and tip them right over. 'Are you going to get out, or are you going to keep ricing?'

"He says, 'Help us out and we'll go.' That's all there is to it, they tip them. Nothing funny. If you want to fight back, he's fighting all the way to shore. If you're fighting back, the others will come. That's the way they used to have it. Those committees, different ones, groups of each will defend their rice, for their children. So it was hard not to obey rules and regulations. You are in trouble when you want to take over."

Since the work of the ricing committee was respected for the most part, such altercations were infrequent. But enforcers were only human, and they were occasionally the target of complaints about actions ranging from nepotism to outright bribery. The practice of electing members anew each year may in part have served to rid committees of undesirables, but it was also a way to cope with the constant changes that the Ojibway faced. Ernestine Friedl saw the uncertainties of the weather, food supply, and game distribution reflected in the election of new rice council members each year: "The wild rice gathering was also frequently managed by different groups each season. The expectation that consequences of any action were likely to be short-lived and that each new situation had to be thought through again was not unrealistic under such conditions, and was perhaps a kind of adaptation to them."[71]

Sometimes the general public on reservations has been critical of decisions about harvest timing. In 1947 at Nett Lake, some ricers who experienced difficulty knocking rice thought the lake had been opened three days too early; using force to dislodge the seed could only hurt the plants, they said. At Bad River, decisions about where and when residents can rice are made by a committee whose structure somewhat replicates the traditional one. It consists of two elders knowledgeable about rice and two members of the tribal council, backed by the tribal game wardens. In 1986 the committee decided to open the Kakagon sloughs on August 17, in conjunction with the annual powwow celebrating the wild rice harvest. Unfortunately, cold, wet weather set in almost immediately and lasted five days. Some criticized the decision as premature, pointing out that after a week they still could harvest only along the Bad River. Ron Parisien, in one of the thirty to fifty boats ricing, told the author it took him four days to collect only 170 pounds of green rice. That year at Lac du Flambeau, only fifty miles southeast of Bad River, the harvest was delayed until after Labor Day.[72]

Some Ojibway have also been critical of decisions about guest ricers. In the late 1960s Fred Jones from Mille Lacs said of Rice Lake: "They got a committee, a ricing committee down there, laid [these rules] out, consists of Indians right down there locally. . . . So they had these rules to go by, they got so that if you wanted rice you registered, and if they like you all right, you got in. If they didn't like you, you didn't get in."[73]

Most such complaints come from outsiders who have been rebuffed on some reservation, though not everyone has had the same experience with a given rice committee. Jones was given guest ricing privileges once at Nett Lake even though he really had no need to rice there. Others were not always so welcome at Nett Lake. About 1944 Dan Raincloud, a noted medicine man from Ponemah on Red Lake Reservation, was brusquely stopped from ricing after two days: "We are supposed to own some of the [Nett Lake] rice bed out there, but I don't know how it went, that we don't own it anymore. . . . But after I heard them say that we're going to keep away from their food, so we just have to keep away from that place. . . . Somebody say, 'You Red Lakers, you better go back and eat up your rice all by yourself.' I didn't like that." Since Raincloud was well respected throughout northern Minnesota, his rebuff suggests that the rice committee miscalculated the size of the harvest and was forced to reduce the number of guest ricers part way through their activities or that a Red Lake resident committed some offense.[74]

Other complaints concerned favoring guest ricers over locals and the occasional acceptance of money by committee members. Jones was hurt to see Leech Lakers allowed to rice at Rice Lake while some East Lakers, who normally riced there, were excluded: "And I think now the East Lakers, they don't want anybody else to rice there. I noticed last year they had some guys from Ball Club [Leech Lake], Indians, ricing there. They deprive their own Indians of the reservation for their rice, but they pick them off another reservation to go in there." He cited two instances in which those in control of the Rice Lake harvest stretched the regulations to accommodate whites. One committee member gave permission to rice to his two white sons-in-law ("'Well, right there they were violating their own rules, you see"). The other instance involved collecting a tax of one hundred dollars per boat from some whites wishing to pay for ricing privileges the following year: " '[W]e needed the money right now,' he says. 'I accepted.' 'George,' I says, 'do you know what you are doing? That's the beginning of the end of ricing for the Indians on that lake.' "[75]

The breakdown in authority of rice chiefs and committees has been comparatively recent and gradual, as economic pressures have driven Indian people to gain what they can for themselves, ignoring the older practice of conserving for the common good. Even a guardsman on the Lac Court Oreilles River, noted James Mustache, cannot be expected to keep a round-the-clock vigil. As a consequence: "that is thinning out too, 'cause we've heard of people going in there at *night,* Indian people, the grabby kind, we've got some of those greedy ones, you know. Yeh, those are the ones who deplete the rice beds."[76]

These sorts of violations, especially by non-Indians, ultimately invited state intervention and the passage of laws controlling all aspects of the harvest. This usurpation of the old system coincided with the decline of the rice camps. In the days when Ojibway were encamped adjacent to their wild rice beds, there was closer scrutiny of potential offenders and a greater conservation of the natural resource, as the decisions of the rice chiefs were backed by public opinion.

SOCIAL LIFE

Because the Ojibway associate wild rice harvesting with some aspects of traditional culture that are disappearing, its mention usually elicits pleasant memories of camp days. Despite the hard work, the harvest was a period of social gatherings, joking and horseplay, storytelling, romance, exchange of news, dancing, and games. Said Frank Jackson, "Yeah, we had a good time when we riced." James Mustache remembered: "They did many things, you know, until just about bedtime. Women exchanged ways of doing things, same way with the men, they'd talk about different things. A lot of things like that they do while waiting for the rice." Camp activities also afforded children an opportunity to learn processing techniques (fig. 12a, 12b). When Hattie Miller of Lac Court Oreilles was small, for instance, her mother took her ricing and made her a tiny winnowing tray.[77]

Teasing and jesting, particularly with close relations, is a favorite Ojibway pastime, and the rice camps provided ample opportunity for indulgence. There are, however, hard-and-fast conventions about whom one may or may not tease; consequently, the Ojibway usually took advantage of condoned opportunities to needle their victims with words—all in good fun, of course. For example, there is no joking relationship with a father-in-law or uncle-in-law, but with a brother-in-law anything goes, and he is not supposed to show anger at the remarks. Paul Buffalo gave a hypothetical example: "Sometimes you'd be paddling along a rice field somewhere and you wonder whose boat that is. Well, then, he's got your sister. Your sister thinks he's all right and is trying to please him. You pull up alongside of him. 'How is he? Do you feed him? [Isn't] he heavy for the amount of work he does? Is he worth what he eats, or how is he on the job? Is he lazy?' You could say that to him. 'I don't think my sister there learned you how to pound rice. And for the winter you're sure that he'll give you enough rice? In the winter, you're sure that later on maybe you don't have to work?; sit down? you'll be so fat and lazy.' "[78]

Clumsiness of any sort during the day's activities is usually subject to ridicule at camp, where ricers relax and the events of the day are recounted. Writers Kathi Avery and Thomas Pawlick cited one exchange from the

FIG. 12a, 12b. Children were exposed to ricing technology at an early age; often they were assigned their own tasks, such as hauling wood for parching or, in the case of young boys, treading the rice.

Sabaskong Ojibway in Canada: "We almost made it to shore, when he decided to stand up. . . . Neee! You looked so funny hanging onto the pole when the canoe kept on going. How does it feel to swim in that loon shit, anyway?"[79]

One focal point of amusement in camp was the *bootaagan,* or stamping pit. Charles Eastman recalled that prizes were offered young men who could hull the quickest and the best, and that in a large rice camp as many as fifty at a time might be dancing rice. This activity also offered the opportunity for a girl to indicate her affection for a boy, by bringing him beaded moccasins and asking him to hull rice for her. Songs were performed to accompany the huller, providing him a cadence for jigging the rice. Apparently, when rice was pounded by several people, a certain amount of communal horseplay took place (fig. 13). It might begin innocently enough: "So the younger class, they got nothing else to do in the evening. Oh boy, and then they'd come, they'll pick up a stick, help the old man. If it's five minutes he'd pound a few, but pretty soon there's a whole bunch of young people, old people, and there they stand talking, visiting, discussing, celebrate and everything, you know. Good will, all of them, then they stir that rice. It was fun. Big, big tubs, big barrels out of the ground. So they knock the hulls out partly, knock the beard loose. They didn't break it, stirred that rice. I'd like to see a picture of that, how we grind them."[80]

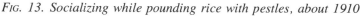

FIG. 13. Socializing while pounding rice with pestles, about 1910

Sometimes, though, if a game were made of it, the ricers might get carried away. Paul Buffalo related: "And when the fun was, when the young people used to get together . . . and I suppose some of them had their girlfriends, and that's where they would have a little fun. They'd dance around there and do all kinds of things in there. Like sometimes they'd put a stick right in the center there and then they'd start pounding it, whichever was the weak side, why I think that stick moved towards them then. They'd start laughing at each other, that they were weaker than the other side, and they had sides. But these people, sometimes they had to watch these young people, because if they don't watch the rice, why he'd get nothing but powder!"[81]

There was other entertainment: lacrosse games for boys or canoe regattas in which both boys and girls could compete. There was plenty of opportunity for courtship as well. Prosper Guibord (born 1874) met his wife-to-be in a rice camp. Working as a lumberer and hay cutter, he once went to see his mother at Rice Lake (Wisconsin) only to find she had gone ricing near Birch Lake: "I hired a rig and got a 4-gallon keg of beer and went up to visit her. They told me at Birch Lake that she had gone up to Lake Chetac to rice, so I went up and found her and met Anna Smith, a Chippewa fullblood, who was in the ricing camp and got acquainted with her." Guibord was kicked out of camp after giving someone a drink of beer (alcohol was illegal for Indians at the time), but he kept up his relationship with Anna.[82]

During courtship, girls in the rice camps developed secret trysting signals to attract boys they were interested in: "These maidens learned to imitate the calls of the different water-fowls as a sort of signal to the members of a group. Even the old women and the boys adopted signals, so that while the population of the village [rice camp] was lost to sight in a thick field of wild rice, a meeting could be arranged without calling any one by his or her own name."[83]

There were other sounds from ricing boats, too. John Mink at Lac Court Oreilles remembered hearing girls play flutes in the rice fields. They could always tell who was playing because each used a different tune for warming up. If their boats were not heard moving through the rice, they might have tired of knocking and taken up their needlework. Men sang powwow songs softly to themselves while poling, and at Bad River in the early 1950s, group singing was the norm as the rice boats headed home, hooked together with rope and towed behind a launch (fig. 14). Almost simultaneously several ricers began to pound on the edge of the ricing boats with their knockers as though they were drumsticks, while the boats acted as resonators, accompanying their song. Said Earl Nyholm: "The songs served purposes, gave the singers an opportunity to sing songs maybe connected with ricing somehow, or traveling on water, and at the same time the buyers waiting down at the landing could

Fig. 14. Harvesters and canoes of rice being towed from the Kakagon sloughs to the landing at Bad River Reservation, 1971

hear us coming for a long ways, could get their scales ready, be all set for us, knew when ricers were coming by hearing the songs."[84]

There was plenty of evening diversion. If their families had retired for the night, younger people could always go visiting at other camps. Many camps would sponsor a woman's dance, or "squaw dance" at night—a traditional circle dance for couples that required reciprocal gifts, no matter how small. While some camps held such dances fairly regularly during harvest, Frank Smart of Odanah on Bad River Reservation said the squaw dances were part of his camp's concluding events. The dances usually began after dark when all work was done, so, according to Frank Jackson, at Bush Landing on Big Rice Lake they used lanterns for illumination. William Baker was sorry to see this aspect of his culture disappear: "The evening, after they get through scorching, big powwow. You don't see that now. They powwow right in the tavern."[85]

Dan White recalled that when he was fifteen (about 1915), if they did *not* have a dance, they gambled, playing the moccasin game—the Ojibway game of chance. This involved one team hiding marked bullets under moccasins and the opposing team guessing where they were hidden, to the accompaniment of special songs. The rice camps offered an opportunity to learn new songs of all genres, for in the course of social gatherings guest ricers invariably performed from their own repertory. As they said at Nett Lake: "If you want to hear new songs, you have to wait for the harvest. When our guests are coming, they bring us new songs for nothing." Lawrence Mitchell told of the sound of drums from various camps on Big Rice Lake at night: "This fellow that lived with my grandmother used to be able to identify those drums. 'Well, that drum is from Ponsford area,' and you'd hear another one way up there somewhere, and it comes from maybe Wisconsin – Hayward, or then you'd have the Mille Lacs drum." The drums were played by singers providing music for informal dancing in the rice camps. (Most dancing in the rice camps took place outdoors as at today's powwows. Where the home village served as the base camp – Nett Lake, for instance – ricers held dances in the community hall, or round house, a traditional structure adopted from Plains tribes in the late nineteenth century and used by the drum societies.)[86]

The frequency of such festivities throughout harvest led some white observers to blame the Ojibway for underproduction. Jenks's correspondent from Pelican Lake, Wisconsin, reported that each family customarily harvested only twelve to fifteen bushels of wild rice and that they would have been able to get much more were it not for all the feasting and dancing. Even some of the more conservative Ojibway were not completely receptive to such conviviality. Paul Buffalo expressed some chagrin at all the talking and laughing on the lake in about 1968, implying that in earlier times the Ojibway took things more seriously. He was also intolerant of noise in the camp: "The Indians, everything wanted a rest. When it was resting time. It's got to be quiet. So anything, any disturbment, you know, we had the authority [as rice committee members] to go on a rice field or at the camps, keep it clean. . . . If you want to celebrate, if you have a special party you want to put on, back in town where you get, not here. We're harvesting here, so let's have it in order."[87]

Ricing might take the Ojibway well into late fall, when all the trees lost their leaves and the first frost appeared. Some people lingered to harvest from late beds, the last to mature. Meanwhile, they sacked the rice, loaded it onto wagons, settled accounts, paid those helping with the harvest, or divided up communally processed rice. In the old days the Indians might bury some of the rice for safekeeping over the winter; then they struck camp, rolling up the wigwam coverings and dismantling the *bootaagan.* Any deliberate sowing of future rice beds was done at this time. The families then returned to their homes to gather produce from their gardens and prepare to move to hunting grounds at the first snow.[88]

Anything resembling the wild rice camp of the past is rare today. Some reasons for its decline have already been mentioned. As wild rice increasingly became a quick source of cash, more people took to the lakes to harvest what they could in a short time, and stiff competition emerged. Most older Ojibway attribute the lack of rice camps today to this haste to earn profits: "Long time ago Indians used to go and camp, maybe ten families they would go to one lake and camp. They would camp there as long as the rice would last. And it used [to last] a month, because they know how to take care of the rice. They know how to go, when to go, and when you should leave it alone. And now we rice, just as soon as the lakes are open [legally] everybody is ricing. . . . They want to get in there and make all the money they can make. I could just say they are greedy now. Long time ago people wasn't like that. They took their time ricing. They got just as much when they took their time."[89]

Such new competition has been especially difficult for older ricers, used to a more leisurely pace. Said George McGeshick: "It's hard on the elders because they could only go out for a little while; they can't stand that boat ride all day like the young people. I know, when I go out, my feet get tired pushing, and [my wife's] shoulders get tired knocking it in." Some also feel that, as greed partly replaced traditional Indian sharing, trust within the community broke down, precluding the communal spirit once prevailing in the rice camps. For instance, in the days "before there were padlocks," said Fred Jones: "Some guys maybe have two boats ricing time, you know; and one guy didn't have no boat, well he'd go down there, he'd walk over there and tell them, 'Well, if you ain't got no boat, you can have that boat of mine.' "[90]

Some changes in Ojibway culture have discouraged the family move to a rice camp. When automobiles replaced teams and wagons, commuting to the rice lake on a daily basis became possible, precluding the need to drag cooking gear and small children to the lakeside (fig. 15). Despite these changes for practical reasons, the spirit of the harvest persists. On many reservations, people still rise with the sun, breakfast, gather in front of their houses to chat, load equipment on their cars, assign their small children to babysitters, then depart in a caravan to drive to the rice lake—not much different from the daily events of earlier ricing. Rather than attending community meetings to learn what ricing areas have been put off limits by the rice chief, harvesters exchange news informally as to the location of good or poor ricing spots. Instead of attending an evening dance near shore, ricers with cash in their hands might celebrate in local taverns but still are up early the next morning to rice again.[91]

A generally happy time, rice harvesting not surprisingly induces feelings of nostalgia. In 1855 Kagagengs, a L'Anse (Michigan) Ojibway, related to Johann Kohl the long story of a vision he had following his mother's death. When the German traveler asked whether he had dreamt of his mother since then, Kagagengs replied: "Yes . . . every autumn, at the time of the rice crop, I dream of her, that I am going on the path of the dead, and see her and speak with her."[92]

Above all, people identify wild rice as a symbol of what it means to be Ojibway. Ernie Landgren of Nett Lake said, "There's a feeling you get out there

FIG. 15. Nett Lake ricers, 1971, preparing to drive the day's harvest to a local processor for sale or home to finish in their yards

that's hard to get other places. You're close to Mother Nature, seeing things grow and harvesting the results of the water and sun and winds. . . . We sort of touch our roots when we're among the rice plants."[93]

Even without the rice camps, the late August harvest has remained a time of special social interaction. This spirit is evident, for example, in Earl Nyholm's recollections of ricing at Bad River during his youth in the early 1950s. As the Nyholms, Ojibway from L'Anse, had strong familial ties with Odanah people, Earl traveled west by bus during ricing season to stay with his mother's great-aunt, Julia Sibayash Bennet, in her old frame house on Kakagon Road. He and other visiting relatives were up by 5:00 A.M. each day. There was no electricity, and two buckets of water—one for drinking, the other for washing up—had to be filled from a well near the Bad River and hauled to the kitchen. Over breakfast—oatmeal with a little grease on it and black coffee—people picked their ricing partners for the day. By 7:00 A.M. all the ricers gathered at the landing, waiting for a tow to the rice fields, a trip of about forty-five minutes. Nyholm remembered Jim La Fernier of Red Cliff Reservation running a kind of charter service with an old eighteen-foot launch that reminded

FIG. 16. Joe Pete and his wife parching rice at Lac Vieux Desert, Wisconsin, 1941; the use of a rectangular metal trough and broom is unusual.

him of the *African Queen.* The inboard towed up to eight boats at a time, returning to retrieve them in the early afternoon.[94]

Although the Bad River people were settled in permanent frame houses, said Nyholm, Kakagon Road resembled a rice camp at that time of year. There was always a pile of green rice drying on a sheet or canvas in every yard, and alongside each house some older woman parched the rice (fig. 16). Nyholm remembered that in the evenings older people collected in his great-aunt's house, conversing only in the Ojibway language. Several women in their eighties wore long black dresses, black caps or bandannas, and white aprons, and sat in rocking chairs playing cribbage and chewing snuff, using baking powder cans as spittoons. On the cool August evenings, the old wood stove blazed, with wild rice cooking on its top. ("It really was a smell you don't get ahold of anymore.") Concluded Nyholm, "It seemed that the old people really enjoyed that time of the year. . . . They would really go about the whole process like it was sacred; they really put themselves into it."

Although the traditional camps have mostly disappeared, the Ojibway recognize ricing as a link with their past. Some Indians, especially urban dwellers who have spent little time on their home reservations, have taken up ricing late in life as a means of reestablishing their roots. One man ricing at Leech Lake in about 1965 took his small sons out on the lake just to show them how it was done. They spent all day harvesting only twenty pounds, all of which they kept. Where signs of a cultural renaissance are evident among the Ojibway today, the urge to return to the rice camp may be among them.[95]

CHAPTER 6

The Economics

A HISTORICAL REVIEW of wild rice in the American economy reveals four basic periods that paralleled changes in the Indians' relationship to Euro-American society. When the Ojibway first moved into the wild rice district in the late seventeenth century, they adopted rice into their subsistence economy as an important new food source. During this early period, contact with Europeans was sporadic, and the Ojibway harvested almost exclusively for their own needs. As the fur trade increased, Indians were gradually induced to produce surplus amounts of wild rice for use in barter. A period of sustained surplus harvesting lasted until the fur trade began to decline after the merger of the Hudson's Bay and North West companies in 1821, shortly after which the reservation era began. With little market for wild rice and restrictions on access to former rice stands, the Ojibway entered occupations such as lumberjacking, and wild rice reverted more closely to a subsistence role. Although the product brought a modest amount of income in a new cash economy, the Ojibway never regained the market control they had during the fur trade.

This third period lasted roughly until whites began to perceive a new demand for wild rice by non-Indians. Spurred by rapid developments in mechanization and scientific research, they entered the market—first as brokers but ultimately as farmers, cultivating wild rice like any other crop. During the last three decades, like tobacco, soybeans, corn, and other "Indian gifts," wild rice has become almost exclusively a non-Indian product, with minimal involvement of the Ojibway or financial rewards for them. This development has rendered the traditional ricing technology nearly obsolete. In this most recent period, wild rice—once the staple of Indian diets—entered modern American agronomy.

Despite the lack of written records, we can assume that precontact wild rice gatherers traded surplus rice with contiguous peoples who moved from the district. After the Sauk were driven from the lands east of the Mississippi and north of the Iowa River in the mid-eighteenth century, for example, they traded for wild rice with the Menominee and Winnebago tribes. As the

French, British, and Americans successively arrived, Indians simply accepted them as new trading partners. The precontact pattern continued, albeit involving larger quantities, as Indians intensified the surplus production of wild rice to fill the subsistence needs of Europeans and thereby acquire trade goods.[1]

THE FUR TRADE

The difficulty of importing the foodstuffs of "civilization" induced Europeans on the frontier to use as much as possible the local natural food supply. Trade goods and supplies could not always be shipped within one season; sometimes they had to be relayed through a series of transportation depots. Settlements along larger waterways such as the Great Lakes were resupplied on a fairly regular basis with canoe shipments from the east; trading posts inland, however, were in a more precarious situation. Sherman Hall, at Lac du Flambeau in 1831, learned of the arduous task of packing in supplies by means of a twenty-four-day portage with 122 stopping places: "Not a pound of flour, or salt, or butter, or lard, or pork or scarcely any other articles of living consumed at the post, except vegetables, a little corn, wild rice and fish, and a small quantity of wild meat, but must be carried across this portage on men's backs."[2]

Wild rice was quickly recognized as a valuable food for sustaining a trading post, so Europeans tended to establish settlements near the plant's natural stands. Wild rice from the Red Cedar and Chippewa rivers was probably part of the diet of those at Fort Pepin, the fur post established by Nicolas Perrot on Lake Pepin in 1686. La Jémeraye built Fort St. Pierre in 1731 at the outlet of Rainy Lake, near a major fishery and rice beds. John Long in 1778 acknowledged the importance of food resources – beyond promising trading prospects – in establishing a post at Lake Schabeechevan (Weed Lake): "On this lake there are about one hundred and fifty good hunters, who make a great many packs of beaver, &c. and this was one inducement for settling here, which was increased by the prospect of a plentiful supply of fish, rice, and cranberries, which are winter comforts of too great consequence to be slighted."[3]

Stephen Long in July 1823 was informed by guides of the remains of former North West Company posts near wild rice fields – two of them on the "Wild-rice river" and one at its mouth. The river "has its rise in a Lake about eighteen miles in diameter, and from the abundance of wild rice growing in it, it is denominated Wild rice [Upper Rice] Lake. The supply of this article of food yielded by the lake is said to be inexhaustible." So vital was this foodstuff that one resident of Fort Frances in 1837 was prompted to proclaim: "[O]ur sole dependence and principal food for the winter: Wild Rice may be truly called the staff of Life, of this post."[4]

For Barter

Before the onslaught of winter, the immediate task of residents of a new post was to begin laying in wild rice. In about 1807 fur trader George H. Monk stressed his reliance on the product: "The [North West] Company have introduced, horses, cats, and hens into this quarter. Hunter's meat is scarce in this country, every possible effort is made in the fall to lay in the necessary stock of provisions for the winter; consequently a quantity of wild rice is purchased from the natives." Traders expectantly awaited the late summer harvest. At Lac la Pluie (Rainy Lake) in 1804, Hugh Faries recorded in his diary on August 26 that the Indians had not yet made any rice; entries beginning on September 8, however, show the continual arrival of canoes laden with freshly processed wild rice. Seasoned traders knew the importance the staple would assume in winter, and they advised appropriately frugal consumption of it. In 1848 Henry Rice wrote George Bonga at Leech Lake: "Your rice you must purchase with ammunition & if the indians will not pay rice for it, let them go without. You must be sparing of it until winter for if you are not the first thing you will know you will be out." So precious was this provision that on September 24 Faries recorded that the clerk Archibald McLellan had "kicked . . . out of the Fort" the Indian Picotté and his wife for selling their portion to the rival XY Company.[5]

Because of their potential populations, some trading posts had to be designed to accommodate considerable provisions as well as trade goods. When Zebulon Pike visited the North West Company post at Leech Lake in 1805, the west end of its main building was occupied by the director of the Fond du Lac Department; in its center was a trading shop, and the east end contained a large store with an ice house beneath it. The most vital architectural feature of the building was its storage area: "The loft extends over the whole building, and contains bales of goods, packs of peltries; also, chests with 500 bushels of wild rice." Traders who had not the buildings to store rice indoors followed the Indian practice of hiding it in the ground. John Sayer's journal shows that on September 27, 1804, he "buried under Ground 3 bags Oats & 60^{lb} flour in case of Necessity the Ensueing Spring." Such supplies were needed by spring, for on April 6 he "at 6 PM sent 2 Men to fetch 3 bags of Oats & [½] Bag of Flour that was hid under Ground last fall in Serpentine [Snake] River."[6]

When laying in rice supplies, post commanders had to keep accurate head counts to estimate winter needs. By October 8, 1833, William Johnston's men were busy purchasing provisions and had already in store 110 sacks of corn and rice—an amount Johnston judged sufficient for the moment, although he could not ascertain the final requirements until more canoes of men and their families arrived. Another trader, Jean Perrault, and his eight men reached the entrance of the Red Cedar River on August 15, 1794. Once the fort was built,

Indians from the Pillager band of Lac de la Sangsue (Leech Lake) began to arrive; from them the trader obtained eighteen sacks of corn and one hundred fawnskins of rice.[7]

Competition among traders sometimes prevented them from purchasing such abundant supplies. Post commanders were advised to hoard provisions because the Indians might change their trading patterns, going elsewhere to sell their rice. Michel Curot of XY Company complained in his journal on February 10, 1804, that he had but one fawnskin of rice left for the winter. His North West Company rival, John Sayer, "did his best To hinder The savages from giving me provisions, and that he could see what provisions I had left to give them." About November 1, 1795, trader Alexander Henry (the younger), Michel Cadotte and his son ("le grand Michel Cadotte, le petit Michel Cadotte"), and a Mr. L'etang arrived at the post of their rival at Pokegama. Short on provisions, L'etang visited the post commander, Perrault, to borrow some. According to Perrault, their initial bargain was short-lived: "I told him that my orders forbade it, but If he wished to make an agreement with me not to send out to The lodges of the Savages in trade that I would get for him some wild rice, at the rate of one plus the fawnskin, and to avoid all uneasiness as much on their part as mine, we included in our Compromise that the first to Break the agreement would be bound to pay the other 100 Otters in good condition. He accepted my proposal, and I let him have 30 fawnskins of wild rice. Everything went according to Contract, until New year's day when I was informed by old la merde au Cul that the other messieurs Had left in the night with 4 men, all well loaded, for Lac de La tortue."[8]

There were other strategies. In times of shortage, a trader might sell surplus rice back to the Indians. The 1861–62 account books of merchants and traders François and Eustache Roussain, for example, showed sales on January 20, 1861, to "Wai-ba-ga-ma-gan, 20# 2.00"; January 18, 1862, "Me-ka-de-wi-gown Rice 1.00"; and January 23, 1862, "Enjmoedang Rice 2.00." By subsisting on a diet of wild rice, Europeans at posts could conserve the seed of imported grains. Having burned land to clear it for gardens at Lake of the Woods, for example, La Vérendrye expressed relief that the abundance of rice permitted his men to plant the seed corn they had brought, thus saving the expense of sending all the way to Fort Michilimackinac (Michigan) for more. Similarly, wild rice supplies at Fort St. Charles allowed La Vérendrye to spare the wheat seed he had saved for planting.[9]

Traders and missionaries who lacked adequate rice supplies sometimes pooled resources or resorted to borrowing or buying from other posts. Thus in 1794 the post commander at Red Cedar River gave twenty-five fawnskins of rice – one quarter of his supply – to fellow trader Michel Cadotte, who was passing through in September, en route to winter quarters at Red Lake. In

April 1838 trader William A. Aitken at Swan River wrote to missionary William Boutwell: "[B]e So Good as to give [us] 18 Bushels [of potatoes] and Six Hoes and 4 Bushels Rice or 5 if the Leech Lake people have brought down the Rice."[10]

Traders repeatedly recorded that, despite their precautions, they, like the Ojibway, sometimes ran short of provisions. On February 10, 1804, Curot wrote that he had reluctantly given Le Jeune Razeur (Young Knife) two pints of rice, "not being able to spare him any more since there is but one fawn-skin left. . . . I told them that I had no desire to Starve them, that they [the Indians] could come back if they chose, But they would stand a pretty good chance of Starving here." After a rice failure in 1824, John Cameron remarked on his luck in buying corn on Plantation Island: "This piece of good fortune has taken a severe thorn out of my side, as I was really at a loss how to make out for the winter." Likewise, facing a bleak winter in 1837, William Aitken wrote to Charles W. Borup, agent of the American Fur Company, about the situation at Sandy Lake: "I can not give you a favourable account of this part of the country. So far it is entirely innundated by water. . . . All the rice we have been able to collect amounts only to 34 Bushels throughout the Department, and we do not get one single fish – So much for the appearance of passing a good winter – on account of the great deficiency in our Cotton, and the very bad quality of our Blankets."[11]

Even with goods to trade, Euro-Americans in the interior suffered from rice failures, for the Indians often had little else to barter. Perrault at Fond du Lac reported that a Mr. Harris, when asked what he had done with his inventory for purchasing provisions, "replied that he had seen very few Indians; that the greater part of them had gone to pass the winter [1783 or 1784] in the prairies west of the Mississippi; that they had no wild rice, the abundant rains having destroyed it."[12]

In short, both traders and Indians utilized nearly identical sources for their food supplies. They shared abundances and lean times alike; occasionally whites depleted their own resources to keep Indians alive and vice versa. In a letter from "Winebagoe Lake, Feby. 4, 1814," Colonel R. Dickson reported that about forty Sauk Indians had arrived, having had nothing to eat for two days, "& had not Askin taken up his Cache & given them foll avoins they must have perished. . . . All I have left at present is 8 handfulls foll avoin – 10^{lbs} Flour – 2 Shanks Deers legs three frozen Cabbages & a few potatoes. The Sauks swept every thing I had & I was obliged to feed them with Sugar."[13]

On August 8, 1823, Major Joseph Delafield at Rainy River recounted how the people stationed there had become resigned to periodic deprivations: "A Mr. Davenport (a young man) was in charge, and three or 4 persons about him, all quite destitute. He told me they had had nothing but fish to live upon, as they might take them, and that for two days, pending the gale they had not been able to take a single sturgeon. He spoke with much sang froid upon the subject, as if used to it, and said shortly they would do well enough, because in about a fortnight the wild rice (folle avoine) would be fit to gather & the Indians would bring it to them."[14]

Curot's journal is particularly instructive of the hardships endured at a trading post in a winter when rice supplies were short. The rice crop failed in 1803; by early fall Curot was exercising other strategies for survival even though his men were laying in wild rice whenever they could. On October 10 he noted with some relief that they had caught enough fish to forgo rice for three days. By March both he and rival Sayer had nearly run out of the staple and were feeling pressure from their employees. Curot described petty bickering at his competitor's post, when only one fawnskin of wild rice was left for six men and two clerks: "Mr. Sayer proposed to his Men to Diminish Their rations by half; they were very unwilling to Consent, Saying that while there was anything left they preferred to have a whole ration of It, and that when there was no longer Anything they would resign themselves, that The rice had been considerably Wasted all The Winter, that they were not willing at present to deprive themselves of a single meal, that they ought to have had the provisions that La prairie had consumed with his family, without even being satisfied with what he had eaten Since after each meal, he no sooner entered his house than he ate again, Either rice that had been Parched, or meat that he found In his wife's kettle." By March 17 Curot had only two days' supply of rice left. When a Mr. Smith demanded his ration, Curot balked, whereupon the angry employee shouted, "Since you are so fond of your rice, go to H– with it," and ran out the door. When, by March 29, his men were threatening to eat the skins they had collected for the company, Curot said he would shoot anyone who tried. Fish kept the post employees alive until mid-May, just before their departure for Lake Superior. On May 13, men arrived in a canoe with "one sack of Corn and another Damaged"—the first grain they had seen in two months. This was sufficient to get them to the St. Croix portage with their furs; there, where the remainder of the corn had been cached, they camped en route to Lake Superior on May 18.[15]

When food supplies *were* sufficient and traders could focus on the business of acquiring furs, considerable amounts of wild rice exchanged hands. The food was essential not only at posts (both within the rice district and those outside of it, mostly to the north and west), but also as sustenance for the canoe brigades of voyageurs who transported furs east and trade goods west. If Zebulon Pike's account of Sandy Lake is representative, the North West Company in about 1805 purchased from twelve thousand to fifteen thousand bushels each year from the Indians at about $1.50 a bushel. A $20,000.00 annual expenditure for wild rice was a substantial budget item. A rough idea of what individual clerks of the company drew from this source can be gleaned from Malhiot's inventory at Lac du Flambeau (October 5, 1804), where among other provisions he listed "40 minots [a bushel plus] of Corn and wild rice."[16]

Whatever a company paid the Indians for rice, there was clearly a markup when the firm sold the rice to whites. In 1837, Frederick Ayer at Pokegama complained in a letter to David Greene that he had been charged $2.50 a bushel for wild rice that year; two years later he estimated among his expenses for the coming year a barrel of rice for $16.50, based on an assessment of the crop. Financial figures are at best sketchy, but a list of inventory prices set by the regulations of the Council of the Northern Department of Rupert's Land about 1843 provides these values (among others):

Corn Indian rough Bus.	3/-
Corn Indian hulled Bus.	4/-
Oil Sturgeon Gall.	2/-
Rice Indian bus.	4/-
Sugar Maple lb.	4d[17]

Throughout the trading period and beyond, *no* rice was harvested or processed by non-Indians. Whereas traders brought their own fishing nets in order to be less dependent on the Indian catch, they never practiced ricing. Perhaps the tedium of gathering, the peculiarities of the processing technology, and the scant reward for the effort discouraged them. Exhaustive investigation by researchers on behalf of Canadian Indians has turned up no evidence of ricing by non-Indians before 1890 at least. The first suggestion of a non-Indian harvesting rice was Gilfillan's report of what a Norwegian immigrant living at White Earth claimed one could make in a day of ricing. It is not clear whether the man referred to himself or an Ojibway.[18]

Whether they desired alcohol, ammunition, or metal wares, the Ojibway continued to use wild rice for purchase. A review of trading patterns before the Ojibway became immersed in a monetary economy provides a perspective on their later position. Establishing fixed value for rice as a commodity during the trade era is nearly impossible, for in the "free market" of the frontier many factors caused exchange rates to fluctuate. Rice failures and abundances raised and lowered rice value from year to year, trader prices were anything but consistent from post to post, and both parties had strategies for obtaining optimum prices. For instance, William Johnston, at Otter Tail Point on Leech Lake in 1833, noticed Indian hesitancy in selling provisions: "We visited the lodges, and purchased fifteen sacks of corn and rice, they were rather backward in selling it; for they thought if they would wait for competition they would get higher prices, for we were alone as yet in purchasing."[19]

Much depended on what the Indians lacked and how badly they desired certain goods in the trader's inventory. On September 15, 1852, Ojibway at the rapids of the Little Sturgeon Weir on the Winnipeg River traded rice with the Reverend Peter Jacobs for tobacco, "of which they were in great want." The next day, at the upper end of Island Portage, Jacobs's party was visited by Ojibway from Islington, a Wesleyan church mission station, who also wanted tobacco in return for rice and fish. Liquor was in great demand; Indians also eagerly sought European firearms for hunting or warfare. William Keating met some Ojibway on the Winnipeg River in 1823 who exchanged their rice for ammunition.[20]

Account books of trading posts provide figures translating into money or beaver skins or both. Thus it is fairly easy to ascertain the relative value wild rice had for whites. Indians traded mostly in maple sugar, wild rice, and furs, while the trading post offered them a fairly large assortment of items, including Old World foodstuffs. As at every outpost, those stationed at the Sandy Lake North West Company post in 1833 relied on a combination of what they could hunt and trap locally and the sugar and rice they bought from the Ojibway: "They have horses procured from Red river of the Indians; raise plenty of Irish potatoes; catch pike, suckers, pickerel, and white-fish in abundance. They have also beaver, deer and moose; but the provision they chiefly depend upon is wild oats, of which they purchase great quantities from the savages, giving at the rate of about one dollar and a half per bushel." The company was willing to trade some of its imported commodities—but only to principals in the trade. Available were flour at 50¢ a pound, salt at $1.00, pork at 80¢, white sugar at 50¢, and tea at $4.50. Thus, an Ojibway needed three bushels of wild rice for a pound of tea—if he could acquire it at all.[21]

Rice for trade was measured in traditional Indian storage containers—fawnskins, cedar-bark bags, *makakoon*—or in bushel sacks provided by the trader; values were translated into beaverskins or cloth. A fawnskin of rice, about two bushels, was worth about four dollars or two beaverskins. (The beaverskin became synonymous with money, and furs from other animals were valued in relation to it. In about 1820 a large beaverskin was worth two average-sized ones or two large otterskins; equivalent to one skin were two prime buckskins, three skins of raccoon, or two of lynx or fisher.) With two sacks of wild rice an Indian could purchase a fathom of stroud (six feet of coarse woolen cloth) or a blanket; the same item could be had for a forty-pound *makak* of maple sugar.[22]

The Ojibway often had the upper hand in dealing with isolated traders, and they took advantage of competition, particularly between Canadians and Americans. John Cameron at Rainy Lake provided this picture of market conditions along the border in 1826: "[T]he Indians were hiding their rice as fast as they could make it, giving out that they had suffered too much the two preceding years from hunger, and therefore would not expose themselves to want again. Rum, Tobacco and ammunition was no inducement and nothing but prime goods would break the resolution they had taken: neither Clouston or the Interpreter ever had so much trouble in a rice [trade] before. It has since appeared that the Lake of the Woods Indians had intentions of carrying their rice to Red River where they expected a much better market. It was still worse with Mr. Sinclair. The Indians he had to deal with were mostly Americans, and all made their Rice within American Territories."[23]

Despite an occasional trade advantage, at times the Ojibway felt the exchange rates were unfair. In a speech at Pokegama in September 1837, Chief Nodin (Wind) complained: "When we take to the Trader Rice and sugar &c in hope to receive something in return . . . Our Father We have to pay our Trader sometimes 2 Boxes of sugar or 4 Bags of Rice for a Blanket. This is too much."[24]

Alcohol and the Trade

One of the sorriest elements in the history of Indian-white trade was the systematic use of liquor for barter to the point of Indian dependency upon it. Here were planted the seeds of excruciating social, economic, and health problems that continue to plague Indian communities. While much the same story can be told about any place along the frontier, the use of liquor for trade in the rice district reached such proportions that Indian people heedlessly traded winter rations for alcohol, leaving many of their families destitute.

Wild rice sales probably did not lead to continual drunkenness on the frontier; rather, the only reports of Indians in such a condition came from people either themselves proffering alcohol or present when Ojibway suddenly came into a great deal of cash from fur and commodity sales or annuities. The state of Indians at other times is rarely mentioned. Similarly, twentieth-century charges of perpetual Indian drunkenness are based on observations made when Social Security checks arrive and certain recipients choose to frequent taverns until their money runs out. That much the same behavior is exhibited by many non-Indians the first of each month is generally overlooked.[25]

Nevertheless, trading alcohol for wild rice was rampant throughout the rice district. For example, the post commander, preparing to acquire food supplies at the entrance of the Red Cedar River in 1794, brought thirteen pieces of cloth and twenty kegs of rum to exchange for rice. Because wild rice was the principal winter staple of both parties, it was usually the first article bartered. In 1880 Paul H. Beaulieu wrote that fifty years earlier: "One five gallon of those spirits would buy more wild Rice in an Indian Camp than $200 worth of any kind of Goods and wild Rice was the Chippewa trader main stay after reaching his trading post and without which subsistence was not assured to them."[26]

Although some whisky was traded, the principal beverage was rum, almost always diluted with water and sometimes with strychnine added for flavor. Alexander Henry at Lake of the Woods in July 1775 began trade with shot, gunpowder, and rum as exchange items: "In a short time, the men began to drink, while the women brought me a further and very valuable present, of twenty bags of rice. This I returned with goods and rum, and at the same time offered more, for an additional quantity of rice. A trade was opened, the women bartering rice, while the men were drinking."[27]

Those Ojibway addicted to drink became obstinate in their trading when alcohol was not offered. Rice failures apparently only compounded the problem. Curot's journal is a sad recitation of alcohol-related difficulties plaguing the St. Croix Ojibway in the winter of 1803–04, when wild rice was in short supply. Certainly the readiness of the trader to deal in spirits immediately after harvest was a contributing factor to the fights, murders, and drunken comportment described so frequently in his journal. On September 16: "Le Grand mâle [Big Buck?] and Le petit Loup [Little Wolf] came to camp opposite us. I gave them Credit. I got from Le petit Loup two fawn-skins of wild rice and one avola [weaselskin?] and a sack full of rice, for this I paid a small Calico shirt, and gave him a small keg of diluted Rum." Three days later Curot traded three pints of mixed rum for a fawnskin of rice; the following day he haggled with Le Grand Razeur (Big Knife), who demanded half a keg for three fawnskins. The 1841 meeting of the Council of the Hudson's Bay Company in London noted that the Lac la Pluie (Rainy Lake) Ojibway would not supply trading posts with wild rice unless they received liquor in return. Accordingly, the Council of the Northern Department of Rupert's Land passed Resolution 43 "to avert such privation, a quantity of Liquor not exceeding 8 Kegs be furnished . . . as gratuities to the Indians." Similar resolutions were passed in the following two years.[28]

François Malhiot's journal at Lac du Flambeau provides a picture of the exchange rates of rice and rum as well as his general attitude. His lists include:

RICE =	RUM
1 sack	keg of four pots [2 gallons]
½ sack and one sack of pumpkins	7 chopines [pints]
1 sack	7 bottles [glass flasks]
1 sack	7 chopines
1 sack	keg of six pots [3 gallons]
3 sacks	half a keg of rum

The rates fluctuated greatly depending upon the inclination of the trader, the time of year, and other factors. On August 25, 1804, noted Malhiot, thirty canoes of Ojibway arrived, apparently with freshly made rice. The trader exchanged a large keg of rum and a brasse of tobacco (a forearm's length of braided or twisted tobacco) for three sacks of wild rice, which earlier had been worth only half a keg of rum.[29]

Traders were in business for profit, and a high exchange rate was in their interest. Malhiot complained that his "timid" employee, Bazinet, had heedlessly raised the ante in the Indians' favor; he had passed Turtle's village and given away two large kegs of rum for only two sacks of rice, whereas shortly thereafter Malhiot was able to purchase four sacks for only half a keg. Among other items Malhiot offered the Ojibway for rice were vermilion in small, flat packages—much valued by Indians for face and body paint—knives, mirrors, branches (strings or bunches) of porcelain beads, and lengths of tobacco. The Ojibway of the area must have traded all the rice they had or were willing to part with by September 5, for after that date corn replaced wild rice in barter.[30]

Much of the trade in alcohol can be attributed to the fierce competition between rival fur companies. The American Fur and Hudson's Bay companies were particularly liberal in dispensing liquor along the border. When the latter handed out medals to gain Ojibway allegiance, the American Fur Company countered by supplying liquor to posts at Pembina, War Road, Rainy Lake, Vermilion Lake, and Grand Portage, despite Aitken's attempts to persuade George Simpson, a Hudson's Bay Company administrator, to stop whisky sales to Indians. Most accounts lay the blame on the Canadian side. In a letter to Jonathan E. Fletcher, Indian agent for the Winnebago and Ojibway, dated November 30, 1848, Henry Rice said: "As soon as the agents of the H. B. Co. found that I was determined to prosecute the trade, they brought a large quantity of ardent spirits to the depot at Rainy lake, and at the time the Indians were gathering their last rice crop, they sent a quantity of liquor within our boundary and gave to our Indians in exchange for rice. I have positive proof of this. . . . The object of the company was to secure all of the surplus rice so that my men would be compelled to abandon the country."[31]

These were the so-called starvation years (about 1850), when rice failures and other food shortages were endemic; still, the liquor trade continued. When Bazil H. Beaulieu, employed as assistant agent for the geological survey of northern Minnesota in the summer of 1848, landed at Crane Lake Portage some twenty miles from the Canadian border: "I found a party of 5 men belonging to the Hudson Bay Company, peddling out liquor to the Indians in exchange for rice, and I saw four drunken Indians on the premises." Beaulieu's indignation did not prevent him from giving money to one of his own men to buy liquor or from sharing a glass of rum himself with the company clerk.[32]

Some traders were bothered about the consequences of providing liquor to the Indians. Paul Beaulieu seemed somewhat relieved when his voyageurs began to subsist on the game and fish they caught, so that "the detested pint cup to measure the Rice and corn feed to the Men is disposed of for a while." Treaty annuities only exacerbated the drinking problem by providing the Ojibway with large amounts of cash on the spot. J. J. Ducatel, at La Pointe during the 1835 payments, claimed that the agents withheld disbursements until the very last day to discourage liquor sales. Still, the problem was too great to control: "The cupidity of a few, however, will defy all laws, and notwithstanding the penalty of confiscation of their entire stock in trade, they contrive to introduce ardent spirits amongst the Indians, which is dealt out somewhat in this style. A whisky vender, standing upon a raised platform behind his groggery, lures them on, one by one, to taste of his 'vinegar,' knowing full well that the unfortunate savage, when he has once tasted of it, can no longer control his thus excited insatiable appetite for more. The vender is of course willing to 'accommodate' him for the trifling sum of fifty cents a gulp, and . . . repeats it until his victim from a savage has become a brute." Some of those intoxicated, wrote Ducatel, burned their lodges, while their frightened wives hastened to conceal knives and other potential weapons. Others also recorded such conditions. Charles Whittlesey witnessed several drunken families in the Vermilion Lake area being plied with rum by two Canadian traders. He contrasted the "wild and haggard look" of such "smoke-dried, sore-eyed creatures" with the Indians of the Grand Fourche band under Chief Wau-nun-nee. The latter had never ceded their lands and persisted in refusing presents from the government; consequently, "No band of Indians in our travels appeared as comfortable or behaved as well as this. Their country is well supplied with rice and tolerably good hunting ground. . . . It was seldom they left their grounds, for they seldom suffered from hunger. They were comfortably clothed, made no importunities for kokoosh [pork] or pequashigon [bread], and in gratifying their savage curiosity about our equipments they were respectful and pleasant." To the credit of both trading parties, Whittlesey traded with Wau-nun-nee's band for wild rice with flour, not rum.[33]

Although their attitudes were at times ambivalent, at least some Ojibway were aware of the dire consequences of trading for alcohol. In meeting with Henry Schoolcraft, Chief Flatmouth enumerated his grievances against the high prices of certain traders and their present unwillingness to sell alcohol: "He complained of the exclusion of ardent spirits, but at the same time admitted, that formerly it was brought in to buy up their wild rice—a practice which left them at the beginning of cold weather, in a destitute condition."[34]

The Indian Nonintercourse Act of 1832 prohibited the sale of alcohol to Indians, but the practice of using wild rice to obtain spirits never really ended.

In the 1940s Charlie Conger of Lac Court Oreilles, a member of the Eagle clan, recalled that he was once out ricing and a woman used totemic insult to cajole him into getting alcohol for her: "A woman who wanted a drink said, 'That eagle is surely dry!' She was joking about his dodem [clan] and wanted a drink, but Charlie didn't know that. His mother told him to sell some rice and get some whiskey. He took some rice to town and got some grain alcohol, and he gave it to the woman, who got very sick and passed out. He gave some more to her later. It made her almost vomit to look at it, but she had to drink it [for having insulted the Eagle clan]. Her husband told her maybe next time she'd keep her mouth shut."[35]

The Credit System

When the Indians could not pay for desired trade goods, they were usually allowed to put them on account. This custom of establishing credit was widespread among traders and lasted well into the twentieth century. In 1733 La Vérendrye encountered a large party of Indians with food to barter, apparently insufficient for the items they wanted in return: "On the 29th of August 150 canoes, with two or three men in each, Cree and Monsoni, arrived laden with meats, moose and bear fat, bear oil and wild oats, the men begging me to have pity on them and give them goods on credit, which was granted them after consultation among those interested."[36]

For the most part, the credit system worked smoothly. Canadian traders informed Johann Kohl at La Pointe in 1855 that: "Although the Indians carry the state of the ledger entirely in their heads, they generally remember all the advances made them, and their own payments on account so accurately, that both statements are usually found unanimous. At times the Indians, when they have no reason to doubt their trader, will accept his reckoning without any examination, and say it is all right."[37]

Borrowing on account eventually proved excessive. Once Indians began to receive annuities for ceded lands, they found their creditors lined up behind the payment coffers to exact their due—as Ducatel euphemistically stated, "the agent having adjusted the rent-roll." Kohl was present at La Pointe when the Lake Superior bands received their first annuities after the treaty of 1854 at La Pointe, in which the Ojibway ceded their land in Minnesota Territory: "At such payments, when the traders expect to find their debtors in funds, they usually lay their detailed account before the government pay-agent, and, if the Indian agree to the items, the amount is deducted from the sum he has to receive and handed to the trader." Kohl related an incident involving a chief from the Chippewa River who once ran up such an enormous bill with a trader that he had to settle for five hundred dollars when annuities were disbursed, and "very little of the tribute was left for the chief." Similar excesses in credit arrangements often left the debtors destitute.[38]

If the Indians sometimes lost in this arrangement, the creditors rarely did. Traders inflated prices with built-in coverage because of Indians who defaulted on loans. Being businessmen they protected themselves by charging as much as 50 percent more for items put on account, assuming that half the outstanding accounts would go unpaid.

By the reservation era, the credit system had become institutionalized, the Ojibway still dealing in natural foodstuffs like wild rice, but also in handcrafts with tourist appeal. With the end of the fur trade and the Ojibway's rapid transition to a money economy, local merchants simply assumed the traders' role. Such a storekeeper was Harry Ayer, whose credit allowances sustained many Mille Lacs Ojibway during hard times. In a midwinter letter in 1919 to Superintendent J. H. Hinton at White Earth, Ayer wrote: "They are nearly all out of money and I find it necessary to carry them over the winter months by allowing them to run accounts in the store which is not only a burden to me but to them as well." Partly to remedy the problem, Ayer established himself as a buyer and seller of Indian handcrafts. In response to a White Earth Agency offer of issuing food to older Mille Lacs Ojibway at Vineland, Ayer wrote to William Dailey: "The old Indians could use the rations all right although they have not been in real want this winter. I have bought all the bead work they could make and it has helped them out fine. Have paid out over $600.00 for moccasins, bead work, baskets, etc. since Nov. 1st."[39]

Wild rice continued to serve as money for the Ojibway until the mid-nineteenth century. With the depletion of game and the abrupt end of competition between major fur companies came the loss in importance of transportation depots such as that at Rainy River; once Indian lands were ceded and reservations established, the Indian economy changed drastically. By the end of the century, the Ojibway had made the transition from subsistence to a cash economy, partly due to the new occupations available to men. In the workplace of the dominant society—particularly in the lumbering industry—Ojibway took jobs alongside recent immigrants and were paid in the cash currency of the United States or Canada. In their new, part-time occupations as fishing and hunting guides, farm hands, and cranberry and bean pickers, the Ojibway were also remunerated in cash.

During this transition period, stirrings of white interest in the potential of wild rice as a commodity began. The next century saw the non-Indian emerge, first as a broker assuming control of wild rice processing and sale, then as a scientific planter and farmer, and ultimately as developer and controller of the industry.

A NON-INDIAN COMMODITY

From the time of their arrival in the western Great Lakes area, Europeans had speculated about the long-range prospects of wild rice as a food source. Jonathan Carver, for example, contemplated wild rice as supporting "the infant colonies" until they were able to cultivate other crops. Still, by the mid-nineteenth century, wild rice was relatively unknown outside the district. Although recognized by connoisseurs for its delicious and unusual flavor, it continued as something of a curiosity. The Englishman W. Gorrie wrote in 1857: "The Wild Rice seems never to have formed an article of regular commerce in the American cities; yet it is invariably deemed an acceptable rarity by the citizens, and a looked-for present from friends returning in the 'fall' from its native localities."[40]

Interest in the possibilities of cultivating wild rice mounted as early sowing efforts were undertaken. Captain John Pope, in 1850 reviewing the prospects for grain farming in the area west of the Mississippi and north of the St. Peter's rivers, found the climate generally too severe and the growing season too short to sustain corn crops. Other cereals, in his opinion, would do well, in particular: "The wild rice abounds in the lakes and streams, and is a favorite article of food with the Indians. It is very palatable and easily collected, and I do not doubt would prove a valuable article of commerce."[41]

Others were skeptical. In 1850 Sherman Hall viewed the removal of the Ojibway to the upper Mississippi as advantageous to the Indians, for their new homeland had an abundance of lakes; he felt, however, that "neither fish nor rice can ever become articles of commerce to much extent." Gilfillan reported that the only people other than the Ojibway eating wild rice at White Earth were missionaries and their families, a few old settlers and traders, and some merchants along the "St. Paul Railroad." This led Jenks to conclude: "If it could be cultivated with any certainty it would long ago have become a staple in America for the white population, as it was a staple for many thousand Indians before them. . . . It must be regretted that so nutritious a cereal was a precarious crop and has not, apparently, warranted extensive cultivation."[42]

Sporadic attempts to sow wild rice, not only within the district but also outside its habitat and even abroad, began quite early. In 1790 Sir Joseph Banks introduced Canadian rice seed into England, where it still grew at his villa in 1819. Some was also planted in Lincolnshire with the notion that the crop might feed the poor, but the rice failed. A citizen of Fort Collins, Colorado, wrote Jenks that wild rice had been tried twice in his state without success. Edmund Ely in a diary entry noted that he had "Exchanged a little salt for some *rough Rice* which I wish to sow as an experiment." In 1848 he received the following inquiry from Nathan Randall: "I wish you to furnish me with any information you can in relation to the *wild rice,* its productiveness if cultivated by the Indians—and extent lakes or regions growing in, mode of cooking gathering &c &c."[43]

At about the same time, Gorrie was experimenting with wild rice seed in England, the results of which inspired him to publish privately an eight-page tract on the subject. He was apparently spurred by earlier, unsuccessful efforts of some Scots, namely a Dr. Neill and Sir G. MacKenzie of Coul in Ross-shire. Their attempts had failed, surmised Gorrie, because "the seeds . . . apparently lost their vitality in their transmission from America." The doctor tried again, planting the seed in a six-inch flowerpot together with another aquatic plant. Although the seed did not sprout immediately, it did germinate the second year, producing an eighteen-inch plant with a few seeds. Gorrie attributed its small size and meager seed production to the possibility that the roots were too densely packed. Undaunted, he proceeded to compare favorably the climate and mean temperature of the British Isles with those in the New World wild rice habitat. Managing to procure a bushel of seed rice from Toronto, Gorrie distributed it in various parts of Britain, including Edinburgh and London, to those interested in trying to start it. Planters were urged to sow immediately on the margins of lakes or sluggish streams; to ensure that the seed sank to the bottom, Gorrie recommended it be rolled into pellets of clay—a practice long familiar to Indians.[44]

By the turn of the century, members of gun clubs actively planted wild rice seed, recognizing the crop's great attraction for migrating wildfowl (fig. 1). In 1899 Currie Brothers of Milwaukee wrote Jenks that "We have sold Wild Rice in a small way for seed about ten years, never selling more than one or two hundred pounds any season. We have never sold it for food that we know of. The principal demand for it has been for sowing in small lakes in the interior, and we have seldom heard the result of such seeding."[45]

Such interest helped spawn the first scientific research on the growth habits of wild rice and led to the publication by the United States Department of Agriculture of such studies as Joseph W. T. Duvel's *The Storage and Germination of Wild Rice Seed.* Duvel was able to offer practical suggestions for improving the germinating capacity of wild rice seed and to correct some hitherto unsuccessful practices. Before his report, it was assumed that the best way to propagate the plant was to emulate nature's way—to gather seed rice at its ripest stage, then broadcast it in the fall. Duvel, however, listed three disadvantages to autumn seeding: ducks would dive to the bottom to eat much of the seed; a good portion would be covered so deeply with mud washed in from shore during the winter that young plants would die of starvation or suffocation before reaching the surface; and many seeds would be carried off by floodwaters and floating ice in the spring. For optimum germination, Duvel recom-

FIG. 1. Wild rice seed packed with moist sphagnum moss into burlap-wrapped balls, used for seeding lakes. Hunting clubs promoted such seeding, and eventually the Minnesota Department of Conservation joined in to increase the state's wild rice acreage. This technique emulated an old Indian method of sowing rice.

mended storing seed in cold water over the winter and sowing it after the spring floods when water levels approached normal.[46]

Interest in transplanting wild rice grew. Because most requests for it were on an ad hoc basis, wild rice seed was purchased from the Indians before they processed it. Harry Ayer, for one, acted as a broker. In August 1919 he received a letter from Will W. Henry, county agent at the State of Washington Extension Service: "Dear Mr. Ayer: I understand . . . you are in a position to give me information in regard to wild rice which grows in the shallow lakes in your County. I have several shallow lakes in this County and I am very anxious to see if I can get some of this wild rice started here. I would be glad to get any information as to where I can secure this seed, when it should be planted, the method of planting, etc." Ayer replied that the time for gathering was near the end of August and asked the agent what quantity he wished, saying the price ranged from twenty-five to forty cents a pound.[47]

In 1920 Ayer wrote to Carlos Avery, state game and fish commissioner: "The Indians are just getting ready for the rice harvest, and next week I think they will be gathering some. Will know then what to expect as to yield." Avery responded, wanting the Mille Lacs Ojibway to quote him a price in advance of the harvest. Another request to Ayer came from A. Lehman of Lompoc, California, in December 1919, asking him about seed rice, which Ayer later supplied at forty cents a pound. In 1920 Lehman placed an order for five pounds, stating: "I don't know whether this is the right time for planting this rice. I am merely trying this out more as an experiment than anything else." Some sixty years later Lehman's home state vastly outproduced in paddies the natural wild rice collected in its original habitat.

Indian Reaction

Euro-American experimentation in cultivating the plant stood in contrast to Indian attitudes about sowing wild rice seed, always somewhat ambivalent because of deep-seated belief in the sacral qualities of *manoomin*. Although Nett Lakers in 1947 expressed astonishment at the concept of sowing rice, half a century earlier Ojibway at Lac Court Oreilles had given Jenks a concise history of their ancestors' involvement in spreading wild rice from one place to another. They identified the first crop on the Red River of the North about 1660. Subsequently, they said, rice was sown in an easterly direction from one body of water to the next until it reached every Ojibway community.[48]

Such recounting shows the Ojibway fully aware that Indians have deliberately sown rice; nevertheless, a certain stigma persists about human involvement with spreading the growth of rice. John Abrahams of Fort Alexander Reserve, Manitoba, when asked whether he knew of anyone planting wild rice, answered: "No one ever planted rice in the past, they only harvested it. I hear from those who planted, there are some across the river, apparently it is not the same when it is planted." Paul Buffalo reported that the "south lakes" were reseeded with larger rice from the "north lakes" to improve yield; he felt, however, that this was somewhat contrary to the natural scheme of things, that lakes should reseed from their own stock: "The germ is there, continue. It build on the same germ, the same seed, seeds its own. It belongs there, but shifting around seed from one place to another, it's hard for the crop." When the Ojibway identify certain wild rice stands as hand sown, they attribute the action to legendary figures such as Spruce (see Chapter 3) or place it in the distant past. Queried about the discovery of wild rice, John Abrahams responded: "[A]ll I heard was they were at it from time immemorial."[49]

Still, many Ojibway not only acknowledge active human sowing but also identify persons responsible and stands from which the seed has been taken. Ojibway near Crandon, Wisconsin, planted wild rice in Rice Lake and tended the beds by weeding out the large, flat aquatic grass competing for space and nutrition. In 1899 at Lac Court Oreilles a woman named Päskin′, said to be more than a hundred years old, remembered when rice was gathered from Red Cedar Lake to seed Lake Chetac, Rice Lake, Bear Lake, Moose-Ear Lake, and the Lac Court Oreilles River. The river had one of the richest stands, sown about 1860 by a couple, whose grandchildren's families were still harvesting it (fig. 2). James Mustache said that much of this seeding took place after the 1854 treaty set reservation boundaries. That most of the sown areas lay outside the reservation suggests that the Ojibway quickly established stands to take advantage later of treaty clauses allowing them to rice on ceded territories. At the very least seeding provided alternate wild rice sources should stands within reservation boundaries be insufficient.[50]

Similar Indian seeding efforts took place in Minnesota and Canada. Ed Burnside said his grandfather came to Nett Lake to take seed for planting "over in his territory by Big Lake"; Pelican Lake rice, he said, was planted in Slim Lake, Nett Lake rice in Little Rice Lake, and Vermilion Lake rice in Ninamos Lake. According to Jenks's research, the Assiniboin Indians west and northwest of Lake Winnipeg sowed rice in marshes: two small lakes near Shoal

FIG. 2. The couple said to have sown wild rice in the Lac Court Oreilles River. Jenks was told that the man was Awa'sa; James Mustache identified the man in this photograph, however, as Bimosegijig (Walking Sky), whose English surname was Butler.

Lake at Rat Portage, Ontario, were sown. Jenks watched one family gather seed to sow a new field for its own use.[51]

The Ojibway have always been aware that wild rice is an annual and that what they did not harvest would seed the rice field for the following season. Their traditional belief—that if they were in harmony with the spirits the crop would always return—helps to explain their fairly limited practice of transplanting rice. Most evidence suggests that rice was deliberately sown only to ensure some family an annual yield for its own needs. Like usufructuary privilege in the sugarbush, a sown field was recognized as a certain family's, whose exclusive right to harvest it was respected. Traditionally, there was no sowing for economic gain. For this reason, the non-Indian farming of wild rice in paddies has been viewed—certainly by many tribal elders—as a desecration, contrary to the laws of nature and the wishes of the supernaturals.

"Underproduction"

White frustrations in propagating wild rice were coupled with general consternation about Indian "underproduction" of this bounteous food. Non-Indians have continually pointed out how little rice the Ojibway harvested. This view was but one facet of the land-use argument of Europeans settling the North American continent; because the Indians were not using the land to its full capacity, they must relinquish their rights to those who would make it more productive. This attitude is clearly reflected in statements such as David Owen's in his report on Cass Lake in 1852: "When it is considered that an acre of this rice is nearly or quite equal to an acre of wheat for sustaining life, the waste of breadstuff in this region, from the indolence and improvidence of the Indians, can be understood." In a similar vein, George Monk, in "Some Account of the Department of Fond du Lac or Mississippi," noted in about 1807 that at Sandy Lake "Wild rice grows spontaneously in all the shallow muddy parts of the lakes and rivers, of which the natives gather a small part." At Leech Lake: "Many of the lakes, Bays & Rivers are muddy and spontaneously produce vast quantities of wild rice, of which the natives gather but a small part."[52]

As wild rice became a cash crop, many whites found it incomprehensible that the Ojibway did not immediately enter the business. At the turn of the twentieth century, one of Jenks's correspondents claimed that feasting and dancing in the rice camps usurped valuable time better spent in reaping larger harvests. The Reverend Gilfillan at White Earth indicted gambling on similar grounds: "The wild rice is such an abundant crop that a Norwegian man (the only white man working there, he being employed for wages), says that a man can make seven dollars a day, at the market price for rice, by gathering it. Here then is a God-send, and something that calls for a great effort. But the fascination of the [moccasin] game is so great that, with the exception of a very few, all the men spend the day lying on the ground gambling. So the golden opportunity is missed."[53]

Later, whites who surveyed the rice district for scientific study and who assembled statistics and harvest calculations were quick to point out the underproduction of wild rice by Indians. In the 1950s a researcher in the Minnesota Department of Conservation's Division of Game and Fish estimated that twice as much rice was processed annually then than in the years from 1860 to 1900, when the Ojibway were its exclusive harvesters. Another cited Minnesota acreage at between twenty thousand and thirty thousand. Given the Ojibway population (also noted in the study), such reports suggest that each Indian had the potential of harvesting as much as one thousand pounds of rice annually – a far cry from Indian need or desire.[54]

MECHANIZATION

Unquestionably the most profound change in the economics of wild rice has come from the development of mechanized processing. Mechanization eventually took over every aspect of wild rice production, including harvest. The time- and labor-saving devices invented to accomplish what for hundreds of years was done by hand eventually shifted the market greatly in favor of the non-Indian. Indians appear to have been the first to adopt such methods, though it is difficult to pinpoint whose idea was first realized and where or when. Novel approaches to replacing centuries-old technologies have spread quickly from one Ojibway community to the next through frequent visiting among area reservations. Many Ojibway now have modest processing operations in their reservation back yards, but in the long run none could successfully compete with the large processing plants that whites with capital resources built to handle large volumes of wild rice.

By Indians

Mechanization was gradual, and its development reflected the Indian way of doing things. Indians typically adapted articles they accepted from another culture to their own needs and tastes, as in unraveling trade blankets and reweaving the yarn, using Indian techniques and designs; converting gun barrels into Indian flutes; using wooden washtubs as frames for drums; and substituting muffin tins for the traditional carved molds for maple sugar cakes.

Almost every step in wild rice processing ultimately saw some change.

Pieces of canvas or even large, raised, concrete blocks replaced birch-bark mats on which rice aboriginally was dried. If a large piece of bark was not available to fashion a winnowing tray, an Ojibway might use heavy cardboard. Anita Soulier at Bad River uses an aluminum mixing bowl in place of a bark tray to toss rice, with equal effect. Rice was once parched in kettles; since the 1940s at Lac Vieux Desert and, more recently, at Lac du Bois, Fort Alexander Reserve, it has been done in sheet-iron troughs. Instead of using the traditional *bootaagan,* Lac du Bois Ojibway hull in concrete pits eighteen inches in diameter and wear rubber-soled shoes instead of moccasins. They do still hold onto a "bucking beam" for support and use a bark *nooshkaachinaagan* for winnowing.[55]

During the 1985 harvest at Lac du Flambeau, the author visited Brian Wiggins, who had a homemade processing plant in his back yard. Next to his modern frame house was green rice drying in fitted sheets laid out on the new asphalt driveway. Nearby, more rice was being air dried in an aluminum rowboat that had a window fan propped up in its bow; the fan was powered through extension cords leading to an electric outlet. On the ground by the boat, folded exactly in the traditional form, was a winnowing tray fashioned of sheet metal and sewn—with rivets.

The two most laborious steps in processing—parching and hulling—were the first to be mechanized. Fairly early in the twentieth century, someone had the notion that a discarded oil drum could be converted to serve the same purpose as the tilted kettle over a low fire, in which small quantities of rice were parched. There were two ways of making such a scorcher. Probably the earlier type was an oil drum fixed to a rod pierced through the center of the drum's two ends, with a door for inserting and removing the rice. The container was suspended lengthwise over a small fire and slowly rotated with a crank or handle at one end of the rod (fig. 3). An improvement on this device involved a stationary oil drum with an opening in its top. A rod with a crank at one end was inserted but not fixed to the barrel; instead, a paddle the length of the barrel and slightly smaller in width than the radius of the drum was attached to the rod. As it was cranked, the paddle stirred the parching rice part way up one side where it fell over the paddle to the bottom, to await the paddle's next revolution. The change meant less weight to turn for the person at the crank. This kind of parching machine is used today in most reservation mechanical processing; other improvements include adding a motor to replace the person cranking and substituting propane-gas blowers for the wood fire. This obviated the need for firewood and stoking and made regulation of the heat source easier.

Such a laborsaving device as the scorcher had immediate economic consequences and social implications for the Ojibway. Because the machine could

FIG. 3. George James (left) *and Bertie Miller of Lac Court Oreilles with James's hand-cranked mechanical winnowing machine, about 1941*

handle large quantities of rice at a time, much more rice could be finished in a far briefer period. William Dudley at Red Lake estimated that it had taken him a full day to parch a sack of rice in the old way, but with a scorcher he could do the same in half an hour (fig. 4).[56]

The accessibility of processing equipment made it easy for Indians to mechanize their operations at home instead of finishing rice by hand near the lakeshore. The new profession of processor emerged – someone who might be paid a percentage of another's rice for processing it. Such inventions hastened the decline of the rice camps and the loss of that special ambiance of sociability.

Hulling machines, which replaced the arduous tramping of rice in a *bootaagan,* were similarly fashioned from oil drums. When the chaff is brittle, slightly burst, and ready to be pounded free from the grain, the parched rice is put through a door into a rotating "thresher" that has hardwood sticks or pegs fixed inside at different angles. The door is closed and the entire barrel is ro-

FIG. 4. William Dudley with his mechanical scorcher, 1969

tated; the action of the barrel and the weight of the rice against the sticks hull the parched grain. Early versions of this machine, belt-driven from a rear axle or a wheel mount, made use of automobile or tractor engines (fig. 5a, 5b). In 1939 the Civilian Conservation Corps published a photo of this device in *Indians at Work,* noting that "sometimes this traditional method [hulling] is supplanted by attaching a barrel, through which has been driven a pronged iron bar, to the back wheel of a 'thunderbuggy.' "[57]

While some Ojibway have been content to accept mechanization for just these two stages of processing, others take the final step, fanning out the broken chaff from the seed with mechanical blowers. Several types have been devised, from those resembling miniature wind tunnels with electric fans at one end to those resembling popcorn poppers, with forced-air jets beneath and exhaust pipes carrying out the chaff from the top.

Since all of this machinery is homemade, probably no two Indian processing devices are alike. Many of them are assembled with parts salvaged from a variety of discarded engines and other mechanical detritus of the dominant society. (One writer aptly described homemade parchers as resembling laundromat dryers.) These machines nevertheless successfully process large quantities of rice in short order. William Morrell spoke of an orphan boy, Russell, whom

Fig. 5a. George James and Bertie Miller with a belt-driven thresher, using a tractor motor for power, Lac Court Oreilles, about 1941

Fig. 5b. Nett Lake children on a truck flatbed, 1947, watching the operation of a mechanical huller; the truck's axle turns the drum of parched wild rice.

he had raised in the Indian ways of ricing, hunting, and trapping. Now living near Big Rice Lake, Russell informed his foster father that he had entered the rice business: "He says, 'I make a machine, I make my profit.' He was very very apt at making things, you know, machinery. He would go around and pick up old parts. . . . And he made his own tractor and his own thresher. He said, 'I am making 1400 [pounds].' He said a lot of rice. 'I'm not selling any of it.' "[58]

James Mustache, who in 1983 helped build Bill Sutton's processing equipment at Lac Court Oreilles ("He's got a dandy . . . does good work, too") told how they went about making it, using the school shop on the reservation. They selected a fifty-five-gallon oil barrel and cleaned it thoroughly; then they inserted a rod, on roller bearings and attached to a small cogwheel, which in turn worked with a larger cogwheel driven by a small motor. They had basswood logs cut into board strips at a local sawmill, three of which they fixed permanently inside the thresher. Following the old way, they spread freshly harvested rice to dry before mechanized processing: "Bill would start up his cooker, take a big dishpan full of that green rice, throw it in the hopper, and cooker, and he'd start it up, go slow, and he'd time it, and he'd have an alarm clock out there, and he'd go out there and look it over. Maybe a little more yet; well, he'd turn it on a little more, and then he'd get that out, and then he's got a thrasher and puts this away so it would dry up, see, and when that's cooled off, then he'd put it in the grinder, the thrasher, and he'd be doing the scorching here and he'd be doing the thrashing over there." The economic advantages of such an operation are obvious. With one person able to carry out three stages of rice processing simultaneously, as Mustache put it, "Nowadays, harvest one day, and it's all done."[59]

The great variety of Ojibway homemade machinery to some degree has paralleled advances in white technology. As noted, before the electric motor was used, the drive shaft of a car engine was often attached to turn the cogwheel. (William Baker disparaged this as "the spinning wheel.") Indian people in the rice business are naturally curious about how other processors' machinery works, and they are attentive to innovations. When Mustache was at Mille Lacs Lake in 1968 for the funeral of a friend, he visited a local mechanized operation: "I know one guy in Mille Lacs, he made his own, but it's more cruder than what Bill's [Sutton] got. Doesn't do a very good job, but it does the job."

Despite all of the automation, some Ojibway still use machinery for only one step of the processing, reverting to traditional methods for the remainder of the work. In one ricing enterprise funded by the Indian Reorganization Act of 1934, fifteen Ojibway rotated oil drums over a fire of poplar slabs to parch the rice, but hulling was done by foot. Today rice may be fanned by pouring it into a long, mesh-bottomed trough to separate chaff from kernel through sieving. It may be further cleaned by hand and graded according to kernel size on a conveyer belt.[60]

Traditional Ojibway are generally suspicious of these new technologies, particularly when applied to natural food staples; many consider the taste of the product to be adversely affected. Alec Everwind (born 1898) of Ponemah, on Red Lake Reservation, commented on the new ways of tapping maple trees for sugar: "They use this new way, see. They use this pounder, drill the tree . . . and they got little spouts, and they drive them in there, and they leak out. It doesn't taste so good . . . like them old ways, that's the best." In Paul Buffalo's opinion, machines did not parch rice properly and were used solely to increase profits by hurrying natural weight reduction. William Baker rejected mechanization outright: "[The whites] don't even do like what the Indians used to do when they processed that. They don't. They got a machine, they got torches, but the Indian has fire, tubs to scorch their rice. . . . They got a big, well you might say a barrel, screen barrel, and then they got blowtorches in that to scorch that and just fan it out at the same time."[61]

Still, mechanization has enabled several entrepreneurial Ojibway on each reservation to start their own processing plants and enter into a modest seasonal business. They process green rice for friends and relatives in return for a percentage of the finished rice, which they then market locally. Vincent Bender, on Bad River Reservation, keeps 20 percent of what he processes for others. He and his wife, Mayda, grade the rice according to quality and package it in one-pound plastic tubs for sale from the back door of their house, located on well-traveled U.S. Highway 2. Bender-processed rice is also retailed at his daughter's convenience store, west on the highway, and by his grandson, Doug Kraft, to the east.

By Whites

When whites developed their own wild rice processing plants, they adopted and refined the Indian inventions to accommodate larger quantities of rice. By 1979 the rice business became profitable enough for six processing plants to be operating in Canada and at least twenty in Minnesota. Some, like Hicks Wild Rice Company of Grand Rapids, began on a modest scale, later enlarging its capacity to more than 2,500 pounds a season. Because it takes about 2½ pounds of green rice to produce a pound of finished rice, Hicks bought nearly 7,000 pounds of lake-harvested rice annually, probably from Leech Lake Ojibway. Most commercial firms follow the traditional Indian method, first drying the green rice in the open on long platforms. One processor in Manitoba, however, dries rice in an airplane hangar, using a suspended air-

FIG. 6. Air drying wild rice in a Manitoba hangar, 1971

craft engine and propeller working as a giant fan to dry large piles of rice that are turned periodically with a pitchfork (fig. 6).[62]

The most controversial device for wild rice production is the harvesting machine, introduced in the 1940s. Several types were devised, almost all of them by whites. Typical is one invented by a Mr. Holliday and H. B. Williams at Lac du Bois, Manitoba. It consists of a thirty-six-foot punt propelled by paddles driven by a car engine. Outriggers on each side support wire-mesh cages opening toward the front, with revolving arms that press the stems of the plants against the cages to catch the falling seed. The rice falls onto moving trays that convey it to the punt, where it is bagged. So thorough is its scooping capacity that the machine collects 90 percent of the rice available. Therein lies its greatest point of criticism, that through *over*production the lake is robbed of seed needed to replenish the crop. Its inventors claimed, however, that the revolving paddles stir up the ooze, thereby improving germination. Another type of mechanical harvester is an airboat or float on pontoons; propelled by an aircraft or small car engine, it has a six- to eight-foot screened-in scoop, or "speedhead," front-mounted to catch the rice as it falls (fig. 7).[63]

FIG. 7. Pontoon-floated, propeller-driven harvester scooping up rice with its front-mounted punt, Manitoba, 1971. The devastation of rice stands caused by such machines led to their prohibition in Minnesota.

Ojibway reaction to these mechanical pickers was at first one of horror. Such machines left little seed, and they plowed through a rice field, uprooting and chopping off most plants at water level—one reason they were banned in Minnesota. Photographs show rice beds harvested by combines desolate and destroyed. Despite Ojibway opposition and because of white competition and government regulations, there was pressure on Canadian Indians to adopt such combines; at Grassy Narrows, Ontario, the Ojibway tried a model made from styrofoam pontoons covered with fiberglass and driven by an aircraft engine; at Osnaburgh Reserve, one hundred miles northeast of Sioux Lookout, Ontario, the band designed its own machine: "[A] speedhead [is mounted] at the front of a motor-driven freight canoe. An underwater panel is attached to the bottom of the canoe at an angle to prevent the motor from uprooting the plant. The Osnaburg[h] style is particularly suited to the thinner stands of their more northerly areas, but not applicable to the thicker, more marshy stands on Lake of the Woods."[64]

The Ojibway vociferously objected to the use of combines to harvest wild rice beds. Because a machine collects in half an hour what one canoe does in a day, most people harvesting in the traditional manner would be put out of work. As Chief Kelly of the Sabaskong band in Ontario declared: "What we are fighting is not only the loss of income but also the soul-destroying effects of unemployment." Attendant was the fear of losing intangible cultural and social values; the Ojibway in the 1940s foresaw that, should harvesting be assumed by machines, they would have little need for their traditional family rice camps. And the limitations of the machinery were apparent: in knocking rice the old way by hand, Indians could gather the best grade of rice because they made repeated runs at different times through the same areas. The mechanical harvester made only one pass at the rice; consequently, its operator had to wait for the optimum ripening period. Unlike the combine, which had to stay in deeper water, the Indians could also gather rice growing near shore.[65]

The potential for both damage to crops and displacement of Indian workers called for compromise in the adoption of mechanical harvesters. At Lac du Bois rice combines operated side by side with Indians in canoes. The Saulteaux in Manitoba permitted use of the machines only after hand-harvesting was finished. Ironically, some of the most successful capitalists in the Manitoba rice industry today are individual Ojibway operating their own combines.

Without mechanization whites probably would not have entered the wild rice business on the scale they did. Those involved might have remained brokers on a limited basis, like Harry Ayer. As wild rice's reputation as a delicacy was spread by hunters and vacationers in the rice district, however, requests for it spread from local storekeepers to retailers and even wholesalers. By 1900 a fledgling market had developed when the Ojibway were still the source of both green and finished rice. Market prices were flexible and ultimately in their hands. By that time considerable amounts of seed rice were being sold, mostly to sow as an attraction for wildfowl. L. L. May & Company of St. Paul answered Jenks's queries (see fig. 9): "In relation to Wild Rice, we handle, we presume, about three thousand pounds of it during the season. We have usually been getting our supply from the Northern part of the state. It is gathered and cured by the Indians, and we find we get a good grade of seed from this source, especially as we have it all thoroughly examined before purchasing. We do not sell any for food."[66]

Harry Ayer, continuing in the role of middleman, received a letter from Griggs-Cooper & Company, of St. Paul, asking: "Can you arrange to ship us down another consignement [*sic*] of wild rice as we will have a few orders next week, which we would like to fill? Perhaps you can see some of the Indians and have them bring some in to you." He had to reply that he could not obtain any more until the next harvest. Similar correspondence was carried on with Rust-Parker Company, a Duluth grocery and coffee wholesale firm. Evidently, Ayer was soliciting business on behalf of the Mille Lacs Ojibway for the forthcoming harvest, as the firm wrote him in August 1920: "We have before us your inquiry of the 16th inst. regarding Wild Rice and while we are not at the present time in position to quote any prices we will be in the market for this product a little later on. . . . In the meantime, we would be pleased to hear from you at any time as to your crop and if you can make us an offer we would be very pleased to give same our consideration." Rust-Parker seemed aware that Indian prices depended on the size of the harvest, for a representative wrote Ayer the following month: "[W]hile we are not familiar with any market having been made on this product or any price, we are in a position to offer you 20¢ per pound at this time. . . . From reports that we have, the crops seem to be rather short but in event that the price gets too high on this product, it is very likely that we will not handle it this season."[67]

Not only did Ayer act as broker for the Indians in such exchanges, apparently he established himself in the mail-order business as well. Responding to a request from D. K. Harting of Little Falls, Minnesota, in 1920, he wrote: "The rice crop in this locality was very short. We have however about 200# and will ship you 25# FOB Onamia for 40¢ per lb." Harting accepted the arrangement and requested that Ayer ship the twenty-five pounds to George Burden of Dubuque, Iowa, presumably as a gift.

The Decline of Indian Processing

This economic picture changed when whites built their own processing plants and began to control the market. Their fledgling industry, however, was not without some birth pangs, as whites experimented with a variety of mechanical procedures to improve the volume and quality of the finished product. From the start, the system was highly competitive; machinery designs and problem solutions are still closely guarded. With the shift in the wild rice market beginning in about 1930 came a new figure—the buyer.

A buyer is quite simply an entrepreneur waiting on the shore of a rice lake with burlap sacks, a scale, cash, and a truck. He begins with a fixed price for the green rice coming off the lake, though the time of the season, the size of the harvest, and competition from other buyers may affect it from day to day, or even within the same day. During rice camp days, the precursor of today's buyer perhaps traded groceries for wild rice instead of paying cash and used a horse and wagon instead of pickup truck. Paul Buffalo reminisced about his family's dealings with this transitional figure: "There was a rice buyer come from Bena [on the Leech Lake Reservation]. He was a postmaster, he was a storekeeper. So this [buyer] would load up groceries, bring it down to the rice camps, and they would deal pretty good with him. . . . On our way home I began to realize the price of rice. . . . We got $6. Then I looked at the groceries. Six dollars worth of groceries and we had a big pile. We was going home. He [the buyer] said, 'I got 6¢ a pound.' That's what he sold them for. It kept raising up to 9¢, see."[68]

Stuart Berde, who spent three weeks at Leech Lake in the ricing season of 1965, described a typical rice buyer—Alvin Jackson (pseudonym). Jackson was otherwise employed outside of harvest time; some of his income was earned selling minnows for bait to fishing resorts. Jackson was in partnership with his cousin. Together they operated three trucks and provided twenty-seven ricing canoes to the Indians; those without transportation were picked up en route to the daily marketplace by the rice lake.[69]

For the duration of the harvest, Ojibway using his boats in effect worked for Jackson—as Berde put it "a sort of partnership akin to a patron-client relationship is formed . . . between the buyer and his ricers." Similar small businesses were established each ricing season by entrepreneurs in many towns in the rice district. Tony Wise of Hayward, Wisconsin, who also ran a ski resort and summer tourist attraction called Historyland, at one time entered the wild rice business with fourteen boats; he hired Lac Court Oreilles Ojibway, paying them a certain amount per pound for what they brought in. Tying the business into his Historyland powwows and its nearby recreated "Indian village," Wise had James Mustache, Bill and John Barber, and Sam Frogg demonstrate traditional rice processing in the tourist park, then sold the finished rice to the tourists.

In exchange for use of a buyer's boat, the ricers were to sell what they harvested exclusively to him. Berde depicted Jackson arriving at the public landing by 6:00 A.M. each day. One of the two docks might already be occupied by his competition. The ricers who came by car parked single file along the narrow road and carried their equipment and boats, if they had them, some distance to the landing. By law, in 1965 the harvest could not begin until 10:00 A.M.; in the interim Jackson took his motorboat to the rice beds to find the best spots for harvest that day. Upon his return, the ricers, with knockers and poles loaded in the boats, were slowly towed by Jackson's motorboat to the fields in a caravan of as many as twenty boats tied in a line. The convoy arrived at the beds by about 9:30 A.M. with half an hour to wait before knocking rice; when the boats were full, they were towed back the same way. A buyer had to exercise caution in pulling such a caravan, especially when the boats were loaded; they could easily tip and lose their valuable contents. (There have been drownings in such accidents, too.)

Back at the landing, ricers usually fill burlap sacks provided by the buyer with the freshly harvested rice. These are weighed on a spring scale hung perhaps from a tree limb or the tail gate of the buyer's truck (fig. 8a, 8b). As he accepts each bag to load on the truck, he tags its weight and gives a receipt

FIG. 8a. Leech Lake teenagers bringing bags of wild rice to a buyer, about 1970

FIG. 8b. Ricers waiting while the buyer examines a sackful of wild rice before weighing it on the spring scale, about 1970; ticket book rests on the tailgate of the truck.

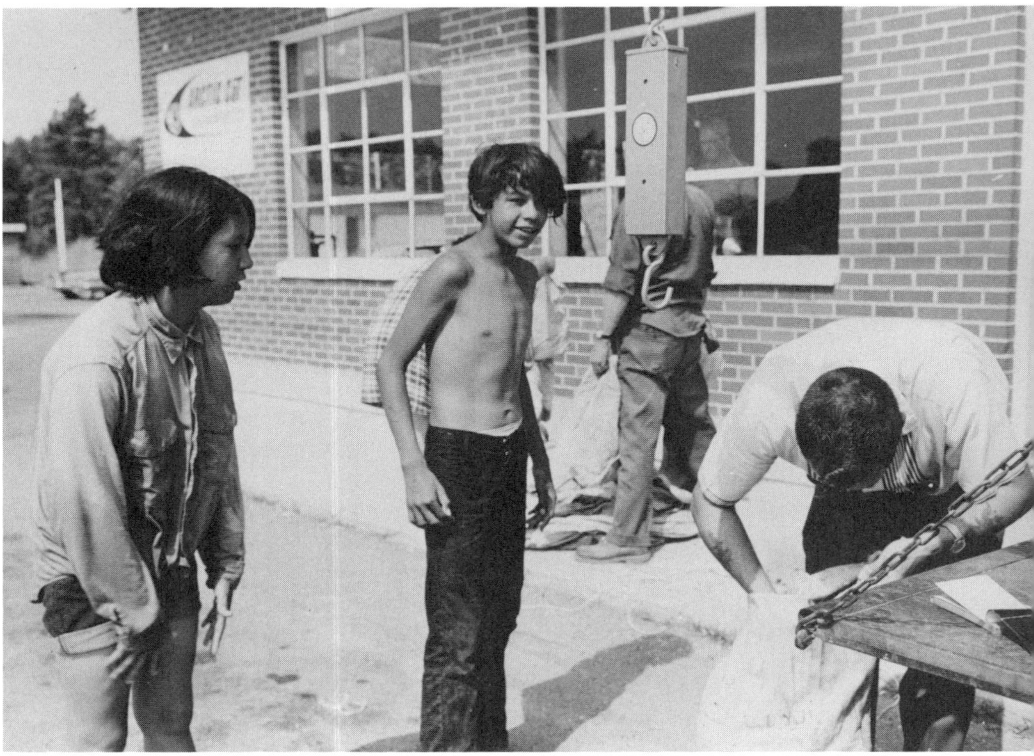

to the ricer, who takes it to the cashier—usually the buyer's partner, holding a metal cashbox in the cab of the pickup. The ricer is paid in cash the going rate for green rice.

Most buyers carry on this transaction at the lakeshore, but when wild rice comes in from many sources, they may conduct business at the processing plant. Since a plant may already have begun to process rice, Indians have the option of exchanging green rice for finished rice at the ratio of about four or five pounds to one. Many trade in this manner for their own use, accepting cash for the rest. If they think they can retail the rice themselves, the Ojibway may trade in all their green for processed rice, taking it home to package in one-pound plastic bags for sale from roadside stands or their houses to tourists.

Although the harvester maintains a certain loyalty to the buyer, who has provided boat, burlap bags, and a tow to the rice fields, competition between buyers may induce ricers to sell elsewhere for more favorable prices. A certain cynicism prevails among ricers, who view buyers generally as fairly ignorant about wild rice. Consequently, cheating to increase poundage—wetting down the rice before sacking it or hiding rocks and other foreign matter in it—is fairly common, even though buyers seem perfectly aware of it. Many simply ignore the deception.[70]

In contrast to the care with which the Ojibway treated rice harvested only for themselves is the attitude at lakeside markets that the buyer must beware. Since the buyer scarcely has time to examine the contents of each sack he weighs, the Indians may give him a good percentage of broken stalks and other detritus. Paul Buffalo deprecated the ability of buyers to perceive quality, saying that one can offer them unripe rice, broken rice, and the like because, to them, rice is just rice. Such brokers are viewed simply as white middlemen—hustling to obtain as much of a commodity as they can. Noted Dan White: "Those buyers there, they just buy whatever they got in the sack there, a lot of time people used to put in some muskrat hollow, or whatever would add weight, and I guess they sold those things to them. And the buyers were so anxious to get as much rice as they can pounded. . . . Those buyers don't care what they buy. And so the person that they hurt would be the processor, for he's getting what these buyers are buying." Such deception is seen as emulating white business dealings. Indian people view it as beating whites at their own game in the world of the almighty dollar. As Berde aptly concluded, "The rice is now out of the Indian's hands, and he has no further responsibility for its treatment."

Little wonder, then, that such a climate discourages the social interaction once characterizing Ojibway rice camps. Instead of feasting, dancing, and gambling, when not on the lake most ricers—reduced to cogs in the machinery of a white business—simply stand around talking with their partners, waiting for the official opening. At selling time, the atmosphere resembles more a commodities exchange than the peaceful setting of campers processing their own rice. Fred Jones recalled the auctions among buyers at Mallard Lake (Minnesota): "When they were getting big money down there for their rice, you know, they went to the landing and watched them and weighed in, and then they auctioned it off. Jerry, the auctioneer down there. Buyers come in there, you know, and he'd get in there and he'd start rattling it off, you know, who pays a cent more, a nickel more, you know, and so on. The highest bidder, and then he buys all the rice."[71]

Some Ojibway have expressed resentment at this procedure, feeling that the greed that has arisen among buyers and harvesters leaves little rice for home consumption. Maggie Hanks Brown of White Earth remembered when rice was only ten cents a pound, and her people were content *not* to sell their rice: "Besides, you could save your rice then, nobody was there to grab your rice, to buy it from you, because they didn't want the rice that bad, see?" Others have complained that pressure from buyers induces the Indians to harvest immature rice: "The people nowadays, they don't really go for the matured rice. They pay a license to hurry up. It's a pressure, $2, $3, it's a pressure to get that wild rice. So they all afraid they ain't going to get enough to pay for the license." Some, like Fred Jones, have viewed the economic situation with mixed feelings. The price of rice was quite high when he was interviewed in 1968 (Mallard Lake green rice brought two dollars a pound at auction, with immediate profits accruing to the Indians), but he was afraid the market might drop without warning: "It was way up high. Boy, I sure like to see that big prices go, keep up there. . . . Just because they can't move it, nobody trying to get that processed [rice] in the northeast corner up to the 1500 pounds. See, we don't pay that kind of money where they're ricing. This is what takes time, you know, it's going to harm us in the long run."[72]

In order to enter commerce each season, buyers often borrow money from local banks. Paul Buffalo acknowledged the affect of financial pressures among the buyers: "Then again become a contest. He's the one that's got a bigger truck, bigger buyer. He can buy [and will pay] more. So that's the way it goes."[73]

Even when paying high prices for green rice, an adventuresome buyer can recover his debt to the bank and still make a profit. Nevertheless, the work is hard and the hours long. Alvin Jackson said he rarely got more than three hours of sleep a night during his six weeks' work as a buyer. Equipment must be loaded and unloaded from the trucks, and many trips must be made to the processing plant. In addition, Indians not part of the normal work crew may arrive at the buyer's home well into the evening, meaning more trips to the processor, perhaps some distance away. Still, in a good year a buyer can make a good amount of money quickly. Jackson claimed he procured as much as 9,700 pounds of rice from a lake in six hours. If accurate, his figure must represent a peak of activity; most boats bring in from eighty-five to one hundred pounds of rice per load, representing about two hours work, so Jackson would have had to buy outside his normal fleet of twenty-seven boats.[74]

Wide fluctuation in prices makes it nearly impossible to arrive at an average paid by buyers for green or finished rice. Green rice, however, rose steadily in value to as high as two dollars a pound in the late 1960s (Table C). One estimate (about 1934) at White Earth was that half the yield of 80,000 pounds was purchased at 14¢ to 20¢ a pound. Finished rice fetched higher prices. At Nett Lake in 1947, when the Ojibway were getting $1.00 a pound for processed rice, buyers fairly shy about intruding on reservation land came only to its borders or to the reservation store to barter. Peter Smith remembered from his childhood that Nett Lakers never received more than 5¢ a pound for rice that they had to deliver themselves by canoe. Their trip required traversing a rapids, unloading the rice, and returning home for another load. In the Nett Lake area about 1955 finished rice retailed for $2.00 to $2.50 a pound. In 1965 Leech Lake buyers paid 65¢ a pound for green rice at the beginning of the season and more than $1.00 by its end. In the middle of the harvest one buyer announced he would raise his price to 80¢ a pound and that each ricer could thereby earn $87.00 that day, suggesting he expected two full loads from each ricing pair. At Leech Lake, early in the 1966 season, ricers received $1.25 a pound for green rice; in 1968 green rice had reached $2.00 per pound in some places. By the mid-1980s finished rice sold for $6.00 to $8.00 a pound on Wisconsin reservations.[75]

Beginning with the period of mechanization, whites entered the buying market in ever greater numbers. The sale of licenses that were eventually required in Minnesota for buyers and harvesters alike reveals a fairly accurate picture of an emerging industry; from 1940 to 1954, the number of harvesters did not quite double (from 2,500 to 4,500), but the number of buyers almost quadrupled from 55 to 203 in 1955, an average of about one for every eleven boats.[76]

These figures imply substantial profit for ricers, too. Remember, however, that this source of income could be counted on but once a year and only for a relatively brief time. Paul Buffalo indicated some of the pressures of the season: "Now the crops are getting shorter. Why? There's so many that like wild rice. People like to eat wild rice. It comes to market. The money, the quick way they get cash to live for their living purposes. The children's got to go to school. They got to have clothes, and everything is on the run, when the harvesting time comes."[77]

At the time Ojibway in Wisconsin and Minnesota received from $1 to $2 a pound for their green rice, their Canadian counterparts were in a much less

TABLE C

Indian Income from Wild Rice

Source	Date	Place	Price
Pike	1805–06	Sandy Lake	approx. $1.50 bushel
Doty	1820	Wisconsin	$4.00 bushel
Pike	1833	Sandy Lake	$1.50 bushel
Ayer	1837	Pokegama	$2.50 bushel
Ayer	1839–40	Pokegama	$16.50 barrel
Cowie	1843	Lac la Pluie district	4 shillings bushel
Brunson	1843	Lake Superior	$1.00 bushel
Bardon	1851–53	?	$5.00 two sacks
Annual Report*	1855	Mille Lacs	$4.00–$5.00 bushel
Gorrie	1855	Canada	4 shillings bushel
Bardon	1861–62	?	$1.00 ten lbs.
Jenks	1864–69	Upper Mississippi, Pillagers, Lake Winnipeg	$4.00–$5.00 bushel (approx.)
Annual Report	1866	Upper Mississippi, Pillagers, Red Lake	$4.00 bushel
Annual Report	1867	Lake Superior	$2.00 bushel
Annual Report	1868	Lake Superior	$2.00 bushel
		Upper Mississippi and Pillagers	$4.00 bushel
Annual Report	1869	Upper Mississippi and Pillagers	$4.00 bushel
Annual Report	1870	Upper Mississippi	$1.50 bushel
Annual Report	1871	Michigan (Menominee)	$4.00–$5.00 bushel
		Nett Lake	$1.00 bushel
Jenks	1898	Bad River	10¢ lb.
		Fond du Lac	6¢–10¢ lb.
		Lac Court Oreilles	8¢–10¢ lb.
		Nett Lake	7¢ lb.
Reagan	1904–14	Nett Lake	30¢–50¢ lb.
SD informants, ca.	1900–40		
Buffalo		Leech Lake	3¢ lb., green; 6¢–9¢, finished
Morrell		Sucker Bay	$1.00 bucket
Jones		Mallard Lake	$2.00 lb. ("high")
Dudley		Red Lake	10¢ lb.
Brown		White Earth	10¢ lb.
Johnson	1932?	White Earth	$1.00–$1.50 lb.

TABLE C

Indian Income from Wild Rice

Source	Date	Place	Price
Jackson	1968	White Earth	$2.00 lb., green
Ayer	1919	Mille Lacs	25¢–40¢ lb., seed rice
	1920	Mille Lacs	30¢–40¢ lb.
Carlson	1924	White Earth	14¢–20¢ lb.
Smith	1924	Mole Lake	25¢–35¢ lb.
Coleman	ca. 1929	White Earth	3¢–6¢ lb., green; $1.25–$1.50, finished
Coleman	ca. 1935	White Earth	20¢ lb.
Hilger	1938	White Earth	10¢ lb., green; 40¢, finished
Burns	1939	Cass Lake	25¢–45¢ lb.
Reed	1943	Hula Lake	20¢–40¢, finished
Lips	1946	Nett Lake	$1.00 lb. ("very high")
Steven	1949	Manitoba, Ontario	10¢–12¢ lb., green; 20¢–60¢, processed (wholesale)
Nyholm	ca. 1950	Bad River	35¢–60¢ lb., green
Brogan	1955	Nett Lake	$2.00–$2.50 lb.
Berde	1965	Leech Lake	65¢–$1.00 lb., green
Jackson	1966	Leech Lake	$1.25 lb. ("high")
Vennum	1985–1987	Bad River	$6.00–$8.00 lb., finished

**Annual Report of the Commissioner of Indian Affairs*

favorable position. Harvest estimates for 1952 from Indian agents in the rice district of Manitoba and Ontario indicate that at the Clandeboye Agency in Manitoba the 250 to 300 Indians ricing earned from $40,000 to $50,000 total, an average of about $170 a person. Since the annual harvest was approximately 250,000 pounds, they must have received under 20¢ a pound for green rice. At Kenora, the situation was somewhat better, with harvesters earning from $200 to $300 each for the season. Whatever the amount, income from wild rice scarcely made up a substantial part of a Canadian family's financial requirements; at Sioux Lookout the sale of green rice accounted for an estimated 5 percent of income. The estimate of the number of Canadian harvesters (850 to 1,050) did not take into account family members involved in the harvest, nor did the figure for the total amount gathered—360,000 pounds—include what the Indians kept for themselves.[78]

After purchasing green rice from the Indians, the buyer sells it to a wholesaler for processing. An initial estimate of the amount is based on the ticket weight that was figured by the buyer when he purchased the rice. Because of natural moisture loss, not to mention the evaporation of the water poured over the rice to increase poundage before bagging, the weight usually "shrinks" by the time the processor receives the rice. Therefore, the rice is reweighed for accuracy; discrepancies become loss to the buyer.[79]

There has never been a consistent policy for marking up wild rice once it is out of Indian hands. Suffice to say that the initial markup is great, and that the more middlemen between buyer and consumer, the higher its price at retail. For instance, in 1949, Ontario green rice bought from the Indians for 10¢ to 12¢ a pound doubled in wholesale price after processing. Manitoba rice bought for 10¢ a pound jumped to 40¢ to 60¢ a pound. The Ojibway usually sold some rice themselves, probably at a lower price than was received off the reservation. For example, Albert Reagan in about 1915 reported that Nett Lake rice was sacked and sold as breakfast food for 30¢ a pound at the village but went for 50¢ in nearby towns. John Johnson in about 1932 seemed to have flexible prices for whites who visited him at White Earth: he asked for $1.00 a pound, though some paid $1.50; apparently his prices diminished for larger quantities, as he sold six pounds for $5.00. Johnson was also aware of the markup on rice in the larger cities; he knew of whites who kept rice in a shed in Minneapolis and sold it for $3.00 to $4.00 a pound. Harry Ayer retained a small profit as he developed strategies to induce Mille Lacs Indians to sell to him. In the fall of 1920, while nearby Onamia merchants paid 18¢ to 25¢ a pound for rice, Ayer offered to buy it for 30¢. Although he realized that Minneapolis retailers got as much as 80¢, he then sold to whites at 40¢. In the summer of 1919 he bought some rice from a white man in Wahbun at 18¢ and held it until the following summer for the Mille Lacs Indians to give their friends during the Fourth of July celebrations, when he let them have it for 25¢ a pound.[80]

Several large towns in the rice district served as principal retail outlets for wild rice before the turn of the twentieth century. Jenks named Rice Lake, Chetek, Cumberland, Bloomer, Shell Lake, and Hayward, in Wisconsin; Bemidji, Park Rapids, Tower, Grand Rapids, and Minneapolis, in Minnesota. At the time of his research, retailers and wholesalers alike did a fairly brisk business. C. W. Moore in Chetek, for instance, sold 1,500 pounds in 1894, and two years later C. H. Oppel & Sons, wholesalers and retailers in Duluth and Tower, did even better. Charles C. Oppel explained the popularity of wild rice: "Most of the cruisers, explorers, and homesteaders take it out into the woods with them. They claim that it is better than tame [white] rice, because it don't take so long to prepare it. We also ship considerable; fact is, we handle from 1 to 2 tons a season."[81]

By 1900 dealers began advertising the product, grading wild rice for size and eye appeal. Currie Brothers of Milwaukee, which sold between one hundred and two hundred pounds a year throughout the 1890s, placed a notice in the *Horticultural Guide for 1899.* In 1898 L. L. May & Company of St. Paul, which had begun to carry an inventory of three thousand pounds of wild rice a season, advertised in its *Farm and Floral Guide* seed catalog under "Grasses, Clovers and other Farm Seeds." The page displayed a somewhat fanciful illustration of a ripe wild rice panicle (fig. 9). Jenks implied the company was selling wild rice for human consumption, but its reply to his query and the advertisement indicated otherwise: "Wild Rice. Valuable as an attraction for wild fowls and is sown in large quantities along the edges of ponds, lakes and streams. Also desirable as a forage plant on inundated lands." The company assured Jenks that it dealt only in a good grade of seed, available for 10¢ per ounce and $1.40 per ten pounds. Meanwhile, the Indians were getting as little as 3¢ to 6¢ a pound for green rice, while the finished product retailed for $1.35 to $1.50 in towns near reservations and higher in larger cities. One Duluth store had various grades for $1.75; another offered "Grade A" wild rice for $2.25.[82]

For the consumer in the late twentieth century, the most expensive way to purchase wild rice has been in small amounts by mail order, usually from some gourmet specialty food outlet far removed from the harvest source. One firm (the Orvis Company, Vermont) has retailed northern Minnesota wild rice for $10.95 a pound. Companies like Gokeys and Eddie Bauer, Inc., which specialize in sporting goods and clothing geared to hunters, have also offered rice at hefty prices. L. L. Bean, Inc., of Maine, has sold "extra-fancy Minnesota long-grain" at $16.00 a pound, shipped in a colorful green canister decorated with canvasback ducks; one could order the rice in a clear plastic bag for $12.00 a pound. Closer to its source, Chieftain Wild Rice Company of Hayward has sold, postpaid, two pounds for $15.95.

Some distributors of gourmet items have cooperated with Indian harvesters. Stressing the rice's natural qualities and traditional harvesting methods, S-M, Inc., of Brattleboro, Vermont, has sold a four-ounce box for $3.99. The product is harvested and packaged by Nett Lake Indians under the Bois Forte Wild Rice Enterprises, Inc., label; the box displays what looks like a Nett Lake official seal and extols: "This natural wild rice is harvested by Indian tribes living in the lakes region of northern Minnesota. No fertilizers or pesticides are used in its growth. No chemicals are used to process it. This natural product of the earth is high in cereal protein, B-vitamins and low in fats. Easy to cook." Sometimes complementary items are offered with the rice to attract gift buyers. The Rainy Lake Wild Rice Company of Ranier, Minnesota, has offered an "executive gift package" for $14.50, including two pounds of rice and four dinner place mats showing northwoods wildlife scenes. Indian peo-

46 L. L. MAY & CO., ST. PAUL, MINN.

MISCELLANEOUS LIST OF

Grasses, Clovers and other Farm Seeds

Grasses and Clovers are Subject to Market Fluctuations. Should our present Stock Become Exhausted we will Fill Orders at Market Prices.

A REQUEST.—Write us for SPECIAL PRICES on Grasses, Clover Seeds and Millet in Large Lots.

Meadow Fescue or English Blue Grass—A splendid pasture grass for sowing with other grasses. Does well in almost any soil. Per lb. 25c, postpaid; by express or freight, 10 lbs. $1.25, 100 lbs. $7.50

Sweet Vernal—Useful for mixing with other grasses. Very sweet scented. Per lb. 35c, postpaid.

Rhode Island Bent Grass—A valuable perennial for lawns and pasturage. Much like Red Top, though smaller. Thrives on light, dry soils as well as on rich, moist ones. For lawn purposes, if used alone, it should be sown at the rate of about forty pounds per acre; for pasture if used alone twenty-four pounds per acre. Per lb. 35c. postpaid. By express or freight, 10 lbs. $1.85, 100 lbs. $17.50.

Perennial or English Rye Grass—A fine grass for permanent pastures or mixing with other grasses for the lawn. Per lb. 20c, postpaid; by express or freight, 10 lbs. 85c, 100 lbs. $8.00.

Creeping Bent Grass—A rapid growing grass, which does best on moist lands. Per lb. 35c, postpaid.

Meadow Foxtail—An erect perennial, in appearance slightly resembling Timothy. Valuable for permanent pastures and does best on good, moderately moist soil. If sown alone use 25 pounds to the acre. Per lb. 35c, postpaid. By express or freight, 25 lbs. $6.00, 100 lbs. $22.50.

Medium Red Clover—Excellent for pasturage or hay, valuable as a green manure, and should be in all grass mixtures. First quality, lb. 25c. postpaid; by freight or express, pk. $2.25, bu. $8.50.

Mammoth Red Clover—Best Grade, lb. 25c, postpaid; by freight or express, pk. $2.25, bu. $8.25.

White Clover—Valuable for mixing with lawn grass. Lb. 35c, 3 lbs. $1.00, postpaid.

Timothy—Carefully cleaned seed. Lb. 20c, postpaid; by express or freight, pk. 75c, bu. $2.50.

Kentucky Blue Grass—Extra Cleaned. Lb. 25c, postpaid; by freight or express, pk. 50c, bu. $1.50.

Orchard Grass—It is a splendid pasturage grass. Extra cleaned seed, lb. 25c, postpaid; by express or freight, pk. 70c, bu. $2 50.

Red Top—(Choice.) Lb. 30c, postpaid; by freight or express, pk. 60c, bu. $2.00.

Improved German Millet—One of the best forage plants there is grown. All kinds of stock are exceedingly fond of it, and eat it readily. Lb. 20c, 3 lbs. 50c, postpaid; by freight or express, pk. 40c, bu. $1.00, bag (2½ bu.) $2.25.

Hungarian Millet—One of the most valuable annual soiling plants. Lb. 20c, 3 lbs. 50c, postpaid; pk 40, bu. $1.00, bag (2½ bu.) $2.35.

Common Millet—The well-known variety. Bu. 85c.

Minnesota Sugar Cane—One of the best green fodder plants. All kinds of stock are exceedingly fond of it. Lb. 25c, postpaid; by freight or express, lb. 15c, 10 lbs. 75c, 42 lbs. (1 bu.) $2.25.

Broom Corn Evergreen—The variety most generally grown. Lb. 25c, postpaid; by freight or express, pk. 75c, bu. (42 lbs.) $2.25.

Broom Corn Japanese—The earliest variety in cultivation Brush is fine and long. Lb. 35c, 3 lbs. $1.00, postpaid; by freight or express, pk. 75c, bu. (42 lbs.) $2.50.

Sainfoin—(Esparcette.) It is a most valuable clover for dry, chalky, sandy soils, and is extensively grown in England. Sow 15 lbs. per acre. Pkt. 5c, lb. 25c, postpaid; freight, 10 lbs. $1 00; 50 lbs. $4.00.

Flax—Per lb. 20c, postpaid. Write for prices on large lots.

Buckwheat, Silver Hull—Grain a light gray color. Pkt. 10c, lb. 25c, postpaid; express or freight, pk. 40c, bu. $1.50.

Buckwheat, Japanese—Wonderfully productive; has been known to yield 100 bushels per acre. Lb. 35c. 3 lbs. $1.00, postpaid; by express or freight, pk. 50c, bu. $1.50.

Spring Rye, Dakota Mammoth—The heaviest yielding variety. Lb. 30c, postpaid. pk. 50c, bu. $1 50.

Giant Spurry—(True.) The great forage plant so extensively advertised of late. Sow 20 lbs. per acre. Will flourish in any soil. Lb. 25c, postpaid; by express or freight, 10 lbs. $1.00, 25 lbs. $2.00.

Spring Vetches or Tares—(Vicia Sativa.) Splendid feed for hogs, and also a most valuable fertilizer. Sow about 150 lbs per acre. Lb. 20c, postpaid; by freight, 10 lbs. 75c, 100 lbs. $5.50.

Lathyrus Silvestris—(Flat Pea). Makes good food for cattle, horses, hogs, etc., and is a great fertilizer. Does well in any soil. Pkt. 10c, oz. 20c, lb. $1.50, postpaid.

Teosinte—A famous annual fodder plant whose yield is surprising the agricultural world. Grows eight or ten feet high and has yielded 50 tons of fodder per acre. Per pkt. 10c, oz. 20c, ¼ lb. 50c, lb. $1.50.

Kaffir Corn—One of the best things offered of late years for a forage plant. The heads contain small white seeds which make an excellent flour. They are greedily eaten by horses and cattle, and make excellent food for poultry either fed in the grain or ground and cooked. Pkt. 2 oz. 10c, lb. 30c, 4 lbs. $1.00, postpaid; by express or freight, 10 lbs. 50c, 50 lbs. $2.00, 100 lbs. $3.50.

Wild Rice—Valuable as an attraction for wild fowls and is sown in large quantities along the edges of ponds, lakes and streams. Also desirable as a forage plant on inundated lands. Per oz. 10c, lb. 30c, 3 lbs. 85c. postpaid; by express or freight, 10 lbs. $1.40, [illegible]0 lb. $12.00.

GREAT WESTERN CORN.

Large ears, fine color, heavy yield and medium early, that's what the Great Western Corn is. It ripened the past season in from 95 to 100 days, so that you can readily see that it is the corn for nearly every section of America, except the extreme north, where only the Dakota Queen Dent Corn can be grown with safety. Too much cannot be said in favor of this variety for such states as Illinois, Ohio, Indiana, Iowa, and in fact, all but the northern tier of states along the Canadian line. Lb. 35c, 3 lbs. $1.00, postpaid; pk. 60c, bu. $2.00, bag (2½ bus.) $4.25.

DAKOTA QUEEN CORN.

It is beyond a doubt, the earliest Dent corn ever introduced, and is the most valuable addition to the list of corn in many years. It is far ahead of Pride of the North, King of the Earlies, Early Butler, and in fact all the Dent varieties in earliness. This new corn can be grown in the extreme Northern states where heretofore only the Flint corn has been raised. It is of a bright yellow color, small ear and cob, with a very long, deep grain. Lb. 35c, 3 lbs. $1.00, postpaid; pk. 60c, bu. $2 00, bag (2½ bush.) $4.25.

May's Famous Grass Mixtures

The Mixtures offered below are made up with the greatest care and include only such grasses as are adapted for the purposes for which they are recommended. We offer no cheap mixtures; they are generally worthless.

NOTICE—At the prices quoted we put the seed up in bags and deliver it on board cars here. If you desire a few pounds by mail, add 8c. per lb. to the price named to cover cost of postage.

		Lbs. per acre.	Per lb.	Per 100 lbs
No. 1.	May's "Rapid Growing" Mixture—This is made up of quick growing grasses and clovers that will produce a big crop in about five months from time seed is sown	20	$0.15	$13 00
No. 2.	May's "Meadow Mixture"—A combination of such varieties as Orchard Grass, Timothy, Red Clover, Can Blue Grass, English Rye and several others desirable for this purpose	18	17	16 00
	PERMANENT PASTURE MIXTURES.			
No. 3.	For Light Soils. A splendid mixture	24	16	14.50
No. 4.	For Medium Soils	22	18	16.50
No. 5.	For moist lands and those occasionally overflowed	22	14	12.50
No. 6.	For pastures on well drained soils	28	22	20.00
No. 7.	For sandy and gravelly soils	35	20	18.50
No. 8.	For pasture in Orchard and shady places	26	18	17.00

FIG. 9. Advertisement for seed rice, L. L. May and Company, St. Paul, 1898

ple, knowing how little the harvesters make, are appalled at these retail prices. Fred Jones in 1968 blamed the high price on get-rich-quick schemes, pointing out that one local firm selling processed rice at more than $9.00 a pound ("People just can't spend that much!") would be able to make a profit at only $3.00 a pound.[83]

A less extravagant approach in wild rice retail has been taken by Lunds, Inc., the Minneapolis-St. Paul grocery chain. For some twenty-five years the firm has reserved rice in advance, bought it in bulk, packaged it on its own, and offered it to regular customers at a fraction above cost as a good will gesture. About 80 percent of its sales are between October and January—mostly to Minnesotans to send as gifts to out-of-state relatives at Christmas. Until about 1970 Lunds purchased processed wild rice from anyone arriving at the back door. Lack of uniformity and quality induced the store to begin dealing directly with harvesters in northern Minnesota and Canada, before endorsing the rice with its own label. Although sales have grown slowly, the company retails annually an average of 250,000 pounds of wild rice. Depending on the crop, the price per pound has fluctuated between about $2.50 and $5.00 ($2.99 in 1986 and $2.49 in 1987), slightly higher for special one- or two-pound gift boxes that accounted for 10 to 15 percent of the Christmas wild rice sales.[84]

TAMING WILD RICE

If mechanization brought substantial change in the traditional economic position of Indian people in the wild rice business, the advent of paddy rice production completely distanced them from the lion's share of the profits. Continuing to harvest lake rice by hand, the Ojibway had at least retained a slender connection with the crop. Once the wild rice plant was successfully moved inland for farming on paddies, mechanical combines replaced Indian people as harvesters, and the wild rice industry fell almost totally into white hands. Quipped George McGeshick: "They're growing it Chinese style!"[85]

Paddy rice production was considered for some time before it was realized in the late 1960s. Agricultural dreamers envisioned crops with greater productivity than natural stands and stable annual yields for a more controlled market. Because water levels in artifical lakes could be accurately managed at all stages of rice plant growth, rice failures due to high spring runoff and sudden flooding would be eliminated; mechanical harvesters (prohibited in natural stands) could be used in the paddies, collecting much more than possible by hand knocking. Furthermore, machine harvesting would cost about one-fourth what hand harvesters were paid. In farms, the wild rice plants could be more easily protected from natural enemies; hybrid strains could be experimented with, and nonshattering grain types could be developed for increased productivity.

Briefly, paddy rice is cultivated on soils ranging from peat to clay, in artificially created fields contained by dikes and ditches. Hybrid, shatter-resistant, weed-free seed is selected for spring planting. The seed is mixed with oats and sown in the fall with a bulk fertilizer spreader and harrow or in the spring, after the fields have been flooded, from an airplane.[86]

Water is pumped into the paddies to the proper level, thereafter maintained with consideration of rainfall and evaporation. Fields are drained in August as rice grains begin to ripen. The ground continues to dry for about two weeks as the kernels mature. By this time the ground is firm enough to support heavy equipment. Standard rice combines modified for use as wild rice pickers (by extending their reel arms) knock the mature kernels into narrow troughs. Special wagons that can traverse still-wet fields transport the rice from the combines to trucks, which carry the rice to open, flat areas where it is spread out and processing is begun. The growing-fields are then allowed to dry further to permit weed eradication and the preparation of new beds for the next year's crop (fig. 10). (Other practices of modern agronomy include using chemicals like 2,4-D amine to control weeds on the dikes; rototilling or mowing; spraying pesticides, such as malathion, to control rice worms and midges; and using sonic devices to discourage blackbirds from attacking the wild rice plants.)

Paddy production began earnestly in 1968 on farms or undeveloped land in the rice district of northern Minnesota, accounting that year for 20 percent of the state's total crop. Some impetus for its development was the continued use of mechanical harvesters in Canada and the fear that the state would not be able to compete if it did not increase its production through similar means. Public funding was crucial. In 1965 scientists at the University of Minnesota had petitioned the state legislature for funding for wild rice studies. In 1969 legislators voted to support this with an initial annual outlay of $75,000 for research into seed production and the development of hybrid plants. Two new strains of seed were soon developed to improve paddy yields. The results from such research were astonishing: in 1968 the 900 acres of paddies produced 90,000 pounds of green rice; by 1973 the acreage had not quite doubled to 17,000 acres and the yield increased to 4 million pounds.[87]

Paddy production helped stabilize the supply and the price of wild rice. From 1971 to 1974 processed wild rice was nationally available in sufficient quantities that it wholesaled for from $2.00 to $2.50 a pound, retailing from $2.70 to $6.00 a pound. A particular boost to the market was the development of new wild rice products by such prominent food corporations as Uncle Ben's, Green Giant Company, and General Foods. At first reluctant to offer unadulterated wild rice, these firms educated the public palate by degrees, mar-

Fig. 10. An airplane spraying a wild rice paddy with insecticide, Minnesota, about 1970

keting a mixture of wild rice and long-grain white or brown rice, thereby saving themselves money as well. The mixed products had a wild rice content of from 12 to 18 percent, thus eliminating the perceived inconvenience of preparing wild rice. Consumers had been convinced that wild rice required long, complicated cooking – a view that persists today. This misperception coupled with high price kept many from trying wild rice. Because manufacturers required wild rice that would cook in the same length of time as the white rice, paddy growers developed a smaller grain with higher moisture content than natural lake rice, making it ideal for a blend. In a mix it produced a larger plate count per pound than lake rice, making it economically attractive, particularly to hotels and restaurants.[88]

Blends and instant frozen rice were only two of the new products to emerge as the industry grew. Soon, various wild rice stuffings, frozen casseroles, cooking pouches, and bread and pancake mixes were on the market. While these were attractive to the middle-class cook intent on trying new recipes, most traditional Indians reacted to such products with skepticism and bemusement. William Baker once received some wild rice mix: "And I got a big bottle of cereal like that, something like a square box. Yeh, they even got recipes! Where the hell is the recipe? There's only one recipe. It's to *cook* it!"[89]

Despite these new products, natural lake-grown rice continued to be accepted in the marketplace and to some degree received beneficial fallout from the general promotion of wild rice as a food. The popularity of natural-foods retail outlets in the late 1960s also encouraged the sale of lake rice. To promote its retail sale—particularly to the local grocery stores, specialty food shops, gift shops, and resorts making up 30 percent of the market—processors packaged wild rice under their own names, such as Gibbs, D'Arcy, or Reese; or, to lend northwoods ambiance to the product they named it Canoe, Caribou, Quiet Water, or Indian. To enhance its attraction, packaging graphics designed to match the romantic brand names showed Indians paddling canoes or quiet lakeside settings. In addition to recipes, a brief history of wild rice and a description of traditional Indian harvesting techniques were supplied. The implicit message was that here was a unique, all-American natural food product through which one might help the Indian economy.

Having successfully introduced paddy production, white entrepreneur farmers wanted to secure their new industry. Accordingly, they founded the Wild Rice Growers Association, Inc., in northern Minnesota in 1969 to promote and protect their interests. (At the time, wild rice was—and in 1988 still is—one of the few grains not governed by a marketing board or commodity exchange; it simply floated in a free market according to supply and demand.) Since forming the association, which became the Minnesota Wild Rice Council in 1974, paddy growers have sought to achieve their goals through standard marketing strategies. Promotional activities have included advertising in trade journals and on radio and television and staffing display booths at conventions with logical market potential (sports shows, food brokers' meetings, and gourmet food shows). Paddy growers have distributed lapel pins and hats extolling the virtues of wild rice; they have offered bumper stickers for sale ("Try it on a bed of wild rice!"), and contracted for the production of films and videos. They were particularly pleased with the publication of a wild rice cookbook (*Wild Rice, Star of the North,* 1986) containing recipes assembled by Lola Perpich, wife of Minnesota's governor, Rudolph G. Perpich, income from which was used to help finance the restoration of the governor's residence. (Governor Perpich, a native of the Mesabi Iron Range and general booster of economic growth in the northern part of the state, has keenly supported the paddy industry.) Growers have encouraged kitchen experimentation with wild rice, adding to the cook's repertory everything from wild rice quiche, lemon-tarragon wild rice, and wild rice au gratin to wild rice-chicken salad. Clearly, the activities and agenda—not to mention food tastes—of the non-Indian growers and those of traditional Ojibway harvesters are worlds apart.[90]

Spurred on by increased supplies at lower prices, what began as a fledgling market has become an ever-expanding industry, complete with middlemen from packers, brokers, and distributors to jobbers—all taking their share. This system, while stabilizing bulk prices, has little impact on small, independent harvesters, including Indians, who process, package, and sell their products locally and are generally oblivious to the larger marketplace. Since they have little overhead and rarely stock inventories beyond the season at hand, they will accept small profits. Indian retailers mostly observe competition within their own communities and set prices accordingly, close to what they think the non-Indian passing through the reservation will pay. As the Ojibway increasingly become aware of gourmet-shop pricing, they tend to raise their prices to something commensurate—say, six or seven dollars a pound—though reservation competition may gradually bring this down. This author has seen wild rice prices fall one dollar a week per pound in some Ojibway communities as small dealers tried to deplete their supplies before the end of the summer tourist season.

Paddy growers, meanwhile, have been equally oblivious to Indian concerns. Beyond their general promotional efforts to expand the market, they operate as a special-interest group in other predictable ways. They are particularly active in political lobbying for laws that will benefit research and increase the land available for operations. Despite the small size of their association—only sixty-five growers in 1981—they have kept in close touch through annual meetings and a monthly newsletter, *Wild Rice News,* published by the Minnesota Wild Rice Council. Among other items, the newsletter introduces recipes using wild rice, asks members to donate sample rice for promotional purposes, advertises requests for seed rice, and announces equipment sales.[91]

Periodic conventions further cement grower ties. With technical presentations by researchers in agronomy economics and plant pathology, the meetings have begun to resemble annual convocations of academic societies. Among the topics addressed at the January 1986 meeting in Grand Rapids, Minnesota, were fertilizer nitrogen losses and placement in peat soils, the latest in wild rice breeding, crayfish control research, and rotary combine and spike tooth versus rasp-bar cylinder performance evaluation.[92]

Gradually the production of wild rice in paddies has come to exceed by far the amount of rice harvested from natural stands in lakes and rivers. In response, in an effort to stigmatize what they perceived as artificial wild rice, processors who purchased from Indian harvesters successfully pressured the Minnesota legislature to pass a law requiring paddy-grown rice to be labeled as such, thereby distinguishing it from natural wild rice. This resulted in considerable bitterness between the two sets of producers, which has only begun to subside in the face of competition from out-of-state growers.[93]

With increased public acceptance of wild rice nationally, the economics of the product changed as paddy production began in other parts of the country.

Minnesotans had consumed two-thirds of the total crop until the mid-1960s, but wild rice began to leave the state in ever-increasing quantities when food corporations began to market paddy rice in mixes. From 1955 to 1972 the Minnesota crop tripled; by 1980 the production of paddy rice—approximately 2.3 million processed pounds that year—was more than double that of lake rice in the state. Wild rice research at the universities in the Twin Cities and Madison increased at a steady pace, supported by taxpayers' dollars. The published results of such research let the genie out of the bottle. As hybrid, nonshattering strains were bred, plant diseases brought under control, harvesting equipment improved, and natural predators eliminated, wild rice suddenly joined the ranks of commercial agronomy. The quickest to seize the opportunity were the California growers—particularly in the Sacramento Valley and in Lake, Mendocino, Shasta, and Lassen counties. Ironically, the West Coast wild rice business was pioneered by Minnesota processors, whose initial two thousand-acre development in California was an attempt to free the industry from dependence on the erratic returns from the annual lake harvest in Minnesota. Due to a white rice glut, California rice farmers had ready-made paddies in set-aside, federally subsidized acres and equipment, which, with minor modification, converted easily to growing and harvesting wild rice for about twice the profit of the earlier crop. Production begun in 1977 reached 800,000 pounds of processed rice by 1982.[94]

By 1986 California was outproducing Minnesota two to one, benefiting from research performed near the natural habitat of the species and funded with Minnesota tax dollars. In 1986 more than 95 percent of the wild rice harvested was paddy grown; the 10 to 11 million pounds glutted the market, dissuading several California growers from planting for 1987. Meanwhile in Minneapolis, finished paddy rice sold for as little as $1.70 a pound.

The California threat had implications for the Ojibway harvester, for the midwestern paddy and lake growers suddenly perceived a common enemy. By 1986 efforts to mend fences were already perceptible. In May 1986 Claude E. Titus represented paddy growers in meetings with Indian groups to obtain Ojibway agreement to rid the state of its label law. While the Indians agreed in principle, they wanted to hold out, using their cooperation as a bargaining chip to get promotional funds from the state to support their own ricing efforts.

What has been the Ojibway response to the gradual take-over of wild rice by whites? In the interest of the Ojibway, non-Indians and state or federal agencies (mostly the latter) have initiated a variety of enterprises to involve the Indians more actively in the business. Where organized exclusively by Ojibway, such activities have been modeled after businesses in the dominant culture. The motivation has been to increase revenue on needy reservations, and the most common approach, the cooperative, has been perceived as closer to the traditional Indian pattern of economy than more capitalistic enterprises. Joint Indian-white wild rice ventures have included the introduction of paddy rice production on reservations.

With some exceptions, most of these efforts have failed. Because the history and sequence of problems are unique for each case, generalizing about the reasons for failure is nearly impossible. Still, examination of a few cases reveals recurrent patterns suggesting that the projects have suffered common flaws and incorrect assumptions and that Indian wild rice businesses on any but a modest scale may be inherently doomed to failure.

Harry Ayer's Mille Lacs Enterprise

As part of his general assistance to Mille Lacs Indians in selling their products, Harry Ayer in the 1920s attempted to generate additional income for them in a wild rice scheme. Previously Ayer had been unsuccessful in getting the Indians started in commercial fishing, as he ran into opposition from local whites. Ayer then encouraged Ojibway families, accustomed to harvesting only for family needs, to gather rice beyond their own requirements and sell the surplus to him. Charles Garbo was named supervisor of the project, and Ayer enlisted participation from Garbo's family and four other groups: the Wadena, Skinaway, Shinodin, and Boyd families. Ayer planned the itinerary, as dictated by the successive ripening of rice in different stands; they began at Onamia Lake, then harvested in turn at Rice Lake, Dean Lake, Mud (Ripple) River, and finally at Platt Lake. The venture was apparently successful until the depression of the 1930s, when it received support from the Works Progress Administration (WPA) for a short while. The project was discontinued along with other WPA projects on the reservation and never resumed.[95]

Nett Lake and the Peavey Company

When the Peavey Company of Minneapolis left the flour milling business, it entered the consumer convenience food market. In 1969, the company approached Nett Lake about building a wild rice processing plant on the reservation. Until then the three non-Indian processors at Nett Lake, although convenient for harvesters, had not contributed much in the way of lease fees for the reservation. The Reservation Business Committee and Peavey negotiated a plan for the company to build a plant adjacent to the lakeshore for easy delivery of green rice from boats. Peavey was to pay the tribe one thousand dollars a year for the lease, hire local help to package and market the rice, and share the profits with the reservation.[96]

Almost immediately there was opposition. Some felt the lakeshore site was inappropriate and that a plant there would ruin the beauty of Nett Lake as well as usurp the only area on shore available for a park. Attendant was the fear that the convenience of "Peavey on the Lake" would give the company a monopoly and drive other processors out of business. The plan provided the company lakeshore rights for twenty years—a privilege held by only one family on the reservation. No sooner had the company poured a concrete slab and begun construction than dissension intensified to the point that a public meeting was convened. By the time Peavey was offered a new site, the company was too discouraged to continue, and it withdrew all interest in the wild rice business. This left reservation opinion about equally divided, with many feeling that Nett Lake had bungled a good economic opportunity.

Man-O-Min Co-op and General Mills

In 1972 the chiefs from Sabaskong, Eagle Lake, Wabigoon, Rat Portage, Shoal Lake, and other Canadian Ojibway reserves formed a cooperative to bring harvesters better prices and give Indians more control over processing and marketing wild rice. The co-op received loans from the Department of Indian Affairs to purchase green rice, and General Mills, Inc., of Minneapolis, wishing to improve its image with minority groups, offered to sell the rice on a nonprofit basis through supermarkets, as part of a self-help program. The rice was shipped green to Nett Lake for processing and to Minneapolis for packaging in six-ounce boxes under the trademark Quiet Water Wild Rice, which General Mills used for both its Anishinahbaig Man-O-Min Co-op (Kenora) and Bois Fort (Nett Lake) Wild Rice Co-op products. In promotional efforts, the company's Betty Crocker kitchen developed new recipes to include wild rice.[97]

The Indians accepted General Mills assistance because of marketing problems in Canada. Shoal Lake Wild Rice, Ltd., owned by Benjamin Ratuski, a close friend of Leo Bernier, the minister of natural resources, had already monopolized the eastern markets. The cooperative tried Canada Safeway for outlets in the west without much success, so in 1973 it approached an independent broker to market the product. General Mills assistance meant crossing the international border to find American markets, but initially spirits were high. The money lent by the Canadian Department of Indian Affairs had enabled the cooperative to begin the season buying green rice from pickers at 55¢ a pound, up to 90¢ by the end of the harvest when the best grade was gathered. This presented stiff competition to white buyers, who offered 30¢ to 45¢ a pound throughout the season. As a further strategy, each reserve designated a buyer and paid him 3¢ a pound for the rice he brought to the co-op. Noted Joe Shebagegit, a director of the Man-O-Min venture, with pride, "For the first time, Indians had something to say about the price of rice."

Soon, however, Man-O-Min—its acronym for Manitoba-Ontario-Minnesota created by Basil Green of Shoal Lake—was faced with problems beyond its control. The Lake of the Woods Water Control Board flooded the rice fields in 1974 (and again in 1975), claiming the need for increased hydroelectric power. To alleviate this problem, in 1974 the chiefs of the reserves met in Thunder Bay with ministers of the Ontario cabinet to explain why wild rice was so important to their economy. The ministers expressed annoyance at the Indians' use of an American firm and asked why they had not sought Canadian provincial help. The Ojibway were completely unaware that Ratuski, their principal competitor, had received not only a $32,000 interest-free loan from the Ontario Development Corporation but assistance from the Ontario Department of Agriculture and Food as well.

Beyond flooding and marketing problems, the fledgling cooperative faced other unanticipated complications. To begin, it did not have enough canoes for harvesting. The Indians were accustomed to borrowing canoes from established white buyers—mostly store owners near the reserves—who for years had purchased green rice for American firms and Shoal Lake Wild Rice, Ltd., extending store credit to the Indians for their rice. Fearing loss of credit if they sold to Man-O-Min, many pickers decided not to risk their established arrangement with the store owners; they continued to use their canoes and sell to them, despite lower prices. In shipping rice to the United States, Man-O-Min lost control of quality grading and processing. Sales did not meet early expectations, and since General Mills sold the product on a nonprofit basis, it was blamed by some for not promoting the product aggressively. Meanwhile, the Canadian government raised the interest on Man-O-Min's loan from 8 to 11 percent. After two years of involvement, General Mills pulled out.

Nett Lake Tries Again

In 1970, the year after Peavey's involvement in the wild rice business collapsed, the Upper Great Lakes Regional Commission and the Iron Range Resources and Rehabilitation Commission obtained funds to experiment with paddy rice at Nett Lake. Fifty acres east of the lake were set aside with plans for paddy construction the first year and production the second. The Reservation Business Committee was to assume control of the established project. After $117,000 had been spent, the first year's harvest yielded only 151 pounds of rice, processed by King Brothers on the reservation—at a cost of nearly $1,000 a pound. Packaging and marketing plans never materialized, and the rice went unsold.[98]

In assessing the situation, Kathren Borgelt sampled reservation opinion. Some felt paddy prices would lower prices generally; others believed the paddy was too small to have any effect; the most cynical cited the paddy failure as proof that no enterprise could succeed on the reservation. Still, Borgelt, who favored Indian paddy production, concluded: "Generally, the effect of commercial harvesting does not appear to be a threat or problem to the Indians' traditional method of harvesting. It appears that only the leaders in the community realize the importance of paddy rice production in Nett Lake's future. . . . Perhaps a better informed residency would be more responsive."

Similar problems have emerged in paddy rice trials on other reservations. In the late 1960s the Bad River Ojibway, with financial help from the Economic Development Administration, set up a cooperative to begin paddy production. After investment by a number of residents the cooperative created levees and dikes in large, open areas on both sides of U.S. Highway 2. There was almost immediate conflict within the community as to the purpose behind "economic development." The cooperative faced an initial debt on equipment that proved ineffective – the harvesting combine tended to break the kernels – and the employment policy was unrealistic – too many were to be hired full time for jobs that fewer employees could do on a seasonal basis. There was little local knowledge about or experience with paddies; the water temperature turned out to be too warm, the water too muddy, and yields consequently low. Seeking professional assistance, the cooperative contracted with a university expert for a high fee, but the general impression was that the professor did little but observe the fields from his car. Still visible, the overgrown and abandoned paddies were cited by William Baker as an example of cooperation falling apart, "just like they tried at Odanah, where they tried to have a plantation. That didn't work."[99]

Canadian Ojibway have not been much more successful. Because land on the eastern side of Lake Winnipeg is marginal for farming, the Department of Indian Affairs decided to convert some of the land to wild rice paddies. Accordingly, it initiated a twenty-four-acre paddy project on the Fisher River Reserve. There were strings attached: most of the funding went not to the Fisher River Ojibway but to research grants for a botanist and management instructor, all of which the community resented. Although the government gave glowing reports about the success of the trainees, very little rice was harvested. One resident said: "Look at that. When an Indian does something good, they single it out. What they mean is that, by golly, these bastards could really do it. . . . To train Indians to grow wild rice is stupid. What we need is not training, but money for our own operations." Generally suspicious of consultants and university authorities provided by the government, the Fisher River Ojibway were outraged: "They give this fellow . . . $30,000 to produce wild rice. You know what he got? Two bags! My God! At least we wouldn't spend $15,000 on a bag of rice."[100]

Whether paddy production will ever succeed on reservations remains to be seen. Lacking capital, the Ojibway have been able to turn to federal sources—usually their only recourse—to pilot such projects. Leech Lake, for example, received $50,000 from the Office of Economic Opportunity and Red Lake, $10,000 from the Bureau of Indian Affairs to plan paddy production and marketing strategies. Leech Lake has had fairly good success with paddies at Steamboat Lake, stabilizing the over-all annual supply from the reservation by mixing paddy rice with the natural lake rice in the market. Since 1969, Red Lake has enlarged its commercial growing area to three hundred acres. Major food companies have expressed a willingness to supply machines and take care of processing if the reservations will assume responsibility for constructing the paddy dikes and seeding them.[101]

Indian wild rice cooperatives that *have* had some measure of success mostly began before the advent of paddy production. Many of them started during the depression of the 1930s with federal money as part of the general Emergency Conservation Work (1933) or, later, under the Indian Reorganization Act of 1934 (IRA), which promoted tribal corporations. Not surprisingly, the initial success of such ventures was reported optimistically in articles like "Chippewa Indians Undertake Cooperation," written by a credit agent about the progress of the Chippewa Indian Cooperative Marketing Association in Cass Lake. His article includes a photograph of the one-pound box label for Chippewa Wild Rice, showing an Indian drum with feathers. This, said the author, was the Indians' first effort in commercial marketing of wild rice. The association elected its own officers, paid harvesters a good wage, and produced eighteen thousand pounds. Members could automatically vote and share in the dividends. The group also marketed handcrafts, maple sugar, berries, and firewood. Even from a hundred miles away, White Earth families participated in the cooperative. White Earth also began a successful rice enterprise, with funding from the IRA. There the agency served as an advisory committee and the Indians acted as buyers, bringing the rice to a central warehouse where it was weighed, processed by fifteen Ojibway using mechanical parchers, and graded. Sister Bernard Coleman commented: "The successful maintenance of this cooperative venture initiated by the Indians themselves is of exceptional interest in view of the fact that in all reservations, except Red Lake, the Minnesota Ojibwa have heretofore shown unwillingness to cooperate with each other in economic matters unless they have been instigated by whites to do so."[102]

Whether from state or private sectors, most ricing assistance from the dominant society has been offered to help the Ojibway get on their feet economically with the ancillary assumption that, once the Indians developed their own wild rice industry, they could be removed from the public dole: "The Nett Lake tribe, to take one area as an example, could with proper management of their lands, be a proud asset of the State, totally self supporting, and devoid of any reason to fear the cultivation of wild rice by neighbors whose skins are prone to sunburn!" Indian people are perfectly aware of this agenda and know that welfare assistance is directly relevant to income from ricing. Fred Jones reported the remarks of one state agent: "The only reason why you Indians can rice here [is] because you're too destitute, and we don't want you running up to the welfare office asking for orders." Many Ojibway have had pension status questioned or welfare checks cut off during a good ricing season. According to Borgelt, "After the ricing season, welfare assistance was resumed for some, while others continued to live on their budgeted 'rice' income." Fred Jones cited the father of a friend, who was deprived of winter fuel assistance, and the Muscadoe family, who, in need of a well, went to the welfare office only to be told: "No, you pay for it out of your pocket. If you done those last year, ricing, take some of that and pay for your well." As a safeguard, many ricers are wisely circumspect about financial returns from the harvest.[103]

Many threats and assistance schemes are based on the assumption that individual Ojibway can make a great deal of money by ricing—simply not the case. This general misperception is based somewhat on the fancy price wild rice brings at the retail level and overlooks the small percentage that the harvester receives. Ojibway tend to resent the impression that they earn much for their labor: "See, the public doesn't know that. They think all the Indians have riced, any would have made that, but they didn't."[104]

A Source of Income

A survey of ricing income since 1850 reveals that, once the fur trade ended, Indian surplus production dropped. As the Ojibway shifted from a food-gathering to a money economy in the last half of the nineteenth century, they entered other work, like lumbering, guiding, and vegetable picking. Accordingly, rice played a less significant role as a source of income. Statistics from the last century indicate that rice provided a much higher percentage of income then than it does today; though they are erratic and difficult to assess, the figures provide a discernible pattern. For instance, in 1864 Pillager, Mississippi, and Lake Winnibigoshish commodity figures show that 5,000 bushels of wild rice valued at $25,000 accounted for about 30 percent of the total production for the year; the combined value of wild rice and maple sugar alone equaled Ojibway income from fur sales.[105]

These figures must be compared with the pattern that emerged in the twentieth century. (Remember that whatever the income from wild rice, it was a once-a-year source based on two to three weeks of labor at most.) In the late 1930s and early 1940s at Lac du Flambeau, off-reservation employment supplemented by income from berries, wild rice, guiding, crafts, and property caretaking amounted to only 23 percent of the band's total income. In 1946 at Nett Lake, beyond personal needs an Ojibway could harvest as much as 400 pounds for sale at $1 a pound, then considered a very high price for finished rice (fig. 11). Of the total annual cash income of $35,000 for New Post (Lac Court Oreilles) families in the early 1950s, only $340—under 1 percent—was earned by gathering greens and selling maple sugar and wild rice. In 1952 at Kenora, each harvester made between $200 and $300 for the season. William Morrell of Leech Lake remembered that one year he kept *no* rice for his own needs but sold all his 600 pounds to whites at $1 a bucket.[106]

Income from ricing must be considered relative to total financial resources. In 1952 at Sioux Lookout, wild rice earnings made up only 5 percent of Ojibway income. In 1966 per capita income at Nett Lake was $600, exclusive of welfare assistance and unreported earnings from hunting, fishing, and ricing. In 1969, a really poor crop year, the twelve Nett Lakers in Borgelt's survey made no more than $100 each. When asked what could be made in a good year, several responded with figures as high as $3,000 to $5,000, probably representing recompense for an entire family's labors. Average income for a Minnesota Ojibway in 1974 from ricing was only $88, but a good harvest, according to the Minnesota League of Women Voters, could bring a family $2,000.[107]

These figures, though random, suggest that even in the most productive years wild rice has been a limited economic resource for the individual Ojibway. That ricing can bring in relatively quick cash is, however, one of its most attractive aspects—*not* because of any great amount of money but because it conforms to traditional Indian subsistence expectations. Missionary Joseph Gilfillan commented perceptively on the government's failure to lure White Earth Ojibway into farming by promising them oxen, plows, and rations. Having learned from a Captain Wallace, who investigated the Mille Lacs Ojibway economy, that their income from all sources, including venison, furs, and wild rice, was greater than that of the average farmer, Gilfillan surmised: "The same is doubtless true of all the Indians. In the course of a year they have up to this time, from various sources, got hold of a great deal of money. It is a mistake to try to force them to be farmers only, as our government has heretofore seemed to try to do. Farming is too hard work, and means too long waiting for returns. They like very much better something which brings *quick returns,* as they had in their old life."[108]

The general picture of Indian underproduction of wild rice must be matched against *over*production by the Ojibway deliberately sustaining fur traders who

Fig. 11. Nett Lake woman selling home-finished wild rice, 1947. Ojibway have long counted on such direct marketing for supplemental income.

needed food. (In the nineteenth century, Indians sold wild rice to lumber camps for the same reason.) Not until European colonies were established well enough to produce their own alternate food commodities did the Indians taper their production of wild rice. Rice became less vital a food source, for example, to the Hudson's Bay Company when the Red River colony began to farm and métis hunters provided the company with meat.[109]

Well into the twentieth century, wild rice and other traditional food products continued as exchange – no longer for trade items like knives, axes, and pails, but, as Ojibway eating habits became increasingly like those of the dominant culture, for food. Alec Everwind of Ponemah went with his father and uncle to the store to trade corn for flour or sugar; Maude Kegg's family exchanged fresh maple sugar cakes for flour, tea, and lard, or they sold berries to whites and used the money for these items as well as for white sugar. Maggie Hanks Brown's family had to travel thirty miles from the reservation to sell wild rice to buy groceries because Rice Lake, where they harvested, was too far away from the stores on the reservation.[110]

Considering the time and labor involved in making rice, the financial returns to Indian people have been small – one reason many diversified their economic activities to work as seasonal laborers on white farms. Poverty never left the reservations, so any economic opportunity was seized. Red Lake corn was the medium of exchange for other staples until the fishery there opened. Thereafter, farming declined; one could earn from $100 to $200 a week at the new factory. For those who entered farming, income from ricing was not a factor at all because the harvest usually arrived at haying time and interfered with laying in fodder for stock. In Wisconsin, cranberry raking offered employment in early September, hard work for $5 to $6 a day. Late summer bean picking on nearby farms was less strenuous but equally unrewarding at 1½¢ a pound; even the best pickers brought in under $5 a day.[111]

Production of traditional crops for sale was not much more profitable. Red Lakers received 10¢ a pound or less for their rice in 1899, Leech Lakers by 1939 only 25¢ to 45¢ a pound, residents of Lac du Flambeau in about 1940, 50¢ a pound, and Nett Lakers in 1946, $1 a pound, which people were willing to pay only because Nett Lake rice was recognized as especially well processed. In short, wild rice, though the principal source of money in late summer, could never be counted on for more than a small part of annual income (see Table C). By the twentieth century most Ojibway had learned to sustain themselves through a traditional pattern of varied seasonal occupations. Prosper Guibord at Lac Court Oreilles is a good example. For forty-five years after he married, his yearly activities consisted of lumber-camp employment during the winter, sugaring in the spring, guiding sports fishermen in summer, and ricing in the fall. As a fall-back strategy, he kept some livestock and chickens, a team of horses, and a small garden.[112]

The winter months continue to find the Ojibway the most pressed, as Ayer emphasized in January 1919 to the superintendent at White Earth: "January and February are the hardest months here during the year as there is no work in this locality and if they contract for wood cutting or tie making, it necessitates the removal of the entire family to wherever they work and their living in temporary wigwams."[113]

Despite government assistance with food stamps, state relief subsidies, county-supplied clothing, and federal poverty programs, Ojibway unemployment continues high. Federal make-work projects, reservation law enforcement, and some tribal clerical work are about all the employment available. Seeking work off the reservation, Indians find themselves in the last-hired/first-fired pool, a situation exacerbated by the fact that most Ojibway reservations are located in already generally depressed economic areas.

Wild rice played its strongest role in a healthy Ojibway economy during the fur trade, when its supply (except for years of failure) was inexhaustible, its requirement by Europeans for subsistence ensured, and its harvesting, processing, and marketing exclusively in Indian hands. Since the middle of the nineteenth century the role of rice in the Indian economy has diminished drastically. Despite attempts to involve themselves in the new, white-monopolized wild rice market, the Ojibway people have generally been unable to compete. Where once they counted on their own surplus production as a source of income, they now view from the sidelines a white industry that, through overproduction, has glutted the market and depressed the value of wild rice. In short, for most Ojibway harvesters, wild rice has reverted to its initial economic role as a subsistence item, with small, surplus amounts traded or sold to contiguous peoples.

CHAPTER 7

The Law

If the cessions extinguished Indian title to the ceded areas, they also would have the effect of abrogating any aboriginal hunting, fishing, trapping, or wild ricing rights. These rights are mere incidents of Indian title, not rights separate from Indian title, and consequently if Indian title is extinguished so also would these aboriginal rights be extinguished.

– United States v. State of Minnesota, 1979[1]

WHEN the American frontier reached the Ojibway, there began an era of land negotiations and agreements regarding Indian rights and the power of the federal government. Through land cessions in numerous treaties the Ojibway found themselves limited in freedom and land on which to pursue subsistence activities. As American states and Canadian provinces were established, new regulations were imposed – sometimes at odds with old ones. Increasingly, the early federal and state statutes are contested in court today; to force test cases, Indian people have deliberately violated certain laws with provocative actions that have strained Indian-white relations. Much earlier, the Ojibway had developed their own system of government and created mechanisms to effect the smooth running of the wild rice harvest. In time, the states usurped many of these functions.

To restrain disruptive intertribal warfare along the frontier, in 1825 the U.S. government brought together Ojibway, Dakota, and other tribes at Prairie du Chien to settle boundary disputes – without giving up land to the United States. That was soon to follow. By establishing tribal boundaries, the government facilitated the next step on its agenda – negotiating with separate Indian tribes for land. In 1837 at the mouth of the St. Peter's River, the Ojibway began to cede areas they had previously occupied, beginning with all land east of the

Mississippi and north to the Crow River; in return, the treaty confirmed their title to many wild rice areas.[2]

Subsistence was uppermost in Indian minds. Records of treaty negotiations show repeated attempts by the Ojibway to explain how vital were their natural resources. Resource management and protection were generally part of the Indian way of life, although government negotiators were often oblivious to this in wording the treaties. In agreeing to the 1837 St. Peter's treaty and those that followed, the Ojibway did not comprehend that federal negotiators wanted the *land,* but thought that the whites wanted only access to resources. According to the recollections of Indian negotiators, they had specified clearly what resources the government could remove and spelled out what it could *not* take (fig. 1). Concerning resources on lands ceded in 1854, one chief recalled: "Very well, I will sell him the Pine Timber as he requests me to, with the usual height of cutting a tree down and upwards to top is what I sell you. I reserve the root of the tree. Again this I hold in my hand the Maple Timber, also the Oak Timber."[3]

In court cases a century later, however, the *intent* of the Indians in signing these agreements has come to be as much a factor in determining their rights as the wording. Tim Holzkamm, who extensively studied Ojibway treaty rights to subsistence resources, wrote: "In reading through many of the records of treaty negotiations I have gotten the feeling that the Ojibway were capable negotiators and were making an attempt to explain the importance of their relationship to resources in an Ojibway context. However, such communication was not always effective or incorporated into the treaty as the native peoples intended. . . . In any case, the binding treaty is not the signed paper, but depends upon the understanding of the signers. In many litigation cases the courts have accepted documents which convey this understanding. Unfortunately, in many cases these documents may not have been preserved."[4]

As land was relinquished, Indian fear of losing traditional food sources mounted. In the negotiations at St. Peter's, Ma-ghe-ga-bo, a Leech Lake Ojibway, requested that his people retain land with maple trees for sugar and sufficient lakes and rivers for fish. He contrasted the power of the whites with the Indians: "I have but few words to say, but they are the words of the chiefs, and very important. The being who created us, made us naked. He gave you and your people knowledge and power to live well. Not so with us; we had to cover ourselves with moss and rotten wood, and you must shew your generousity towards us." Lawyers arguing Indian treaty rights have cited Ma-ghe-ga-bo's statement as an example of figurative speech, intended not to represent the Indians' position as weak in bargaining but to elicit the government's generosity in annuity payments.[5]

In *Early Life Among the Indians,* Benjamin G. Armstrong, interpreter in

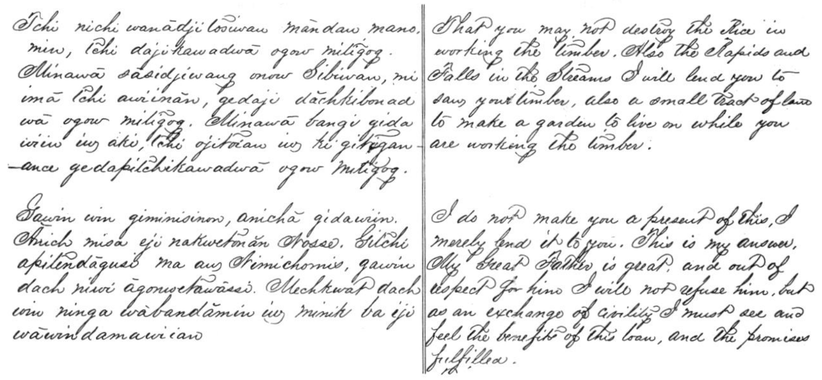

Tchi nichi wanādjitōiwaw māndaw manomin, Tchi dajikawadwā ogow mitigog. Minawā sāsidjiwang onow Sibiwan, mi imā Tchi awinān, gedaji dāchkibonadwā ogow mitigog. Minawā bangi gida iwin iu aki, Tchi ojitoiaw iu ki gitigan-ance gedapitchikawadwā ogow mitigog.	That you may not destroy the Rice in working the timber. Also the Rapids and Falls in the Streams I will lend you to saw your timber, also a small tract of land to make a garden to live on while you are working the timber.
Gawin win giminisinon, anichā gidawiin. Anich misa eji nakwetonān Nosse. Gitchi apitendāguso ma au Pimichomis, gawin dach niwi āgonwetawāsi. Mechkwat dach iwi ninga wābandāmin iu minik ba eji wāwindamawiiaw	I do not make you a present of this, I merely lend it to you. This is my answer. My Great Father is great, and out of respect for him I will not refuse him, but as an exchange of civility I must see and feel the benefits of this loan, and the promises fulfilled.

FIG. 1. Portion of the manuscript Ojibway chiefs brought in vain to Washington, D.C., in February 1865 to explain their *understanding of the terms of the 1854 treaty. The statement was recorded by a young Ojibway and later translated into English by Joseph Gurnoe, a mixed-blood Ojibway.*

treaty negotiations, stressed deceptions by government representatives and the Indians' complete misunderstanding of what they were relinquishing. Regarding the 1842 treaty at La Pointe, he said: "No conversation that was had at this time gave the Indians an inkling or caused them to mistrust that they were ceding away their lands, but supposed that they were simply selling the pine and minerals, as they had in the treaty of 1837."[6]

Clearly, Indian signatories to the 1842 treaty did not fully understand its implications. A protest from Martin, a chief representing the Ottawa Lake (Lac Court Oreilles), Chippewa River, and Lake Chetac bands, was attached to a letter, dated January 6, 1843, from Alfred Brunson, Indian agent at La Pointe, to James D. Doty, governor of Wisconsin territory: "We have no objections to the white man's working the mines & the timber & making farms. But we reserve the birch bark & cedar, for canoes, the Rice and Sugar trees & the privilege of hunting without being disturbed by the whites." Fearful that white encroachment would abrogate what they understood as their treaty rights, the head chiefs of sixteen Lake Superior bands petitioned Congress on February 7, 1849, for twenty-four sections of land at seven specified places, "covering the graves of our fathers, our sugar orchards, and our rice lakes and rivers."[7]

Article 5 of the 1837 treaty (fig. 2) had specifically granted to the Ojibway, conditional on good behavior, the rights of "hunting, fishing and gathering the wild Rice upon the lands, the Rivers and the Lakes, including in the territory ceded"; Article 2 of the 1842 treaty likewise promised "the right of hunting on the ceded territory, with the other usual privileges of occupancy, until required to remove by the President." The Ojibway understood these usufructuary rights to last as long as they lived in the ceded area. At the time the treaties were signed, no one on the government side expected the land to be settled for some time. The Ojibway were told in 1842 that "You will never see the day when whites want your land," but soon the attractions of mineral deposits, timber, and potential farm land caused the area that is now Wisconsin to fill with enough citizens to qualify for statehood. Similarly, in the territory that was to become Minnesota, exploratory expeditions in the 1820s and 1830s by Cass, Schoolcraft, Nicollet, and others had drawn national attention to the rich resources of the area, and its population grew, too. Inevitably, as Indian people exercised what they believed their rights to be, sufficient tension arose along the frontier for state legislatures to petition the federal government for the removal of the Indians. Accordingly, in 1850 President Zachary Taylor revoked the "privileges" granted in 1837 and 1842 and ordered the Ojibway off ceded lands.[8]

FIG. 2. Page from the St. Peter's treaty, 1837; signatories included various witnesses, agents, interpreters, and Ojibway leaders.

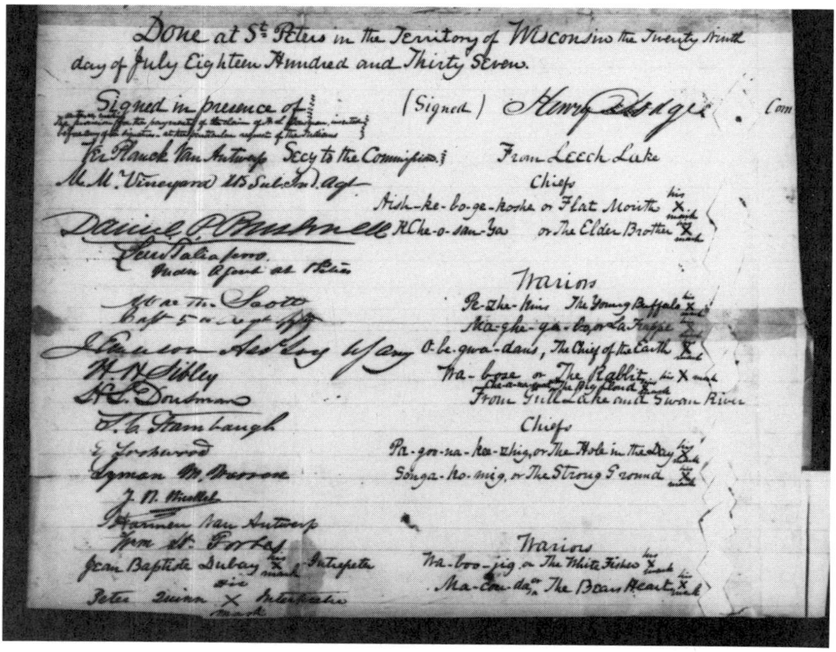
Done at St Peters in the Territory of Wisconsin the Twenty Ninth day of July Eighteen Hundred and Thirty Seven.

Signed in presence of — (Signed) Henry Dodge . Com

Verplanck Van Antwerp Secy to the Commissioner

M. M. Vineyard U.S. Sub Ind. Agt

Daniel P. Bushnell

Law Taliaferro Indian Agent at St Peters

H. H. Sibley

H. L. Dousman

Lyman M. Warren

J. N. Nicollet

Harmen Van Antwerp

Jean Baptiste Dubay his x mark Interpreter

Peter Quinn his x mark Interpreter

From Leech Lake
Chiefs
Aish-ke-bo-ge-koshe or Flat Mouth his x mark
R-Che-o-sau-ya or The Elder Brother his x mark
Warriors
Pe-zhe-kins The Young Buffalo his x mark
Ma-ghe-ga-bo or La Trappe his x mark
O-be-gwa-dans, The Chief of the Earth his x mark
Wa-bose or The Rabbit his x mark
From Gull Lake and Swan River
Chiefs
Pa-goo-na-kee-zhig, or The Hole in the Day his x mark
Songa-ko-mig, or The Strong Ground his x mark
Warriors
Wa-boo-jig or The White Fisher his x mark
Ma-cou-da or The Bear Heart his x mark

The order sent shock waves through the disbelieving Indian population. Sherman Hall wrote the American Board of Commissioners of Foreign Missions in 1850: "In view of the contemplated removal, the [government] farmer at Bad River was dismissed last winter and the teams and farming utensils were removed, and they [the Ojibway] ordered to make no more improvement there. They however went on and planted their ground as usual, and have nearly as large fields of corn and potatoes as formerly, though they had to dig their ground with the hoe. Most of them say they are not prepared to remove & shall not the present season."[9]

The rescission in 1852 of the removal order was the result of the visit of Chief Buffalo (Bizhiki) to Washington, of a letter-writing campaign on behalf of the Ojibway by missionaries like Hall, as well as of a resolution against removal by the Wisconsin state legislature. The Treaty with the Chippewa, 1854, also negotiated at La Pointe, addressed the earlier request for lands to be set aside for exclusive Ojibway use. Accordingly, boundaries were drawn for many of the present reservations: along the south shore of Lake Superior at L'Anse, Bad River, and Red Cliff; at its west end, Fond du Lac; and on its north shore, Grand Portage. Subsistence resources were taken into account to some degree. For example, the La Pointe Ojibway removed to Bad River retained a slender strip of land at the northeast end of Madeline Island for fishing. Indians did not immediately grasp the implications of their signatures. When Na-gon-a-bi was asked in 1855 by an Indian agent whether he understood the treaty terms he had assented to the year before, he replied: "My father, I was here last year, when the treaty was made, and I swallowed the words of the treaty down my throat, and they have not yet had time to blister on my breast." Not until a century later did the Indians begin to test their rights in court, winning such landmark battles as the Voigt decision (1983, see page 276), which continues to be contested by the Wisconsin Department of Natural Resources and white interest groups such as game-hunting enthusiasts.[10]

As the Ojibway slowly realized that their own understanding of treaty agreements was ignored by the government, they attempted in vain to correct the record. During the winter of 1864–65, the chiefs of the Bad River and Lac Court Oreilles bands met in council to prepare for a delegation to Washington. Relying on their recollection of treaty details, they drafted a statement and took it to the nation's capital in February (see fig. 1). They could have saved themselves the trip. They presented the document to Indian commissioner William P. Dole, who had it logged but dismissed it as "the same old chronic complaint." He returned the paperwork to the delegation, which took it to Senator James R. Doolittle of Wisconsin, who "wrote some lines to the commission which ended the matter."[11]

No sooner had Ojibway reservations been established in return for the vast tracts ceded than the ownership of those lands came under dispute. Several reservations, supposedly created by the 1854 treaty, were not to be exactly located until a later date. (Lac du Flambeau was not surveyed until 1871, Lac Court Oreilles not until 1876, and the St. Croix and Mole Lake reservations not until the 1930s.) Without clearly demarcated boundaries, it was impossible for Indians to protect many of their resources. Armstrong described how Indian access to traditional food staples declined as the land base eroded: "[I]t was only a few years after they were set apart that white men came and claimed to own every sixteenth section of their land under the state school land laws. Following these came men who claimed to have acquired title to all the swamp and overflowed lands on the reservations, depriving the Indians of their rice fields, cranberry marshes and hay meadows."[12]

What sort of land did the Ojibway give up and what was the nature of the property reserved for them? From the government viewpoint, the land selected for reservations was for the most part useless to whites, so nothing valuable was lost in the exchange. Minnesota governor Alexander Ramsey, in his report on the 1863 treaty with the Red Lake and Pembina bands of Ojibway contrasted "primitive" with "civilized" land requirements in describing what had been set aside for the Red Lake people: "[T]he tract reserved for their future occupancy, while abounding in game, fish, fields of wild rice, and other resources adapted to the primitive wants of the Indian, is, from the nature of the surface, which may be generally described as a series of impassable swales, entirely valueless to a civilized people."[13]

Ramsey's opinion aside, compared to other bands the Red Lake Ojibway were fortunate in retaining land that would continue to provide traditional sources of subsistence. Ojibway chiefs from other communities expressed alarm at the particular lands they were about to be removed to. Neb-a-wash of the Pillagers, objecting to their move to Cobmubbi (?), pointed out that: "[T]here is nothing there to hunt for. Whenever there is a rise in the water our rice fields are destroyed and we are left without any provisions at all to live upon."[14]

Not all Ojibway, however, were willing to acquiesce to treaty terms; in fact, many communities saw their signatories to the treaties as having sold out. The famous Hole-in-the-Day, chief of some 1,200 Mississippi Ojibway and a signatory, upon reflection was angered by the treaty's terms: "It requires many of us to give up good homes for poor ones, the very poorest ones that can be selected in the whole northwest. . . . gives us little but swamps or marshes, where locations can be selected, that combine all these elements of comfort and content to our people; that is, good land, game, fish, rice, and sugar. . . . True, we may find a little rice and a few fish, but not sufficient for my people, not enough to save them from starvation." Murders of chiefs by their people for signing away valuable land in exchange for swamps and other areas unsuitable for cultivation are confirmed in a letter by Catholic missionary Francis X. Pierz of July 6, 1863. He said that the chiefs of Hare and Red Cedar lakes had already been killed and that he had been hiding three chiefs from Mille Lacs for two weeks.[15]

Forcibly moving one group of Ojibway usually meant relocating them where other Ojibway already lived. The potential chain reaction of displaced peoples seems to have been recognized by government planners. When Major John S. Watrous, agent at La Pointe, wrote to Ramsey in 1850 that the Leech Lake area would be an ideal location for the Lake Superior bands because of the area's abundant fish, rice, sugar, and game, he cautioned that the Pillager band already living there would have to be compensated for the influx.[16]

SUBSISTENCE

Once settled on reservations, the Ojibway quickly found their subsistence needs were not adequately filled, and the establishment of reservation boundaries marked the beginning of their problems with access to rice beds. Even though ricing rights were never mentioned in most treaties, the general belief was that wild rice was necessary for Indian survival. Had the Indians abdicated their ricing rights, they would surely have been compensated in the wording of the treaties. Some reservations—White Earth, Leech Lake, and Bad River, for example—contained sizable rice stands. But the placement of others left the Indians bereft of ricing lakes or rivers. This happened at Fond du Lac. After Indian agent C. K. Drew visited in October 1858, he wrote: "The Indians at this place are disappointed and sore with regard to the boundary lines of their reserve. They state that the 'Rice Lakes' [especially Perch Lake] which were to be included in their reservation have been entirely overlooked and left out, and they are unwilling to relinquish their claim to them." The Fond du Lac Ojibway expressed willingness to trade a large part of the reservation if the lakes to the south could be included within new boundaries. The land was resurveyed and the oversight was corrected.[17]

Other rice gatherers were not so fortunate. When the Menominee were removed to their reservation in 1854, they were separated from one of their traditional sources of wild rice at Shawano Lake. Because their treaty did not reserve usufructuary rights for them in ceded territory, the Menominee head chief, Oshkosh, had to request special permission from the agency superintendent for his people to rice on the lake, eight miles south of the reservation, the year after their removal. By the end of the century their crop diminished to fewer than one hundred bushels annually because whites who owned land adjacent to the lake forbade them to set up rice camps. The Menominee people, who bore the name of North America's native cereal, eventually saw wild rice disappear as a staple.

The problem of access to off-reservation rice lakes continues to plague the Ojibway, who must often depend on the whims or good will of non-Indian landowners. Many of these lakes have become resort areas, surrounded by the summer cabins of urban whites who enjoy recreational motorboating and fishing. The Sokaogon Ojibway riced in the Pickerel Lake area until homeowners there deliberately began to weed the lakes of wild rice plants to discourage Indians from coming to harvest. One farmer at Lake Pakweiwong, knowing the Lac Court Oreilles Ojibway were about to arrive there to rice, went out with a boat and cut down the crop for hay. William Baker complained that whites owning land on his reservation required Indians to pay with rice for the privilege of access to the lakes: "You couldn't even go in there unless you gave them some rice . . . I suppose half. I never did, I give them nothing; they never give me anything."[18]

Some white landowners, however, were generous in letting Indians camp on their property during ricing season. James Mustache said that at most off-reservation places his people were welcome to rice, and that at Lake Chetac and Gull Lake there were landings they could use. He recalled one bachelor farmer at Lake Pakweiwong who was particularly helpful to the Indians during ricing. When they were ready to set up camp the farmer moved his young stock back in with the regular herd to make room for the ricers. He also brought them firewood, corn, potatoes, cabbage, and milk. Such benevolent actions of white landowners, however, have been the exception more than the rule, as many with property abutting rice lakes forced Indians to pay for access in cash or rice.[19]

In a few instances the federal government assisted the Ojibway in protecting and ensuring access to their rice stands. Almost invariably this help has led to legal confrontation with the state. Realizing that most of the land surrounding one rice lake on White Earth Reservation no longer belonged to the Indians as a result of the Dawes Allotment Act of 1887, Congress in 1926 enacted Public Law No. 418, legislation that created a protected area to be known as the Wild Rice Lake Indian Reserve, "setting aside Rice Lake and contiguous lands in Minnesota for the exclusive use and benefit of the Chippewa Indians of Minnesota." The state of Minnesota, however, wished to convert it to a public hunting ground and game refuge because the luxuriant rice growth attracted wildfowl. Ignoring the federal legislation of 1926, Minnesota began condemnation hearings in 1934 to acquire ownership of the land. After a court petition was denied, Congress in new legislation (Public Law No. 217, in 1935) restated the earlier act and authorized the secretary of the interior, "in his discretion, to establish not to exceed three additional wild-rice reserves in the State of Minnesota, which shall include wild-rice-bearing lakes situated convenient to Chippewa Indian communities or settlements." The secretary was also empowered to control water levels to conserve the rice beds. The costs of implementing the new law were to be paid out of Ojibway trust funds in the federal treasury.[20]

In the ensuing legal battle with Minnesota, the federal government reviewed its position that Indians had necessarily been made wards of the nation in order for the United States to regulate commerce with them. Siding with the federal government and citing a nineteenth-century decision, the Sixth District Court of Minnesota made note of the status of Indians in this paternalistic relationship: "They are communities *dependent* on the United States; dependent largely for their daily food; dependent for their political rights. They owe no allegiance to the States, and receive from them no protection. Because of the local ill feeling, the people of the States where they are found are often their deadliest enemies."[21]

Developing the "commercial clause" argument, the court went on to note: "If the establishment of such a relationship is within the purview of the constitutional provision, it would seem that the attempt of the Government to acquire a reserve for the Indians so that they can have access to a huge wild rice bed is likewise within the scope of the constitutional power. Congress must have assumed that the procuring of this wild rice bed would aid and assist the Indians in obtaining that which to them is a very important source of livelihood. If this is true, the efforts of the Government may prevent this tribe from becoming an indigent and pauperized group, and any enhancement or improvement in their economic situation unquestionably will have an effect upon, and bear a direct relationship to, the commerce which is carried on with the Indian tribes." The government had specifically pointed out that, since Indian people sold it, wild rice was an article of commerce.[22]

Not only did treaties exclude the Ojibway from many of their former ricing waters, but the location and timing of annuity payments interfered with the rice harvest as well. While Washington authorities appear to have been oblivious to Indian subsistence patterns, officials in the immediate vicinity were sensitive to the hardships that government decisions imposed on the Ojibway and repeatedly recommended changes. David P. Bushnell's report from the La Pointe subagency (September 30, 1840) expressed the belief that Indian subsistence means were gradually failing and that the October payment time interfered with fall hunting and prevented upper Mississippi Ojibway from returning home before freeze-up. A letter from Alfred Brunson to Governor Doty on January 10, 1843, urged payment before the rice harvest, preferably no later than July 1: "If taken away from their Rice harvests they loose [*sic*] more than the whole payment amounts to, say about $7 per head." Because of the distances many had to travel, some Ojibway leaders balked at the request to come to La Pointe to be paid their due. Said Chief Na-naw-ong-ga-be: "I . . . concluded it would not be proper to advise my young men to leave immediately, while we were all busily engaged in collecting wild rice, to provide for my people against hunger and famine."[23]

As "civilization" closed in on the Ojibway, other kinds of "official time" inevitably affected the wild rice harvest. After establishing reservations, the federal government built schools for Indian children to hasten assimilation into American society. The timing of fall back-to-school requirements for children who would otherwise have been in the rice camps deprived them of their traditional role in the harvest. Some eventually petitioned unsuccessfully to have school openings postponed until after the harvest in schools with a majority of Indian pupils. Boarding schools were not always successful in holding Ojibway children at such crucial times of year. Maggie Hanks Brown of White Earth remembered that about 1901 she lasted only a year at the mission school before her family took her out. An enforced roundup of truants in the rice camps brought her back: "[W]e were out there ricing with my folks at that time, when some people came around there picking up children to go to school, so that's where I was picked up to come to school here." Truancy became such a problem that one Minnesota priest purchased a Model-T Ford to capture those who escaped his mission school.[24]

So long as the Ojibway pursued traditional subsistence patterns, they could not be easily brought into white society. Converting the Indians to nonmigratory agriculturists was one strategy not readily accepted, at least by Ojibway males. In a speech at the time of La Pointe annuity payments in 1835, Chief Buffalo made it clear that his men deprecated gardening in the white manner as woman's work. The La Pointe Indians found it easier to steal potatoes from the gardens of whites.[25]

Once on reservations, Ojibway people tried to continue ricing much as their ancestors had, yet they found themselves increasingly subject to the laws of the dominant society. Eventually its regulations extended to the wild rice harvest, supplanting traditional Indian law. Just as Europeans owned possessions, so did Indians. They owned things they had made for themselves or inherited, such as canoes or hunting equipment, cooking utensils, and clothing, though they were typically generous about sharing. Resource management, however, was often more practically handled through communal rather than individual efforts. Consequently, native North American groups developed cooperative stategies for hunting, fishing, and gardening: the communal hunt on the northern plains to corral a buffalo herd using fire or stampede it over a cliff, the drives of Paiute Indians to ensnare rabbits in long nets, and the large community cornfields of Iroquois and Pueblo Indians. Among the Ojibway some of these old patterns of obtaining food supplies never completely died out. Well into the twentieth century, for instance, relatives still hunted in co-residential groups, each on its specific ground. Another group activity was the trapping of fish during ricing. Those encamped at Lake Chetac, for example, built a large trap between Chetac and Flat lakes; older members of the families sat by the trap to catch bluegills and other fish that got stranded on the platform.[26]

In Ojibway food production, clear distinctions have been made between group and individual modes of harvesting. Some late fall hunting for deer was communal. The scarcity of floor vegetation in the northern forest region, however, resulted in a fairly thin distribution of the herd; consequently, for *all* to survive, hunting grounds were staked out to individuals or family groups. In this sense, then, specified grounds were regarded as a hunting property, with trespassing prohibited.[27]

In the sugarbush, clear usufructuary laws were also in effect. Like trapping grounds, each maple stand was recognized as a certain family's; it could not be sold but would be passed on to descendants. This plot could be rented—that is, if one were unable to use the trees he (or she) could allow others to work them in return for a portion of the sugar. Someone who discovered a good, unclaimed stand would blaze each tree with an ax, leaving a distinctive ownership mark to declare the family's usufructuary rights to the sap. No one would think of violating these rights. Somewhat the same principle extended to late spring planting, done individually. Typically gardens were modest affairs; the produce belonged to the individual gardener for family use.

With the arrival of summer, the concept of property rights pertaining to food production relaxed considerably. Berry picking throughout the season took place *wherever* one found them growing. No one claimed ownership of water, so fishing with spears from a canoe or with nets overnight was open to all through the year.

North American tribal legal systems pertaining to property were an abiding focus of the Lipses' studies. Wild rice culture illustrated several theories distinguishing hunting-and-gathering societies from harvesting societies. Among hunters and gatherers, Julius Lips saw boundary lines clearly defined and rigorously defended. To trespass on the property of another meant certain death. With harvesters, however, boundary restrictions were lifted under certain conditions—the wild rice harvest was one. The rice fields belonged to all, and since the crop was of dominant importance to the economy, the law found its most important expression in a territorial principle that denied personal property rights to the cropland—in this case, areas of water where rice grew.[28]

Eva and Julius Lips saw the rice fields as the center of life for the Ojibway, since their economy was based upon the staple. This explained why living close to rice beds was desirable and why land lost its value the farther it was from the lake. (After treaty cessions, the removal of the Ojibway from waterfronts was—and still is—a constant source of frustration to them.) Communal ownership of the rice fields meant that the band's property boundaries were relaxed. In loosening boundary restrictions and deemphasizing territoriality in favor of communal rice production, Ojibway groups entered a changed relationship with their neighbors. No longer were they enemies. In times of surplus they were invited to share in the harvest as guests; they were expected to reciprocate when the host community experienced hard times. Ultimately this led to a sort of intergroup insurance, with a network of communities sharing in the general good.

Because the rice beds belonged to all, the Ojibway developed the mechanisms necessary to control the harvest for the common good through the appointment of the rice chief and his committee. Thus a legal situation prevailed that was somewhere between the usufructuary rights of the sugarbush and the divisions of communally hunted game. As Lips stated, under these circumstances work created property; what one harvested from the common source was one's own. Despite the communal social life of the rice camps, each individual was free to harvest as much or as little as desired and, for the most part, to process and retain it in the family. Except for donations to the rice fund or where the division of finished rice was prearranged, it was the individual ricer's property to use as food or sell. To this degree, then, while the rice fields were communally owned, their products were not.[29]

There were three ways to create property in this system: sowing, binding, and harvesting. The custom of recognizing established areas as belonging to certain families goes back for centuries among rice gatherers. In 1670 Claude Dablon wrote about the Mississippi Dakota: "They are content with a kind of marsh rye which we call wild oats, which the prairies furnish them naturally,—they dividing the latter among themselves, and each gathering his own harvest separately, without encroaching on the others." M. Inez Hilger, in particular, told of sowing deliberately to gain exclusive privilege to rice in a certain spot. The only exception she could remember was at Lac du Flambeau in 1935. There people scattered rice seed on the lakeshore a few days after the harvest, saying it was for future generations.[30]

Jenks's information on sowing came from responses to a questionnaire. R. Pither at Rat Portage suggested that sowing was done with excess seed once the Indians' needs were taken care of. Prosper Guibord identified for anthropologist Robert Ritzenthaler various people who had sown rice beds with seed imported from other lakes: John Mink had his at the south end of Lake Chetac; Guibord's parents and relations had theirs halfway up the west side of the lake.

In times of plenty they invited others to their rice field; otherwise, said Guibord, one never thought of approaching another's rice stand.[31]

Binding also marked a ricer's individual territory. While there was no visible evidence of a particular rice patch being sown by hand, there was no mistaking the neatly bound rows of sheaved rice as the marking of someone's property. Not until the twentieth century did the ownership of sown and bound fields cease to be respected. Economic motives drove people to harvest whatever they could, and former family plots—particularly if bound—were easy targets.

Such unwritten Indian laws evolved and were practiced at a time when, except for rice failures, rice grew in amounts more than sufficient for Indian subsistence. Inevitably the collision of traditional Ojibway concepts of land use and property with those of Europeans led to conflict. For example, much of the current dilemma facing Ojibway ricers is the constant pressure to increase productivity to satisfy the dominant society's need for land-use justification. Where whites have succeeded in gaining control of the production of staples formerly Indian (in the commercial overfishing of sturgeon in the boundary waters area, for instance), the results have often been ecologically disastrous. The Indians' whole legal system in regard to wild rice involved protecting it; from their vantage, whites seem interested only in exploiting the product by whatever means, including enacting laws to gain the upper hand.[32]

The "underproduction" of wild rice by Indian people was a source of consternation to Europeans from the time they arrived in the rice district. Unable to appreciate the deeper meaning of *manoomin* in Ojibway life, they paid little attention to its ceremonial use, were oblivious to the role of wild rice in legends, regarded the rice camps as mere social diversions interfering with the harvest, and generally considered the lack of concentrated effort to gather every grain possible an indication of Indian indolence or stupidity. "What percentage of the available crop is harvested?" was high on the list in Jenks's questionnaire of 1898; the answers and unsolicited comments he received from government farmers and Indian agents were predictable. The 1,200 Bad River Ojibway gathered only 200 bushels, about half the available crop, said Roger Patterson from Odanah. Peter Phalon, government farmer at Cloquet, Minnesota, estimated the potential crop to be 150,000 bushels annually. Presumably this would allow each of the fifty families ricing to bring in 3,000 bushels of rice: "Much rice could be gathered in a good season if the Indians could be induced to work. One Indian with the help of his wife, gathered in five days, 20 bushels and then quit, rice enough; this Indian and his Squaw, worked on an average of 9 hours ber [*sic*] day."[33]

The situation was clearly ripe for Europeans to apply the rationale of land-use justification to an aquatic crop that many saw as a potential economic benefit being wasted by the Indians. The Minnesota Department of Natural

Resources even criticized Indian harvest methods as "inefficient" because some rice was inadvertently knocked into the water and "lost." The Ojibway, of course, see this as good conservation, needed for reseeding the lakes.[34]

STATE REGULATION

Increasing interest—of whites and Indians—in wild rice as a profitable crop and the erosion of tribal control over ricers led to excessive and potentially ruinous harvest practices. Although the principal and most far-reaching wild rice legislation was not passed in Minnesota until 1939, there was earlier, sporadic action to protect the crop as a natural resource ("public property"). Because of the adverse effects of high water, for example, there was a temporary court order in 1924 to control the water level on Rice Lake at White Earth. In 1929 the Minnesota Department of Conservation expressed concern about ricing practices to the commissioner of game and fish, holding that "wild rice and rushes growing in public water are the property of the state in trust for the public generally." The legislature in 1931 passed its first wild rice law, Chapter 373, "an act relating to the protection of wild rice in the public waters of this state." Section 2 reads: "It shall be unlawful wantonly or unnecessarily to break down or otherwise injure or destroy any wild rice plants in any public waters of this state; provided, that such unavoidable breakage or injury as may occur when wild rice is harvested with reasonable care in a lawful manner shall not be deemed a violation of this section." Breaking this law was a misdemeanor, restrainable with an injunction by state attorney general or any county attorney.[35]

Until this period, Indian people had little legal recourse in trying to protect wild rice growing off reservations in "state waters." (They were not made citizens until 1924.) Even within reservation boundaries they faced competition from white landowners, for, following the passage of the Dawes Act of 1887 allotting plots to individuals, many Indians had sold their land. The large percentage of reservation tracts falling into white hands resulted in the so-called checkerboard pattern of property ownership that exists today. At White Earth, for instance, the Ojibway own scarcely 8 percent of the original reservation. Much of the property bought by whites abutted reservation lakes, prompting new owners, oblivious of techniques protecting the crop and assuring its annual replenishment, to take part in harvesting the wild rice there. Not only property owners but also visitors had access to the rice lakes from public boat landings or through lake channels. Even after attaining citizenship, many Ojibway spoke little or no English and thus did not comprehend the dominant legal system. Several decades passed before Indian people became lawyers, trained to attend to tribal interests and legally challenge whites about treaty rights, mineral exploitation, incursions on Indian property, and other external threats to their land. In the meantime, Indians had to count on sympathetic whites to represent their interests.[36]

Already experienced in offering assistance and understanding to Indians, Harry Ayer at Mille Lacs frequently corresponded with state officials about ricing matters, particularly in regard to the harvesting of immature rice—specifically at Squaw, Bowstring, and Leech lakes. In 1935 Ayer wrote J. W. Kauffman, agricultural extension agent for the U.S. Indian Field Service at Cass Lake: "There has been some complaint among the Indians here about the premature harvesting of wild rice. It is said that certain ones enter the rice fields before it [is] any where near the proper stage for taking, thus causing a great loss in weight, and the standing rice to become lodged so that it is never again available."[37]

That day Ayer also wrote Charles Morrison at White Earth: "Would like your opinion on the idea of having the State Game and Fish Div. take up the matter of establishing a date limiting the time of the starting of the Wild Rice Harvest. The law, I believe[,] already covers the matter, but it seems to be a question of enforcement. There are complaints here of 'sooners' [harvesters of premature rice] spoiling a lot of rice and no doubt you have the same trouble there." Ayer received an immediate reply from Kauffman: "It is very difficult to serve an injunction against those harvesting the crop before it is fully mature, but I believe your plan to have the State regulate the dates that various lakes could be entered and have the same policed with wardens from the Game and Fish Commission might help to solve the problem." Kauffman promised to take up the matter at a meeting of the directors of the Indian Cooperative Marketing Organization at Cass Lake. In his reply to Ayer he also enclosed a copy of a letter from the Minnesota Department of Conservation, which stated that any evidence of premature harvesting should be presented to county attorneys.

Ayer was certainly not alone in advocating protection of Indian harvest methods, but his voice must have had some impact. In any case, the situation had gradually so deteriorated that by the end of the decade, without controls, commercial harvesting machines had already demonstrated their power to devastate rice beds. In 1939 the Minnesota legislature passed Chapter 231, "an act relating to the protection and regulation of wild rice in the public waters of the State, declaring an emergency and granting certain rights and privileges to the Indians of Minnesota." Although no mention of treaty rights was included, the state recognized that wild rice was vital to the Indian economy. Legislators adapted the new laws as much as possible to traditional Indian harvesting methods by outlawing machine harvesters on public waters and specifying ricing equipment that conformed to Indian standards. Following Ayer's (and undoubtedly others') suggestion, the Division of Game and Fish was to oversee the wild rice harvest. The new post of director of the rice harvest was created, through whom the Department of Conservation would control the timing of the harvest.[38]

Section 1 recognized the centuries-old value of wild rice—"from time immemorial"—in Indian subsistence and its importance in the Indians' future economy; it acknowledged increasing abuses against the crop through non-Indian harvesting methods, including machinery, and contrasted them with nondestructive Indian techniques; it recognized high water levels as a threat to the harvest and the need for addressing the problem; it foretold hunger and impoverishment for the Indians and the danger of their being forced onto welfare rolls should controls not be imposed; and it declared the "moral obligation" to grant Minnesota Indians exclusive ricing rights on all public waters within reservation boundaries of White Earth, Leech Lake, Nett Lake, Vermilion Lake, Grand Portage, Fond du Lac, and Mille Lacs. (Red Lake was not included as that band never agreed to the Nelson Act of 1889, which allotted reservation lands in Minnesota to individuals. As a result of the refusal to accept allotment, Red Lake remained a "closed" reservation, in common tribal ownership, exempt from county and state jurisdiction.)

Section 2 made it illegal for anyone except Indians and non-Indians living on reservations to harvest on the waters listed. (The initial termination date—November 1, 1943—was subsequently extended indefinitely.)

Section 3 specified equipment that could be used for harvesting on all public waters in the state. Powerboats were excluded and only hand-poled or paddled canoes, skiffs, or boats were allowed. They could be no more than 30 inches wide and 16 feet long. Hand-operated flails no longer than 30 inches and no heavier than 1 pound were to be used for harvesting.

Section 9 forbade harvesting, selling, or purchasing unripe rice, that having more than 15 percent of its seeds still in the milk state.

Section 10 set a curfew on ricing from 6:00 P.M. to 8:00 A.M. and required ricing poles to terminate in forks of no more than 12 inches.

Section 11 enabled the commissioner to appoint as director of the harvest someone of proven ricing experience, responsible for testing the ripeness and enacting further regulatory measures as needed. The director would report to the commissioner the opening and closing dates for each lake or rice bed—such dates to be made public five days before harvest.

Section 12 empowered the commissioner to restrict ricing in public waters or completely forbid it where, in his judgment, it was necessary to protect the rice.

The Department of Conservation's game wardens would enforce these regulations and direct the harvest. The new system would be financed through annual license fees required of all ricers and buyers. Since 1939 the statutes have been slightly but not substantially changed, in amendments extending the termination date of Indian harvesting rights, raising license and dealers' fees, requiring residence documentation for purchase of a license, empowering the commissioner to harvest seed for research and reseeding of depleted beds, extending the length of ricing boats to 18 feet, and requiring them to have smooth, rounded bottoms.

Ironically, the legislation seemingly favorable to the Indian cause was no sooner pending than objections by Indians began. Generally, the Indian point of view was that the state had simply usurped the traditional Ojibway system for policing the wild rice harvest. The new rice chief was a white commissioner who knew nothing of wild rice and sat in St. Paul; his new rice committee consisted of game wardens already disliked by most Indians for their control of Ojibway fishing and hunting practices that had been uncontested for centuries; the rice fund meant to meet the needs of poorer members of the tribe became a licensing collection agency with coffers in the state capitol. The harvest would be supervised by wardens, and the Ojibway resented their presence; areas listed as off limits were frequently near white settlements—exactly where abuses by whites prompting the legislation were most frequent. In short, while the Indians were receptive to new controls placed on whites, they were unhappy with the legislation applying to them.[39]

Take, for instance, the issue of harvesting licenses. While the fee was initially modest—one dollar for each ricer and five dollars for each buyer in 1939—the Indians immediately voiced suspicion about where the money was going. Naomi Warren LaDue complained about having to travel that year from White Earth to Bemidji just to pay her fee to the game warden: "And I said to him, 'I think it is terrible for Indians to have to buy a ricing license now.' I said, 'I wonder who in the world,' I said, 'is the state going to make money off of it or who?' " Many Ojibway simply disregarded the licensing requirement, which invariably got them into conflicts with wardens demanding to see their licenses. There was no clear understanding of where a license permitted harvest, so the guest-ricer issue became confused. Fred Jones recalled: "[W]e had a party go up from here, see, you want to go up there and rice at Leech Lake. We got relations up in there so they generally go and rice. Well, this one fall, why they kinda stopped them and told them they couldn't go, and of course this guy pulled out his license. He had a license to show that he could go ricing anywheres where there was rice. And the fellow asked him where he was from. He said he was from Mille Lacs. He said, 'Oh, oh, I thought you was a Nett Laker.' See, apparently they are kicking all the Nett Lakers off the

Leech Lake." There was also feeling that the state was earning money without improving ricing conditions as expected.[40]

By the time of the 1939 legislation, the Ojibway perceived a real threat to their traditional wild rice economy. Some indication of the number of whites already ricing is provided by the figures for license sales that first year: 1,521 ricing licenses were issued for whites compared to 993 for Indians. While this does not reflect the actual number of Ojibway harvesting—one Indian license permitted a whole family's participation, whereas each white had to have an individual license—or show the number of whites ricing illegally, it does indicate the sizable number of non-Indians who had begun to rice for themselves. By 1970 only 25 percent of those harvesting were Indian.[41]

Licensing only exacerbated Indian resentment of white participation in the harvest. Although many whites had harvested for years, the 1939 legislation officially sanctioned the practice and encouraged newcomers. Whether out of curiosity, for sport, or for profit, their participation meant even more competition for a dwindling Indian resource. In 1965 only 150 of the 1,900 white residents of Leech Lake Reservation purchased licenses, while the general Indian impression was that most whites riced without them. Furthermore, the price of the license rose; by 1969 it cost four dollars. Ultimately, Indians were given the right to harvest on reservations without licenses, although a new law was enacted requiring buyers to pay one dollar for purchases up to one thousand pounds, and twenty-five dollars for more. Resentment was not directed at white buyers, however, on whom the Ojibway had come to depend for income. In fact most buyers, having formerly had a completely free hand in the open market, shared the Indians' dislike of state intrusion in their business.[42]

Few Indians thought whites were skilled harvesters; indeed, whites had demonstrated that they were a destructive force in the rice beds. Unable to distinguish immature from ripe rice, they knocked the stems too hard to dislodge the seeds. Leech Laker William Morrell reflected on what happened when the ricing legislation went into effect. At the time he was about fifty-five years old: "The state controlled the rice in all these lakes, but we Indians tried to stick these lakes with our reservations from the white people, but we can't do it. . . . They come in before the rice ripens, before it matures and they just cut the heads off, off from the stalk of the rice and then it doesn't reseed itself . . . what little bit left, that don't mature, see. Kept the stalk from growing, it deadened the rice. I told the conservation department, 'If you keep this practice in 15 years time,' I said, 'we won't have no rice in the state of Minnesota.' "[43]

Many Ojibway, already unhappy that reservation whites could rice legally, were certain the nonreservation whites joined the harvest illegally. Some who did not fully comprehend the new laws were under the mistaken impression that the local Indian council was empowered to remove white harvesters from reservation lakes.[44]

The requirement for a license to rice, in fact, was little more than a symbolic annoyance. On the other hand, state game wardens, as well as other state officials "meddling" in wild rice matters (biologists restricting areas for experiments or Highway Patrol officers enforcing regulations), were regarded with mild disdain to real enmity. The situation at Mille Lacs Lake was fairly typical, with whites as culpable in illicit trading—usually for alcohol—as Indians were in hunting and fishing out of season. The Indians could cite cases of entrapment, even by their own people working for the state. Fred Jones, in discussing illicit trade at Mille Lacs, noted: "They got rid of the whole bunch [of game wardens] but one guy that was mixed up with the state, Indian work up north. He's the guy that went up and bought a fish from him. The guy wanted to give it to him for nothing. You know, give him a dollar, then he turned him in." Harry Ayer was fully aware of such trafficking at Mille Lacs, but he blamed local whites as well. In a draft of a letter to C. V. Peel, special agent at White Earth, he wrote: "The Indians have broken the game and fish laws. I know of Indians who have illegally caught pike from Mille Lac waters and taken them to whites who illegally bought them. The same is true of duck, partridges and deer." Two sentences, crossed out by Ayer, follow: "I can prove that signors [*sic*] of aforesaid petition [a letter of complaint against traditional Indian subsistence practices, sent by white residents near Mille Lacs] have done the same. If necessary, I will give the names." On the other hand, Ayer defended the local Ojibway against the accusation that they hunted without licenses, saying that he had personally assisted in the applications of nearly all those eligible.[45]

The conflicts between Indians and game wardens at times resembled tug of war. Jones noted that the local warden had tried to arrest Indians hunting ducks in June, even though they were on reservation land. Such harassment extended to the wild rice harvest. In 1953 Public Law 280 gave Minnesota legal jurisdiction over all reservations but Red Lake. Technically the law did not empower the state to regulate reservation usufructuary rights, which had been explicitly exempted from the grant of criminal jurisdiction to the state. It did serve as an excuse for game wardens to enforce all regulations of the Department of Conservation, including those related to rice harvest. "Indian time" and the clock of the whites have never been closely synchronized, so it was perhaps inevitable that game wardens arrested forty Ojibway for starting to rice five minutes ahead of the officially scheduled opening of the lake. When Fred Blessing visited George Boyd's family at Mille Lacs in 1968, "they were in an uproar because the day before . . . a game warden had taken the wild rice away from Mrs. Boyd (83 years) for picking it on an illegal day."[46]

RIGHTS AND LITIGATION

State control of the wild rice harvest has been tested in court cases touching on Indian treaty rights and demonstrating cultural differences in perception of property. In late August 1972, two Ojibway, Everett Keezer and James Kier, tried to rice on Neds Lake (Anoka County) before the season opening. They were apprehended by a state conservation officer and cited for violating the Minnesota law requiring them to have a license to rice on public waters outside reservation boundaries. The two were convicted and fined twenty-five dollars each, touching off a six-year legal battle finally resolved in a seven-to-two Minnesota Supreme Court decision against the Indians. In a review of the decision, attorney Brian A. Hawley faulted the majority of the court and agreed with the dissenting minority that the majority conclusions had been colored by "culturally-bounded conceptions of property rights" and that the majority had failed to observe the "canons of construction" governing treaty rights recognized in the first part of the court's opinion.[47]

The defendants based their case on aboriginal rights of hunting, fishing, and foraging (including ricing), which they claimed were guaranteed in the Treaty of Greenville (1795) and the treaty at Prairie du Chien (1825). They argued that they could not be required to hold a license on any land that was unceded Indian property in 1795. The state countered with the claim that the Ojibway did not receive these rights in the Northwest Territory (created by the Treaty of Greenville), and that in any case, whatever rights they might have obtained in 1795 were nullified by later treaties with the government.

The Minnesota Supreme Court's ruling centered on its interpretation of the distinctions made by the United States Supreme Court between the concepts of *relinquishment* and *cession* in defining Indian title. This interpretation held that many treaties had dual purposes: when they recognized the right of Indians to occupy lands, it was a *relinquishment* by the federal government to the Indians of claims held by the United States; when they were intended to gain territory for the United States, it was a *cession* of lands from the Indians to the federal government. Cession treaties, reasoned the state court, therefore "are construed as a grant from the Indians . . . and as reserving to the Indians rights not [expressly] granted [away by them]," but when the treaty's purpose was to recognize Indian occupancy rights, by virtue of its sovereignty the United States *gave* recognition to Indian title, and the Indians reserved only those rights *expressly given* in the wording of the treaty.[48]

The defendants argued that the wording of Article 5 of the 1825 treaty was ambiguous and, according to the canons of construction, should be interpreted as favorable to them. Hunting, fishing, and foraging rights should be seen as retained by all tribes signatory to the treaty; therefore, the defendants had ricing rights throughout Minnesota and need not possess a state license to exercise them.

In considering the 1825 treaty, as Hawley pointed out, the state supreme court brought forth culturally bound arguments to decide against the Indians. The defendants claimed that Article 13 gave them permission to rice in the Neds Lake area today. That article included the following passage: "[T]he Chiefs of all the tribes have expressed a determination, cheerfully to allow a reciprocal right of hunting on the lands of one another, permission being first asked and obtained, as before provided for." The majority opinion held that the government did not intend to create one huge reservation in the Northwest, where Indians would retain hunting rights. Citing United States v. Northern Pacific Ry. Co. (1940), the court implied that the very size of the territory was too vast and, had it been intended for a reservation, the government would have given more land per person than the Indian population reasonably would require: "In the case of one of the tribes, if the treaty were considered to create a technical reservation it would have alloted to each man, woman, and child in the tribe more than eighteen square miles."[49]

In assessing Indian land needs the court clearly applied Euro-American concepts of individual property ownership, ignoring completely Indian traditions of communal use of the land for its natural resources. Eighteen square miles was more than a farmer would need to grow corn but not necessarily enough for a hunter to keep his family alive through the winter. Further undermining the position of the defendants, the court took the view that the treaty of 1825 was not really *with* the United States, that the government was simply acting in the neutral role of facilitating a treaty *between tribes* to establish boundaries and put a halt to bloodshed; consequently, the canons of construction did not apply. Reciprocal hunting rights, even if granted by the various signatory tribes in 1825, were negated because the warfare between them continued. Additionally, the court argued, rights that might have existed in the 1825 treaty were nullified by the government's later treaties with the Dakota (1837, wherein the Indians ceded all land east of the Mississippi) and the Ojibway (1854, granting them reservation land). The Neds Lake area, where Keezer and Kier were apprehended, was occupied by the Dakota in 1837. When the Dakota ceded lands at that time, they did not expressly retain hunting, fishing, and foraging rights and so could not have transferred such rights to the Ojibway. Despite the Minnesota Supreme Court's ruling against the defendants in that case, the rule adopted by a "slight majority of all jurisdictions" has been to the contrary, that relinquishment of real property interests does not constitute relinquishment of hunting, fishing, and foraging rights as well.[50]

In Wisconsin the Ojibway were more successful. On March 8, 1974, two Lac Court Oreilles Ojibway were arrested while ice fishing on Chief Lake by

Wisconsin wardens of the Department of Natural Resources (DNR). They were charged with and found guilty of possessing a spear and occupying a fish shanty without a proper tag showing the owner's name and address. A year later, the reservation brought suit against Lester P. Voigt, then secretary of the DNR, for attempting to interfere with Indian exercise of off-reservation hunting and fishing treaty rights. The legal team for the Indians was led by Wisconsin Judicare, a federally funded assistance program; Voigt was simply a symbolic target, representing the state, the DNR and its wardens, and the Sawyer County sheriff. The case examined the fundamental issue of whether or not the relinquishment of land constitutes surrendering subsistence rights on such land as well. Some treaties contain clear language on the matter. Article 5 of the 1837 Ojibway treaty of St. Peter's (see fig. 2), for instance, proclaimed: "The privilege of hunting, fishing, and gathering the wild Rice, upon the Lands, the Rivers and the Lakes, included in the territory ceded, is guarantied [*sic*] to the Indians, during the pleasure of the President of the United States."[51]

After a long period of litigation, on January 25, 1983, a three-judge panel of the U.S. Court of Appeals for the Seventh Circuit ruled that the Lake Superior Ojibway retained rights to hunt, fish, and forage on lands ceded to the United States in the treaties of 1837 and 1842 – encompassing nearly the entire northern third of Wisconsin. (Foraging included the harvesting of wild rice.) The court remanded the case to Judge James Doyle in Madison to consider "the permissible scope of the State regulation of ceded lands." In July 1983 Wisconsin appealed the case to the United States Supreme Court, which on October 3 denied its appeal, letting the lower court's ruling stand and leaving the state to work out the details.

To cope with the implications of the decision, the six Wisconsin tribal bands directly affected joined with the four Minnesota and Michigan bands of Lake Superior Ojibway to form the "Voigt Inter-tribal Task Force," chaired by attorney James H. Schlender, an officer on the Lac Court Oreilles tribal governing board. With assistance from the U.S. Bureau of Indian Affairs, the task force began to plan for tribal enforcement, resource management, the hiring of biologists to assess the ecological status of reservation lands, and a much-needed public information program.

The last item on the task force agenda continues to be a priority. The decisions prompted a rash of media attention, much of it confusing and misinformed. The general public was given the mistaken impression that the Ojibway had been granted "unlimited rights," at the same time that the DNR announced it would not enforce game laws against the Indians. Writers for sports journals and gun-hunters' groups painted a picture of Indian assault on game and consequent depletion of the state's natural resources, as latent anti-Indian sentiment began to percolate.

In compliance with the court's intentions, the state and the tribal groups began to negotiate interim agreements about how treaty rights were to be exercised off the reservations, what compromises were needed to protect natural resources, and what the role of tribal and state game wardens was to be. By mid-1984 they successfully arrived at four agreements, concerning deer hunting, ice fishing, trapping, and open-water fishing.

The confrontations between Indians and whites over hunting and fishing are important to understand because off-reservation ricing rights, yet to be tested, are covered in the Voigt decision. The turbulence over Indian deer-hunting rights has subsided somewhat. Open-water fishing is a far more sensitive issue, for several reasons. The army of gun hunters who descend on northern woods each fall is there for a limited period, whereas fishing season is much longer and, compared to deer hunting, of greater economic importance to the region as a component of the tourism and resort business. The anticipated "slaughter" of deer by Indians on off-reservation lands has proved vastly exaggerated. Despite the longer hunting season worked out for them, in 1984 Ojibway took fewer than 700 deer, less than .3 percent of the total kill for the state. There do remain areas of controversy – tribal insistence, for example, on permission to carry uncased weapons in cars and to hunt from moving vehicles.[52]

The fishing issue, however, pits Indian subsistence directly against the desires of people who fish for sport and is consequently seen as affecting tourism adversely. Whereas gun hunters of all races use the same weapons and follow much the same tactics in pursuit of their prey, the traditional, aboriginal Ojibway methods of harvesting fish – with gill nets and spears – fly in the faces of non-Indian sport fishers who, in their search for trophy fish, are limited by state game laws to lure-and-line fishing, with strictly enforced size and number restrictions and limited hours. Whites are also adamantly against Indian fishing during spawning.

Indian deer and fish kills are almost exclusively for subsistence, as they were traditionally. To be sure, over the years some Ojibway have attempted illegally to sell venison or walleye pike for personal profit. For the most part, however, they use deer and fish for food on reservations, where the low per-capita income is reflected in the starch-heavy, protein-deficient diet characteristic of many of America's poor. (From years of association with Indian people, this author can safely state that food in reservation households is rarely if ever wasted.)

Laws affecting wild rice in Wisconsin were drafted later than those already mentioned, partly because harvests were comparatively small and the bulk of the crop was customarily retained by Indians for home consumption and modest sales. (Wisconsin from 1960 to 1970 accounted for only 5 percent of wild rice in the world commercial market.) Incursions into the rice business by non-Indians in that state were not particularly disruptive until after World War II, when whites began to realize the potential profit of the crop. Many of the same problems emerged that had in Minnesota. Most non-Indians held full-time jobs and had only weekends free for harvest. When they had the chance, they tended to knock rice around the clock—some staying on the lakes all night long. The Sokaogon Ojibway complained that whites using rowboats far too wide cut destructive swaths through the rice fields: "They would leave a big trail and all the rice would be pushed down. They would use broom sticks, and the weight of the sticks would break the stalks."[53]

Wisconsin enacted state laws, similar to those in Minnesota, forbidding motorboats and setting restrictions on the size of boats and ricing sticks. Indians were given exclusive rights to harvest within reservation boundaries, although they needed licenses to rice on public waters outside the reservations. The harvest season on many lakes was set by the DNR in consultation with the various Indian rice committees. In the wake of the 1983 Voigt decision recognizing off-reservation treaty rights, the department enacted even more positive regulations to protect the rice beds, asking Ojibway to identify lakes most needing attention. Harvest license fees were increased and funds earmarked for reseeding projects.

Problems common to Indian harvesters in the United States have occurred north of the border as well. The situation in Canada, however, is considerably different, reflecting the general legal status of Canadian Indians dealing with the government. In 1873 the Canadian government signed Treaty Number Three with twenty-five bands of Ontario Indians. The agreement applied to an area of 55,000 square miles, where some 7,500 Indians (mostly Ojibway) live today. Although the official version of the treaty does not mention ricing rights, the Indians possess a document that (they claim) does. Signed by the two métis interpreters for the Ojibway during treaty negotiations, it states explicitly that "The Indians will be free as by the past for their hunting and rice harvest." The Indian power of appeal was greatly weakened in 1888, when a court ruling gave the province rather than the national government jurisdiction over natural resources, including wild rice. An 1894 agreement between the national and provincial governments further clarified the reserve boundaries, including water boundaries as part of reserve lands. These were to be surveyed from one headland to another by the province, but the surveys have never been done, leaving in question which rice stands belong to the reserves. Indians hoped the 1959 Wild Rice Harvesting Act would clarify the issue, but it did not. The act created ten "block areas" as wild rice harvesting sections, which Indians interpreted as government recognition of their ricing rights. Actually, the act only left the question of boundaries and ricing privileges in limbo, vulnerable to later assault by non-Indian ricing interests and the Ministry of Natural Resources.[54]

Many of the Canadian Indian ricing problems can be attributed to the energy concerns of Canada's growing population and economy. Lake of the Woods—traditionally an Ojibway ricing area—is part of a huge water system now managed by a control board representing both national and provincial interests. The system is overseen by engineers of Environment Canada, the Ontario Ministry of Natural Resources, Ontario Hydro, and Manitoba Hydro, charged with ensuring multiple use of the water "for domestic and sanitary purposes, navigation, fishing, power, irrigation and reclamation." Under their control, Lake of the Woods is used as a holding tank for water producing 30 percent of northwestern Ontario's power and 25 percent of Manitoba's. The control board is permitted level variances to 5¼ feet—between 1,056 and 1,061¼ feet. Because of the drastic effects of improper water levels on wild rice growth, the crop fluctuates in size annually according to the whims of the board. In about 1973 the board flooded the wild rice fields, claiming that higher water was needed to generate hydroelectric power. In 1977 there was a bumper crop, but the following year the board kept the lake two feet higher, resulting in total crop failure. The Ontario Ojibway managed to glean fifteen thousand pounds of rice from nearby rivers, solely because the rice there was protected by water-control structures. Ironically, this happened at a time when the government was using the argument of Indian underproduction to urge development of a wild rice industry. Chief Fred Copenace of Big Grassy Reserve pointed out the government's duplicity: "On the one hand the Ministry of Natural Resources says there's a 20 million dollar crop of wild rice on Lake of the Woods. Then they allow the Board to raise the water levels and drown the rice!"

Indian complaints about water levels on the lake led to a debate with the Lake of the Woods Control Board. The latter insisted that the 1978 crop failure was due to weather, arguing that ricing had also been poor on unregulated lakes that year. The Ontario Ojibway chiefs had statistics to back their claim that water levels *had* to be at fault. For the period 1966 to 1976 they showed that, whereas the annual Manitoba rice harvest, unaffected by water controls, fluctuated in yield from approximately 115,194 to 593,000 pounds, the Kenora (Lake of the Woods) crop showed a fluctuation of from near zero, total crop failure, to 1,127,000 pounds—clear proof that water control was the problem.

In the meantime, Ontario rice processors had been watching developments across the border in Manitoba and particularly in Minnesota, where the paddy rice industry appeared to be booming. For topographical and ecological reasons, the Ontario rice area did not lend itself to paddy development, but the argument of Indian underproduction continued, and processors began to lobby the provincial legislature to encourage commercial development by granting more harvesting licenses to non-Indians and seeding new lakes. The Ministry of Natural Resources responded in 1977 with a proposal for a new wild rice act to facilitate industrial growth of the rice business. The proposed act would have undermined totally the ricing rights, however vaguely worded, achieved by Indians in the 1959 Wild Rice Harvesting Act. It called for elimination of the block system and ending *de facto* recognition of the Indians' exclusive harvesting rights in many of their most traditional waters—Lake of the Woods, for example. The new act would have given a monopoly to Ontario rice processors by establishing their right of first refusal for all green rice harvested in the province. The proposal met with immediate opposition from Indians, whose cause was joined by many whites. The joint outcry was sufficient to prompt an investigation by the Ontario Royal Commission on the Northern Environment, which ultimately recommended a freeze on changes in the existing statutes and a five-year moratorium on granting new licenses to non-Indian harvesters: "[T]he government of Ontario should not implement any new policy on wild rice which would weaken the Indians' position in this industry. During the next five years, the Indians should be given the opportunity to develop a viable wild rice industry on their own." To assist the Indians the government decided to fund the research necessary to develop a stable reserve economy based on the wild rice industry.

This compromise did little to satisfy either side. On one hand, it produced backlash cries of "reverse discrimination" from rice processors, who hastened to form the Ontario Wild Rice Producers' Association. Although the association gained the support of three ministers, it failed to divide Indian opposition by soliciting nonstatus Indians (for example, women who, due to marriage with whites, were not recognized by the Canadian government as part of a designated band) and métis to join. These native people preferred to maintain alliance with the Ontario chiefs and continue ricing with the Ojibway bands. On the other hand, the Indians perceived the five-year moratorium to develop a viable industry as a deadline, which made them justifiably nervous. Reassurances from the province that "traditional harvesting areas" (only a few selected bays in each block) would remain in Indian hands had little calming effect. Even if the Indians could achieve a functioning industry by the end of five years, the remainder of the waters with dam control and seeding supported by the government would be open to harvesting by anyone, and the competition would be overwhelming. Meanwhile, rice processors continued to press for industry development on "Crown lands," which the Indians had always considered their territory.

Behind all such efforts of the white majority to open up "Indian territory" for economic development is the old land-use argument of Euro-Americans – a justification still asserted in promoting the interests of the non-Indian wild rice industry. In the mid-1970s, Leo Bernier, minister of natural resources and member of the Ontario provincial parliament since 1966, issued reports purporting to show Indian underutilization of the available wild rice crop. The figures of 20 percent harvested for 1975 and 10 percent for 1976 created the impression that the Indians were squandering a valuable natural resource and that Indian lands should therefore be opened to others for wild rice harvesting. The Grand Council Treaty Three, an organization of chiefs, questioned the validity of the statistics. Many of the ministry's figures were obtained through aerial photographs of known and suspected rice stands. After acreage was calculated, the plants in one-meter plots and the seeds on each plant head were counted. The Indians stressed that genetic differences in rice stands affect poundage and that "available amount" estimates were optimal, without taking into account what could actually be harvested. The figures ignored that some stands were inaccessible and that others might not mature. Beyond that, the ministry counted on statistics provided by the rice buyers; when the figures were not forthcoming, the ministry simply guessed. Buyers who gave figures did not include what the Ojibway harvested themselves to sell on the side. Even by the ministry's own report, noted its opponents, only 40 to 60 percent of the crop could be harvested, given maximum effort and no losses to wind or rain. The ministry's proposal to take over Indian land because of perceived underproduction was likened "to telling a farmer that a temporarily fallow field on his land, or a section he planned to put in oats next year, would be taken away from him because oats were not growing on it at the moment or were not growing thickly enough."

Throughout the period of new proposals and adverse Indian reaction, the newly formed Ontario Rice Producers' Association grew more and more eager to begin competition on a grander scale with neighbors. Association member Hugh Carlson said, "My main beef is that while Ontario is dilly-dallying about policies and regulations, Manitoba and Minnesota are going ahead developing a thriving industry."

Throughout the period of government-imposed regulations on ricing, Ojibway people for the most part have been driven by the need for self-protection and by anger that age-old rights and harvest controls were usurped by the state. In various testimony, elders in the twentieth century have expressed astonishment at the course of events and revealed a general naïveté concerning settlements between their ancestors and the whites. Dan White of Leech Lake, for example, spoke vaguely about some treaty in the distant past in which the chief had ceded away land but with certain restrictions: "On that treaty he said that he didn't want the white man to have the privilege to rice . . . it never entered to the white man's mind that, he never ate rice or had any rice or have anything to do with that at that time."[55] It remains, however, for the closer scrutiny of treaty rights and new legal cases to clarify many of the unresolved legal issues concerning wild rice.

CHAPTER 8

The Future

Persistence of traditional modes of camp life until quite recently and continued uses of traditional forms of leadership . . . stand alongside a growing participation in the cash economy of the white-dominated wild rice industry. Although the traditionally accepted boundaries for the exploitation of wild rice have been disputed, the critical factor of long term Indian-white interdependence in this realm was recognized early. . . . Any consideration of "aboriginal" patterns in the utilization of wild rice will have to come to grips with this symbiosis. It is especially crucial to contemporary Ojibwa culture, a part [of] which involves a pattern of political jockeying for scarce resources. —*Robert Jarvenpa, 1971*[1]

WHAT ROLE can the Ojibway expect wild rice to play in their future? Paddy rice production has exploded into a white-controlled industry, and decisions by state and federal legislatures and courts continue to affect the Ojibway land base, harvesting activities, treaty rights, and general economy. Because many issues remain unresolved, a kind of limbo exists, in which Indian people rice with little clear idea of how thereby to improve their economic status. Neither is it clear that all Ojibway desire to exploit this resource. Some, such as Chief Peter Kelly in Ontario, have watched their people's land and fish resources dwindle and see ricing as the last, best hope for a native industry: "Manomin belongs to the Anishinahbaig. . . . Wild rice is our tradition, our right. It is non-negotiable." But many others persist in more conservative attitudes and express feelings about the significance of wild rice in their lives beyond economics; there is some resentment at the intrusion of the market place into the cultural sphere of wild rice. Although economic destitution induced the Ojibway to sell rice for supplemental income, most had modest, informal rice dealings. In the 1960s, when paddy production became a reality and wild rice became big business, the small size and informality of Indian sales became so disadvantageous that many people stopped selling rice altogether. When Kathren Borgelt sampled public opinion about the introduction of paddy rice at Nett Lake, one resident told her, "It will knock out the husband and wife who go out ricing." This reply reflects as much a *cultural* as an economic concern. Generally the more conservative Ojibway—those closest to the traditional culture—are less involved in selling their wild rice than the more entrepreneurial Indian citizens.[2]

Statistics from White Earth are revealing. A 1937 survey of the type of housing families occupied reflected several patterns indicating a conservative-progressive split in the community. The conservatives most likely still spoke principally or exclusively the native language, eschewed mission churches for the medicine lodge, adhered to a traditional diet, and showed greater efforts at self-support, with less dependence on government handouts. (Homemade furniture was an indicator.) That fall, forty-three of the 150 families on the reservation went ricing. By far the preponderance of the ricers lived in tarpaper shacks—thirty-five versus eight families living in more modern, frame houses. Although both groups saved at least some rice for their own use, only four of the thirty-one families actively selling rice in the informal wild rice market at White Earth lived in the poorer housing. Since only eight families who riced lived in frame houses, this total meant that an additional nineteen "progressive" families were no longer harvesters of wild rice but simply brokers in the business, interested in profits, however small they might be.[3]

The cards seem stacked against Ojibway wishing to assume a greater share of the wild rice market. The industry is now almost completely out of their hands, and they will probably suffer economically from this monopoly. (Estimates of the Indian share of the market in 1986 were as low as 2 to 3 percent.) Because governments and courts still fail to take decisive positions, the situation may already have reached that point of no return: "Unresolved issues suggest that the wild rice controversy will continue until governmental initiatives lead to a comprehensive resource management policy that deals with the various interests at stake, or until one of the interests succeeds in dominating wild rice cultivation, processing, and distribution."[4]

While economic and legal issues remain unresolved, threats to the wild rice crop and the Indians' rights to harvest it continue. Some of these, such as tourism, are recent. Other problems, like fluctuating water levels and pollution, have been around for some time.

TOURISM

In 1986 Congress passed legislation adding Long Island in Lake Superior to the Apostle Islands National Lakeshore, managed by the National Park Service. Of the twenty-two islands in the group, both Madeline and Long islands had been excluded from the establishing bill (1967) – the former because it was considerably populated and developed, the latter by accident. The southernmost of the Apostles, Long Island is a narrow, 2½-acre sandy spit forming the northern boundary of Chequamegon Bay and sheltering it somewhat from the ravages of lake action. According to changes in Lake Superior water levels and currents bearing sand, the island has at times been connected to the mainland, forming a peninsula – hence the Ojibway have referred to it as the sandy point where the water breaks.

Wisconsin Democrats in Congress introduced legislation intended to add the island to the park system. In economically depressed northern Wisconsin, the national lakeshore had proven a business boom to the nearby town of Bayfield, much less so to Ashland and Washburn, situated too far south on Chequamegon Bay to reap much benefit from increased tourism. With two marinas in place, a third under construction, and projections for increased boat activity in the area generally, Ashland and Washburn business interests clearly would be served by Long Island's incorporation in the national lakeshore. The island provided spectacular long beaches on both sides, but access was legally prohibited. Because it had been recently discovered as a breeding area for the piping plover – an endangered species – drafters of the legislation were able to enlist the support of the National Audubon Society, the Wilderness Society, and the Sierra Club, despite the clear intentions of developing the island for recreation. Ignoring the lack of much local enthusiasm at a preliminary public hearing in Ashland and a resolution of the Bad River Ojibway tribal council strongly opposing the bill, its sponsors represented it as having broad support.

The Indians were justifiably concerned. To begin with, Long Island has played a vital role in their culture as historic, sacred land. The site of a key battle with the Dakota, it was also an important resting place in the Ojibway legend of the migration along the south shore of Lake Superior. Sacred songs mentioning the peninsula in this trek were known by priests of the medicine lodge as far west as White Earth Reservation, who had never seen Long Island but knew it from oral tradition.[5]

Perhaps even more important were the ecological and economic implications of the legislation, for the island acts effectively as a protective reef for wild rice stands in the Kakagon sloughs, just to its southeast, where Ojibway have harvested rice each fall for more than a century. In recent years the rice crop has shown signs of deterioration, and the increase of motorboat traffic, mostly by non-Indians fishing for sport in the sloughs, has been suspected as one culprit. Because passages through the sloughs are technically navigable state waters, the Ojibway are powerless to control boat traffic. Excessive boat speeds can effect wake damage to the wild rice plant, to say nothing of water pollution by gasoline engines. Additional boat traffic to Long Island is certain to spill over into the rice beds, hence the tribe's concern.

Various conservation groups testifying on behalf of the bill focused attention exclusively on saving the piping plovers' nesting areas, while congressional supporters, in what seems a contradictory position, extolled potential tourist attractions of the island – not only its fine beaches but also the abandoned lighthouse, which might be restored as a historic site. They rehearsed the island's importance in American history, beginning with the missionaries and fur traders. Since the Bad River Ojibway were not invited to testify, no one ever mentioned the role of Long Island in Indian history, even though it had once been the homeland of the Ojibway.

Beyond the island's cultural value to the Ojibway generally and to the Bad River band specifically, the economic aspects of the legislation posed a more immediate threat. Particularly in the crucial summer months – exactly when tourism is at its peak in the area – the wild rice plant cannot tolerate pollution or the constant action of boat wakes. Many people at Bad River, with incomes already well below the poverty line, count on wild rice to supplement other food sources and get them through the winter. A few sell modest amounts of rice to tourists passing through the reservation on U.S. Highway 2. As a product harvested on Indian land, this rice costs the taxpayer nothing and, it might be argued, actually decreases federal welfare costs.

Congress passed the bill (H.R. 2182, S. 1019) in 1986, albeit with language more protective than that of the original House version. What the future holds for the Bad River wild rice stands is uncertain, but this example illustrates how the interests of tourism endanger existing rice beds. Earlier, in other locations, whites who bought vacation homes on lakes in the north woods wanted sport fishing, water-skiing, and motorboating, and they frequently weeded out the rice and prevented Indians from harvesting. Should seeding new lakes to increase the crop available be undertaken on public waters, as the Wisconsin DNR and Great Lakes Indian Fish and Wildlife Commission have suggested, restrictions against other types of human activity may be required to ensure proper wild rice growth and Indian access to harvest.

Another threat is the potential for wild ricing to become a totally recreational activity. Wildfowl once hunted for food became so scarce by the late nineteenth century that stiff conservation measures, such as the section of Public Law 430, known as the Federal Migratory Bird Treaty Act (1913), were enacted. This law empowered the United States Department of Agriculture to set open seasons and punish violations, thereby discouraging market shooting. Another solution to that problem, also still in operation, made hunting a totally recreational sport, with licenses and strict time and bag limits; the average duck hunter gets only a small harvest for home consumption. Non-Indians have long been licensed to take part in the wild rice harvest; many of them have found it enjoyable and return to it as a yearly activity. No one has yet seriously offered "ricing for fun" as a lure for tourists, but should the total natural stand of rice on public waters diminish, there is bound to be increased pressure on existing beds, as more ricers, Indians and whites alike, compete for the crop.[6]

POLLUTION

Throughout the treaty period, the federal government offered the Indians goods, services, or cash in exchange for timber, minerals, or food resources it wished to exploit. Government promises of exchange were not always kept. As whites clear-cut virgin forests, drilled for and extracted minerals, or otherwise removed what they wanted from the land, they were rarely careful to clean up, often leaving ore tailings, sawmill wastes, and other ecologically unsound residue. In many instances such pollution has had an adverse effect on traditional food resources. After the 1873 Treaty Number Three opened the Rainy River area to settlement, for example, wastes from lumbermills in addition to commercial overfishing by non-Indians using pound nets severely damaged the breeding population of sturgeon. As wastes from the Fort Frances, Ontario, pulpmill were pumped into the river from 1905 to 1910, the spawning grounds of the fish were further polluted, causing a decrease in sturgeon population from which it has never fully recovered. Mercury dumping by the Reed International paper mill at Dryden, Ontario, has caused pollution to the English-Wabigoon-Winnipeg river system so severe that all commercial fishing has been banned. This deprived the Grassy Narrows Ojibway of food and income directly and indirectly: in the wake of the disaster, summer resorts were closed, and Indians were no longer hired as fishing guides.[7]

In negotiating treaties with Indians, the government usually selected for reservations land it foresaw serving no other useful purpose. The land given the Menominee, for example, was of no particular use for farming because it was so rocky. It is a great irony that a century later the Wolf River batholith attracted attention as a potential dumpsite for nuclear wastes. As crystalline rock has been judged the most suitable containment for storing nuclear waste material, it is not surprising that five of the twelve sites initially selected by the U.S. Department of Energy turned out to be on Indian land. The Menominee have protested the selection as a violation of their treaty rights and have been adamant about preventing the federal government from entering the reservation to drill test holes.[8]

Ojibway elders today are of the general impression that when they were younger, natural resources were in greater supply and of better quality. Although they may not atttribute this to pollution per se, they are in agreement that white presence is responsible. William Baker regretted the loss of the "rice bird," in profusion when his family was in the rice camp: "Things died out . . . look at that rice bird, we used to go out and shoot them with slingshots, and I caught about four or five of them, and maybe my grandmother used to take them and then cook them right in that wild rice. You don't see that no more."[9]

Such complaints include those about the quality of wild rice harvested today. Paul Buffalo remembered when the seed-bearing panicles of rice stalks were as long as nine inches and so loaded with grain that the heads of the plant bent back, hanging over the water. He suggested that artificial fertilizers (runoff from nearby farms) and a decline in the quality of the air have been responsible for less bounteous rice crops today. In interviews with residents at Nett Lake in 1970 Borgelt heard similar complaints about the deterioration of the rice. Not only had there been four times as many canoes harvesting earlier, but "At one time you knew where to go on the lake to get better rice, but not anymore. There is no consistent size. It is all mixed," or "Bumper crops looked like wheat fields that were four miles wide. Then you couldn't see the water and you could start picking at the shoreline. Not like that anymore." As ricing for profit increased, sloppy habits led to pollution of lakes with soft-drink cans and other debris. Buffalo issued a warning in his 1968 interview: "We got to cooperate with the whites and the Indians both, but I think the practices should be handed down with somebody that's experienced in ricing. . . . We got to study and practice on rice a little more. Got to bring it back. See, that rice is going to be a thing of the past, and it's going to go the way it is. They say it takes seven years to mature, but very little rice can be got now. The crop is getting shorter. The water is getting shorter. The fish is getting shorter. . . . Game is getting shorter. So we're losing a lot of game, we're going to lose rice too, if we're not careful."[10]

Exxon and Mole Lake

The Sokaogon Ojibway in Wisconsin, through an accident of history, were not included in the negotiations of the 1854 treaty at La Pointe. They began separate discussions with the federal government, which promised them a twelve-square-mile tract centered on Rice Lake. This area encompassed several good rice lakes, but the Sokaogon people ultimately acquired only one of them; in 1939, when the government granted them tribal status, Chief Willard Ackley managed to obtain for his people most of the land surrounding Rice Lake. Rice Lake is thus the very heart of the community, much like Nett Lake is in Minnesota. The Sokaogon Ojibway have always recognized it as a valuable resource, have systematically reseeded it to improve the stands, and have gone to court to protect the quantity and quality of its water.[11]

In May 1976 Exxon Company USA, Inc., announced the discovery of one of the world's largest sulfide ore deposits—the so-called Crandon Deposit—about two miles upstream from Rice Lake beneath the headwaters of the Wolf River, just south of the town of Crandon. The company estimated that at least seventy million tons of zinc and copper, with lesser amounts of lead, silver, and gold, lay ripe for extraction. Crandon, in an economically depressed area, entertained visions of becoming a boom town while the state pondered what mineral development could do for its coffers.

The potential for water pollution by mineral by-products, borne down Swamp Creek directly to Rice Lake, was clear to the Sokaogon people. The tribal council requested an immediate socioeconomic and environmental impact study by the Department of Commerce's Economic Development Administration. Anthropologist Robert Gough, who researched the issue extensively, wrote: "For the Sokaogon, whose community would be most immediately affected by the proposed mineral development, issues of sovereignty, self-determination, treaty rights and the federal government's trust responsibility transcend the state's mineral development interests and Exxon's corporate timetable."

At the time of this writing, the Mole Lake issue had been put on hold. Citing depressed market prices for metals, Exxon in December 1986 suspended its application process with the state of Wisconsin. Whether other such mineral strikes are likely to occur in the wild rice habitat cannot be anticipated. The Ojibway's only recourse to the threat of pollution, however, has been through the federal government and its agencies in court. Even in early treaty negotiations, the Ojibway addressed the issue of pollution. In recalling negotiations for the St. Peter's treaty of 1837, which allowed whites to clear pine timber from the land, one chief emphasized Indian concern for protecting adjoining resources: "This Straw which I hold in my hands, Wild Rice is what we call this. These I do not sell. That you may not destroy the Rice in working the Timber, Also the Rapids and Falls in the Streams I will lend you to saw your timber. . . . I do not make you a present of this, I merely lend it to you."[12] Safeguarding the rice fields will continue to be an important part of Ojibway long-term strategy for cultural survival.

WATER LEVELS AND RECLAMATION

Government and industry control of water levels has in nearly every instance proven disastrous to wild rice crops. All changes in the customary water climate of rice stands affect the plants, as seen repeatedly in this study. Problems began when lumbering interests built coffer dams so that logs could be floated downstream to mills. An official in the Indian office at Fort Frances, Ontario, told why the Rainy River harvest was slim in the 1890s: "[L]umbermen have been damming up the creeks, and then letting the water out and raising the water in the lakes and killing the growing rice stems." In Wisconsin, the rice crop at Lac Vieux Desert was destroyed one year by raising the water level with a dam. In the early 1920s the Northern States Power Company developed a flowage along the Chippewa River, which submerged entire villages, forcing resettlement (people from Old Post now live at New Post), and drowning many old rice stands. The government tried to compensate for this by setting aside forty-acre lots adjacent to rice lakes for use by Lac Court Oreilles Ojibway as rice camps. The rice crop in the Kakagon sloughs on the south shore of Lake Superior already shows signs of decline, perhaps partly due to the changes in water levels controlled at Sault Ste. Marie by the Great Lakes Commission, which uses Lake Superior as a holding tank for the lower lakes; in 1986 the levels were the highest on record.[13]

Canadian Ojibway face similar problems. Fort Alexander Reserve Indians rice at Lac du Bois, near the mouth of the Winnipeg River. To reach it, they must paddle fifty miles upstream, portaging around hydroelectric dams en route. Stanjigoming Bay in Rainy Lake was good for ricing until the Fort Frances dam was installed and rice beds were flooded. Ricers then moved across the lake to Redgut Bay, but in 1932 the water there had also become too high. Partly for this reason many Rainy Lake people began to renew their Bois Fort band affiliations and rice in the United States.[14]

Interference with the Mississippi headwaters, traditionally a rich ricing area for the Pillager band, shows just how vulnerable to governmental pressures are Indian lands and subsistence sources. Under the aegis of "stream management," the U.S. Army Corps of Engineers undertook water-control projects that confiscated Indian land for agricultural and commercial development. Among their activities, beginning in the 1880s, were drainage efforts that destroyed rice beds to make room for farms and building sites, changing the courses of waterways to aid in land development, widening and channeling stream beds, and constructing locks and dams – all to reduce flood damage to communities along the Mississippi River. Widening and channeling the slowly moving currents in the streams and lakes feeding into the Mississippi destroyed the rice stands; the dams, meant to facilitate navigation when the Mississippi was low in summer, never really accomplished that goal, but they did create reservoirs out of lakes and drown the wild rice. The harvest at Lake Winnibigoshish, once a major rice lake, now results in a mere fraction of earlier yields. On the other hand, where dams might have helped maintain water levels conducive to rice growth, Ojibway requests fell on deaf ears. To no avail the Ojibway repeatedly petitioned Minnesota for the construction of dams at various lakes on White Earth Reservation—Sargent, North Twin Lakes, and Little Rice—and a reconstruction of the dam on the Mississippi near Ball Club on Leech Lake Reservation.[15]

While the engineers became a destructive force in the wild rice habitat, other federal agencies sought to repair the environment. In the general spirit of cooperation during the depression of the 1930s, some dam construction projects were initiated to improve the harvest in other ways—specifically through the creation of brand new rice campsites at White Earth. There had been concern that the lack of sanitary facilities in the old rice camps caused sickness among many White Earth residents immediately following the ricing season. Consequently, sanitation was uppermost in the minds of the planners. The work on six projects provided the Ojibway with jobs as part of Indian Emergency Conservation Work (IECW), paying laborers about $2.35 a day. As E. J. Carlson, forest supervisor for the Indian service, said, the new camps "have the appearance of parkways. Each site was chosen in a heavy stand of timber, necessitating forest stand improvement which resulted in the removal of all dead trees, slash, bushes and other forest debris and fifty percent of the standing timber. A fire lane was made around each camp. Streets twenty feet wide were installed every one hundred feet across the grounds and, on each side of the streets, lots were cleared off and numbered. At one end of each street two latrines were constructed, in accordance with State regulations." (One wonders where the camp occupants were supposed to find firewood.) Additionally, 500-foot to 1,600-foot docks were erected over the swamp, pole-marked trails to the mainland were cleared, and 6-foot-wide canals dredged alongside the docks to facilitate the unloading of canoes close to shore. In all, noted Carlson, the project "saved the rice pickers a six mile walk." The caption provided for one historical photograph accompanying Carlson's article underlined the new improvements: "A Typical Rice Pickers' Camp Of The Old-Style Without Conveniences Or Provision For Health. Today The Indians Can Set Up Their Teepees By The Lakes And Still Have Pure Water And Health Facilities, Thanks To IECW." Despite the best of the federal government's paternalistic intentions, one has to wonder about the social ramifications of scientifically created "Indian rice camps."[16]

In some places Indian people have taken the initiative to enhance wild rice as a resource. At Red Lake Reservation they set up two large wildlife areas on eight thousand acres in the late 1960s. Part of their effort went to seeding wild rice in the area. Dan Needham was clearly pleased: "[T]hat's going back into wildlife, such as muskrat, and beaver, mink, ducks and so on. That'd be good for the Indians, they like to trap, you know, trap and hunt. And there is wild rice in those areas being seeded. So they can harvest the wild rice and in the wintertime trap for fur-bearing animals. And that is what the Indian likes to do."[17]

Meanwhile, the problems presented by tourism, incorrect water levels, and pollution to lakes will have to be decided in the courts. Although irresolution has characterized the decisions of the past, we may expect increasing litigation regarding treaty rights applying to ricing issues. Where this will lead is uncertain. As increasing numbers of politicians propose treaty abrogations, the termination policies begun under President Dwight D. Eisenhower may surface again. In July 1987 Senator Robert W. Kastenmeier (Republican, Wisconsin) mailed a "Special Report on Indian Treaty Rights" to his constituents, urging forced negotiations to nullify Indian treaty rights and threatening to cut off federal aid to tribal programs. Later that month, Congressman F. James Sensenbrenner, Jr., (Republican, Wisconsin) went even futher. Testing the political waters in his potential bid for retiring Senator William Proxmire's seat, he introduced legislation in the House (H.R. 3034) that would totally abrogate all Indian hunting, fishing, and gathering rights. Clearly, the Voigt decision supporting foraging rights and Minnesota's action against harvesting wild rice off reservations are at odds. In summarizing his review of State v. Keezer, Brian Hawley concluded: "[I]nconclusiveness characteriz[es] the more than 70 years of judicial activity in this area of the law since United States v. Winans was decided in 1905. The majority opinion does little to aid in the clarification of an already confusing and increasingly turbulent area of the law, and breathes life into these culturally-bound attitudes which have served to systematically deprive Native Americans first of their land and then of their livelihood. In short, the opinion does nothing to redress the injustice perpetrated on the only native Americans."[18]

Everett Keezer and James Kier were caught in the act of "trespassing" to harvest rice without a license on waters belonging to the "people of Minnesota" in Anoka County, an area without a large Indian population. Their arrest, incarceration, and ultimate conviction may have been due in part to the old image that persists among whites, that is, that Indians are *different* by nature, with all the pejorative connotations that word may hold. Having failed to turn Indians into farmers or induce them otherwise to conform to the life styles of Euro-Americans, the dominant society, still not ready to accept Indians for who they are, perceives their culture as foreign. This attitude is more openly expressed closer to the reservations; in towns bordering them, it surfaces repeatedly in blatant racism and open confrontation, sometimes resulting in violence.

When Harry Ayer responded to C. V. Peel in 1919 in defense of Mille Lacs Indians pursuing ancient foraging patterns for subsistence, he was answering the complaint of local whites about the seminomadism of the Ojibway. The Mille Lacs whites objected to Ojibway living in temporary shelters rather than in permanent homes. Implicit was the notion that unsettled Indians were likely to maraud or prepare sneak attacks on settlers—themes still hammered into the white subconscious by Hollywood. In trying to explain the behavior of Mille Lacs Ojibway, Ayer raised the obvious question: "Why there should be an objection to Indians taking advantage of these material gifts [berries, rice, maple sugar, etc.], and placing on the market products that would otherwise be absolutely wasted, is not clear, and to camp and live close to nature while thus occupied constitutes no harm to others and is benificial [*sic*] to them. That they move to the wild rice producing lakes is also true. They are the only producters [*sic*] of a valuable table delicacy that brings them hundreds of dollars. I have heard no complaints of their trespassing on the occasion of the wild rice harvest. On the contrary many desire them to camp on their land for the privilege of obtaining a supply of rice."[19]

The image problem, while continuing to plague Indian people, has economic implications for future involvement of the Ojibway in the wild rice industry. The state of Minnesota's first enactment of protective wild rice legislation, in 1939, was not particularly controversial because the motives behind it were conservation-directed rather than economic, and the new laws had only a slight impact on the marketing of wild rice. Charlene L. Smith and Howard J. Vogel saw the 1939 laws as a form of benevolent paternalism toward the Ojibway, one abandoned when paddy rice entered the picture: "As a result, there has been a recent shift—ostensibly for good reasons such as the development of the state's agricultural economy—from supporting the Indian people's conception of wild rice management to favoring the entrepreneurs." This policy is evident in the funding of University of Minnesota research concentrating on the commercial production of wild rice: "The University contends that any improvement in paddy rice will benefit the natural stands, yet the University is committed to conducting studies only on grains that will become field crops." Smith and Vogel perceived these developments as the classic colonial pattern of exploiting indigenous peoples to bring economic gains for the colonial majority.[20]

Smith and Vogel forwarded some practical suggestions for resolving some of the issues that remain in limbo. Recognizing the lack of financial resources available to the Ojibway, their proposals depended exclusively on state and federal assistance to promote lake rice harvested by Indian people. Still, the authors feared that unless the Indians entered the paddy business, they would face total exclusion from the economic benefits of the industry.

The labeling law passed by the Minnesota legislature has not been enforced, and it would not be effective since California is now outproducing the state in wild rice and is not required to stigmatize its product as "paddy grown." Recognizing this law as negative–it is still a source of irritation to paddy growers–Smith and Vogel suggested positive steps in *promotional* labeling of lake rice. The paddy growers have in fact begun to put small stickers on their packaging to emphasize it as a Minnesota product, "the official state grain." Smith and Vogel would go a step farther with lake rice, stressing that it is *not* domesticated but wild, hand-harvested from waters that are naturally clean and chemically balanced, that no fertilizers, pesticides, or fungicides have been applied to it, and so on. They suggested Minnesota Farmstead Cheese as a model, a venture that has promoted a cottage industry among state dairy farmers. To market their product under this label farmers must use a special cheese culture developed by the Governor's Rural Development Council and the University of Minnesota Agricultural Extension Service and must use milk from the farm where the cheese is made. Along the same lines, Smith and Vogel suggested that harvesters and distributors of lake rice incorporate as a nonprofit cooperative association, to take advantage of centralized billing and shipping. Their product could then be aggressively sold to the gourmet market, with advertising in magazines like the *New Yorker,* presumably aimed at a class of readers interested in natural foods and willing to pay extra for them.

Smith and Vogel's second major suggestion was the ecologically based management of wild rice to prevent unrestricted harvesting that might impair growth and propagation. On the positive side, they pointed out that environmental mandates now apply to all federal agencies, including the U.S. Army Corps of Engineers. The corps, for instance, has had to rethink its policies on the Mississippi headwaters. Its 1982 *Mississippi River Headwater Lakes in Minnesota Feasibility Study* at least encouraged the agency to consider the effects of water levels on reservation rice stands, which led to proposals for a mutual agreement on levels during the growing season, as well as a six-year data base study of rice production. Likewise, the U.S. Department of the Interior moved to study the broader ecological picture and funded a research team in the Sherburne Wildlife Sanctuary in Minnesota, in 1979, to consider human impact as well as animal and bird uses of lake rice.

While these signs of change and suggestions for improvements are promising, they do not address the immediate, fundamental economic problem: to what extent and by what means can Ojibway expect to reap financial reward from their wild rice crop? One solution occasionally forwarded by Indian people frustrated with government regulations and competition from non-Indian ricers has been to return *all* the ricing business to the Ojibway. Roderick Skead of Rat Portage Reserve said, "You can't fight for the rice in the board room. That's playing the government game. There's only one way to save the rice. Get the families camped out there on the rice fields, picking and stopping anyone else from picking." A resolution calling for complete Indian control of wild rice was adopted by the 1969 Tribal Leadership Conference in Duluth, with these words: "Wild rice should be a 100% Indian enterprise. After all, you gave Germany and Japan back their peaceful enterprises after you defeated them in war. Why not the Ojibway Indians?" A recipe book published in Minneapolis in 1940 carried this message from its author, Chief May-Zhuc-Ke-Ge-Shig (Clearing Sky): "We who gave to the white world Tobacco for its markets, offer now Mah-No-Min, more delectable and of greater worth to all. BUT we entreat you, White Folk of State and Nation, to leave to us, men, if you will, of the plains and forests, this our only remaining native industry. . . . Let Mah-No-Min live and give our Ojibways this their final chance to live and enjoy, by making the caring for this gift from the 'Prince of Harvests,' his exclusive right."[21]

Indian people are aware that their ancestors knew how to use natural resources to their fullest without depleting them. A recent study has shown that the Rainy River Ojibway produced sustained yields of sturgeon over a sixty-year period far above what commercial non-Indian fishermen using pound nets achieved over the next sixty years. Ojibway have always viewed government intrusion into the traditional economy with suspicion. As Lake of the Woods Ojibway told Avery and Pawlick: "Any inroad by the government into the traditional Ojibway use of the resource, and that resource is soon taken away. It's happened with trapping, hunting, and fishing."[22]

Some argue that the wild rice business has simply developed too much for consideration of exclusive Indian rights—particularly since paddy production. The Minnesota League of Women Voters pointed out that Indians had already begun their own paddy enterprises. It warned that should the price of wild rice drop, Indians hand picking lake rice could no longer be paid at even present levels.[23]

Sometimes non-Indians suggest that the domestication of wild rice by whites was inevitable. Smacking of assumptions of "Manifest Destiny" and tinged with evolutionist paternalism and a thinly veiled desire to get Indians off the public dole, an appendix in the recently published *A Study of Wild Rice in Minnesota* said, "To take the attitude of some sociologists and welfare agents that 'the rice should be left to the Indian' is to close the eyes to facts. Once the white man tasted the grain it was no longer left to him—it became a delight of anyone's diet. So the white man will eventually domesticate the grain! To curb the trend by stubborn, lethargic, do-nothingness will be to lose the business to another state with vision and the will to prosper its agricultural community. If the Indian is to be raised to a level of equality, respectability and become a self-supporting part of Minnesota economy, it is criminal neglect to let him waste his heritage and make no effort to better the one natural resource that is uniquely his."[24]

WILD RICE AND THE OJIBWAY PEOPLE

Ojibway who remember the past are generally critical of changes in the harvest and processing of wild rice. Most say that earlier people knew how "to take care of the rice." Ignatia Broker's reaction to the mechanization of processing and abdication to white regulations was that: "To the Ojibway, the new system was a desecration, for the first rice to ripen was to be offered to the Gitchi Manito [Great Spirit] and be carried on the wind." Other complaints concerned the cleanliness of the rice—formerly a measure of expertise and care: "They knew how to harvest, not like now, they did not dirty it, they even put on new moccasins while harvesting. Of course they were slow years ago; their containers were small. There was only one woman parching all day. Husking was only done in the evening."[25]

These attitudes are critical of the haste shown by today's harvesters, who work under strict time limits to pick as much as possible. That this has had social implications is apparent in complaints that people are too busy to talk to each other except perhaps to discuss where their boats should be aimed: "When the lake used to be really filled with rice, it was a happy, festive time. Everybody knew each other. People would be singing, laughing, or telling stories. And about four o'clock or so, the old Indians used to get off the lake and say, 'Tomorrow's another day,' having just gathered enough rice." Tribal elders look back with nostalgia at a more leisurely pace of ricing, when financial gain was not everything: "We used to only rice for one month, and then leave it. If there was any more, they just left it. They riced only at a certain time. Now they rice for so many hours out of each day, every other day. That doesn't do any good anyhow. They still wreck it."[26]

At Sabaskong Reserve older people related that before the 1930s they camped out for two months, picking one bay after another, allowing the rice to rest for a week before returning. All that has changed, said Shawahn Copenace: "We only camp one or two weeks now." Paul Buffalo complained that since wild rice had become a cash commodity, harvesters were interested only in immediate profits and not in conservation of the crop: "We want to leave some so it will germinate for the next year. . . . The generation nowadays never figures far enough ahead, when next year, and wild rice becomes wild rice, there's so much money involved in that."[27]

Inherent in all of these attitudes is the idea that wild rice continues to symbolize the old Ojibway culture: it is part of the Indian world, distinct from the white. The Indians exchanged timber from their allotments for lumber with which to build new frame houses and camped in tents while picking berries, but in the wild rice camps they continued to use wigwams. Harvesting techniques are at least three centuries old, and part of the traditional belief system is intricately bound up with the rice crop. Peter Kelly, chief of the Sabaskong band, claimed that the migration story of the Ojibway, documented on birchbark medicine scrolls, told of his people sowing wild rice wherever they traveled.[28]

Just as the Ojibway distinguished between Indian diseases and those of Euro-Americans, so, too, are the two worlds of foodways distant. Many believe the Great Spirit meant wild rice solely for the Indians. Even for those living outside the rice district, wild rice provides a certain identity; Michigan Ojibway near Mount Pleasant regularly sell wild rice at their pageants, even though none grows in the lower peninsula where they live. Insensitive to food preferences and distinctions among the poorer classes, the federal government has sometimes included American-grown white rice in rations provided the Ojibway. This is rejected just as when it has been donated to Southeast Asians. Paddy rice in particular is avoided as a creation of whites; some say it has a slight oily taste from the harvesting machinery; others complain that it is difficult to cook and becomes mushy. (Even non-Indians have been persuaded that there is a difference in taste. Former harvest director Ron Libertus, in a Minnesota Senate subcommittee hearing on the labeling law, convinced legislators to support the bill by preparing and serving samples of lake and paddy rice.) When a food store in St. Paul unwittingly donated paddy rice to the American Indian Center for its 1982 Thanksgiving meal: "The Indians refused to take the free rice, even though it meant their children might go hungry, because the paddy rice offended their cultural and religious sensibilities. Labeling the paddy rice as wild rice was analogous to misrepresenting non-kosher food as kosher."[29]

Older Ojibway remember their former diet and show continuing preference for the old foods. Dan White lived with his grandparents in a shack on Leech Lake and was proud to say they always had enough to eat of wild rice, venison, ducks, and fish: "I never knew them to waste any food that they got from the land and I never seen these people run to the store, only just once in a great while." In 1947 John Nett Lake, then about ninety and living in a wigwam, was particular about sticking to his "wild diet" and held in contempt all non-Indian foods that came in cartons or bags, considering them poisonous to his people. John Mink at Lac Court Oreilles preferred traditional food: "The Old Man often expressed a strong craving for the native Ojibwa foods and after a long denial would eat ravenously of such delicacies as fresh-killed venison, bear fat or wild rice."[30]

William Baker identified the period of wild foods as one characterized by sharing: "What they used to do—they had wild foods, *opiniig* [wild potatoes], hemlock, meat, *waashkesh* [venison], bearmeat, muskrat, woodchuck, they had everything. Now we ain't got that. We got porkchops, now, and everything you go and buy, porkchops, pork, steak, or liver or something, but when they kill a deer, they got everything, and then they divide it up, too . . . everybody hogs everything now . . . everything greedy, greedy."[31]

Giving food away was part of the older life style as was sharing generally. Alec Everwind's father lent his plow and team as needed, and his people at Red Lake worked communally in hoeing and hulling corn; Red Lakers with extra nets fished for relatives unable to do so for themselves.[32]

Sharing extended to all aspects of the rice harvest. Thomas Shingobe even explained that the Ojibway, by not harvesting all the available rice, were sharing some of the seed with the birds and crows. The rice fund at Nett Lake provided a certain social security; the physically handicapped and the widows without relatives got their yearly supply from it. Paul Buffalo at Leech Lake and James Mustache at Lac Court Oreilles confirmed that rice was given to those who could not take part in the harvest. This author was told of one family that each year arrived very late at the rice camp due to drinking problems of two of its members; as they tried to harvest the little rice left, the other ricers in camp donated rice to them out of sympathy. Although wild rice was never sold among the Ojibway, one might reciprocate with a gift. Or one might offer rice from the family larder in the course of preparing a communal meal: "We never sold, gave it, gave it away. And sometimes they'd have these big powwows, you know, maybe the women would get together and find out what this woman is going to cook. Well, maybe my grandmother would cook a big pot full of rice, one of them big pots. Each woman had a different item to cook." In such an atmosphere of generosity, reciprocity was expected, and people were supposed to offer their fair share. One Cass Lake woman asserted that, while a certain degree of thrift was prudent, idleness was frowned upon: "[I]t was never to an Ojibwa's credit to lack food, especially rice, and if he were persistently idle, he was grudgingly served, and made to understand that he was expected to supply his own needs."[33]

Because ricing is such a deeply rooted activity, most Ojibway build harvest time into their annual schedules as a matter of course. Many urban Indians return to their home reservations for ricing; others leave regular jobs in nearby towns for the harvest, even though it can mean financial loss. It is not unusual during harvest for an Indian to request time off or call in sick to get enough rice for the family table. Most who rice are culturally motivated; while ten of fourteen Leech Lakers interviewed by Stuart Berde in 1965 sold all their rice, eleven in the group said they would go ricing even if no money were to be made. In 1986 twenty-one of twenty-two Mole Lakers said the same. Of those who rice for sale, most keep five to ten pounds for special home occasions or ritual use. Ricing is also an activity that older people continue to participate in. When Paul Buffalo retired, ricing was the *only* work he still did.[34]

For cultural reasons alone, the Ojibway people will probably never give up ricing willingly. Norma Smith of Mole Lake summed up her feelings:

> We have a deep feeling of satisfaction and gratitude as we sack up the rice again toward evening. We do not feel the ache in our arms as we anticipate the gain. If the rice is light, we will sell it for seed. If it is heavy, we will take it home to cure for eating. And tomorrow we will be back again for another day of picking. . . . I often wonder what my children will do when the rice is gone forever. What will take its place when this last tradition is gone?[35]

Reference Notes

ABBREVIATIONS

ABCFM	American Board of Commissioners of Foreign Missions, Papers, Houghton Library, Harvard University, Cambridge, Mass.
Folklife Archives	Office of Folklife Programs Archives, Smithsonian Institution, Washington, D.C.
GPO	Government Printing Office
Jesuit Relations	Reuben G. Thwaites, ed., *The Jesuit Relations and Allied Documents: Travels and Explorations of the Jesuit Missionaries in New France, 1610–1791.* 73 vols. (Cleveland: The Burrows Brothers Co., 1896–1901)
MHS	Minnesota Historical Society, St. Paul
MPM	Anthropology Section, Milwaukee Public Museum
SD	University of South Dakota American Indian Research Project, Part 2, microfiches of typed manuscripts, South Dakota Oral History Center, Vermillion

Introduction

1. Other than as they appear in citations, the spelling of Ojibway words throughout this text conforms to the system used in John Nichols and Earl Nyholm, eds., Minnesota Archaeological Society, *Ojibwewi-Ikidowinan: An Ojibwe Word Resource Book,* Occasional Publications in Minnesota Anthropology no. 7 (St. Paul, 1979) and revised in Maude Kegg, *Nookomis Gaa-inaajimotawid: What My Grandmother Told Me,* ed. and transcribed by John D. Nichols, Minnesota Archaeological Society, Occasional Publications in Minnesota Anthropology no. 11 (St. Paul, 1983). The single exception is the spelling *Ojibway,* which follows Minnesota Historical Society Press style. Nichols and Nyholm have provided spellings for words not included in their *Resource Book* and restorations for longer phrases mistranscribed in other sources.

2. Leo G. Waisberg, "An Ethnographic and Historical Outline of the Rainy River Ojibway," in *An Historical Synthesis of the Manitou Mounds Site on the Rainy River, Ontario,* vol. 1, *Archaeological and Ethnographic Evidence,* ed. William C. Noble (1984), 122–23, manuscript on file, Parks Canada, Ontario regional office.

3. Here and below, see Robert E. Ritzenthaler field notes, Book 5, p. 43, Robert E. Ritzenthaler

Papers, MPM (unless otherwise noted, all Ritzenthaler materials are in this collection). In his many years of field work Ritzenthaler compiled numerous notebooks which he dated, numbered, and paged inconsistently; citation here follows the originals Ritzenthaler later wrote that the Ojibway operated within a fifty-mile radius of their summer village base; see "Southwestern Chippewa," in *Handbook of North American Indians,* ed. William C. Sturtevant, vol. 15, *Northeast,* ed. Bruce G. Trigger (Washington, D.C.: Smithsonian Institution, 1978), 746.

4. *Jesuit Relations* 56 (1899): 121. Bay des [Gens] Puans (Stinkards' Bay) was so-called because of the stench caused by mud and mire each summer as well as dead fish in the lower course of the Fox River; see *Jesuit Relations* 59 (1900): 99. The words for Winnebago in the Ojibway, Menominee, and Potawatomi languages mean "people of the dirty water," suggesting some association of Winnebago with this bay (Ojibway, *wiinibiigoog*).

5. George I. Quimby, *Indian Life in the Upper Great Lakes, 1100 B.C. to A.D. 1800* (Chicago: University of Chicago Press, 1967), 111; William W. Warren, *History of the Ojibway People* (1885; reprint, St. Paul: Minnesota Historical Society Press, Borealis Books, 1984), 33; Walter J. Hoffman, "The Menomini Indians," in *Fourteenth Annual Report of the Bureau of American Ethnology, 1892–93* (Washington, D.C.: GPO, 1896), 1:12–14. In their own language the Menominee name for themselves is of unclear etymology and is *not* derived from their word for wild rice—Hoffman, Jenks, and others to the contrary. See Albert E. Jenks, "The Wild Rice Gatherers of the Upper Lakes: A Study in American Primitive Economics," in *Nineteenth Annual Report of the Bureau of American Ethnology, 1897–98* (Washington, D.C.: GPO, 1900), 2:1022–24.

6. See, for instance, Huron H. Smith, *Ethnobotany of the Ojibwe Indians,* Bulletin of the Public Museum of the City of Milwaukee, vol. 4, no. 3 (1932), 403; Ives Goddard to the author, July 3, 1986.

7. Frank Siebert, Jr., "Resurrecting Virginia Algonquian from the Dead: the Reconstituted and Historical Phonology of Powhatan," in *Studies in Southeastern Indian Languages,* ed. James M. Crawford (Athens: University of Georgia Press, 1975), 414; John Smith, "A Map of Virginia With a Description of the Country, the Commodities, People, Government and Religion," in *The Jamestown Voyages Under the First Charter, 1606–1609,* ed. Philip L. Barbour (Cambridge, Eng.: Cambridge University Press, 1969), 2:347. The symbols θ, 8, and the raised dot are from the orthographies of the sources cited above.

8. Aubery Manuscript, 64, in the museum of the Société historique d'Odanak, Quebec Province; *Jesuit Relations* 44 (1899): 247; Reuben G. Thwaites, ed., "Radisson and Groseilliers in Wisconsin," *Collections of the State Historical Society of Wisconsin* 11 (1888): 64n1, 78. Aubery's translation has been questioned; see Pauleena M. Seeber, "The Bird Names of Aubery and Rasles," in *Papers of the Sixteenth Algonquian Conference,* ed. William Cowan (Ottawa: Carleton University, 1985), 171–81.

9. See Elliott M. Coues, ed., *The Expeditions of Zebulon Montgomery Pike* (New York: Francis P. Harper, 1895), 1:38n44. For sixty popular synonyms in French, English, German, and Indian languages, see Jenks, "Wild Rice Gatherers," 1022–24. The Indian agent at Portage la Prairie, Manitoba, wrote Jenks that old guides at Rat Portage still called wild rice "la folle avoine"; Albert E. Jenks Papers, State Historical Society of Wisconsin Archives Division, Madison. The term *wild rice* was included in F.Lamson-Scribner, *Useful and Ornamental Grasses,* United States Department of Agriculture Bulletin no. 3 (Washington, D.C., 1896), thus giving it a federal mark of approval.

10. *Report of the Secretary of the Interior,* 31st Cong., 2d sess., 1850, H. Doc. 1, p. 86 (Serial 595). Jean Baptiste Franquelin, *Partie de l'Amerique Septentrionale,* 1699, copy in Lowery Collection, Library of Congress; Warren, *History of the Ojibway,* 38–39.

11. *Jesuit Relations* 58 (1899): 273, 289; Johann G. Kohl, *Kitchi-Gami: Life Among The Lake Superior Ojibway* (1860; reprint, St. Paul: Minnesota Historical Society Press, Borealis Books, 1985), 117–18; Coues, ed., *Expeditions of Pike* 1:117, 120.

12. *Jesuit Relations* 51 (1899): 57, 59; Alexander Henry, *Travels and Adventures in Canada and the Indian Territories Between the Years 1760 and 1776* (New York: I. Riley, 1809), 250.

13. See the manuscript from about 1743, Public Archives of Canada, ms618, B12. Harold

Hickerson, "Land Tenure of the Rainy Lake Chippewa at the Beginning of the 19th Century," *Smithsonian Contributions to Anthropology* 2 (Washington, D.C.: GPO, 1967): 45, infers Ojibway occupancy from La Vérendrye's 1736 manuscript, although his position has been challenged. Adolph Greenberg and J. Morrison, among others, have taken a fresh approach. Their study, "Group Identities in the Boreal Forest: The Origins of the Northern Ojibwa," cited in *Historical Synthesis,* ed. Noble, 85, concludes: "What has been seen as migration, or a general population movement is, in fact, the diffusion of the term 'Ojibwa' to ethnic units known at contact under a host of different names—among them Kilistinons or Cree, Monsoni, Muskego, and Gens de Terres." Hickerson minimizes the role of wild rice in the "contested zone" and attributes most of the fighting to conflicts over hunting resources, especially Virginia deer; see *The Chippewa and Their Neighbors: A Study in Ethnohistory* (New York: Irvington Publications, [1970]), 106–19. In this author's opinion Hickerson vastly underrates the importance of wild rice to the Dakota in this struggle.

14. Thwaites, ed., "Radisson and Groseilliers," 83, 89; *Jesuit Relations* 51 (1899): 53; *Jesuit Relations* 54 (1899): 191, 193.

15. Jonathan Carver, *Travels through the Interior Parts of North America in the Years 1766, 1767, and 1768* (3rd ed., 1781; reprint, Minneapolis: Ross & Haines, 1956), 262; Coues, ed., *Expeditions of Pike* 1:47, 76. See also Gary C. Anderson, *Little Crow, Spokesman for the Sioux* (St. Paul: Minnesota Historical Society Press, 1986), 14; George Catlin, *Letters and Notes on the Manners, Customs, and Condition of the North American Indians* (1841; reprint, Minneapolis: Ross & Haines, 1965), 2: sketch 278, facing p. 208; Henry R. Schoolcraft, *Historical and Statistical Information Respecting the History, Condition and Prospects of the Indian Tribes of the United States* (Philadelphia: Lippincott, 1853–57), 2:97. These marshes were noted a century earlier on Carver's 1769 map; Jenks, "Wild Rice Gatherers," 1047.

16. Jonathan Carver, map (1769), additional manuscript 8949, folio 42, British Library, London, copy in Library of Congress, Washington, D.C.; Coues, ed., *Expeditions of Pike* 1:233–34; Warren, *History of the Ojibway,* 308–14; Jenks, "Wild Rice Gatherers," 1042, 1062n3.

17. Eliza Morrison, *A Little History of My Forest Life,* ed. Austin J. McLean (La Crosse, Wis.: Sumac Press, 1978), 7; Harold Hickerson, *The Southwestern Chippewa: An Ethnohistorical Study,* American Anthropological Association, Memoir 92 (Menasha, Wis., 1962): 22–23. Ojibway were not the only ones to threaten the Dakota. Nicollet wrote on September 20, 1838, that the Wahpekute "cannot bring themselves to leave the country in spite of the continual danger they run of being attacked by the Sauk and Fox. At this moment they are scattered in little bands of 3 to 6 lodges in *les bois francs* around the lakes to gather wild rice." Edmund C. Bray and Martha C. Bray, trans. and eds., *Joseph N. Nicollet on the Plains and Prairies: The Expeditions of 1838–39 with Journals, Letters and Notes on the Dakota Indians* (St. Paul: Minnesota Historical Society Press, 1976), 125.

18. J. W. Powell, "Report of the Director," in *Nineteenth Annual Report of the Bureau of American Ethnology* (Washington, D.C.: GPO, 1900), 1:liv.

Chapter 1

1. *Jesuit Relations* 59 (1900): 93, 95.

2. The taxonomic history of wild rice is confused. Botanists continue to define further varieties, the most recent being *Z. aquatica subbrevis.* See Suzanne I. Warwick and Susan G. Aiken, "Electrophoretic Evidence for the Recognition of Two Species in Annual Wild Rice (*Zizania,* Poaceae)," *Systematic Botany* 11 (July/September 1986): 465. Generally speaking, the wild rice in the present study is of the *palustris* species. Eva Lips, *Die Reisernte der Ojibwa-Indianer: Wirtschaft und Recht eines Erntevolkes* (Berlin: Akademie Verlag, 1956), 55, 65. Professor J. Matsumura of Japan claimed wild rice is identical to a plant in Japan, Formosa, and eastern China; see Jenks, "Wild Rice Gatherers," 1021. See also K. C. Chang, ed., *Food in Chinese Culture* (New Haven: Yale University Press, 1977), 217, 331.

3. Jenks, "Wild Rice Gatherers," 1022, 1025; Henry A. Gleason and Arthur Cronquist, *Manual of Vascular Plants of Northeastern United States and Adjacent Canada* (Princeton, N.J.: Van Nostrand, 1963), 97.

4. Carl von Linné, *Species Plantarum* (1753; reprint ed., London: Ray Society, 1959), 991. Lips, *Reisernte,* 62, 64, wrote that many botanical handbooks incorrectly give Latin variations for wild rice, such as *Zizania effusa.* For her discussion of etymology, see p. 59–65.

5. Lips, *Reisernte,* 67.

6. Lips, *Reisernte,* 72; John B. Moyle, "Wild Rice in Minnesota," *Journal of Wildlife Management* 8 (July 1944): 180.

7. Moyle, "Wild Rice," 178.

8. Here and below, see Trevor Lloyd, "Wild Rice in Canada," *Canadian Geographical Journal* 19 (November 1939): 291; Thomas Pawlick, "Riz Sauvage," *Harrowsmith* 3 (1979): 52.

9. Catherine P. Traill, *The Backwoods of Canada: Being Letters from the Wife of an Emigrant Officer* (London: Charles Knight, 1836), 237.

10. Moyle, "Wild Rice," 177; SD, tape 350, p. 16–17. Most plants have but a single stalk; in shallow water, however, "stooling" may occur, with one plant producing five or six tillers. Lips, admittedly no expert in botany, felt that the time of blossoming had to do with the degree of daylight. She classified wild rice as one of the "short day plants" because of the long nights in northern Minnesota. It was her impression that the blossoms would appear when the daily dark period reached or surpassed a certain length of time; Lips, *Reisernte,* 64.

11. SD, tape 350, p. 16.

12. Here and below, see Moyle, "Wild Rice," 177; J. Sharpless Fox, ed., "Letters on the Fur Trade 1833 by William Johnston," *Historical Collections and Researches Made by the Michigan Pioneer and Historical Society* 37 (1909, 1910): 178; Jenks, "Wild Rice Gatherers," 1026; Albert B. Reagan, "Plants used by the Bois Fort Chippewa (Ojibwa) Indians of Minnesota," *Wisconsin Archeologist,* New Series 7 (July 1928): 247; James D. Doty, "Northern Wisconsin in 1820," *Report and Collections of the State Historical Society of Wisconsin* 7 (1876): 199. Jenks's figures seem extreme. Wild rice is not normally found in water deeper than six to seven feet, and it usually reaches a height of no more than six to ten feet above the water level.

13. Moyle, "Wild Rice," 181, claims that a given stand's ripening fluctuates by no more than two to three days over a period of years; Lawrence J. Burpee, ed., *Journals and Letters of Pierre Gaultier de Varennes de la Vérendrye and His Sons* (Toronto: The Champlain Society, 1927), 221.

14. SD, tape 350, p. 18; Moyle, "Wild Rice," 181.

15. Lips, *Reisernte,* 71.

16. SD, tape 332, p. 15; Schoolcraft, *Information* 3:63; SD, tape 350, p. 17.

17. Schoolcraft, *Information* 3:63.

18. Moyle, "Wild Rice," 180; SD, tape 262, p. 2.

19. Reagan, "Plants," 247; Lips, *Reisernte,* 74; Warren, *History of the Ojibway,* 308–10; Robert Gough, "Wild Ricing," *Wisconsin Trails* 24 (September/October 1983): 22; Jenks, "Wild Rice Gatherers," 1035; Doty, "Northern Wisconsin," 199.

20. George W. Featherstonhaugh, *A Canoe Voyage up the Minnay Sotor* (1847; reprint, St. Paul: Minnesota Historical Society, 1970), 1:184, 190; Henry Youle Hind, *Narrative of the Canadian Red River Exploring Expedition of 1857 and of the Assiniboine and Saskatchewan Exploring Expedition of 1858* (1860; reprint, New York: Greenwood Press, 1969), 1:116.

21. Cloeter, "First Report of Missionary Cloeter, Kabitawigama, Sept. 27, 1858," p. 3, English translation of article in the German language, probably from *Der Lutheraner* (St. Louis), copy in Grace Lee Nute, comp., Manuscripts Relating to Northwest Missions, 1810–1896 (hereafter cited as Nute, Manuscripts), MHS; David D. Owen, *Report of a Geological Survey of Wisconsin, Iowa, and Minnesota* (Philadelphia: Lippincott, Grambo & Co., 1852), 321.

22. Jenks, "Wild Rice Gatherers," 1052; Lucile M. Kane et al., eds., *The Northern Expeditions of Stephen H. Long* (St. Paul: Minnesota Historical Society Press, 1978), 205.

23. John D. Cameron, cited in Waisberg, "Ethnographic and Historical Outline," 141; Hind, *Narrative* 1:118–19; Jean Baptiste Perrault, "Indian Life in the North-Western Regions of the

United States, in 1783," cited in Schoolcraft, *Information* 3:356; *Annual Report of the Commissioner of Indian Affairs,* 31st Cong., 1st sess., 1849–1850, H. Doc. 5, p. 1040 (Serial 570); *Annual Report of the Commissioner of Indian Affairs,* 31st Cong., 2d sess., 1850, H. Doc. 1, p. 121 (Serial 595).

24. Taylor A. Steeves, "Wild Rice—Indian Food and a Modern Delicacy," *Economic Botany* 6 (1952): 111, 124. For rice failures elsewhere, see Jenks, "Wild Rice Gatherers," 1095. Jenks's information came from government farmers at Lac Court Oreilles, Vermilion Lake, Bad River, and Fond du Lac, among other places. His correspondent from Grass Lake, Illinois, insisted that there had not been a rice failure there in sixty years.

25. Reuben G. Thwaites, ed., "A Wisconsin Fur-Trader's Journal, 1803–04," *Collections of the State Historical Society of Wisconsin* 20 (1911): 403–4 (hereafter cited as Thwaites, ed., "Curot"); Lips, *Reisernte,* 70.

26. Jenks, "Wild Rice Gatherers," 1027.

27. Lips, *Reisernte,* 70. See Charles E. Chambliss, "The Botany and History of Zizania aquatica L. ('Wild Rice')," in *Annual Report of the Board of Regents of the Smithsonian Institution . . . For the Year Ended June 30, 1940* (Washington, D.C.: GPO, 1941), 373; for types of vegetation sharing the wild rice habitat, see Moyle, "Wild Rice," 177.

28. Ayer to P. R. Wadsworth, August 13, 1922, Harry D. Ayer and Family Papers, MHS; Sister Bernard M. Coleman, "The Ojibwa and the Wild Rice Problem," *Anthropological Quarterly* 26 (July 1953): 87, who called Big Rice "Tice" Lake.

29. L. A. Paddock to Albert Jenks, January 20, 1899, Jenks Papers.

30. Hind, *Narrative* 1:93; Jenks, "Wild Rice Gatherers," 1027. Moyle, "Wild Rice," 182, identified the rice worm as the "army worm" (*agrotis* sp.), an idea challenged by more recent researchers. See A. G. Peterson et al., *Insects of Wild Rice in Minnesota,* University of Minnesota Agricultural Experiment Station, Miscellaneous Report 157 (St. Paul, 1981), 3.

31. *Jesuit Relations* 54 (1899): 215, 219.

32. Gardner P. Stickney, "Indian Use of Wild Rice," *American Anthropologist* 9 (April 1896): 120; William Bineshi Baker, Sr., transcript of taped interview, September 4, 1985, Lac Court Oreilles Reservation, p. 6, Folklife Archives.

33. Jenks, "Wild Rice Gatherers," 1026–27, 1099.

34. Lips, *Reisernte,* 73n1; William Baker transcript, 6. Similarly, paddy rice growers have tried using sonic disturbances to drive off birds.

35. *Annual Report of the Commissioner of Indian Affairs,* 41st Cong., 3rd sess., 1870, H. Doc. 1, p. 773 (Serial 1449).

36. Jenks, "Wild Rice Gatherers," 1077; Coleman, "Ojibwa and Wild Rice," 87; Carver, *Travels*, 525; Thomas L. McKenney, *Sketches of a Tour to the Lakes* (Baltimore: Fielding Lucas, Jr., 1827), 337.

37. SD, tape 347, p. 1.

38. Moyle, "Wild Rice," 182.

39. SD, tape 141, p. 2.

40. *Annual Report of the Commissioner of Indian Affairs,* 34th Cong., 1st sess., 1855, H. Doc. 1, p. 373 (Serial 840).

41. SD, tape 155, p. 106.

42. Lips, *Reisernte,* 241; Kathi Avery and Thomas Pawlick, "Last Stand in Wild Rice Country," *Harrowsmith* 3 (1979): 44.

43. Caleb Atwater, *The Indians of the Northwest* (Columbus, Ohio: C. Atwater, 1850), 181.

44. Quimby, *Indian Life,* 2.

45. See Grace Rajnovich, "A Study of Possible Prehistoric Wild Rice Gathering on Lake of the Woods, Ontario," *North American Archaeologist* 5 (1984): 204; Quimby, *Indian Life,* 3.

46. See, for instance, Richard A. Yarnell, *Aboriginal Relationships Between Culture and Plant Life in the Upper Great Lakes Region,* Museum of Anthropology, University of Michigan, Anthropological Papers, no. 23 (1964), 65, 78. With the exception of the Kettle Hill Cave site in Ohio, almost all archaeological evidence for the prehistoric use of wild rice has been found since Yarnell's monograph appeared. His excellent study remains a useful introduction to the topic. See

Richard I. Ford and David S. Brose, "Prehistoric Wild Rice from the Dunn Farm Site, Leelanau County, Michigan," *Wisconsin Archeologist,* New Series 56 (March 1975): 9–15, for a burial site containing wild rice grains dating from 400–600 B.C.

47. Jenks, "Wild Rice Gatherers," 1034. Rajnovich, "Prehistoric Wild Rice Gathering," 204.

48. Martha Coleman Bray, ed., *The Journals of Joseph N. Nicollet, A Scientist on the Mississippi Headwaters* (St. Paul: Minnesota Historical Society, 1970), 74–75.

49. The Nett Lake-Little Fork-Rainy River connection typically made this a trade route. Kane et al., eds., *Northern Expeditions,* 218 (see also Long's description of Lac qui Parle, 167); Cloeter, "First Report," 4.

50. Chambliss, "Botany and History," 375–76.

51. Carver, *Travels,* 38–39; on the abundance of rice on this river, see p. 536. John J. Bigsby, *The Shoe and the Canoe, or Pictures of Travel in the Canadas* (London: Chapman and Hall, 1850), 2:256; Featherstonhaugh, *Canoe Voyage,* 190.

52. Sherman Hall, Journal, [45v–46], undated, but probably late September 1832, ABCFM.

53. *Jesuit Relations* 59 (1900): 105; see also, Grace Lee Nute, ed., "A Description of Northern Minnesota by a Fur Trader in 1807," *Minnesota History Bulletin* 5 (February 1923): 37.

54. Warren, *History of the Ojibway,* 309.

55. Jenks, "Wild Rice Gatherers," 1034.

56. Warren Upham, *Catalogue of the Flora of Minnesota,* in Geological and Natural History Survey of Minnesota, Annual Report of Progress for the Year 1883 (Minneapolis, 1884), 159; Owen, *Report,* 325; Hind, *Narrative* 1:118–19.

57. *Jesuit Relations* 59 (1900): 99; Pierre François Xavier de Charlevoix, *Journal of a Voyage to North America* (1761; reprint, Chicago: Caxton Club, 1923), 2:56.

58. Here and two paragraphs below, see Jenks, "Wild Rice Gatherers," 1028–30, Plate 66, facing p. 1033; Carl S. Scofield, *The Salt Water Limits of Wild Rice,* United States Department of Agriculture, Bureau of Plant Industry Bulletin 72, pt. 2 (Washington, D.C., 1905), 7; C. W. Mathews to Albert Jenks, December 15, 1898 and Simon Pokagon to Jenks, December 16, 1898, both in Jenks Papers.

59. Ford and Brose, "Prehistoric Wild Rice," 9–15; Jenks, "Wild Rice Gatherers," 1036.

60. A. L. Kroeber, "Cultural and Natural Areas of Native North America," *University of California Publications in American Archaeology and Ethnology* 38 (1938): 89; Lips, *Reisernte,* 54.

61. Jenks, "Wild Rice Gatherers," fig. 48, p. 1106; D. Wayne Moodie, "Historical Geographical Perspectives on the Ojibway Exploitation of Wild Rice," paper read at the American Society for Ethnohistory meeting, Oakland, California, November 1987.

62. Carver, map (1769); Lips, *Reisernte,* 126.

63. Jenks, "Wild Rice Gatherers," 1045; Coues, ed., *Expeditions of Pike* 1:344; Bray and Bray, eds., *Nicollet on the Plains,* 48, 115.

64. Thwaites, ed., "Radisson and Groseilliers," 83; Jenks, "Wild Rice Gatherers," 1047.

65. See Melvin R. Gilmore, "Uses of Plants by the Indians of the Missouri River Region," *Thirty-Third Annual Report of the Bureau of American Ethnology, 1911–1912* (Washington, D.C.: GPO, 1919), 67; Jenks, "Wild Rice Gatherers," 1032n1, 1069–70.

66. Stickney, "Indian Use of Wild Rice," 116; SD, tape 291, p. 1; James Mustache, Sr., transcript of taped interview, September 4, 1985, Hayward, Wis., p. 1, Folklife Archives.

67. Warren, *History of the Ojibway,* 304. Jenks apparently did not consult Franquelin's map. Jenks, "Wild Rice Gatherers," 1117, using Carver's map published in his travel narrative (1778, 1781), located the village on the St. Croix River, but Carver's map of 1769 clearly represents the village with a small tepee at the north end of one headwater lake surrounded by marshes and flowing into the Red Cedar River. Lake Chetac was at one time an important ricing lake for the Ojibway.

68. Joseph A. Gilfillan, *Minnesota Geographical Names Derived from the Chippewa Language,* in Geological and Natural History Survey of Minnesota, Fifteenth Annual Report of Progress for the Year 1886 (Minneapolis, 1887), 471; Lawrence Mitchell to the author, April 30, 1985.

69. Edwin James, ed., *A Narrative of the Captivity and Adventures of John Tanner* (1830; reprint, Minneapolis: Ross & Haines, 1956), 159; Warren, *History of the Ojibway,* 308–9.
70. Jenks, "Wild Rice Gatherers," 1126.

Chapter 2

1. Jenks, "Wild Rice Gatherers," 1083 and "Table D—Composition of cereals and Indian foods," 1081–82. His statistics for wild rice are drawn primarily from chemical tests, one made in 1862 and another in 1899, the latter at the Agricultural Experiment Station in Madison, Wisconsin. See also Edward Taube, "Wild Rice," *Scientific Monthly* 73 (December 1951): 375. Like most cereals, wild rice cannot be considered a complete food, as it is relatively low in protein and certain vitamins and minerals.
2. Jenks, "Wild Rice Gatherers," 1106, 1108–10, included five statistical tables estimating the number of Indians inhabiting the district. He drew on various sources, such as Schoolcraft, Pike, and an 1882 report to the secretary of war and relied considerably on Stephen S. Hebberd's *History of Wisconsin under the Dominion of France* (Madison: Midland Publishing Co., 1890).
3. H. Clyde Wilson, "A New Interpretation of the Wild Rice District of Wisconsin," *American Anthropologist* 58 (1956): 1059–64, argued a good case for dropping at least five of the twelve tribes Jenks designated as wild rice harvesters—the Sauk, Fox, Mascouten, Potawatomi, and Kickapoo—thereby reducing the figures considerably. His reassessment of the rice district is supported by Gertrude D. Kurath in "Wild Rice Gatherers of Today: A Sequel Note," *American Anthropologist* 59 (1957): 713. This author questions Wilson's assertion (p. 1060) that the rice district was *over*populated at the time of contact. He based this on Jesuit reports of Indian starvation but failed to take into account typical, periodic rice failures. The missionaries, it should be remembered, were prone to depicting Indians in a destitute condition, needing salvation. The fact that Indians ate dogs as reported in the *Jesuit Relations* may have had more to do with Indian religious practices than hunger.
4. See, for example, Hickerson, *Southwestern Chippewa.*
5. Jenks, "Wild Rice Gatherers," 1085–86, probably described a four-day medicine dance followed by a four-day drum dance, the traditional fall seasonal rites; he photographed both events extensively. See Thomas Vennum, Jr., *The Ojibwa Dance Drum: Its History and Construction,* Smithsonian Folklife Studies 2 (Washington, D.C.: Smithsonian Institution Press, 1982), 113, 114 (fig. 34), 115 (fig. 35).
6. Stephen Gheen to Albert Jenks, November 15, 1898, Jenks Papers; SD, tape 350, p. 24–25; Mustache transcript, 4.
7. Lawrence Mitchell, transcript of taped interview, April 30, 1985, Washington, D.C., p. 3, Folklife Archives; Jenks, "Wild Rice Gatherers," 1087; Henry, *Travels and Adventures,* 211; see also, George Catlin, *Illustrations of the Manners, Customs, and Condition of the North American Indians* (London: Henry G. Bohn, 1845), 1:122. Hickerson, *Chippewa and Their Neighbors,* 106–19, misperceived the place of horticulture in the Ojibway economic cycle; see Tim E. Holzkamm, "Subsistence Factors in the Spread of Ojibway Horticulture in the Upper Mississippi and Boundary Waters Region During the 19th Century," paper read at the 17th Algonquian Conference, Montreal, October 1985.
8. Holzkamm, "Subsistence Factors," 5. Similarly, describing a corn and potato failure in 1897, the government farmer at Lac Court Oreilles said that residents "would be in very hard circumstances if it had not been for a uncommon large crop of wild rice as it is the most nutritious food the Indians eat"; N. D. Ordman to Albert Jenks, November 11, 1898, Jenks Papers.
9. Holzkamm, "Subsistence Factors," 9. See also John D. Speth and Katherine A. Spielmann, "Energy Source, Protein Metabolism, and Hunter-Gatherer Subsistence Strategies," *Journal of Anthropological Archaeology* 2 (March 1983): 21. In various sources, Lac la Pluie is also called Lac de la Pluie and Rainy Lake.
10. Holzkamm, "Subsistence Factors," 6–11.

11. Henry, *Travels and Adventures,* 238–39.

12. See Yarnell, *Aboriginal Relationships,* 48; Frederic Baraga, *A Dictionary of the Otchipwe Language* 2 (Montreal: Beauchemin & Valois, 1880): 221, 71, 404.

13. Joseph B. Casagrande, "John Mink, Ojibwa Informant," *Wisconsin Archeologist* 36 (December 1955): 110; Lips, *Reisernte,* 36. According to Frances Densmore, "Uses of Plants by the Chippewa Indians," *Forty-Fourth Annual Report of the Bureau of American Ethnology, 1926–1927,* (Washington, D.C.: GPO, 1928), 306, the Ojibway "cooked and ate all trapped animals except the marten."

14. Sherman Hall to David Greene, September 17, 1831, and Hall, Journal, items 42–45, ABCFM.

15. McKenney, *Sketches of a Tour,* 253, 378; "Report of Lieutenant Allen, of the Army, of H. R. Schoolcraft's Exploration of the Country At and Beyond the Sources of the Mississippi, on a Visit to the Northwestern Indians in 1832," *American State Papers: Military Affairs* 5:324, emphasis added.

16. J. J. Ducatel, "A Fortnight Among the Chippewas of Lake Superior," in *The Indian Miscellany,* ed. W. W. Beach (Albany, N.Y.: J. Munsell, 1877), 369–70; Kohl, *Kitchi-Gami,* 50–51. It is possible that the Kakagon sloughs were intensively seeded with wild rice following the removal of La Pointe Indians to Bad River Reservation, as mandated in 1854.

17. Early reports of corn cultivation at Red Lake attest to the abundance of the crop, with a sizable annual surplus for trade; William T. Boutwell, "Schoolcraft's Exploring Tour of 1832," *Collections of the Minnesota Historical Society* 1 (1902): 126; "Report of Lt. Allen," 327. On the irregular rice returns at Red Lake, see Paula Brown, "Changes in Ojibwa Social Control," *American Anthropologist* 54 (January 1952): 58; Erwin F. Mittelholtz, *Historical Review of the Red Lake Indian Reservation* (Bemidji, Minn.: General Council of the Red Lake Band of Chippewa Indians and the Beltrami County Historical Society, 1957), 17; Mary A. Sagatoo, *Wah Sash Kah Moqua: Or, Thirty-Three Years Among the Indians* (Boston: C. A. White, 1897), 109, 116.

18. Ignatia Broker, *Night Flying Woman: An Ojibway Narrative* (St. Paul: Minnesota Historical Society Press, 1983), 29; Baker transcript, 6. At some earlier point in their history the Ojibway must have practiced stone-boiling, as it is mentioned matter-of-factly in their legends.

19. Jenks, "Wild Rice Gatherers," 1086; H. Smith, *Ethnobotany of the Ojibwe,* 404; Smith made the same observation of the Menominee but said the opposite of the Potawatomi; *Ethnobotany of the Forest Potawatomi Indians,* Bulletin of the Public Museum of the City of Milwaukee, vol. 7, no. 1 (1933), 102.

20. Lips, *Reisernte,* 75; Jenks, "Wild Rice Gatherers," 1086; Reagan, "Plants," 248; Edward D. Neill, "Memoir of the Sioux," in *Macalester College Contributions,* First Series (St. Paul: The College, 1890), 236.

21. SD, tape 350, p. 24–25.

22. Ritzenthaler field notes, Book 5, p. 5; SD, tape 267, p. 62. See also the Petit Jean or Pti-zha tale of the Nez Perce Indians in Jarold Ramsey, ed., *Coyote was Going There: Indian Literature of the Oregon Country* (Seattle: University of Washington Press, 1977) in which the hero cuts out a monster's tongue. Anthropologist Ruth Landes, about 1930, collected "The Story of Twin Boys," a close variant of Jones's tale; Ruth Landes Papers, National Anthropological Archives, Smithsonian Institution, Washington, D.C.

23. See Thomas Vennum, Jr., "The Ojibwa Begging Dance," in *Music and Context: Essays for John M. Ward,* ed. Anne D. Shapiro (Cambridge, Mass.: Harvard University Press, 1985), 65–66.

24. Maude Kegg, *Gabekanaansing/At the End of the Trail: Memories of Chippewa Childhood in Minnesota,* ed. and transcribed by John D. Nichols, Linguistics Series, Occasional Publications in Anthropology no. 4, University of Northern Colorado (Greeley: Museum of Anthropology, [1978]), 67–68.

25. John McLoughlin, cited in Waisberg, "Ethnographic and Historical Outline," 143–44; see also G[eorges A.] Belcourt to Bishop of Quebec, August 3, 1841, original in Archives of Archdiocese of Quebec, Quebec City, copy and English translation in Nute, Manuscripts.

26. McLoughlin, cited in Waisberg, "Ethnographic and Historical Outline," 144.

27. SD, tape 350, p. 25.

28. Baker transcript, 3; Jenks, "Wild Rice Gatherers, 1094; see also Louis Hennepin, *A New Discovery of a Vast Country in America* (1697; reprint, Chicago: A. C. McClung and Co., 1903), 1:224.

29. Stickney, "Indian Use of Wild Rice," 119; *Jesuit Relations* 59 (1900): 95; J[ohn] Long, *Voyages and Travels of an Indian Interpreter and Trader* (1791; reprint, Toronto: Coles Publishing Co., 1974), 6l; Mitchell transcript, 5; Baker transcript, 1–2; Janet Fontaine, et al., comps., "Making It at Sagkeeng," typescript, 1976, on file at Fort Alexander, Manitoba, 82. See also Fox, ed., "Letters on the Fur Trade," 178.

30. Ducatel, "Fortnight Among the Chippewas," 372; James W. Biddle, "Recollections of Green Bay in 1816–17," *Collections of the State Historical Society of Wisconsin* 1 (1888): 63; SD, tape 340, p. 14; Kegg, *Nookomis,* 86. The etymology of *tassimanonny* is not certain. *Manonny* could be a corruption of *manoomin.*

31. Baker transcript, 6.

32. Lips, *Reisernte,* 237; Doty, "Northern Wisconsin," 199; Mitchell transcript, 4; John Gyles, "Memoirs of Odd Adventures, Strange Deliverances, Etc.," in *Puritans Among the Indians: Accounts of Captivity and Redemption, 1676–1724,* ed. Alden T. Vaughan and Edward W. Clark (Cambridge, Mass.: Harvard University Press, 1981), 122.

33. Manuscript no. 61, p. 28–29, Landes Papers.

34. Frances Densmore, *Chippewa Music—II,* Bureau of American Ethnology Bulletin 53 (Washington, D.C.: GPO, 1913), 291. Other non-Indian flavorings include milk and cane syrup.

35. Ducatel, "Fortnight Among the Chippewas," 372; Hind, *Narrative* 1:97; Stickney, "Indian Use of Wild Rice," 119; *Chippewa Indians as Recorded by Rev. Frederick Baraga in 1847,* Studia Slovenica, vol. 10 (New York: League of Slovenian Americans, 1976), 64; Ritzenthaler field notes, Book 5, p. 35; Doty, "Northern Wisconsin," 199. Reagan, "Plants," 248, cited Doty anonymously. The Ojibway ate skunk on occasion, but they always took the animal far into the woods to remove its skin and glands. Highly dubious is the claim by Elizabeth Ayer that Pokegama Ojibway in 1841, having killed several Dakota warriors, added their flesh to a wild rice stew. See Frances E. Babbitt, "Illustrative Notes Concerning the Minnesota Odjibwas," *Proceedings of the American Society for the Advancement of Science* 36 (1887): 307.

36. See Carrie A. Lyford, *The Crafts of the Ojibwa (Chippewa),* Indian Handcrafts Series No. 5 ([Washington, D.C.]: Office of Indian Affairs, 1943), 27; Hoffman, "The Menomini," 291; Sister M. Inez Hilger, *Chippewa Child Life and Its Cultural Background* (Washington, D.C.: GPO, 1951), 145.

37. Dablon cited in Stickney, "Indian Use of Wild Rice," 119; *Jesuit Relations* 59 (1900): 93; J. Long, *Voyages and Travels,* 146.

38. SD, tape 279A, p. 14; Hilger, *Chippewa Child Life,* 146; Lips, *Reisernte,* 238.

39. A. F. Chamberlain, "Notes on the History, Customs, and Beliefs of the Mississauga Indians," *Journal of American Folk-Lore* 1 (July–September 1888): 155.

40. Hilger, *Chippewa Child Life,* 148; Broker, *Night Flying Woman,* 15; Newton H. Winchell, *The Aborigines of Minnesota* (St. Paul: Minnesota Historical Society, 1911), 593; Schoolcraft, *Information* 3:63; Mitchell transcript, 5; George and Mary McGeshick, taped interview, September 22, 1986, Crystal Falls, Michigan, tape in Folklife Archives.

41. Coues, *Expeditions of Pike* 1:47; J. P. B[ardwell], in *Oberlin* (Ohio) *Evangelist,* September 12, 1849, p. 148; Charles Whittlesey, "Among the Otchipwees II," *Magazine of Western History* 1 (January 1885): 177–78.

42. *Jesuit Relations* 51 (1899): 53; *Jesuit Relations* 59 (1900): 95.

43. Hennepin, *New Discovery* 1:224, 252, 295–96, 298, 258. Winchell, *Aborigines,* 496, mistakenly translated *Bluez* as whortleberries.

44. Chrysostom Verwyst, "Historic Sites on Chequamegon Bay," *Collections of the State Historical Society of Wisconsin* 13 (1895): 429. For place names see Verwyst, "A Glossary of Chippewa Indian Names of Rivers, Lakes and Villages," *Acta et Dicta* 4 (July 1916): 253–74; for grammar, see Verwyst, *Chippewa Exercises* (1901; reprint, Minneapolis: Ross & Haines,

1971); Joseph A. Gilfillan, "Wild Rice Gathering in Minnesota," *Spirit of Missions* (November 1876): 543.

45. Henry Schoolcraft to Lewis Cass, October 24, 1831, U.S. Office of Indian Affairs, Letters Received, 1831–58, Record Group 75, National Archives, microfilm copy at MHS; E. Morrison, "Little History," 26.

46. R. G. Thwaites, ed., "A Wisconsin Fur-Trader's Journal, 1804–05," *Collections of the State Historical Society of Wisconsin* 19 (1910): 165n22, 198, 199, 202, 206 (hereafter cited as Thwaites, ed., "Malhiot").

47. J. B. Tyrrell, ed., David Thompson's Narrative of his Explorations in Western America 1784–*1812* (Toronto: The Champlain Society, 1916), 274; Fox, ed., "Letters on the Fur Trade," 138.

48. R. G. Thwaites, "The Fur-Trade in Wisconsin, 1812–25," *Collections of the State Historical Society of Wisconsin* 20 (1911): 135; Atwater, *Indians of the Northwest,* 181; Robert R. Reed, *Wild Rice: America's First Grain* (1943; reprint, *Quarterly Bulletin of Winona State College,* August 1962), 10.

49. Mitchell transcript, 10.

50. Hilger, *Chippewa Child Life,* 147; SD, tape 340, p. 10; Mustache transcript, 5; McGeshicks, interview.

51. Thwaites, ed., "Radisson and Groseilliers," 89; Jenks, "Wild Rice Gatherers," 1086; Baker transcript, 6; Stickney, "Indian Use of Rice," 120n17.

52. See Robert E. Ritzenthaler, *Chippewa Preoccupation with Health: Change in a Traditional Attitude Resulting from Modern Health Problems,* Bulletin of the Public Museum of the City of Milwaukee, vol. 19, no. 4 (1953): 226; SD, tape 332, p. 7; SD tape 241, p. 24.

53. Carver, *Travels,* 523, 38; Charles Whittlesey, "Recollections of a Tour Through Wisconsin in 1832," *Collections of the State Historical Society of Wisconsin* 1 (1855): 74. Lloyd, "Wild Rice," 298, claimed that at least eleven species of ducks feed on rice and that it is the mallard's favorite food in the fall.

54. Jenks, "Wild Rice Gatherers," 1099.

55. M. Catesby, *The Natural History of Carolina, Florida, and the Bahama Islands* (London: M. Catesby, 1731), cited in S. Dillon Ripley, *Rails of the World: A Monograph of the Family Rallidae* (Boston: David R. Godine, 1977), 249; Elisha J. Lewis, *The American Sportsman* (rev. ed., Philadelphia: J. B. Lippincott & Co., 1906), 269; Harry Ayer to Francis Netwig, June 25, 1920, Ayer Papers; Gilfillan, "Wild Rice Gathering," 544.

56. SD, tape 310, p. 12; Mitchell transcript, 1–2.

Chapter 3

1. Lips, *Reisernte,* 77. Johnson's indication that the couple thought they were absent eight days, when it was actually eight years, seems to derive from teachings of the *midewiwin.* As in freemasonry, one advanced through this Indian society by degrees, each requiring additional learning. The eighth degree was the highest attainable, and few reached it; the instruction was total. Humans chosen as guardians of so much knowledge would have had to serve a long apprenticeship.

2. Charlene L. Smith and Howard J. Vogel, "The Wild Rice Mystique: Resource Management and American Indians' Rights as a Problem of Law and Culture," *William Mitchell Law Review* 10 (1984): 748. At the time of his writing, Jenks was unaware of the spiritual role of wild rice in Ojibway tales.

3. Kegg, *Gabekanaansing,* 71.

4. E. James, ed., *John Tanner,* 95, 104–5; Calvin Martin, *Keepers of the Game: Indian-Animal Relationships and the Fur Trade* (Berkeley: University of California Press, 1978), 136–41; Lips, *Reisernte,* 130.

5. Stuart Berde, "Wild Ricing: The Transformation of an Aboriginal Subsistence Pattern," in

Anishinabe: 6 Studies of Modern Chippewa, ed. J. A. Paredes (Tallahassee: University Presses of Florida, 1980), 121 (hereafter cited *Anishinabe,* ed. Paredes).

6. Catharine Holt, *Shasta Ethnography,* Anthropological Records, vol. 3, no. 4 (Berkeley: University of California Press, 1946), 327.

7. Hoffman, "Menomini Indians," 40–41; Jenks, "Wild Rice Gatherers," 1092–93. Chief Pokagon of the Bear clan wrote Jenks: "There is some old legend I do not fully understand . . . about an exchange of fire and corn for 'Rice' "; Pokagon to Jenks, November 16, 1898, Jenks Papers. Also in these papers is information from Winnebago people at Elroy, Wisconsin, who said that the Great Spirit gave wild rice and maize simultaneously to one man. From these "sacred gifts" stories he concluded that the various Menominee clans had rice very early, before their larger tribal organization, and that the Winnebago and Potawatomi obtained it later. Christopher Vecsey to the author, 1986, suggested that the representations of Bear, a land animal, and Sturgeon, a water being, as the owners of wild rice may reflect its position as a water crop, making it a land-water boundary-crosser.

8. Lips, *Reisernte,* 77–78.

9. Christopher Vecsey, *Traditional Ojibwa Religion and Its Historical Changes,* Memoirs of the American Philosophical Society, vol. 152 (Philadelphia: The Society, 1983), 94; see also Christopher Vecsey and John F. Fisher, "The Ojibwa Creation Myth: An Analysis of its Structure and Content," *Temenos: Studies in Comparative Religion* 20 (1984): 66–100; Jenks, "Wild Rice Gatherers," 1093; Schoolcraft, *Information* 2: 197. Bill Johnson of Nett Lake told Lips in 1947 that rice, as well as all edible wildlife, was created solely for the Indians; *Reisernte,* 77.

10. Here and below, see Jenks, "Wild Rice Gatherers," 1094. The material chosen for the canoe seems unusual; normally the bark would be from a birch. Lips, *Reisernte,* 78, gave the same story, conflating Jenks's version with other sources, including those she heard at Nett Lake fifty years later.

11. For a discussion of dream songs, see Frances Densmore, *Chippewa Music,* Bureau of American Ethnology Bulletin 45 (Washington, D.C.: GPO, 1910), 126–37.

12. Jenks, "Wild Rice Gatherers," 1094–95. The west-to-east direction, from one Ojibway band to the next, has parallels in Ojibway culture. The ceremonial dance drum also was passed along in this direction; Vennum, *Ojibwa Dance Drum,* 70–75.

13. The traditional *midewiwin* teaching is that the path of life, usually designated by a straight line on birch-bark instructional scrolls, is constantly interrupted by temptations which divert one from goals. These are represented by branchlike lines in the pictographs. Vecsey pointed out a recurrent theme of certain foods being disgusting or poisonous in contrast to wild rice, which has only the sublimest properties; Vecsey to the author, 1986.

14. See Laura Makarius, "The Crime of Manabozo," *American Anthropologist* 75 (June 1973): 663, 667.

15. Vecsey, *Traditional Ojibwa Religion,* 97.

16. Here and below, see Thomas W. Overholt and J. Baird Callicott, *Clothed-in-Fur and Other Tales: An Introduction to an Ojibwa World View* (Lanham, Md.: University Press of America, 1982), 128–30.

17. Paul Radin and A. B. Reagan, "Ojibwa Myths and Tales," *Journal of American Folklore* 41 (January-March 1928): 83–84. The use of heated stones for cooking suggests that this story is very old.

18. Jenks, "Wild Rice Gatherers," 1094.

19. While some rice seed may survive the alimentary canal intact or adhere to birds' feathers, it is probably insufficient to establish new wild rice beds. Some Indian people believe that ducks do their share of reseeding. One resident of Mole Lake, Wisconsin, noted: "Your ducks will eat, will gather rice and then go, probably sit on a lily pad and probably drop a few kernels, just like they're planting too, you know"; Robert Gough, "Wild Rice and the Sokaogon Chippewa: A Study in Cultural Ecological Adaptation," unpublished manuscript in Gough's possession.

20. See "Mänäbus Visits his Little Brother, Red Squirrel" in Alanson Skinner and John V. Satterlee, *Folklore of the Menomini Indians,* Anthropological Papers of the American Museum of Natural History, vol. 13, pt. 2 (New York, 1915), 282–84. The same tale was collected by

Leonard Bloomfield, *Menomini Texts,* Publications of the American Ethnological Society 12 (New York, 1928), 191, 207.

21. Makarius, "Crime of Manabozo," 669.

22. Victor Barnouw, *Wisconsin Chippewa Myths & Tales and Their Relation to Chippewa Life* (Madison: University of Wisconsin Press, 1977), 77–80; Ritzenthaler field notes, Book 11, p. 29–30.

23. Overholt and Callicott, *Clothed-in-Fur,* 57; Barnouw, *Chippewa Myths & Tales,* 102. Legends collected most recently are fragmentary in comparison to earlier versions.

24. Jenks, "Wild Rice Gatherers," 1093; Lips, *Reisernte,* 76–77.

25. SD, tape 268, p. 15.

26. Ritzenthaler field notes, Book 13, Book 7, p. 1.

27. Kegg, *Gabekanaansing,* 73–74.

28. Lips, *Reisernte,* 131–34.

29. SD, tape 268, p. 23.

30. Lips, *Reisernte,* 136.

31. Dan Brogan, "Wild Rice Harvest," *Frontiers* 20 (October 1955–June 1956): 131. The "half sea lion and half fish" may be the Ojibway mythical "underground panther."

32. Hilger, *Chippewa Child Life,* 28–29, 51; Mustache transcript, 3; Joseph B. Casagrande field notes, John Mink entry, July 30, 1941, Joseph B. Casagrande Papers, MPM (unless otherwise noted, all Casagrande materials are in this collection); Kegg, *Nookomis,* 14. See also Kegg, *Gabekanaansing,* 28.

33. Lips, *Reisernte,* 46–47, 222, 289.

34. Here and below, see SD, tape 268, p. 13–15. Vecsey to the author, 1986, noted that the normal sky/underground dichotomy in Ojibway mythology seems reversed in Burnside's tale.

35. Manuscript no. 30, p. 19, Landes Papers.

36. Barnouw, *Wisconsin Chippewa Myths & Tales,* 154.

37. Sister Bernard M. Coleman, "The Religion of the Ojibwa of Northern Minnesota," *Primitive Man* 10 (July & October 1937): 35–36; Joseph B. Casagrande, "Ojibwa Bear Ceremonialism: The Persistence of a Ritual Attitude," in Sol Tax, ed., *Acculturation in the Americas,* Proceedings of the 29th International Congress of Americanists (Chicago: University of Chicago Press, 1952), 114.

38. Casagrande, "Ojibwa Bear Ceremonialism," 115–16. See also Vennum, "Ojibwa Begging Dance," 66.

39. Sister Bernard Coleman et al., *Ojibwa Myths and Legends* (Minneapolis: Ross & Haines, 1962), 57; Kegg, *Nookomis,* 94, 96; Kegg, *Gabekanaansing,* 61; see also SD, tape 341, p. 47–48; Edmund F. Ely, Diary no. 16, March 22, 1841, Northeast Minnesota Historical Center, Duluth, copy in Edmund F. Ely and Family Papers, MHS.

40. See also Vennum, *Ojiwba Dance Drum,* 44–76; SD, tape 279A, p.9.

41. Hilger, *Chippewa Child Life,* 38–39; Ritzenthaler, *Chippewa Preoccupation with Health,* 207–8; Casagrande, "John Mink," 117. The dewclaws once strung on the war rattle used in the Chief Dance (see Vennum, *Ojibwa Dance Drum,* fig. 1) were later replaced with tin jingles.

42. Hilger, *Chippewa Child Life,* 67; SD, tape 311, p. 24.

43. Hilger, *Chippewa Child Life,* 68; Kohl, *Kitchi-Gami,* 51; Ernestine Friedl field notes, Book 1, July 2, 1943, Book xvi, July 28, 1942, Ernestine Friedl Papers, MPM (unless otherwise noted, all Friedl materials are in this collection).

44. Lips, *Reisernte,* 212.

45. Here and below, see Lips, *Reisernte,* 238–39, 265; Ritzenthaler field notes, Book 3760, Book 5, p. 86. See also Kegg, *Nookomis,* 94, 96; Mustache transcript, 7; Avery and Pawlick, "Last Stand," 33.

46. See Jenks, "Wild Rice Gatherers," 1085–86; SD, tape 258, p. 82; see also William E. Culkin, "Tribal Dance of the Ojibway Indians," *Minnesota History Bulletin* 1 (August 1915): 83–93; U.S. Department of the Interior, Census Office, *Report on Indians Taxed and Indians Not Taxed in the United States* (Washington, D.C.: GPO, 1894), 346.

47. Vivian J. Rohrl, "The People of Mille Lacs: A Study of Social Organization and Value

Orientations" (Ph.D. diss., University of Minnesota, 1967), 71; Broker, *Night Flying Woman,* 48, 117.

48. Lips, *Reisernte,* 229. The participation of children in the dancing, the wearing of "jingle dresses," and the "rabbit hop" dance step Lips described all suggest a secular rather than a sacred event.

49. See, however, SD, tape 256, p. 36, where anthropologist Timothy Roufs asked Paul Buffalo to sing "The Ricing Song." No transcription of the music and no text, however, appear in the transcript.

50. Albert B. Reagan, "The Bois Fort Chippewa," *Wisconsin Archeologist,* New Series 3 (September 1924): 131–32; Sylvia Cloud to the author, August 1986. Kurath, "Wild Rice Gatherers," 713, learned of "threshing songs" remembered at Baraga, Michigan; Mustache transcript, 2.

51. Berde, "Wild Ricing," 121; SD, tape 347, p. 1-2; Coleman, "Ojibwa and Wild Rice," 79.

52. SD, tape 344, p. 50; Hilger, *Chippewa Child Life,* 146; Ritzenthaler, *Chippewa Preoccupation with Health,* 211; Avery and Pawlick, "Last Stand," 35. See also Rohrl, "People of Mille Lacs," 71, for the Mille Lacs custom of sprinkling tobacco onto the lake before going out onto it.

53. Thomas Hariot, *Narrative of the First English Plantation of Virginia* (London: B. Quaritch, 1893), 25; Jenks, "Wild Rice Gatherers," 1091; Mustache transcript, 6.

54. Sherman Hall, Journal, Jan. 30, 1833, ABCFM; Ely, Diary no. 2, October 22, 1833, Northeast Minnesota Historical Center, Duluth, copy in Ely Papers.

55. Reagan, "Bois Fort Chippewa," 131–32; Hilger, *Chippewa Child Life,* 80–81; see also Hoffman, "Menomini," 239; Ford and Brose, "Prehistoric Wild Rice," 11. The thirty-three carbonized grains were found in burned organic matter with human bone. Because of the popped and twisted condition of the grains, researchers concluded that the rice had been fresh and unparched, and dated the burial to late August or early September.

56. Densmore, *Chippewa Music–II,* 153–57.

57. Hilger, *Chippewa Child Life,* 86–87; Ritzenthaler field notes, Book 5, p. 17.

58. SD, tape 267, p. 8; Mustache transcript, 7.

59. Ritzenthaler field notes, John Bisonette entry, Book '44.

60. See Baraga, *Dictionary of the Otchipwe Language,* 236; Peter Grant, "The Sauteux Indians about 1804," in *Les Bourgeois de la Compagnie du Nord-Ouest,* ed. L. R. Masson (New York: Antiquarian Press, 1960), 2:360.

61. Rohrl, "People of Mille Lacs," 71; Hilger, *Chippewa Child Life,* 52. See also Kegg, *Nookomis,* 94, 96; Ritzenthaler, *Chippewa Preoccupation with Health,* 212; Mustache transcript, 7-8; Baker transcript, 5.

Chapter 4

1. *Jesuit Relations* 48 (1899): 121, 123. Although Lalemant described Ottawa ricing techniques, they apply generally to all wild rice harvesters.

2. See Thwaites, ed., "Fur-Trade," 91; Elliott M. Coues, "The Wild Rice of Minnesota," *Botanical Gazette* (1894): 505. Some Ojibway say in English they "pick rice."

3. Ritzenthaler field notes, Book '44, Book No. 3750, Book 5, p. 86.

4. Carver, *Travels,* 524; Jenks, "Wild Rice Gatherers," 1059; Baker transcript, 4.

5. Frances Densmore, *Chippewa Customs* (1929; reprint, St. Paul, Minnesota Historical Society Press, Borealis Books, 1979), 128; see also Coleman, "Ojibwa and Wild Rice," 80; Mustache transcript, 1; Ritzenthaler field notes, Book 8, p. 47.

6. Stickney, "Indian Use of Wild Rice," 117; George McGeshick to the author, September 22, 1986.

7. Ritzenthaler field notes, Book '44.

8. SD, tape 350, p. 2; Lips, *Reisernte,* 221–22.

9. Doty, "Northern Wisconsin," 200; Hilger, *Chippewa Child Life,* 147–48; Jenks, "Wild Rice Gatherers," 1059, 1060, fig. 47; Stickney, "Indian Use of Wild Rice," 116; James Mustache, Sr.,

to the author, August 27, 1986; Charles A. Eastman, in "Life and Handicrafts of the Northern Ojibwas," *Southern Workman* (Hampton, Va.) 40 (May 1911): 274, wrote that at Rainy Lake rice was bound by August 1, a month before it was harvested.

10. Densmore, "Uses of Plants," 313 and plates 36–39 for photographs of binding rice; Jenks, "Wild Rice Gatherers," 1060. On binding at Cass Lake, see J. P. B[ardwell], in *Oberlin Evangelist,* September 12, 1849, p. 148.

11. Ellis, "Fifty-Four Years' Recollections of Men and Events in Wisconsin," *Collections of the State Historical Society of Wisconsin* 12 (1873–76): 265.

12. Lips, *Reisernte,* 221; Mustache transcript, 1.

13. Jenks, "Wild Rice Gatherers," 1059, 1063.

14. Hennepin, *New Discovery* 1:224; E. S. Seymour, *Sketches of Minnesota, the New England of the West* (New York, 1850), 183; Edward Van de Vorst to the author, November 18, 1987.

15. Densmore, "Uses of Plants," 313–14; Baker transcript, 6; see also Lips, *Reisernte,* 222.

16. Daniel Stanchfield, "History of Pioneer Lumbering on the Upper Mississippi and Its Tributaries, With Biographic Sketches," *Collections of the Minnesota Historical Society* 9 (1901): 331.

17. Jenks, "Wild Rice Gatherers," 1062. See, however, Harry D. Ayer to P. R. Wadsworth, August 13, 1922, Ayer Papers.

18. Bigsby, *Shoe and Canoe* 2:247; Jenks, "Wild Rice Gatherers," 1063–64; A. Ellis, "Fifty-Four Years' Recollections," 265; Stickney, "Indian Use of Rice," 117. Lips, *Reisernte,* 81, incorrectly identified Stickney as the only source on cutting the sheaves.

19. SD, tape 291, p. 27.

20. See Charles A. Eastman, *From the Deep Woods to Civilization: Chapters in the Autobiography of an Indian* (1916; reprint, Lincoln: University of Nebraska Press, 1977), 174; Ritzenthaler field notes, Book 12, p. 31; Jenks, "Wild Rice Gatherers," 1058; Mitchell transcript, 1.

21. Lips, *Reisernte,* 89.

22. McGeshicks, interview; John B. Moyle, "Wild Rice – Pioneer Food and Modern Delicacy," *Conservation Volunteer* 19 (January–February 1956): 12; Ritzenthaler field notes, Book 12, p. 31; Mustache transcript, 2.

23. SD, tape 141, p. 16; Baker transcript, 1.

24. Earl Nyholm, tape, June 1986, Folklife Archives.

25. See Lips, *Reisernte,* 232–34, for a description of Nett Lakers preparing to knock rice on the opening day, September 1, 1947; Berde, "Wild Ricing," 104; Barbara D. Jackson, "A Peyote Community in Northern Minnesota," in *Anishinabe,* ed. Paredes, 152.

26. SD, tape 350, p. 3–4.

27. SD, tape 350, p. 12; Mitchell transcript, 13.

28. Quimby, *Indian Life,* 143; Schoolcraft, *Information* 3:63. Sherman Hall reported from La Pointe that canoes varied in length from 10 to 30 feet; Journal, August 5, 1831, ABCFM.

29. Edwin T. Adney and Howard I. Chapelle, *The Bark Canoes and Skin Boats of North America,* United States National Museum Bulletin 230 (Washington, D.C.: Smithsonian Institution, 1964), p. 124, fig. 115, p. 125; G. A. Belcourt to Bishop of Quebec, August 3, 1841, Nute, Manuscripts; Charles A. Eastman, *Indian Boyhood* (Boston: Little Brown and Co., 1902), 235.

30. Jenks, "Wild Rice Gatherers," 1059; "The Narrative of Peter Pond," in *Five Fur Traders of the Northwest,* ed. Charles M. Gates (St. Paul: Minnesota Historical Society, 1965), 36; Adney and Chapelle, *Bark Canoes,* 124–25; Hilger, *Chippewa Child Life,* 117.

31. S. N. McKinsey, "Chippewa Indians Undertake Cooperation," *Indians at Work,* April 1, 1937, p. 13; Mark L. Burns et al., " 'Manomin,' The Wild Rice of the Lake Country," *Indians at Work,* January 1939, p. 29; Ritzenthaler field notes, Book '42.

32. Mitchell transcript, 2; Lips, *Reisernte,* 168.

33. Jenks, "Wild Rice Gatherers," 1062; Otis T. Mason, *The Origins of Invention: A Study of Industry Among Primitive Peoples* (London: Walter Scott Ltd., 1895), 190; Lyford, *Ojibwa Crafts,* 27; Hazel H. Wahlberg, *The North Land: A History of Roseau County* (Roseau: Roseau County Historical Society, 1975), 27; Stanchfield, "Pioneer Lumbering," 332.

34. Paul Buffalo, SD, tape 350, p. 1; Jackson, "Peyote Community," 152; Lips, *Reisernte,* 85.

35. According to Mark Burns of Cass Lake, paddles or forked poles were used, depending on

the density of the rice field; Lips, *Reisernte,* 93. Sometimes a pole and a long paddle were used together.

36. Berde, "Wild Ricing," 105, said that 22 feet is the maximum permissible length. It is doubtful that any poles approached that length.

37. Berde, "Wild Ricing," 105; Lips, *Reisernte,* 169; Fred K. Blessing, *The Ojibway Indians Observed: Papers of Fred K. Blessing, Jr., On The Ojibway Indians, from* The Minnesota Archaeologist, Occasional Publications in Minnesota Anthropology no. 1 (St. Paul: Minnesota Archaeological Society, 1977), 23; Vennum, *Ojibwa Dance Drum,* 227, and figs. 88, 93; Jackson, "Peyote Community," 152. George McGeshick carved his fork from soft maple and attached it to the shaft with brass screws because nails would rust.

38. Berde, "Wild Ricing," 105–6; Avery and Pawlick, "Last Stand," 42.

39. Carver, *Travels,* 524–25; Lips, *Reisernte,* 26; A. Ellis, "Fifty-Four Years' Recollections," 265.

40. Mitchell transcript, 11; Blessing, *Ojibway Indians Observed,* 23; see also Lips, fig. 93, for sketches of four variations in Nett Lake carving designs.

41. *New Yorker,* December 23, 1967, p. 38, 40; Norma Smith, "What Ricing Means to Me," *Wisconsin Trails* 24 (September/October 1983): 25. For film footage of standard ricing techniques, see Greg Bezat and John Knutson, producers and editors, *Wild Rice: The Taming of a Grain* (Minneapolis: Waterstone Films, 1987).

42. McGeshicks, interview; Fontaine, "Making It," 88.

43. SD, tape 350, p. 2–3.

44. Mitchell transcript, 6.

45. N. Smith, "What Ricing Means," 25.

46. For example, Stickney, "Indian Use of Wild Rice," 117, asserted that one of the two knockers was sometimes fashioned with a curve or hook at one end to facilitate pulling the stalks over into the boat, and that after doing this, the ricer repeated the action reversing the hands—an unlikely and curiously laborious technique. The curved stick he described must be the sickle-shaped stick used in *binding,* not knocking. For other questionable reports, see Daniel W. Harmon, *A Journal of Voyages and Travels in the Interiour of North America* (Andover, Mass.: Flagg and Gould, 1820), 142; H. Smith, *Ethnobotany of the Ojibwe,* 404.

47. Schoolcraft, *Information* 3:63.

48. See photo of John Buckanaga and his wife on Rice Lake in Tamarac National Wildlife Refuge, *Minneapolis Tribune,* September 1, 1946, *Picture Magazine,* 1; see also the photograph in *Indians at Work,* September 1941, p. 14. Mitchell transcript, 7; Frank Jackson (born 1900), also of White Earth, remembered the same arrangement, and he, too, was at a loss to explain when and why the change took place (SD, tape 228, p. 3); Gilfillan, "Wild Rice Gathering," 544; Cloeter, "First Report," 3. See also Lloyd, "Wild Rice," 294, for the same practice at Lac du Bois in Manitoba; Edward Tanner cited in Jenks, "Wild Rice Gatherers," 1061. Other published anomalies concerning ricing techniques include Chamberlain, "Notes on the History of the Mississagua," 155; Adam Maurizio, *Die Geschichte unserer Pflanzennahrung von den Urzeiten bis zur Gegenwart* (Berlin: Paul Parey, 1927), 43; Lyford, *Ojibwa Crafts,* plate 10.

49. *Jesuit Relations* 59 (1900): 95; Henry, *Travels and Adventures,* 242; Coues, ed., *Expeditions of Pike* 1:39n44; SD, tape 350, p. 2.

50. SD, tape 279A, p. 11–12.

51. Berde, "Wild Ricing," 106; SD, tape 350, p. 19.

52. Chambliss, "Botany and History," 377; Gough, "Wild Ricing," 25; William H. Keating, *Narrative of an Expedition to the Source of St. Peter's River, Lake Winnepeek, Lake of the Woods, &c. &c* (Philadelphia: H. C. Carey & I. Lea, 1824), 2:160; Coleman, "Ojibwa and Wild Rice," 81; Yngreg Lithman, *The Capitalization of a Traditional Pursuit: The Case of Wild Rice in Manitoba,* Manitoba University Center for Settlement Studies, Series 5, Occasional Papers no. 6 (Winnipeg, 1973), 14 (seven hundred pounds a day for one boat seems highly unlikely); Avery and Pawlick, "Last Stand," 38. The Minnesota Department of Agriculture uses this "rule of thumb": processed rice weighs roughly sixty pounds per bushel, seed rice, approximately twenty-five pounds per bushel; telephone call by author, October 29, 1987.

53. Mustache transcript, 1; Baker transcript, 8; Gilfillan, "Wild Rice Gathering," 544.

54. Lips, *Reisernte,* 81; Jenks, Table A, "Statistical view of wild-rice production," 1075–77; Owen, *Report of a Geological Survey,* 324. This author questions Lithman's assertion, *Capitalization of a Traditional Pursuit,* 14, that Manitoba harvesters collect only 10 percent of the rice.

55. Joseph A. Gilfillan, "The Ojibways in Minnesota," *Collections of the Minnesota Historical Society* 9 (1901): 123–24; Jenks, "Wild Rice Gatherers," 1061, 1072–73; Hilger, *Chippewa Child Life,* 147; Schoolcraft, *Information* 3: 62–63; Lucy and William Lewis to Br[other] James (J. R. Wright), January 10, 1844, William Lewis Papers, MHS.

56. Thwaites, ed., "Malhiot," 197; Jenks, "Wild Rice Gatherers," 1063; Keating, *Narrative of an Expedition* 2:160; W. Vernon Kinietz, *Chippewa Village: The Story of Katikitegon,* Cranbrook Institute of Science Bulletin 25 (Bloomfield Hills, Mich., 1947), 58; Gilfillan, "Ojibways," 124; SD, tape 279A, p. 11. See also Fox, ed., "Letters on the Fur Trade," 178.

57. McGeshicks, interview; Berde, "Wild Ricing," 105, 118; Lips, *Reisernte,* 93; Mustache transcript, 5.

58. Mustache transcript, 5. Gough's statistics for Sokaogon Ojibway in 1986 show that well over one-third of the ricers customarily harvested with their spouses; more than two-thirds said they usually riced with the same partner (Gough, "Wild Rice and the Sokaogon Chippewa").

59. Lips, *Reisernte,* 94–95, 240–41; *Jesuit Relations* 48 (1899): 121.

60. Baker transcript, 1, 3–4.

61. Mitchell transcript, 7.

62. SD, tape 350, p. 25–26; E. James, ed., *John Tanner,* 199; Densmore, "Uses of Plants," 315. Tanner called the birch-bark sheets "puk-kwi."

63. Mitchell transcript, 3; Densmore, "Uses of Plants," 315; Jenks, "Wild Rice Gatherers," 1064; Brogan, "Wild Rice Harvest," 132.

64. SD, tape 331, p. 15; SD, tape 190, p. 8–9. Hilger, *Chippewa Child Life,* 148, is the only source to claim that the Ojibway dried rice on flat rocks heated over a fire, although some Potawatomi may also have used this method.

65. Winchell, *Aborigines,* 593; Densmore, "Uses of Plants," 315; Lips, *Reisernte,* 96; N. D. Rodman to Albert Jenks, March 1, 1899, Jenks Papers. Parching destroys the kernel's capacity to germinate; sun drying, apparently, does not.

66. *Jesuit Relations* 59 (1900): 95; Carver, *Travels,* 525; George Bonga to William Boutwell, copy in Nute, Manuscripts.

67. Thwaites, ed., "Curot," 427.

68. Doty, *Northern Wisconsin,* 200; Winchell, *Aborigines,* 592; Stickney, "Indian Use of Wild Rice," 118; Chamberlain, "Notes on the History of the Mississagua," 155; Jenks, "Wild Rice Gatherers," 1065, 1066; Keating, *Narrative of an Expedition* 2:160; Fox, ed., "Letters on the Fur Trade," 178; Bear Lake manuscript in Ritzenthaler Papers, MPM.

69. Stickney, "Indian Use of Wild Rice," 118; Bear Lake manuscript, Ritzenthaler Papers; *Jesuit Relations* 59 (1900): 93.

70. Lips, *Reisernte,* 96; Stickney, "Indian Use of Wild Rice," 118, echoed Charles C. Trowbridge's 1820 observation; see Charles C. Trowbridge, "The Journal and Letters of Charles Christopher Trowbridge, Expedition of 1820," in *Narrative Journal of Travels Through the Northwestern Regions of the United States . . . in the Year 1820,* ed. Mentor L. Williams (Lansing: Michigan State College Press, 1953), 483.

71. Lips, *Reisernte,* 99–100.

72. Kegg, *Gabekanaansing,* 61–62.

73. Brass kettles at Cass Lake are mentioned in B[ardwell], in *Oberlin Evangelist,* September 12, 1849, p. 148. These may have been the "man kettles" that Densmore mentioned as fur trade items (*Chippewa Music—II,* 222). Jenks, "Wild Rice Gatherers," 1069–70; Brogan, "Wild Rice Harvest," 132; Lips, *Reisernte,* 99; Kegg, *Nookomis,* 90. Lips disputed Jenks's claim that copper kettles were used, saying he was the only source in the literature and that she never saw any such kettles.

74. Kegg, *Nookomis,* 88; see also SD, tape 241, p. 27.

75. SD, tape 279A, p. 13; McGeshicks, interview; George Warren manuscript on treaty interpretations, Chippewa Indians collection, State Historical Society of Wisconsin.

76. Densmore, "Uses of Plants," 315; Fontaine, "Making It," 90; McGeshicks, interview.
77. Lips, *Reisernte,* 236.
78. Densmore, "Uses of Plants," 315; SD, tape 279A, p. 12–13.
79. Jenks, "Wild Rice Gatherers," 1065–66.
80. Jenks, "Wild Rice Gatherers," 1065.
81. Lips, *Reisernte,* 100.
82. Rajnovich, "Prehistoric Wild Rice Gathering," 204; Guy E. Gibbon, "The Old Shakopee Bridge Site: A Late Woodland Ricing Site On Shakopee Lake, Mille Lacs County, Minnesota," *Minnesota Archaeologist* 35 (1976): 2–56; Eastman, "Life and Handicrafts," 274; Jenks, "Wild Rice Gatherers," 1067; Reagan, "Plants," 247.
83. A. Ellis, "Fifty-Four Years' Recollections," 266; *Jesuit Relations* 59 (1900): 95; Schoolcraft cited in Jenks, "Wild Rice Gatherers," 1067.
84. Jenks, "Wild Rice Gatherers," 1067; Mitchell transcript, 11; Kegg, *Gabekanaansing,* 65–66; Blessing, *Ojibway Indians Observed,* 22; Winchell, *Aborigines,* 593.
85. Mitchell transcript, 1.
86. Jenks, "Wild Rice Gatherers," 1069; Mustache transcript, 2–3. See also Brogan, "Wild Rice Harvest," 132.
87. Fox, ed., "Letters on the Fur Trade," 178; Jenks, "Wild Rice Gatherers," 1068; Lips, *Reisernte,* 237; SD, tape 331, p. 16.
88. Jenks, "Wild Rice Gatherers," 1067, and plate 75B, facing p. 1068.
89. See, for example, Gilfillan, "Wild Rice Gathering," 544; Lorraine Slaebbert to the author, September 1985.
90. Seymour, *Sketches of Minnesota,* 183–84; Stickney, "Indian Use of Wild Rice," 119; A. Ellis, "Fifty-Four Years' Recollections," 266; Lips, *Reisernte,* 237.
91. Lips, *Reisernte,* 237; McGeshicks, interview; Mitchell transcript, 7.
92. Winchell, *Aborigines,* 593; Densmore, *Chippewa Customs,* 124, fig. 14, and "Uses of Plants," 315–16; Jenks, "Wild Rice Gatherers," 1069; Mustache transcript, 2; Baker transcript, 5.
93. SD, tape 350, p. 12; SD, tape 279A, p. 13; Fontaine, "Making It," 78. For Menominee and Winnebago methods, see Jenks, "Wild Rice Gatherers," 1068–69.
94. Densmore, *Chippewa Customs,* 128, and "Uses of Plants," 316; Kegg, *Gabekanaansing,* 62–63; Coleman, "Ojibwa and Wild Rice," 80.
95. Jenks, "Wild Rice Gatherers," 1068; Mustache transcript, 2; A. C. Stuntz to Albert Jenks, Jenks Papers.
96. Keating, *Narrative of an Expedition* 2:160; Jenks, "Wild Rice Gatherers," 1070; Lips, *Reisernte,* 102; Brogan, "Wild Rice Harvest," 132.
97. SD, tape 228, p. 1. See Hilger, *Chippewa Child Life,* 134, and plate 24 for specimens from Red Lake, Vermilion Lake, and Lac Court Oreilles; the American Museum of Natural History has had on display a bark winnowing tray that is 24 inches wide at its top.
98. SD, tape 293, p. 36–37; Mustache transcript, 4; Jenks, "Wild Rice Gatherers," 1070–71.
99. Warren, *History of the Ojibway,* 186; SD, tape 241, p. 26.
100. Schoolcraft, *Information* 3:63; Henry, *Travels and Adventures,* 241–44.
101. E. James, ed., *John Tanner,* 261–62, 213; Thwaites, ed., "Malhiot," 193.
102. Quimby, *Indian Life,* 133.
103. Hoffman, "Menomini Indians," 290–91; Doty, "Northern Wisconsin," 200–01.
104. SD, tape 350, p. 13; Buffalo's own figures are somewhat contradictory.
105. *Jesuit Relations* 3 (1897): 107, 109.
106. Lips, *Reisernte,* 12.
107. Carver, *Travels,* 525; Winchell, *Aborigines,* 593–94; Jean Baptiste Perrault, "Indian Life," in Schoolcraft, *Information* 3:359. For a more detailed version of the incident, see John S. Fox, ed., "Narrative of the Travels and Adventures of a Merchant Voyageur . . . by Jean Baptiste Perrault," *Historical Collections and Researches Made by the Michigan Pioneer and Historical Society* 37 (1909, 1910): 524.
108. Thwaites, ed., "Curot," 406, 411, 443.
109. Fox, ed., "Narrative," 562.

110. Kegg, *Gabekanaansing,* 63. Lips, *Reisernte,* 27–28, claimed that sub-Arctic hunters near Lake Winnipeg carried enormous amounts of rice for months at a time.

111. Lips, *Reisernte,* 242.

112. SD, tape 190, p. 10; SD, tape 268, p. 78; Kegg, *Nookomis,* 102; J. Long, *Voyages and Travels,* 117.

113. Fontaine, "Making It," 102. For the construction of *makakoon,* see Densmore, "Uses of Plants," 388. Near Mille Lacs in 1847, Stanchfield, "Pioneer Lumbering," 332, recorded ½ to 1 bushel as their storage capacity. See also Avery and Pawlick, "Last Stand," 33.

114. Ely Diary No. 3, December 23, 1833, Northeast Minnesota Historical Center, copy in Ely Papers; William Dudley, SD, tape 331, p. 17.

115. SD, tape 255, p. 13.

116. Friedl field notes, June 17, 1942; Belcourt to Bishop of Quebec, August 3, 1841, copy in Nute, Manuscripts; Lips, *Reisernte,* 151.

117. Densmore, *Chippewa Customs,* 157–58, plates 64a-b; Jenks, "Wild Rice Gatherers," 1072; Schoolcraft, *Information* 3:63. Winchell, *Aborigines,* 592, shows an illustration of this "mode of forming the edge of the rice bag." The same finishing method was used on the Menominee cedar-bark bag; the American Museum of Natural History has on permanent display an example each of an Ojibway and Menominee woven cedar-bark rice bag, identically made, although the latter is three times the size of the Ojibway specimen.

118. On Elizabeth Ellet, see Jenks, "Wild Rice Gatherers," 1104; Kinietz, *Chippewa Village,* fig. 25.

119. Mary Rowlandson, "The Sovereignty and Goodness of God," and Gyles, "Memoirs," both in *Puritans Among the Indians,* ed. Vaughan and Clark, 48–49 and 105, respectively. Ojibway from the Cass Lake area in 1939 recalled that the caches below the frost line were never touched until spring; Burns et al., " 'Manomin,' " 27.

120. Catlin, *Illustrations* 1:122; Rajnovich, "Prehistoric Wild Rice Gathering," 205; *Jesuit Relations* 8 (1897): 77, 79.

121. Thwaites, ed., "Malhiot," 214; Perrault, "Indian Life," in Schoolcraft, *Information* 3:366. The same incident appears in Fox, ed., "Narrative," 533.

122. SD, tape 268, p. 4–5.

123. *Jesuit Relations* 7 (1897): 223; Jenks, "Wild Rice Gatherers," 1071; *Jesuit Relations* 3 (1897): 109; Waisberg, "Ethnographic and Historical Outline," 129.

124. Hilger, *Chippewa Child Life,* 149; Thwaites, ed., "Curot," 416.

125. Ritzenthaler field notes, Book '42.

126. Hilger, *Chippewa Child Life,* 149–50; Mitchell transcript, 5.

127. Lips, *Reisernte,* 170, 242; Thomas Shingobe in Smith and Vogel, "Wild Rice Mystique," 760n53.

128. Mitchell transcript, 5; Baker transcript, 6. Baker's estimate may be exaggerated. Frank Jackson of White Earth said *his* family got through the winter on fifty pounds of rice but admitted they did not eat it steadily; SD, tape 228, p. 10–11.

129. SD 350, p. 14; Mustache transcript, 4; SD, tape 228, p. 10–11. Buffalo's figures jibe with those of Gilfillan, "Ojibways," 124, who noted that at White Earth a family could bring back twenty-one large sacks of rice.

130. Harry Ayer to Blanche La Du, February 10, 1933, Ayer to Wadsworth, August 13, 1922, Ayer Papers.

131. Hickerson, *Southwestern Chippewa,* 14–15.

Chapter 5

1. Lips, *Reisernte,* 233.
2. Gough, "Wild Ricing," 24.
3. Peel to Ayer, November 7, 1919, Ayer Papers.

4. Here and below, see Hall, Journal, November 27, 1831, December 27, 1831, February 1832, March 6, 11, 1832, ABCFM.

5. Sister Carol Berg, cited in Gerald Vizenor, *The People Named the Chippewa* (Minneapolis: University of Minnesota Press, 1984), 104; Cloeter, "Second Report of Missionary Cloeter, Kabitawigama, Nov. 7, 1858," 8, original published in German in *Der Lutheraner* [?], copy and English translation in Nute, Manuscripts.

6. Frederick Ayer to David Greene, August 4, 1839, October 8, 1838, originals in ABCFM, copies in Nute, Manuscripts.

7. *Report of the Commissioner of Indian Affairs,* 38th Cong., 1st sess., H. Doc. 1, 1863, p. 597 (Serial 1182); Hall to David Greene, June 14, 1832, ABCFM.

8. William Dailey to Ayer, October 10, 1921; Ayer to Manager, Kimball Base Ball Team, August 16, 1920, Ayer Papers.

9. E. James, ed., *John Tanner,* 205, 211.

10. Kegg, *Gabekanaansing,* v.

11. Hickerson, *Southwestern Chippewa,* 34–35.

12. Hall, Journal, October 1, 1932, [49v–50].

13. Alex[ander] J. Russell, *The Red River Country, Hudson's Bay & North-West Territories, Considered in Relation to Canada* (Montreal: G. E. Desbarats, 1870), 168.

14. Jenks, "Wild Rice Gatherers," 1089; Verwyst, *Chippewa Exercises,* 408–9n2.

15. Paul Radin, "The Winnebago Tribe," in *Thirty-Seventh Annual Report of the Bureau of American Ethnology* (Washington, D.C.: GPO, 1923), 77; Lips, *Reisernte,* 29, citing Peter Rosen, *Pa-Ha-Sa-Pah, or, The Black Hills of South Dakota* (St. Louis: Nixon-Jones Printing Co., 1895), 108.

16. SD, tape 279A, p. 14.

17. McGeshicks, interview.

18. Ruth Landes, *Ojibwa Sociology,* Columbia Contributions to Anthropology, vol. 29 (New York: Columbia University Press, 1937), 101; Nyholm tape; N. Smith, "What Ricing Means," 25.

19. SD, tape 338, p. 16. Thirteen of Berde's eighteen informants said they had lived in rice camps earlier in their lives; Berde, "Wild Ricing," 121.

20. Sister M. Inez Hilger, *A Social Study of One Hundred Fifty Chippewa Indian Families of the White Earth Reservation of Minnesota* (Washington, D.C.: Catholic University of America Press, 1939), 21.

21. Kegg, *Gabekanaansing,* 60; Baker transcript, 1; Mustache transcript, 1. Rohrl, "People of Mille Lacs," 70, mentioned about six families grouped along Mille Lacs Lake in the early 1940s; possibly these were Point Indians.

22. Kegg, *Gabekanaansing,* 73; Baker transcript, 1; SD, tape 241, p. 26–27.

23. Reed, *Wild Rice,* 10–11.

24. Mitchell transcript, 1; Landes, *Ojibwa Sociology,* 101–2.

25. E. Morrison, "A Little History," 14–15; SD, tape 290, p. 3.

26. Warren, *History of the Ojibway,* 309; Gilfillan, "Ojibways," 123–24; Kegg, *Gabekanaansing,* 70; McGeshicks, interview; SD, tape 228, p. 6–7; SD, tape 279A, p. 14.

27. SD, tape 211, p. 2; SD, tape 279A, p. 11.

28. Robert McElroy and Thomas Riggs, eds., *The Unfortified Boundary: A Diary of the first survey of the Canadian Boundary Line from St. Regis to the Lake of the Woods by Major Joseph Delafield* (New York: Privately printed, 1943), 435; Bray, ed., *Journals of Joseph N. Nicollet,* 105; Harry Ayer to W. F. Dickens, August 9, 1919, Ayer Papers.

29. Coleman, "Ojibwa and Wild Rice," 84; SD, tape 196, p. 7; SD, tape 331, p. 15; Mitchell transcript, 12.

30. Densmore, "Uses of Plants," 316–17; SD, tape 228, p. 9; SD, tape 331, p. 15; Mitchell transcript, 12.

31. Avery and Pawlick, "Last Stand," 38; SD, tape 196, p. 9.

32. Kegg, *Gabekanaansing,* 16; Ritzenthaler, *Chippewa Preoccupation with Health,* 177; Hilger, *Chippewa Child Life,* 138, 140.

33. Mustache transcript, 1; Kegg, *Gabekanaansing,* 4; SD, tape 228, p. 1–2.
34. SD, tape 350, p. 22.
35. SD, tape 257, p. 58–59; SD, tape 287, p. 1–2.
36. Mustache transcript, 1.
37. Kegg, *Gabekanaansing,* 67.
38. SD, tape 350, p. 10.
39. SD, tape 350, p. 11–12; Lips, *Reisernte,* 235.
40. SD, tape 228, p. 5.
41. Lips, *Reisernte,* 234; SD, tape 279A, p. 11, 14.
42. Kegg, *Gabekanaansing,* 62; SD, tape 228, p. 5.
43. Densmore, "Uses of Plants," 316; SD, tape 228, p. 2.
44. Ritzenthaler field notes, Book 8.
45. Lips, *Reisernte,* 81.
46. Gene Weltfish, *The Lost Universe* (New York: Basic Books, 1965), 210; Alfonso Ortiz, "San Juan Pueblo," in *Handbook of North American Indians*, vol. 9, *Southwest,* ed. Alfonso Ortiz (Washington, D.C.: Smithsonian Institution, 1979), 282–87.
47. Alanson Skinner, *Social Life and Ceremonial Bundles of the Menomini Indians,* Anthropological Papers of the American Museum of Natural History, vol. 13, pt. 1 (New York, 1915), 25; Felix M. Keesing, *The Menomini Indians of Wisconsin: A Study of Three Centuries of Cultural Contact and Change* (1939; reprint, Madison: University of Wisconsin Press, 1987), 40; Hickerson, *Southwestern Chippewa,* 52. In certain remote areas rice chiefs are reported still to be functioning—among the St. Croix Ojibway, for instance; Kathryn L. Tierney to the author, June 19, 1986.
48. Lips, *Reisernte,* 269; Broker, *Night Flying Woman,* 117.
49. Schoolcraft, *Information* 1:194.
50. See Warren, *History of the Ojibway,* 316–19; Kinietz, *Chippewa Village,* 16.
51. Vennum, "Ojibwa Begging Dance," 56; see also Schoolcraft, *Information* 3:62; Vennum, *Ojibwa Dance Drum,* 269.
52. On the Pueblo hunt chief's responsibilities, see Florence H. Ellis, "Isleta Pueblo," in *Handbook of North American Indians* 9:362; see also Hickerson, *Chippewa and Their Neighbors,* 110–11; Lips, *Reisernte,* 254.
53. Lips reviewed the official government list of Nett Lake chiefs with her informants, who pointed out errors and omissions; *Reisernte,* 254–55.
54. Here and three paragraphs below, see Lips, *Reisernte,* 259.
55. Lips, *Reisernte,* 260.
56. Reagan, "Plants," 247.
57. Lips, *Reisernte,* 262–64.
58. SD, tape 228, p. 1; Mitchell, 5; Baker transcript, 3; Vennum, *Ojibwa Dance Drum,* 269. James Mustache named Tony Butler as guardsman for Lake Chetac and the Lac Court Oreilles River, although sometimes it was Willy Billy Boy.
59. Ruth Landes, "The Ojibwa of Canada," in *Cooperation and Competition Among Primitive Peoples,* ed. Margaret Mead (New York: McGraw-Hill, 1937), 96.
60. Here and two paragraphs below, see Lips, *Reisernte,* 256; Smith and Vogel, "Wild Rice Mystique," 753; Kegg, *Gabekanaansing,* 63–64.
61. Reed, *Wild Rice,* 14–15; SD, tape 241, p. 27.
62. Here and below, see Lips, *Reisernte,* 232, 240–41; Mustache transcript, 1.
63. Here and below, see Lips, *Reisernte,* 230.
64. Public Archives of Canada, "Report Of S. J. Dawson—1870," Colonial Office Records 42, vol. 698; SD, tape 155, p. 88.
65. See F. Ellis, "Isleta Pueblo," 361.
66. Lips, *Reisernte,* 224.
67. Lips, *Reisernte,* 224.
68. SD, tape 350, p. 22; Fontaine, "Making It," 76, 84; Lips, *Reisernte,* 226.
69. Lips, *Reisernte,* 90; Skinner, "Social Life," 26.

70. For Buffalo's experiences, here and below, see SD, tape 350, p. 4–10. Buffalo also implied that the committee had some jurisdiction over fishing and duck hunting (p. 7).

71. Ernestine Friedl, "Persistence in Chippewa Culture and Personality," *American Anthropologist* 58 (1956): 818.

72. Lips, *Reisernte,* 237; Ron Parisien to the author, August 1986.

73. SD, tape 155, p. 82.

74. SD, tape 155, p. 88; SD, tape 262, p. 1–3.

75. SD, tape 155, p. 88–89, 93.

76. Mustache transcript, 5.

77. SD, tape 228, p. 10; Mustache transcript, 3; Ritzenthaler field notes, Book 3760, Book 3, p. 27.

78. SD, tape 258, p. 43.

79. Avery and Pawlick, "Last Stand," 38.

80. Eastman, *Indian Boyhood,* 237; SD, tape 350, p. 12–13.

81. SD, tape 279A, p. 14–15.

82. Eastman, *Indian Boyhood,* 235–37; Ritzenthaler field notes, Book 5, p. 43, Book 6.

83. Eastman, *Indian Boyhood,* 234–35. Mothers were typically cautious about sending daughters unattended to harvest. Ritzenthaler wrote that "Lucy Begay's mother gave her three pieces of *wike* (flagroot) tied in a string to take to the rice fields to protect her from snakes"; Book '46.

84. Casagrande field notes, John Mink entry; Eastman, *Indian Boyhood,* 234; Nyholm tape.

85. Kurath, "Wild Rice Gatherers," 713; SD, tape 228, p. 8; Baker transcript, 5. "Squaw" is an Anglicized form of the Algonquian word for woman (for example, *ikwe* in the Ojibway language); it is usually considered derogatory when used by non-Indians.

86. SD, tape 279A, p. 7; Lips, *Reisernte,* 275. Albert Reagan recorded Canadian singers at Nett Lake in 1914, possibly while there ricing. See also Vennum, *Ojibwa Dance Drum,* 113–26.

87. W. L. Motzfeldt to Albert Jenks, "Wild Rice Gatherers," December 3, 1898, Jenks Papers; SD, tape 228, p. 9.

88. Kegg, *Gabekanaansing,* 64; Warren, *History of the Ojibway,* 266.

89. SD, tape 241, p. 27.

90. McGeshicks, interview; SD, tape 156, p. 36.

91. See B. Jackson, "Peyote Community," 153, for a description of ricing preparations at Leech Lake.

92. Kohl, *Kitchi-Gami,* 209.

93. Edmund J. Danziger, Jr., *The Chippewas of Lake Superior* (Norman: University of Oklahoma Press, 1978), 184.

94. Here and below, see Nyholm tape.

95. J. Anthony Paredes, "Chippewa Townspeople," in *Anishinabe,* ed. Paredes, 360.

Chapter 6

1. Jenks, "Wild Rice Gatherers," 1051.

2. Hall, Journal, September 1831, [40–40v], ABCFM.

3. William W. Folwell, *A History of Minnesota,* rev. ed. (St. Paul: Minnesota Historical Society, 1956), 1:36–37, 48; J. Long, *Voyages and Travels,* 108–9.

4. Kane et al., ed., *Northern Expeditions,* 177–78; Waisberg, "Ethnographic and Historical Outline," 149.

5. Nute, ed., "Description of Northern Minnesota," 38; "The Diary of Hugh Faries," in *Five Fur Traders,* ed. Gates, 206, 208, 211; Henry Rice to George Bonga, August 23, 1848, letterbook 1, Henry M. Rice and Family Papers, MHS.

6. Coues, ed., *Expeditions of Pike* 1:282. John Sayer's journal was mistakenly attributed and published under the title "The Diary of Thomas Connor," in *Five Fur Traders,* ed. Gates, 245–78; for this paragraph, see "Connor [Sayer]," 252, 275.

7. Fox, ed., "Letters on the Fur Trade," 184; Fox, ed., "Narrative," 570.

8. Thwaites, ed., "Curot," 441; Fox, ed., "Narrative," 571.

9. Ledger Book 6, labeled "Current With Roussain & Brother," John A. Bardon Papers, MHS; see also Quimby, *Indian Life,* 148; Burpee, ed., *Journals of La Vérendrye,* 97, 104.

10. Fox, ed., "Narrative," 570; William Aitken to William Boutwell, April 23, 1838, Nute, Manuscripts.

11. Thwaites, ed., "Curot," 441; John Cameron cited in Leo G. Waisberg, "Ojibway Commercial Production," in *Historical Synthesis,* ed. Noble, 115; William Aitken to Charles Borup, October 24, 1837, copy in American Fur Company Papers, MHS.

12. Perrault, "Indian Life," in Schoolcraft, *Information* 3:356–57.

13. Thwaites, ed., "Dickson and Grignon Papers – 1812–1815," *Collections of the State Historical Society of Wisconsin* 11 (1888): 289, 292.

14. McElroy and Riggs, eds., *Unfortified Boundary,* 434.

15. Thwaites, ed., "Curot," 413, 450, 452, 458, 467–68.

16. Coues, ed., *Expeditions of Pike* 1:139–40; Harmon, *Journal of Voyages and Travels,* 142–43; Thwaites, ed., "Malhiot," 225.

17. Frederick Ayer to David Greene, October 4, 1837, August 4, 1839, originals in ABCFM, copies in Nute, Manuscripts; Isaac Cowie, ed., "The Minutes of the Council of the Northern Department of Rupert's Land, 1830–1843," *Collections of the State Historical Society of North Dakota* 4 (1913): 842–43.

18. Tim Holzkamm to the author, July 3, 1986; Gilfillan, "Ojibways," 124.

19. Fox, ed., "Letters on the Fur Trade," 182.

20. *Journal of the Reverend Peter Jacobs, Indian Wesleyan Missionary* (New York: P. Jacobs, 1857), 76–77; Keating, *Narrative of an Expedition* 2:97.

21. Coues, ed., *Expeditions of Pike* 1:139–40.

22. Taube, "Wild Rice," 374; but see Doty, "Northern Wisconsin," 200, 205, who says a bushel sack, worth $2, would fetch two skins. Trowbridge, in *Narrative Journal,* ed. Williams, "Journals and Letters," 487, sets the price of a skin at $2.

23. See Waisberg, "Ethnographic and Historical Outline," 150.

24. Nodin's speech transcribed by Frederick Ayer as part of "Speech of Sundry Chippeway Chiefs met in Council at Snake River (or Pokegama), Sept. 25, 1837," copy in Nute, Manuscripts.

25. See Nancy O. Lurie, "The World's Oldest On-Going Protest Demonstration: North American Indian Drinking Patterns," in *The American Indian: Essays from the Pacific Historical Review,* ed. Norris Hundley, Jr. (Santa Barbara, Calif.: Clio Books, 1974), 55–76. For a slightly different interpretation of the use of alcohol in the fur trade, see Bruce M. White, " 'Give Us a Little Milk': The Social and Cultural Meanings of Gift Giving in the Lake Superior Fur Trade," *Minnesota History* 48 (Summer 1982): 60–71, and "A Skilled Game of Exchange: Ojibway Fur Trade Protocol," *Minnesota History* 50 (Summer 1987): 229–40.

26. Fox, ed., "Narrative," 570; Paul H. Beaulieu, "The Fur Trade," in *Escorts to White Earth, 100 Year Reservation, 1868–1968,* ed. Gerald R. Vizenor (Minneapolis: Four Winds Press, 1968), 89.

27. Henry, *Travels and Adventures,* 242; see also Harold Hickerson, ed., "Journal of Charles Jean Baptiste Chaboillez, 1797–1798," *Ethnohistory* 6 (Summer 1959): 275; Gates, ed., "Connor [Sayer]," 253.

28. Thwaites, ed., "Curot," 400, 409, 410; Waisberg, "Ethnographic and Historical Outline," 149; Cowie, "Rupert's Land," 798.

29. Thwaites, ed., "Malhiot," 193, 216–17.

30. Thwaites, ed., "Malhiot," 200–201, 216–17.

31. Henry R. Schoolcraft, *Personal Memoirs of a Residence of Thirty Years with the Indian Tribes on the American Frontiers* (Philadelphia: Lippincott, Grambo & Co., 1851), 354–55; *Report of Major Wood,* 31st Cong., 1st sess., 1850, H. Doc. 51, p. 8 (Serial 577).

32. *Report of Major Wood,* 31st Cong., 1st sess., 1850, H. Doc. 51, p. 7.

33. Beaulieu, "Fur Trade," 88; Ducatel, "Fortnight among the Chippewas," 373; Whittlesey, "Among the Otchipwees," 340–41.

34. Philip P. Mason, ed., *Schoolcraft's Expedition to Lake Itasca: The Discovery of the Source of the Mississippi* (East Lansing: Michigan State University Press, 1958), 55.
35. Casagrande field notes, September 10, 1941.
36. Burpee, ed., *Journals of La Vérendrye,* 140.
37. Kohl, *Kitchi-Gami,* 78.
38. Ducatel, "Fortnight among the Chippewas," 363; Kohl, *Kitchi-Gami,* 79–80.
39. Harry Ayer to J. H. Hinton, January 7, 1919, Ayer to William Dailey, March 31, 1921, Ayer Papers.
40. Carver, *Travels,* 523; W. Gorrie, *Zizania Aquatica: The Wild Rice of the Canadian Lakes* (London: W. Gorrie, 1857), 5.
41. *Report of the Secretary of War,* 31st Cong., 1st sess., 1850, S. Doc. 42, p. 8 (Serial 558).
42. Sherman Hall to S. B. Treat, August, 1850, original in ABCFM, copy in Nute, Manuscripts; Gilfillan, "Ojibways," 124; Jenks, "Wild Rice Gatherers," 1105.
43. Jenks, "Wild Rice Gatherers," 1037, 1029; Ely Diary No. 16, March 22, 1841, and Nathan Randall to Ely, October 15, 1848, originals in Northeast Minnesota Historical Society, copy in Ely Papers.
44. Gorrie, *Zizania,* 6–8.
45. Currie Brothers to Albert Jenks, May 6, 1899, Jenks Papers.
46. Joseph W. T. Duvel, *The Storage and Germination of Wild Rice Seed,* United States Department of Agriculture, Bureau of Plant Industry Bulletin 90 (Washington, D.C.: GPO, 1906): 7.
47. Here and below, see Will W. Henry to Harry Ayer, August 13, 1919, Ayer to Henry, July 21, 1920, Ayer to Carlos Avery, August 25, 1920, Avery to Ayer, August 28, 1920, Ayer to A. Lehman, July 21, 1920, Lehman to Ayer, July 27, 1920, Ayer Papers.
48. Jenks, "Wild Rice Gatherers," 1094–95.
49. Fontaine, "Making It," 94, 106; SD, tape 350, p. 28–29.
50. Jenks, "Wild Rice Gatherers," 1057–58; Mustache to the author, August 1986.
51. SD, tape 268, p. 1–2; Jenks, "Wild Rice Gatherers," 1057.
52. Owen, *Report,* 324; Nute, ed., "Description of Northern Minnesota," 36, 37.
53. Jenks, "Wild Rice Gatherers," 1074; Gilfillan, "Ojibways," 124.
54. Moyle, "Wild Rice," 179; William Burnson, "Wild Rice: Wilderness Staple Through the Ages," *Minnesota Volunteer* 44 (September–October 1981): 44, 46, 48.
55. Lloyd, "Wild Rice," 294.
56. SD, tape 331, p. 16.
57. Burns et al., " 'Manomin,' " 27, 28.
58. Avery and Pawlick, "Last Stand," 40; SD, tape 287, p. 7.
59. Here and below, see Mustache transcript, 4–5.
60. Coleman, "Ojibwa and Wild Rice," 84–85. She seems to have the sequence wrong in describing "blowers" having auto engines attached to a drive shaft.
61. SD, tape 169, p. 56; SD, tape 350, p. 26; Baker transcript, 1.
62. Coleman, "Ojibwa and Wild Rice," 83.
63. Lloyd, "Wild Rice," 295.
64. Avery and Pawlick, "Last Stand," 42.
65. Here and below, see Avery and Pawlick, "Last Stand," 42; Lloyd, "Wild Rice," 295; Forrest G. English to the author, June 1987.
66. L. L. May & Co. to Albert Jenks, May 10, 1899, Jenks Papers. The rice L. L. May & Co. purchased could not have been "cured"; such rice will not germinate.
67. Here and below, see R. P. Warner to Harry Ayer, April 11, 1921, Ayer to Warner, April 22, 1921, Rust-Parker Co. to Ayer, August 17, September 7, 1920, Ayer to D. K. Harting, November 18, 1920, Harting to Ayer, November 20, 1920, Ayer Papers.
68. SD, tape 350, p. 14–15.
69. Here and two paragraphs below, see Berde, "Wild Ricing," 102–8.
70. Here and below, see Berde, "Wild Ricing," 107; SD, tape 350, p. 19; SD, tape 279A, p. 12; author's field notes. Earl Nyholm said that in the early 1950s younger people intent on selling

all their rice to buyers scooped up water to wet it down while their boats were being towed to the landing at Bad River; Nyholm tape.

71. SD, tape 155, p. 90–91.

72. SD, tape 196, p. 8; SD, tape 350, p. 18; SD, tape 155, p. 91.

73. SD, tape 350, p. 19.

74. Berde, "Wild Ricing," 102–3, 108.

75. E. J. Carlson, "Indian Rice Camps, White Earth Reservation," *Indians At Work* 2 (November 15, 1934): 23; Lips, *Reisernte,* 241; Brogan, "Wild Rice Harvest," 133; Berde, "Wild Ricing," 102; SD, tape 228, p. 11.

76. Brogan, "Wild Rice Harvest," 134.

77. SD, tape 350, p. 20.

78. Steeves, "Wild Rice," 122–23.

79. Berde, "Wild Ricing," 107.

80. Steeves, "Wild Rice," 125; SD, tape 236, p. 14; Harry Ayer to Mr. Wadsworth, draft, n.d., probably late October 1920, Ayer Papers.

81. Jenks, "Wild Rice Gatherers," 1105.

82. *Farm and Floral Guide,* 46; L. L. May & Co. to Jenks, May 10, 1899, Jenks Papers; Coleman, "Ojibwa and Wild Rice," 83.

83. Forrest G. English, "The Marketing of Wild Rice," typescript, dated 1975, p. 51, copy in author's possession; SD, tape 155, p. 91.

84. Author's interview with Frank E. Gleeson, December 1985, notes in author's possession; figures for 1986 and 1987 from telephone conversations.

85. George McGeshick to the author, September 1986.

86. Here and below, see E. A. Oelke et al., *Commerical Production of Wild Rice,* University of Minnesota Agricultural Extension Service Extension Folder 284 (St. Paul, 1973): 4–7; Duvel, *Storage and Germination,* 9–10; see also Lloyd, "Wild Rice," 296. For film footage of paddy production, see Bezat and Knutson, *Wild Rice.*

87. The legislature increased funding in 1973 to $105,000. The United States Department of Agriculture provided $100,000 in 1972 for similar projects at the Northern Research Laboratory in Peoria, Illinois. Whereas Minnesota in the 1960s produced 60 percent of the world's wild rice crop, due to the success of paddy rice, by 1973 this figure had climbed to 81 percent, based on a record 2.15 million pounds of finished rice; see English, "Marketing of Wild Rice," 5, 44.

88. English, "Marketing of Wild Rice," 33.

89. Baker transcript, 2.

90. The intention of this study is not to fault the paddy growers, who are industrious and dedicated, having entered into a precarious and untried business in an economically depressed area of the Upper Midwest. At least initially there was little profit, and some growers left the business soon after entering it; English, "Marketing of Wild Rice," 49.

91. A 1985 issue proudly displayed a photograph of the council's officers and Minnesota Senator Rudolph E. Boschwitz handing President Ronald Reagan a jar of wild rice in the Oval Office, noting that Reagan promised to include wild rice in formal dinners at the White House. (The administration lived up to this promise shortly thereafter by serving wild rice mixed with walnuts to accompany cornish game hen at a state dinner for India's Prime Minister Rajiv Gandhi—a truly "gamey" meal scarcely consistent with Asian Indian notions of refined cuisine!)

In an effort to improve their image with duck hunters, paddy growers claimed that their rice stands attracted wildfowl and "produced 4 to 5 times as many young birds reaching maturity" as federal waterfowl management areas; see Claude E. Titus, "Wild Rice Paddies Aid Waterfowl," *Jim Peterson's Outdoor News* (Golden Valley, Minn.), June 6, 1986, p. 1.

92. *Wild Rice News* (Grand Rapids, Minn.), January 1986, p. 1–2.

93. *Wild Rice News,* September 1985, p. 1.

94. Here and below, see English, "Marketing of Wild Rice," 7, 27; Elizabeth H. Winchell and Reynold P. Dahl, *Wild Rice: Production, Prices, and Marketing,* University of Minnesota Agricultural Experiment Station, Miscellaneous Publication 29 (St. Paul, 1984), 5–6, 18; Smith

and Vogel, "Wild Rice Mystique," 792n221; *Minneapolis Star and Tribune,* December 21, 1980, p. 4B; *St. Paul Pioneer Press and Dispatch,* November 24, 1986, business sec., p. 8.

95. Coleman, "Ojibwa and Wild Rice," 83–84.

96. Here and below, see Kathren J. Borgelt, "Wild Rice in the Cultural Landscape of Nett Lake Indian Reservation" (Master's thesis, Mankato State College, 1970), 75–81.

97. Here and three paragraphs below, see Avery and Pawlick, "Last Stand," 43–44; English to the author, October 1987.

98. Here and below, see Borgelt, "Wild Rice," 81–90.

99. Corky West to the author, December 15, 1986; Baker transcript, 5.

100. Lithman, "Capitalization of a Traditional Pursuit," 26–29; the unattributed quotations are from his field notes.

101. Smith and Vogel, "Wild Rice Mystique," 770n95; League of Women Voters of Minnesota, *Indians in Minnesota* (St. Paul: The League, 1971), 124.

102. McKinsey, "Chippewa Indians Undertake Cooperation," 12–13; Coleman, "Ojibwa and Wild Rice," 84–85.

103. Armando DeYoannes, "History of Wild Rice Research at Wilderness Valley Farms," in F. Robert Edman, *A Study of Wild Rice in Minnesota,* Minnesota Resources Commission Staff Report, no. 14 (St. Paul, 1975), vii; SD, tape 155, p. 94–95; Borgelt, "Wild Rice," 69–70.

104. SD, tape 155, p. 96; for historical perspective on ricing and "standard of life," see Jenks, "Wild Rice Gatherers," 1079.

105. Jenks, "Wild Rice Gatherers," 1078.

106. Danziger, *Chippewas,* 150, 162; Lips, *Reisernte,* 178; Steeves, "Wild Rice," 122; SD, tape 291, p. 24. Only recently have wild rice statistics provided an accurate picture. For example, there was no standard weight per bushel of wild rice, with reports varying widely from sixteen to sixty pounds per bushel (Moyle, "Wild Rice—Pioneer Food," 12, used fifty pounds as the correct weight). Given the source of the data, Jenks's own tables are difficult to disentangle—many bands are lumped together, for instance—and he himself admitted the problem. Indian affairs reports varied in accuracy, he pointed out, because agents were frequently changed, and some were disinterested. Reports were sometimes submitted before or during the harvest, so they lacked any reference to wild rice; at times the reports made no distinction between wild rice and other cereals.

107. Steeves, "Wild Rice," 122; Borgelt, "Wild Rice," 61–62, 67–68; League of Women Voters, *Indians in Minnesota,* 124.

108. Gilfillan, "Ojibways," 56–57, 72, emphasis added.

109. Waisberg, "Ojibway Commercial Production," 108–9.

110. SD, tape 355, p. 13; Kegg, *Gabekanaansing,* 13, 39; SD, tape 196, p. 9–10.

111. SD, tape 211, p. 1; see Cecilia Rock (born 1901), SD, tape 275, p. 3; Ritzenthaler field notes, Book 13, p. 25.

112. G. A. Morrison to Albert Jenks, February 21, 1899, Jenks Papers; Burns et al., " 'Manomin,' " 29; Ritzenthaler Expense Book, 53, and Ritzenthaler field notes, Book 6, p. 16; Lips, *Reisernte,* 178.

113. Harry Ayer to J. H. Hinton, January 7, 1919, Ayer Papers.

Chapter 7

1. United States v. State of Minnesota, 466 F. Supp. 1385 (1979).

2. For the text of these treaties, see Charles J. Kappler, comp. and ed., Indian Affairs. *Laws and Treaties* (Washington, D.C.: GPO, 1904) 2:250–55, 491–93.

3. George Warren manuscript, Chippewa Indians collection, State Historical Society of Wisconsin. Pine roots yielded sewing materials used in canoe construction.

4. Tim Holzkamm to the author, May 23, 1986.

5. "Proceedings of a Council with the Chippewa Indians," in *Iowa Journal of History and Politics* 9 (1911): 424–25; Tierney to the author, June 19, 1986.

6. Benjamin G. Armstrong, *Early Life Among the Indians* (Ashland, Wis.: A. W. Bowron, 1892), 12.

7. Letter cited in Jenks, "Wild Rice Gatherers," 1096 (Martin [possibly Marten] is mistakenly identified as an Ottawa Indian); *Petition of the Head Chiefs of the Chippewa Tribe of Indians on Lake Superior,* 30th Cong., 2d sess., 1849, H. Doc. 36, p. 1 (Serial 544).

8. Kappler, comp. and ed., *Laws and Treaties* 2:492, 542. Language in the published treaties varies slightly from the manuscript version.

9. Sherman Hall, "Mission to the Ojibwas," enclosed with Hall to ABCFM, August 2, 1850, original in ABCFM, copy in Nute, Manuscripts.

10. Edmund J. Danziger, "They Would Not Be Moved: The Chippewa Treaty of 1854," *Minnesota History* 43 (Spring 1973): 175–85; Richard F. Morse, "The Chippewas of Lake Superior," *Collections of the State Historical Society of Wisconsin* 3 (1857): 344.

11. George Warren to L. C. Draper, November 9, 1882, Chippewa Indians collection.

12. Tierney to the author, June 19, 1986; Armstrong, *Early Life,* 81.

13. Alexander Ramsey to William P. Dole, October 1863, 38th Cong., 1st sess., 1863, Executive P., Confidential, p. 10. See also Stanchfield, "Pioneer Lumbering," 331; *Report of the Commissioner of Indian Affairs,* 31st Cong., 2d sess., 1850, H. Doc. 1, p. 94 (Serial 595).

14. Documents Relating to the Negotiations of Ratified and Unratified Treaties with Various Indian Tribes, 1801–69, Record Group 11, National Archives, Washington, D.C.

15. *Report of the Secretary of the Interior,* 38th Cong., 1st sess., 1864, H. Doc. 1, p. 449–50 (Serial 1182); Francois [*sic*] Pierz to Alexander Ramsey, July 6, 1863, translation of original, Alexander Ramsey Papers, MHS.

16. John Watrous to Alexander Ramsey, July 2, 1850, U.S. Office of Indian Affairs, Minnesota Superintendency, Letters Received and Letters Sent, 1849–1856, Record Group 75, National Archives, microfilm copy in MHS.

17. League of Women Voters, *Indians in Minnesota,* 124–25; *Report of the Secretary of the Interior,* 35th Cong., 2d sess., 1859, S. Doc. 1, p. 400 (Serial 974); Jenks, "Wild Rice Gatherers," 1097.

18. Gough, "Wild Ricing," 24. East Lake Ojibway lost Rice Lake to a fenced-in wildlife refuge; SD, tape 155, p. 86–87; Mustache transcript, 5; Baker transcript, 2. See also Ayer to Wadsworth, draft, n.d., probably late October 1920, Ayer Papers.

19. Mustache transcript, 1–2.

20. State of Minnesota v. United States, 125 Federal Reporter, 2d series, 636 (1942); United States v. 4,450.72 Acres of Land, Clearwater County, State of Minnesota et al., 27 F. Supp. 167 (1939); *United States Statutes at Large,* vol. 44, pt. 2 (Washington, D.C.: GPO, 1927), 763, and vol. 49, pt. 1 (1936), 496–97. See Carlson, "Indian Rice Camps," 21. In acquiring the White Earth property, Minnesota acted quickly, as it already owned much of the contested area as "swamp land," and other tracts had reverted to the state through failure of owners to pay taxes.

21. United States v. Kagama and Mahawaha, United States Supreme Court Reports 30 (Rochester, N.Y.: Lawyer's Co-operative Publishing Co., 1887): 231. See also State of Minnesota v. United States, 125 Federal Reporter, 2d series, 636; United States v. 4,450.72 Acres, 27 F. Supp. 174.

22. United States v. 4,450.72 Acres, 27 F. Supp. 174.

23. D. P. Bushnell report, U.S. Office of Indian Affairs, Wisconsin Superintendency, Records, 1836–1848, Record Group 75, National Archives, microfilm copy in MHS; Brunson cited in Jenks, "Wild Rice Gatherers," 1096–97. Two years earlier Bushnell had expressed the same concern; see *Report of the Commissioner of Indian Affairs,* 25th Cong., 3d sess., 1839, H. Doc. 2, p. 468 (Serial 344). See also Kohl, *Kitchi-Gami,* 112–13; Morse, "Chippewas of Lake Superior," 342; F. Pierz to Alexander Ramsey, June 21, 1863, translation, Ramsey Papers.

24. SD, tape 196, p. 24; Vecsey, *Traditional Ojibwa Religion,* 46.

25. Ducatel, "Fortnight Among the Chippewas," 364.

26. Ritzenthaler field notes, Book 8, p. 43–46.

27. Hickerson, *Chippewa and Their Neighbors,* 108–9. On hunting and trapping rights, see Baraga, *Chippewa Indians,* 24–25; Grant, "Sauteux Indians," 326; Waisberg, "Ethnographic and Historical Outline," 177–78.

28. Here and below, see Lips, *Reisernte,* 267–68.

29. See Landes, "Ojibwa in Canada," 98.

30. *Jesuit Relations* 55 (1899): 169; Jenks, "Wild Rice Gatherers," 1073; Schoolcraft, *Information* 3:62–63; Hilger, *Chippewa Child Life,* 147. The Menominee prohibited sowing rice for religious reasons. They believed that its spiritual properties caused it to appear wherever they settled.

31. R. Pither to Albert Jenks, December 5, 1898, Jenks Papers; Ritzenthaler field notes, Book 8, p. 47.

32. Tim Holzkamm and Michael McCarthy, "Lake Sturgeon (*Acipenser fulvescens*) in the Returns of the Hudson's Bay Company Lac La Pluie District 1," unpublished paper, May 1986, copy in author's possession.

33. On Indian "laziness" in regard to ricing, see, for example, Paul Kane, *Wanderings of an Artist Among the Indians of North America* (Toronto: Radisson Society of Canada, Ltd., 1925), 313; Roger Patterson to Albert Jenks, December 5, 1898, and Peter Phalon to Major W. W. Campbell, Indian agent at Fond du Lac, December 27, 1898, both in Jenks Papers.

34. Tierney to the author, June 19, 1986.

35. Carlson, "Indian Rice Camps," 21; *Session Laws of the State of Minnesota . . . 1931* (St. Paul: Secretary of State, 1931), 480; copy of opinion to commissioner of game and fish, September 12, 1929, enclosed in Frank N. Whitney to W. T. Cox, August 31, 1932, Ayer Papers.

36. League of Women Voters, *Indians in Minnesota,* 31.

37. Here and below, see Harry Ayer to J. W. Kauffman, and to Charles Morrison, both April 17, 1935, and Kauffman to Ayer, April 18, 1935, Ayer Papers.

38. Here and seven paragraphs below, see *Session Laws of the State of Minnesota . . . 1939* (St. Paul: Secretary of State, 1939), 321–25.

39. Lips, *Reisernte,* 216.

40. SD, tape 223, p. 16–17; SD, tape 155, p. 89–90; this may have been in retaliation for the stringent restrictions on guest ricers at Nett Lake. See also SD, tape 350, p. 21.

41. Coleman, "Ojibwa and Wild Rice," 83; League of Women Voters, *Indians in Minnesota,* 123.

42. Berde, "Wild Ricing," 121; League of Voters, *Indians in Minnesota,* 123; Coleman, "Ojibwa and Wild Rice," 86.

43. SD, tape 291, p. 27.

44. See SD, tape 226, p. 10 for Josephine L. Norcross (born 1887) of Red Lake on Indians' misunderstanding of the rice council's powers.

45. SD, tape 155, p. 8; Harry Ayer to C. V. Peel, [November–December? 1919], undated response to letter of November 7, 1919.

46. See SD, tape 155, p. 13–14, for the story of Fred Jones's shooting at a game warden for cutting his fishnets; see also *United States Code, 1970 Edition,* title 18, no. 1162b, title 25, no. 1321b, and title 28, no. 1360; League of Women Voters, *Indians in Minnesota,* 125; manuscript no. 39, [p. 11–12], Fred Blessing manuscripts, in private possession.

47. Here and below, see Brian A. Hawley, "Treaty Interpretation—Off Reservation Rights," *Hamline Law Review* 4 (January 1981): 373–74. Because of the ambiguous wording in many Indian treaties, American court decisions have developed over the years certain "canons of construction" applying in treaty interpretation and Indian law in general. Only in cases where the original wording of a treaty is so clear that its intention cannot be challenged are these canons not followed.

48. Here and below, see Hawley, "Treaty Interpretation," 374–75. In its dissent, the minority of the court took strong exception to the relinquishment/cession dichotomy developed by the majority, saying that it deliberately weakened the application of the canons of construction.

49. Hawley, "Treaty Interpretation," 377, 384; Kappler, comp. and ed., *Laws and Treaties,* 253–54.

50. Hawley, "Treaty Interpretation," 376–78, 384, 386–87; SD, tape 291, p. 28.

51. Here and four paragraphs below, see *Masinaigan: A Chronicle of the Lake Superior Ojib-*

way (Odanah, Wis.), Special Ed.: Open Water Agreement, July 1984, p. 1; Kappler, comp. and ed., *Laws and Treaties,* 492; on anti-Indian sentiment in Wisconsin, see, for example, *Newsweek,* September 30, 1985, p. 35.

52. Totals on Wisconsin deer kill from author's telephone call to the Wisconsin DNR, September 1986.

53. Here and below, see Gough, "Wild Ricing," 24.

54. Here and seven paragraphs below, see Avery and Pawlick, "Last Stand," 36–38, 43–46.

55. SD, tape 279A, p. 10.

Chapter 8

1. Robert Jarvenpa, "Political Entrenchment in an Ojibwa Wild Rice Economy," *Journal of the Minnesota Academy of Science,* vol. 37, no. 2–3 (1971): 71.

2. Avery and Pawlick, "Last Stand," 36; Smith and Vogel, "Wild Rice Mystique," 765; Borgelt, "Wild Rice," 89.

3. Hilger, *Social Study,* 187.

4. *St. Paul Pioneer Press and Dispatch,* November 24, 1986, business sec., p. 8; Smith and Vogel, "Wild Rice Mystique," 789.

5. Thomas Vennum, Jr., "Ojibwa Origin-Migration Songs of the *mitewiwin,*" *Journal of American Folklore* 91 (July–September 1978): 753–91.

6. *Statutes at Large,* vol. 37, pt. 1 (Washington, D.C.: GPO, 1913), 847–48. More funds were appropriated in 1918 to continue the program; *Statutes at Large,* vol. 40, pt. 1 (Washington, D.C.: GPO, 1919), 995.

7. Holzkamm and McCarthy, "Lake Sturgeon," 10–11n3; Avery and Pawlick, "Last Stand," 35–36; see also Vecsey, *Traditional Ojibwa Religion,* 199–201.

8. Ben A. Franklin, "Indians Angry that U.S. Puts Lands on Nuclear Dump List," *New York Times,* April 18, 1986.

9. Baker transcript, 5.

10. Borgelt, "Wild Rice," 47; SD, tape 350, p. 17, 30.

11. Here and two paragraphs below, see Robert Gough, "Sokaogon Chippewa: Protecting a Heritage From Mining Development," *Anthropological Resource Center Newsletter* (Cambridge, Mass.) 4(1980): 24–25.

12. Warren manuscript, Chippewa Indians collection, State Historical Society of Wisconsin.

13. Jenks Papers; Kinietz, *Chippewa Village,* 68; Ritzenthaler field notes, No. 3670, Book 5, p. 89; James Meeker to the author, August 1986.

14. Lloyd, "Wild Rice," 291; Landes, *Ojibwa Sociology,* 101.

15. Smith and Vogel, "Wild Rice Mystique," 756–57n45; Coleman, "Ojibwa and Wild Rice," 88.

16. Carlson, "Indian Rice Camps," 12, 16–20, 22.

17. SD, tape 211, p. 11.

18. *Masinaigan,* August 1987, p. 2; Hawley, "Treaty Interpretation," 389.

19. Harry Ayer to C. V. Peel, [November–December? 1919], Ayer Papers.

20. Here and three paragraphs below, see Smith and Vogel, "Wild Rice Mystique," 773, 767, 790–93, 784–86n200, 201.

21. Avery and Pawlick, "Last Stand," 107; League of Women Voters, *Indians in Minnesota,* 122; William Madison, *Mah-No-Min (Wild Rice): Ojibway's Native Food Recipes* (Minneapolis: W. Madison, 1940), [2].

22. Holzkamm and McCarthy, "Lake Sturgeon," 8; Avery and Pawlick, "Last Stand," 107.

23. League of Women Voters, *Indians in Minnesota,* 124.

24. DeYoannes, "History of Wild Rice Research," vii.

25. Broker, *Night Flying Woman,* 118; Fontaine, "Making It," 76.

26. Gough, "Wild Ricing," 25; SD, tape 141, p. 16–17.

27. Avery and Pawlick, "Last Stand," 38; SD, tape 350, p. 20–29.
28. Avery and Pawlick, "Last Stand," 35.
29. Kurath, "Wild Rice Gatherers," 713; Smith and Vogel, "Wild Rice Mystique," 794.
30. SD, tape 276, p. 1; Lips, *Reisernte,* 149; Casagrande, "John Mink," 124.
31. Baker transcript, 3.
32. SD, tape 171, p. 35, 40; SD, tape 191, p. 12.
33. Smith and Vogel, "Wild Rice Mystique," 760n53; Mustache transcript, 3; Coleman, "Ojibwa and Wild Rice," 81.
34. Berde, "Wild Ricing," 116; Gough, "Wild Rice and the Sokaogon Chippewa"; SD, tape 257, p. 25.
35. N. Smith, "What Ricing Means to Me," 25.

Glossary of Selected Ojibway Ricing Terms

The following terms relating to wild rice culture have been culled from a number of speakers and sources listed in the bibliography of this volume, including Baraga, Lips, and the unattributed manuscript from Bear Lake, Wisconsin. The words have been checked with native speakers in Wisconsin and Minnesota; all spellings have been converted to the system developed in the mid-twentieth century by Charles Fiero, a missionary to the Ojibway in Ontario. Transitive verbs are given in imperative (prefixless) forms and translated that way; intransitive verbs are translated without a subject.

aaba′oodoon	untying the rice
abwaajigan (var. abwaajiganaak)	rack for smoke drying rice
aniib	elm bark
apakwaan, -ag	birch-bark covers sewn together, on which rice is sometimes spread out to dry
bawa′iganaak, -oon	wooden ricing stick(s); "knocker(s)"
bootaagan	tramping pit
bootaaganaak, -oon	pole(s) or pestle(s) used to dehusk rice
chi-manoomin	black, i.e., spoiled rice
makak, -oon	bark pail(s)
manoomin	wild rice
manoomin daabishkoo bakwezhigan	ground rice used in making bread
manoominiig	wild rice people; the Menominee Indians
manoominikewin	harvesting wild rice; "making rice"
manoominike-giizis	rice moon; August
manoominikeshiinh	rice bird resembling a snipe
manzaan	chaff or fine rice

manzaanens	small chaff or fine rice particles; first winnowings after the final tramping, containing much small rice that must be removed
mashkimod, -an	bag(s), sack(s)
nooshkaachinaagan, -an	winnowing or fanning tray(s)
okaadakik	cast-iron parching kettle
ozhaawashko-manoomin	green rice
wiigob	inner bark of basswood (used for binding the rice)
wiigwaasapakwaan, -ag	birch-bark strips sewn together, used on wigwams or drying racks

Bibliography

MANUSCRIPTS

Anthropology Section, Milwaukee Public Museum, Milwaukee, Wisconsin
Joseph B. Casagrande Papers
Ernestine Friedl Papers
Robert E. Ritzenthaler Papers. Field notes and unattributed manuscript from Bear Lake, Wisconsin
Houghton Library, Harvard University, Cambridge, Massachusetts
American Board of Commissioners of Foreign Missions, Papers
Minnesota Historical Society, St. Paul, Minnesota
American Fur Company Papers
Harry D. Ayer and Family Papers
John A. Bardon Papers
Edmund F. Ely and Family Papers
John McLoughlin Papers. Description of Indians living in the region between Fort William, Ontario, and the Lake of the Woods (copy)
Grace Lee Nute, comp. Manuscripts Relating to Northwest Missions, 1810–1896
Alexander Ramsey Papers
Henry M. Rice Papers
U.S. Office of Indian Affairs, Minnesota Superintendency, Letters Received and Letters Sent, 1849–1856 (microfilm); Wisconsin Superintendency, Records, 1836–1848 (microfilm)
National Anthropological Archives, Smithsonian Institution, Washington, D.C.
Ruth Landes Papers
National Archives, Washington, D.C.
Record Group 11, Documents Relating to the Negotiations of Ratified and Unratified Treaties with Various Indian Tribes, 1801–69
Newberry Library, Chicago, Illinois
Edward E. Ayer collection. Herman Haupt, Jr., "North American Indians.

Ethnology of the Dakota-Sioux—and Ojibway-Chippeway—Indians. 1897."
Public Archives of Canada, Ottawa, Ontario
Report of S. J. Dawson. Colonial Office Records 42, vol. 698
Société historique d'Odanak, Quebec, Canada
Joseph Aubery, manuscript Abenaki-French dictionary
State Historical Society of Wisconsin, Archives Division, Madison, Wisconsin
George Boyd Papers
Alfred Brunson Papers
Albert E. Jenks Papers
Chippewa Indians collection. George Warren manuscript on treaty interpretations

INTERVIEWS

Office of Folklife Programs Archives, Smithsonian Institution, Washington, D.C.
William Bineshi Baker, Sr., transcript of taped interview, September 4, 1985, Lac Court Oreilles, Wisconsin
Lawrence Mitchell, transcript of taped interview, April 30, 1985, Washington, D.C.
James Mustache, Sr., transcript of taped interview, September 4, 1985, Hayward, Wisconsin
George and Mary McGeshick, taped interview, September 22, 1986, Crystal Falls, Michigan
Earl Nyholm, taped recollections, June 1986
South Dakota Oral History Center, University of South Dakota, Vermillion
American Indian Research Project, taped interviews ca. 1960–68 and transcripts

MAPS

Jonathan Carver. Unpublished map dedicated "To the Rt. Honble the Earl of Hillsborough." 1769
——. *A Plan of Captain Carvers Travels in the interior Parts of North America in 1766 and 1767.* 1778
Jean Baptiste Louis Franquelin. *Partie de l'Amerique Septentrionale.* 1699

NEWSPAPERS AND NEWSLETTERS

Jim Peterson's Outdoor News (Golden Valley, Minn.), 1986
Masinaigan: A Chronicle of the Lake Superior Ojibway (Odanah, Wis.), 1984–87
Wild Rice News (Grand Rapids, Minn.), 1978–86

BOOKS, ARTICLES, AND UNPUBLISHED MATERIALS

Adney, Edwin T., and Howard J. Chapelle. *The Bark Canoes and Skin Boats of North America.* United States National Museum Bulletin 230. Washington, D.C.: Smithsonian Institution, 1964.

Allen, Lieutenant James. "Report of Lieutenant Allen, of the Army, of H. R. Schoolcraft's Exploration of the Country At and Beyond the Sources of the Mississippi, on a visit to the Northwestern Indians in 1832." *American State Papers: Military Affairs.* Vol. 5, p. 312–44. Washington, D.C., 1860.

Anderson, Gary C. *Little Crow, Spokesman for the Sioux.* St. Paul: Minnesota Historical Society Press, 1986.

Anderson, R. A. "Wild Rice: Nutritional Review." *Cereal Chemistry* 53 (1976): 949–55.

Armstrong, Benjamin G. *Early Life Among the Indians.* Ashland, Wis.: A. W. Bowron, 1892.

Arnold, John B., comp. *A Story of Grand Portage and Vicinity . . .* Minneapolis: Harrison & Smith Co., 1923.

Atwater, Caleb. *The Indians of the Northwest.* Columbus, Ohio: C. Atwater, 1850.

Avery, Kathi, and Thomas Pawlick. "Last Stand In Wild Rice Country." *Harrowsmith* 3 (1979): 33, 35–40, 43–46, 107.

Babbitt, Frances E. "Illustrative Notes Concerning the Minnesota Odjibwas." *Proceedings of the American Society for the Advancement of Science* 36 (1887): 303–07.

Babcock, Willoughby M. "With Ramsey to Pembine: A Treaty-Making Trip in 1851." *Minnesota History* 38 (March 1962): 1–10.

Baraga, Frederic. *Chippewa Indians as Recorded by Rev. Frederick Baraga in 1847.* Studia Slovenica, vol. 10. New York: League of Slovenian Americans, 1976.

——. *A Dictionary of the Otchipwe Language.* 2 vols. Montreal: Beauchemin & Valois, 1880.

Barnouw, Victor. *Wisconsin Chippewa Myths & Tales and Their Relation to Chippewa Life.* Madison: University of Wisconsin Press, 1977.

Barrett, S. A. *The Dream Dance of the Chippewa and Menominee Indians of Northern Wisconsin.* Bulletin of the Public Museum of the City of Milwaukee 1 (1911): 251–415.

Beltrami, Giacomo C. *A Pilgrimage in Europe and America, Leading to the Discovery of the Sources of the Mississippi and Bloody River . . .* 2 vols., London: Hunt and Clarke, 1828.

Berde, Stuart. "Wild Ricing: The Transformation of an Aboriginal Subsistence Pattern." In *Anishinabe: 6 Studies of Modern Chippewa,* ed. Anthony J. Paredes, 101–26. Tallahassee: University Presses of Florida, 1980.

Bessey, Charles E., and Herbert J. Webber. *Report of the Botanist on the Grasses and Forage plants and the Catalogue of Plants.* Lincoln, Neb.: State Journal Company, Printers, 1890.

Biddle, James W. "Recollections of Green Bay in 1816–'17." *First Annual Report and Collections of the State Historical Society of Wisconsin* 1 (1855): 49–63.

Bigsby, John J. *The Shoe and the Canoe, or Pictures of Travel in the Canadas.* 2 vols. in 1. London: Chapman and Hall, 1850.

Blackbird, Andrew J. *Complete Both Early and Late History of the Ottawa and Chippewa Indians of Michigan . . .* Harbor Springs, Mich.: Babcock & Darling, 1897.

Blackwood, Beatrice. "Tales of the Chippewa Indians." *Folk-lore* 40 (1929): 315–44.

Blair, Emma H., ed. *The Indian Tribes of the Upper Mississippi Valley and Region of the Great Lakes.* 2 vols. Cleveland: Arthur H. Clarke Co., 1911.

Blessing, Fred K., Jr. *The Ojibway Indians Observed: Papers of Fred K. Blessing, Jr., from* The Minnesota Archaeologist. Occasional Publications in Minnesota Anthropology no. 1. St. Paul: Minnesota Archaeological Society, 1977.

Bond, J. Wesley. *Minnesota and Its Resources . . .* Philadelphia: Charles Desilver, 1857.

Boutwell, William T. "Schoolcraft's Exploring Tour of 1832." *Collections of the Minnesota Historical Society* 1 (1872): 153–76.

Bray, Edmund C., and Martha C. Bray, trans. and eds. *Joseph N. Nicollet on the Plains and Prairies: The Expeditions of 1838–39 With Journals, Letters, and Notes on the Dakota Indians.* St. Paul: Minnesota Historical Society Press, 1976.

Bray, Martha Coleman, ed. *The Journals of Joseph N. Nicollet: A Scientist on the Mississippi Headwaters, With Notes On Indian Life, 1836–37.* Trans. André Fertey. St. Paul: Minnesota Historical Society, 1970.

Breck, James Lloyd. *Chippeway Pictures from the Territory of Minnesota, 1857.* Hartford, Conn.: Church Missions Publishing Co., 1910.

Brogan, Dan. "Wild Rice Harvest." *Frontiers: A Magazine of Natural History* 20 (June 1956): 131–35.

Broker, Ignatia. *Night Flying Woman: An Ojibway Narrative.* St. Paul: Minnesota Historical Society Press, 1983.

Brooks, Edwin R. *A Survey of the Current and Potential Wild Rice Production, Processing, and Marketing on the White Earth, Nett Lake, and River Indian Reservations in Minnesota, and the Mole and the Bad River Indian Reservations in Wisconsin.* University of Minnesota Institute of Agriculture, Department of Agronomy and Plant Genetics. St. Paul, 1966.

Brown, Paula. "Changes in Ojibwa Social Control." *American Anthropologist* 54 (January 1952): 57–70.

Brown, Samuel R. *The Western Gazeteer; Or, Emigrant's Directory, Containing a Geographical Description of the Western States and Territories . . .* Auburn, N. Y.: Printed by H. C. Southwick, 1817.

Burns, Mark L., et al. " 'Manomin,' The Wild Rice of the Lake Country." *Indians at Work* 6 (January 1939): 26–29.

Burnson, William. "Wild Rice: Wilderness Staple Through the Ages." *Minnesota Volunteer* 44 (September–October 1981): 44–51.

Burpee, Lawrence J., ed. *Journals and Letters of Pierre Gaultier de Varennes de la Vérendrye and His Sons.* Toronto: The Champlain Society, 1927.

Burton, Frederick R. *American Primitive Music, with Especial Attention to the Songs of the Ojibways.* New York: Moffat, Yard and Co., 1909.

Bushnell, David I. *Burials of the Algonquian, Siouan and Caddoan Tribes West of the Mississippi.* Bureau of American Ethnology Bulletin 83. Washington, D.C.: GPO, 1927.

——. *Native Cemeteries and Forms of Burial East of the Mississippi.* Bureau of American Ethnology Bulletin 71. Washington, D.C.: GPO, 1920.

Calkins, Hiram. "Indian Nomenclature of Northern Wisconsin, with a Sketch of the Manners and Customs of the Chippewas." *First Annual Report and Collections of the State Historical Society of Wisconsin* 1 (1854): 119–26.

Canniff, William. *History of the Settlement of Upper Canada (Ontario), with special Reference to the Bay Quinté.* Toronto: Dudley & Burns, 1869.

Carlson, E. J. "Indian Rice Camps, White Earth Reservation." *Indians at Work* 2 (November 15, 1934): 16–25.

Carr, Lucien. "The Food of Certain American Indians and Their methods of preparing It." In American Antiquarian Society *Proceedings* 10 (1896): 155–90.

Carver, Jonathan. *Travels through the Interior Parts of North America in the Years 1766, 1767, and 1768.* 3rd ed., 1781. Reprint. Minneapolis: Ross & Haines, 1956.

Casagrande, Joseph B. "John Mink, Ojibwa Informant." *Wisconsin Archeologist* 36 (December 1955): 106–28.

——. "Ojibwa Bear Ceremonialism: The Persistence of a Ritual Attitude." In *Acculturation in the Americas: Proceedings and Selected Papers of the XXIXth International Congress of Americanists,* ed. Sol Tax, 113–17. Chicago: University of Chicago Press, 1952.

Catlin, George. *Illustrations of the Manners, Customs, and Condition of the North American Indians . . .* 2 vols. London: Henry G. Bohn, 1845.

——. *Letters and Notes on the Manners, Customs, and Condition of the North American Indians.* 2 vols. 1841. Reprint. Minneapolis: Ross & Haines, 1965.

Chamberlain, Alexander F. "Maple Sugar and the Indians." *American Anthropologist* 4 (1891): 381–84.

——. "Notes on the History, Customs, and Beliefs of the Mississagua Indians." *Journal of American Folk-Lore* 1 (July–September 1888): 150–60.

Chambliss, Charles E. "The Botany and History of Zizania Aquatica L. ('Wild Rice')." In *Annual Report of the Board of Regents of the Smithsonian Institution . . . For the Year Ended June 30, 1940* (Washington, D.C., GPO, 1941): 369–82.

Charlevoix, Pierre François Xavier de. *Journal of a Voyage to North America,* ed. Louise Phelps Kellogg. 2 vols. 1761. Reprint. Chicago: Caxton Club, 1923.

"Chippewa Indians Harvest Rice in Minnesota Marshes." *Indians at Work,* October 1939, p. 28–29.

Cleland, Charles E. "A Research Report on the 19th Century Patterns of Resource Use and Economic Strategy of the Lake Superior Chippewa." 1985. Copy of typescript in author's possession.

Coleman, Sister Bernard M. "The Ojibwa and the Wild Rice Problem." *Anthropological Quarterly* 26 (July 1953): 79–88.

——. "Religion and Magic among the Cass Lake Ojibwa." *Primitive Man* 2 (1929): 52–55.

——. "The Religion of the Ojibwa of Northern Minnesota." *Primitive Man* 10 (1937): 33–57.

——, et al. *Ojibwa Myths and Legends.* Minneapolis: Ross & Haines, 1962.

Cooper, Leland R. "Wild Rice Gathering and Processing." *The Naturalist* 3 (1953): 57–60.

Copway, George. *Recollections of a Forest Life* . . . London: C. Gilpin, 1850?

——. *The Traditional History and Characteristic Sketches of the Ojibway Nation.* London: C. Gilpin, 1850.

Coues, Elliott M., ed. *The Expeditions of Zebulon Montgomery Pike* . . . 3 vols. New York: Francis P. Harper, 1895.

——. "The Wild Rice of Minnesota." *Botanical Gazette* 19 (1894): 504–6.

Cowie, Isaac, introduction. "The Minutes of the Council of the Northern Department of Rupert's Land 1830 to 1843." *Collections of the State Historical Society of North Dakota* 4 (1913): 644–838.

Culkin, William E. "Tribal Dance of the Ojibway Indians." *Minnesota History Bulletin* 1 (August 1915): 83–93.

Danziger, Edmund J., Jr. *The Chippewas of Lake Superior.* Norman: University of Oklahoma Press, 1978.

Dawson, S. J. *Report on the Exploration of the Country between Lake Superior and the Red River Settlement and between the Latter Place and the Assiniboine and Saskatchewan.* Toronto: J. Lovell, Printer, 1859.

Densmore, Frances. *Chippewa Customs.* 1929. Reprint. St. Paul: Minnesota Historical Society Press, Borealis Books, 1979.

——. *Chippewa Music.* Bureau of American Ethnology Bulletin 45. Washington, D.C.: GPO, 1910.

——. *Chippewa Music–II.* Bureau of American Ethnology Bulletin 53. Washington, D.C.: GPO, 1913.

——. "Material Culture among the Chippewa." In *Explorations and Field-Work of the Smithsonian Institution in 1918,* Smithsonian Miscellaneous Collections, 70 (1919): 114–18.

——. "Study of Chippewa Material Culture." In *Explorations and Field-Work of the Smithsonian Institution in 1917,* Smithsonian Miscellaneous Collections, 68 (1918): 95–100.

——. "Uses of Plants by the Chippewa Indians." In *Forty-Fourth Annual Report of the Bureau of American Ethnology, 1926–27, 275–397.* Washington, D.C.: GPO, 1928.

Dickinson, Dennis. "A Selected and Annotated Bibliography on Wild Rice." *Plains Anthropologist* 13 (May 1968): 90–99.

Dore, William G. *Wild Rice.* Canada, Department of Agriculture, Research Branch, Publication 1393 (1969).

Doty, James Duane. "Northern Wisconsin in 1820." *Report and Collections of the State Historical Society of Wisconsin* 7 (1876): 195–206.

Ducatel, J. [T.] "A Fortnight Among the Chippewas of Lake Superior." In *The Indian Miscellany . . .*, ed. W. W. Beach, 361–78. Albany, N.Y.: J. Munsell, 1877.

Duvel, Joseph W. T. *The Storage and Germination of Wild Rice Seed.* United States Department of Agriculture, Bureau of Plant Industry, Bulletin 90 (1906): 5–13.

Eastman, Charles A. *From the Deep Woods to Civilization: Chapters in the Autobiography of an Indian.* 1916. Reprint. Lincoln: University of Nebraska Press, 1977.

——. *Indian Boyhood.* Boston: Little Brown and Co., 1902.

——. "Life and Handicrafts of the Northern Ojibwas." *Southern Workman* (Hampton, Va.) 40 (May 1911): 273–78.

Edman, F. Robert. *A Study of Wild Rice in Minnesota.* Minnesota Resources Commission Staff Report, no. 14. St. Paul, 1975.

Ellet, Elizabeth F. *Summer Rambles in the West.* New York: J. C. Riker, 1853.

Ellis, Albert G. "Fifty-Four Years' Recollections of Men and Events in Wisconsin." *Report and Collections of the State Historical Society of Wisconsin* 7 (1873–76): 207–68.

English, Forrest G. "The Marketing of Wild Rice." 1975. Typescript, copy in author's possession.

Featherstonhaugh, George W. *A Canoe Voyage up the Minnay Sotor* . . . 2 vols. 1847. Reprint. St. Paul: Minnesota Historical Society, 1970.

Flint, Charles L. *Grasses and Forage Plants: A Practical Treatise* . . . Rev. ed. Boston: Lee and Shepard, 1888.

Folwell, William W. *A History of Minnesota.* Vol. 1. Rev. ed. St. Paul: Minnesota Historical Society, 1956.

Fontaine, Janet, et al., comps. "Making It at Sagkeeng." Photocopy of typescript in author's possession. 1976. Cultural Education Centre, Sagkeeng Education Authority, Fort Alexander, Manitoba.

Ford, Richard I., and David S. Brose. "Prehistoric Wild Rice from the Dunn Farm Site, Leelanau County, Michigan." *Wisconsin Archeologist,* n.s. 56 (March 1975): 9–15.

Fox, John Sharpless, ed. "Letters on the Fur Trade 1833." *Historical Collections and Researches Made by the Michigan Pioneer and Historical Society* 37 (1909–10): 132–207.

——. "Narrative of the Travels and Adventures of a Merchant Voyageur. . . " *Historical Collections and Researches Made by the Michigan Pioneer and Historical Society* 37 (1909–10): 508–619.

Friedl, Ernestine. "Persistence in Chippewa Culture and Personality." *American Anthropologist* 58 (1956): 814–25.

Fyles, Faith. *Wild Rice.* Canada, Department of Agriculture, Bulletin 42, 2d series (1920).

Gates, Charles M., ed. *Five Fur Traders of the Northwest.* St. Paul: Minnesota Historical Society, 1965.

Gibbon, Guy. "The Old Shakopee Bridge Site: A Late Woodland Ricing Site on Shakopee Lake, Mille Lacs County, Minnesota." *Minnesota Archaeologist* 35 (1976): 2–56.

Gilfillan, Joseph A. *Minnesota Geographical Names Derived from the Chippewa Language.* In Geological and Natural History Survey of Minnesota, Fifteenth Annual Report of Progress for the Year 1886, p. 451–77. Minneapolis, 1887.

——. "The Ojibways in Minnesota." *Collections of the Minnesota Historical Society* 9 (1901): 55–128.

——. "Wild Rice Gathering in Minnesota." In *Spirit of Missions* 41 (November 1876): 543–45.

Gillin, John, and Victor Raimy. "Acculturation and Personality." *American Sociological Review* 5 (1940): 371–80.

Gilmore, Melvin R. "Some Chippewa Uses of Plants." *Papers of the Michigan Academy of Science, Arts, and Letters* 17 (1932): 119–43.

——. "Uses of Plants by the Indians of the Missouri River Region." In *Thirty-Third Annual Report of the Bureau of American Ethnology, 1911*–1912, 43–154. Washington, D.C.: GPO, 1919.

Godsell, Philip H. "The Ojibwa Indian." *Canadian Geographical Journal* 4 (1932): 50–66.

Gorrie, W. *Zizania Aquatica: The Wild Rice of the Canadian Lakes.* London: W. Gorrie, 1857.

Gough, Robert. "Sokaogon Chippewa: Protecting a Heritage from Mining Development." In *Anthropological Resource Center Newsletter* (Cambridge, Mass.) 4 (1980).

——. "Wild Rice and the Sokaogon Chippewa: A Study in Cultural Ecological Adaptation." ca. 1985. Typescript, copy in author's possession.

——. "Wild Ricing." *Wisconsin Trails:* 24 (September–October 1983): 22–25.

Grant, Peter. "The Sauteaux Indians about 1804." In *Les Bourgeois de la Compagnie du Nord-Ouest* . . ., ed. L. R. Masson, 303–66. 2 vols. 1889–90. Reprint. New York: Antiquarian Press, 1960.

Grist, Donald Honey. *Rice.* London: Longmans, Green, 1953.

[Halkett, John]. *Statement Respecting the Earl of Selkirk's Settlement upon the Red River*, . . . London: J. Murray, 1817.

Hallowell, A. Irving. "Concordance of Ojibwa Narratives in the Published Works of Henry R. Schoolcraft." *Journal of American Folklore* 59 (1946): 136–53.

Harmon, Daniel W. *A Journal of Voyages and Travels in the Interiour of North America.* Andover, Vt.: Flagg and Gould, 1820.

Hart, Irving Harlow. "The Story of Beengwa, Daughter of a Chippewa Warrior." *Minnesota History* 9 (December 1928): 319–30.

Hawley, Brian A. "Treaty Interpretation—Off Reservation Rights." *Hamline Law Review* 4 (January 1981): 373–89.

Hebberd, Stephen S. *History of Wisconsin under the Dominion of France.* Madison: Midland Publishing Co., 1890.

Hennepin, Louis. *A New Discovery of a Vast Country in America . . .* 2 vols. 1697. Reprint. Chicago: A. C. McClung and Co., 1903.
Henry, Alexander. *Travels and Adventures in Canada and the Indian Territories Between the years 1760 and 1776.* New York: I. Riley, 1809.
Hickerson, Harold. *The Chippewa and Their Neighbors: A Study in Ethnohistory.* Studies in Anthropological Method. New York: Holt, Rinehart & Winston, 1970.
——, ed. "Journal of Charles Jean Baptiste Chaboillez, 1797–1798." *Ethnohistory* 6 (Summer, Fall 1959): 265–316, 363–427.
——. "Land Tenure of the Rainy Lake Chippewa at the Beginning of the 19th Century." *Smithsonian Contributions to Anthropology* 2 (Washington, D.C.: GPO, 1967): 41–63.
——. *The Southwestern Chippewa: An Ethnohistorical Study.* American Anthropological Association, Memoir 92. Menasha, Wis., 1962.
Hilger, Sister M. Inez. *Chippewa Child Life and Its Cultural Background.* Bureau of American Ethnology Bulletin 146. Washington, D.C.: GPO, 1951.
——. "Chippewa Customs." *Primitive Man* 9 (1936): 17–24.
——. "Chippewa Pre-Natal Food and Conduct Taboos." *Primitive Man* 9 (1936): 46–48.
——. *A Social Survey of One Hundred Fifty Chippewa Indian Families of the White Earth Reservation of Minnesota.* Washington, D.C.: Catholic University of America Press, 1939.
Hind, Henry Youle. *Narrative of the Canadian Red River Exploring Expedition of 1857 and of the Assiniboine and Saskatchewan Exploring Expedition of 1858.* 2 vols. 1860. Reprint. New York: Greenwood Press, 1969.
Hoffman, Walter J. "Ein Besuch bei den Ojibwa im Noerdlichen Minnesota." *Globus* 60 (1891).
——. "The Menomini Indians." In *Fourteenth Annual Report of the Bureau of American Ethnology, 1892–93,* 1: 11–328. Washington, D.C.: GPO, 1896.
——. "The Midē'wiwin or 'Grand Medicine Society.'" In *Seventh Annual Report of the Bureau of American Ethnology, 1885–86,* 143–300. Washington, D.C.: GPO, 1891.
——. "Notes on Ojibwa Folk-Lore." *American Anthropologist* 2 (1889): 215–23.
——. "Pictography and Shamanistic Rites of the Ojibwa." *American Anthropologist* 1 (1888): 209–29.
Holt, Catharine. *Shasta Ethnography.* Anthropological Records, vol. 3, no. 4. Berkeley: University of California Press, 1946.
Holzkamm, Tim E. "Subsistence Factors in the Spread of Ojibway Horticulture in the Upper Mississippi and Boundary Waters Region During the 19th Century." Paper presented at the Seventeenth Algonquian Conference, Redpath Museum, McGill University, Montreal, October 25, 1985. Photocopy in author's possession.
——, and Michael McCarthy. "Lake Sturgeon (*Acipenser fulvescens*) in the Returns of the Hudson's Bay Company Lac La Pluie District 1." May 1986. Typescript, copy in author's possession.
Hrdlička, Aleš. "Anthropology of the Chippewa." In *Holmes Anniversary Volume: An-*

thropological Essays Presented to William Henry Holmes . . ., 198–227. Washington, D.C.: Privately published, 1916.

Hunter, John D. *Memoirs of a Captivity among the Indians of North America, from Childhood to the Age of Nineteen . . .* 3d ed. London: Printed for Longmans, Hurst, Rees, Orme, Brown, and Green, 1824.

"In The Fashion Of Their Forefathers – Chippewas Gather Wild Rice." *Indians at Work* September, 1941, 14–20.

Jackman, Sydney W., and John F. Freeman, eds. *American Voyageur: The Journal of David Bates Douglass.* Marquette: Northern Michigan University Press, 1969.

Jackson, Barbara D. "A Peyote Community in Northern Minnesota." In *Anishinabe: 6 Studies of Modern Chippewa,* ed. Anthony J. Paredes, 127–93. Tallahassee: University Presses of Florida, 1980.

Jacobs, Peter. *Journal of the Reverend Peter Jacobs, Indian Wesleyan Missionary, from Rice Lake to the Hudson's Bay Territory and Returning . . .* New York: P. Jacobs, 1857.

James, Edwin, ed. *A Narrative of the Captivity and Adventures of John Tanner . . .* 1830. Reprint. Minneapolis: Ross & Haines, 1956.

Jarvenpa, Robert. "Political Entrenchment in an Ojibwa Wild Rice Economy." *Journal of the Minnesota Academy of Science* 37 (1971): 66–71.

——. "The Wild Rice Gatherers of Rice Lake, Minnesota: A Brief Note on Cultural Historical Indicators." *Minnesota Archaeologist* 31 (1971): 71–105.

Jenks, Albert E. "The Wild Rice Gatherers of the Upper Lakes: A Study in American Primitive Economics." In *Nineteenth Annual Report of the Bureau of American Ethnology, 1897–98*, 2:1013–1137. Washington, D.C.: GPO, 1900.

Jenness, Diamond. *The Ojibwa Indians of Parry Island, Their Social and Religious Life.* National Museum of Canada, Bulletin no. 78, Anthropological Series no. 17. Ottawa: J. O. Patenaude, printer, 1935.

Johnson, Frederick. "Notes on the Ojibwa and Potawatomi of the Parry Island Reservation, Ontario." *Indian Notes* (Museum of the American Indian, Heye Foundation) 6 (July 1929): 193–216.

Jones, J. A. "Key to the Annual Reports of the United States Commissioner of Indian Affairs." *Ethnohistory* 11 (1959): 58–64.

Jones, Volney H. "Notes on the Preparation and Uses of Basswood Fiber of the Indians of the Great Lakes Region." *Michigan Academy of Science Papers* 22 (1936): 1–14.

Jones, William, comp. *Ojibway Texts,* ed. Truman Michelson. 2 vols. American Ethnological Society Publications 7. Leyden, Netherlands and New York: E. J. Brill and G. E. Stechert, 1917–19.

Kane, Lucile M., et al., eds. *The Northern Expeditions of Stephen H. Long . . .* St. Paul: Minnesota Historical Society Press, 1978.

Kane, Paul. *Wanderings of an Artist Among the Indians of North America.* Toronto: Radisson Society of Canada, Ltd., 1925.

Keating, William H. *Narrative of an Expedition to the Source of St. Peter's River, Lake Winnepeek, Lake of the Woods, &c . . .* 2 vols. Philadelphia: H. C. Carey & I. Lea, 1824.

Keesing, Felix M. *The Menomini Indians of Wisconsin: A Study of Three Centuries of Cultural Contact and Change.* 1939. Reprint. Madison: University of Wisconsin Press, 1987.

Kegg, Maude. *Gabekanaansing/At the End of the Trail: Memories of Chippewa Childhood in Minnesota,* ed. and transcribed by John D. Nichols. Linguistics Series, Occasional Publications in Anthropology no. 4, University of Northern Colorado. Greeley: Museum of Anthropology, 1978.

——. *Nookomis Gaa-inaajimotawid: What My Grandmother Told Me,* ed. and transcribed by John D. Nichols. Minnesota Archaeological Society, Occasional Publications in Minnesota Anthropology no. 11. St. Paul, 1983.

Kennedy, Cornelia. "Nutritive Properties of Wild Rice (Zizania Aquatica)." *Journal of Agricultural Research* 27 (1924): 219–24.

Kinietz, W. Vernon. *Chippewa Village: The Story of Katikitegon.* Cranbrook Institute of Science Bulletin 25. Bloomfield Hills, Mich., 1947.

——. *The Indians of the Western Great Lakes, 1615–1760.* Museum of Anthropology, University of Michigan, Occasional Contributions no. 10 (1940).

Kinzie, Juliette A. *Wau-Bun, the "Early Day" in the North-West.* New York: Derby & Jackson, 1856.

Kohl, Johann G. *Kitchi-Gami: Life Among The Lake Superior Ojibway.* 1860. Reprint. St. Paul: Minnesota Historical Society Press, Borealis Books, 1985.

Kurath, Gertrude D. "Wild Rice Gatherers of Today: A Sequel Note." *American Anthropologist* 59 (1957): 713.

Laidlaw, George E. "Ojibway Myths and Tales." In *Annual Archaeological Report, Ontario Provincial Museum* (1915): 71–90; (1920): 66–85; (1921–22): 84–99. Toronto, 1915–22.

Lamson-Scribner, F. *American Grasses, 1.* United States Department of Agriculture, Division of Agrostology, Bulletin 7. Rev. ed. Washington, D.C., 1898.

——. *Useful and Ornamental Grasses.* U.S. Department of Agriculture, Division of Agrostology, Bulletin 3. Washington, D.C., 1896.

Landes, Ruth. "The Ojibwa of Canada." In *Cooperation and Competition among Primitive Peoples,* ed. Margaret Mead, 87–126. New York: McGraw-Hill, 1937.

——. *Ojibwa Religion and the Midéwiwin.* Madison: University of Wisconsin Press, 1968.

——. *Ojibwa Sociology.* Columbia University Contributions to Anthropology, 29. New York: Columbia University Press, 1937.

——. *The Ojibwa Woman.* Columbia University Contributions to Anthropology, 31. New York: Columbia University Press, 1938.

——. Review of *Die Reisernte der Ojibwa-Indianer . . .,* by Eva Lips. *American Anthropologist* 59 (1957): 1097–98.

Lapham, Increase A. "The Grasses of Wisconsin, and . . . the Territory of Minnesota, and the Regions about Lake Superior." In *Transactions of the Wisconsin Agricultural Society* 3 (1854): 397–488.

Lathrop, Stanley Edwards. *A Historical Sketch of the "Old Mission", and Its Mission-*

aries to the Ojibway Indians on Madeline Island, Lake Superior, Wisconsin. Ashland, Wis.: S. Lathrop, 1905.

League of Women Voters of Minnesota. *Indians in Minnesota.* St. Paul: The League, 1971.

Lips, Eva. *Die Reisernte der Ojibwa-Indianer: Wirtschaft und Recht eines Erntevolkes.* Berlin: Akademie Verlag, 1956.

——. "Wanderungen und Wirtschaftsformen der Ojibwa-Indianer." *Wissenschaftliche Zeitschrift der Universität Leipzig,* no. 1 (1951).

Lithman, Yngreg. "The Capitalization of a Traditional Pursuit: The Case of Wild Rice in Manitoba." Manitoba University Center for Settlement Studies, Series 5, Occasional Papers, no. 6 (1973).

Lloyd, Trevor. "Wild Rice in Canada." *Canadian Geographical Journal* 19 (November 1939): 288–99.

Long, J[ohn]. *Voyages and Travels of an Indian Interpreter and Trader.* 1791. Reprint. Toronto: Coles Publishing Co., 1974.

Lurie, Nancy Oestreich. "The World's Oldest On-Going Protest Demonstration: North American Indian Drinking Patterns." In *The American Indian: Essays from the Pacific Historical Review,* ed. Norris Hundley, Jr. Santa Barbara, Calif.: Clio Books, 1974.

Lyford, Carrie A. *The Crafts of the Ojibwa (Chippewa).* Indian Handcrafts Series no. 5. [Washington, D.C.]: Office of Indian Affairs, 1943.

McAtee, W. L. "Three Important Wild Duck foods." U.S. Department of Agriculture, Bureau of Biological Survey, Circular no. 81. Washington, D.C.: GPO, 1911.

McElroy, Robert, and Thomas Riggs, eds. *The Unfortified Boundary: A Diary of the First Survey of the Canadian Boundary Line from St. Regis to the Lake of the Woods by Major Joseph Delafield . . .* New York: Privately printed, 1943.

McKenney, Thomas L. *Sketches of a Tour to the Lakes . . .* Baltimore: Fielding Lucas, Jr., 1827.

MacKenzie, Alexander. *Voyages from Montreal, on the River St. Laurence, through the Continent of North America to the Frozen and Pacific Oceans . . .* London: T. Cadell, Jun. and W. Davies, 1801.

McKinsey, S. N. "Chippewa Indians Undertake Cooperation." *Indians at Work,* April 1, 1937, p. 12–13.

Madison, William. *Mah-No-Min (Wild Rice): Ojibway's Native Food Recipes.* Minneapolis: W. Madison, 1940.

Makarius, Laura. "The Crime of Manabozo." *American Anthropologist* 75 (June 1973): 663–75.

Marshall, G. E. "Wild Rice." *American Forests* 34 (1928): 279–80.

Mason, Otis T. *The Origins of Invention: A Study of Industry Among Primitive Peoples.* London: Walter Scott Ltd., 1895.

Mason, Philip P., ed. *Schoolcraft's Expedition to Lake Itasca: The Discovery of the Source of the Mississippi.* (East Lansing: Michigan State University Press, 1958).

Maurizio, Adam. *Die Geschichte unserer Pflanzennahrung von den Urzeiten bis zur Gegenwart.* Berlin: Paul Parey, 1927.

Memorial of the Chippeway, Pottawatomy, and Ottawa Indians, of Walpole Island! Touching Their Claim of the Huron Reserve, Fighting, Bois Blanc, Turkey, and Point au Pelee Islands. To His Excellency the Governor in Council. Sarnia, Ont.: Printed at the "Canadian" Book & Job Office, 1869.

Minnesota. Governor's Interracial Commission. *The Indian in Minnesota.* St. Paul?, 1947.

Minnesota Chippewa Tribe. *Corporate Charter of the Minnesota Chippewa Tribe of the Consolidated Chippewa Agency: Ratified November 13, 1937.* Washington, D.C.: GPO, 1938.

Mittelholtz, Erwin F. *Historical Review of the Red Lake Indian Reservation.* Bemidji, Minn.: General Council of the Red Lake Band of Chippewa Indians and the Beltrami County Historical Society, 1957.

Moodie, D. Wayne. "Historical Geographical Perspectives on the Ojibway Exploitation of Wild Rice." Paper presented at the American Society for Ethnohistory meeting, Oakland, California, November 1987.

Morriseau, Norval. *Legends of My People, the Great Ojibway,* ed. Selwyn Dewdney. Toronto: Ryerson Press, 1965.

Morrison, Eliza. *A Little History of My Forest Life,* ed. Austin J. McLean. La Crosse, Wis.: Sumac Press, 1978.

Morse, Jedidiah. *Report to the Secretary of War of the United States on Indian Affairs* . . . New Haven, Conn.: S. Converse, 1822.

Morse, Richard F. "The Chippewas of Lake Superior." *Third Annual Report and Collections of the State Historical Society of Wisconsin* 3 (1857): 338–69.

Moyle, John B. "Manomin – Minnesota's Native Cereal." *Conservation Volunteer* (January–February 1945): 29–31.

——. "Wild Rice in Minnesota." *Journal of Wildlife Management* 8 (July 1944): 177–84.

——. "Wild Rice – Pioneer Food and Modern Delicacy." *Conservation Volunteer* 19 (January–February 1956): 11–14.

——, and Paul Krueger. *Wild Rice in Minnesota.* Minnesota, Department of Conservation, Division of Game and Fish, Section of Research and Planning, Special Publication no. 18 (1964).

Neill, Edward D. "History of the Ojibways, and Their Connection with Fur Traders, Based upon Official and Other Records." *Collections of the Minnesota Historical Society* 5 (1885): 395–510.

——, ed. "Memoir of the Sioux – A Manuscript in the French Archives . . ." *Macalester College Contributions* 1 (1890): 223–40.

Neville, Ella Hoes, et al. *Historic Green Bay. 1634–1840.* Green Bay, Wis.: The authors, 1893.

Nicollet, Joseph N. *Report Intended to Illustrate a Map of the Hydrographical Basin of the Upper Mississippi River.* Washington, D.C., 1843.

Noble, William C., ed. *An Historical Synthesis of the Manitou Mounds Site on the Rainy River, Ontario.* Vol. 1. *Archaeological and Ethnographic Evidence.* 1984. Manuscript on file, Parks Canada, Ontario regional office.

Nute, Grace Lee, ed. "A Description of Northern Minnesota by a Fur-trader in 1807." *Minnesota History Bulletin* 5 (February 1923): 28–39.

O'Brien, Frank G. *Minnesota Pioneer Sketches: From the Personal Recollections and Observations of a Pioneer Resident.* Minneapolis: H. H. Rowell, 1904.

Oelke, E. A., et al. *Commercial Production of Wild Rice.* University of Minnesota Agricultural Extension Service, Extension Folder 284. St. Paul, 1973.

Overholt, Thomas W., and J. Baird Callicott. *Clothed-in-Fur and Other Tales: An Introduction to an Ojibwa World View.* Lanham, Md.: University Press of America, 1982.

Owen, David D. *Report of a Geological Survey of Wisconsin, Iowa, and Minnesota.* Philadelphia: Lippincott, Grambo & Co., 1852.

Palmer, Edward. "Plants Used by the Indians of the United States." *American Naturalist* 12 (1878): 593–606, 646–55.

Paredes, J. Anthony, ed. *Anishinabe: 6 Studies of Modern Chippewa.* Tallahassee: University Presses of Florida, 1980.

——. "Chippewa Townspeople." In *Anishinabe,* ed. Paredes, 324–96.

Pawlick, Thomas. "Ben & Leo: A Curious Relationship." *Harrowsmith* 3 (1979): 48–50.

——. "Riz Sauvage." *Harrowsmith* 3 (1979): 51–53.

Perrault, Jean Baptiste. "Indian Life in the North-Western Regions of the United States, in 1783." In *Historical and Statistical Information,* ed. Schoolcraft, vol. 3, p. 351–69.

Peterson, A. G., et al. *Insects of Wild Rice in Minnesota.* University of Minnesota Agricultural Experiment Station, Miscellaneous Report 157. St. Paul, 1981.

Pike, Zebulon M. "Pike's Explorations in Minnesota, 1805." *Collections of the Minnesota Historical Society* 1 (1872): 368–416.

"Proceedings of a Council with the Chippewa Indians." *Iowa Journal of History and Politics* 9 (July 1911): 408–37.

Quimby, George I. *Indian Life in the Upper Great Lakes, 1100 B.C. to A.D. 1800.* Chicago: University of Chicago Press, 1968.

Radin, Paul. "Ojibwa and Ottawa puberty dreams." In *Essays in Anthropology Presented to A. L. Kroeber in Celebration of His Sixtieth Birthday, June 11, 1936,* ed. Robert H. Lowie, 233–64. Berkeley: University of California Press, 1936.

——. "Ojibwa Ethnological Chit-Chat." *American Anthropologist* 26 (1924): 491–530.

——. *Some Aspects of Puberty Fasting among the Ojibwa.* Canada, Department of Mines, Geological Survey, Museum Bulletin no. 2, Anthropological Series, no. 2. Ottawa: Government Printing Bureau, 1914.

——. "The Winnebago Tribe." In *Thirty-Seventh Annual Report of the Bureau of American Ethnology, 1915–1916,* 35–560. Washington, D.C.: GPO, 1923.

——, and A. B. Reagan. "Ojibwa Myths and Tales." *Journal of American Folk-Lore* 41 (January–March 1928): 81–146.

Radisson, Pierre Esprit. *Voyages . . . Being an Account of His travels and Ex-*

periences among the North American Indians from 1652 to 1684. Boston: The Prince Society, 1885.

Rajnovich, Grace. "A Study of Possible Prehistoric Wild Rice Gathering on Lake of the Woods, Ontario." *North American Archaeologist* 5 (1984): 197–215.

Ray, Arthur J. *Indians in the Fur Trade: Their Role as Trappers, Hunters, and Middlemen in the Lands Southwest of Hudson Bay, 1660–1870.* Toronto: University of Toronto Press, 1974.

Reagan, Albert B. "The Bois Fort Chippewa." *Wisconsin Archeologist,* New Series 3 (September 1924): 101–32.

——. "Plants Used by the Bois Fort Chippewa (Ojibwa) Indians of Minnesota." *Wisconsin Archeologist,* New Series 7 (July 1928): 230–48.

——. "Rainy Lake Indians." *Wisconsin Archeologist,* New Series 2 (July 1923): 125–50.

——. "Some Chippewa Medicinal Recipes." *American Anthropologist* 23 (1921): 246–49.

——. "Some Notes on the Grand Medicine Society of the Bois Fort Ojibwa." *America* 27 (1933): 502–19.

——. "Wild or Indian rice . . ." *Proceedings of the Indiana Academy of Science* (1919): 241–59, 347–58.

Reed, Robert R. *Wild Rice: America's First Grain.* 1943. Reprint. *Quarterly Bulletin of Winona State College* (August 1962).

Richardson, John. *Arctic Searching Expedition: A Journal of a Boat-Voyage through Rupert's Land and the Arctic Sea, in Search of the Discovery Ships under Command of Sir John Franklin.* Vol. 1. London: Longman, Brown, Green, and Longmans, 1851.

Riley, C. V. "Insects Affecting the Rice Plant." In "Report of the Entomologist," in *Report of the Commissioner of Agriculture for the Years 1881 and 1882,* 127–38. Washington, D.C.: GPO, 1882.

Ritzenthaler, Robert E. *Chippewa Preoccupation with Health: Change in a Traditional Attitude Resulting from Modern Health Problems.* Bulletin of the Public Museum of the City of Milwaukee 19, no. 4 (1953): 175–257.

——. "Southwestern Chippewa." In *Handbook of North American Indians,* ed. William C. Sturtevant, vol. 15, *Northeast,* ed. Bruce G. Trigger, 743–59. Washington, D.C.: Smithsonian Institution, 1978.

Roueché, Berton. "Ricing." *New Yorker,* December 23, 1967, p. 34–38, 40–42.

Russell, Alexander J. *The Red River Country, Hudson's Bay & North-West Territories, Considered in Relation to Canada, with Two Last Reports of S. J. Dawson . . . on the Line of Route between Lake Superior and the Red River Settlement.* Montreal: G. E. Desbarats, 1870.

Sagatoo, Mary A. *Wah Sash Kah Moqua: Or, Thirty-Three Years Among the Indians.* Boston: C. A. White, 1897.

Schoolcraft, Henry R. *Algic researches, Comprising Inquiries Respecting the Mental Characteristics of the North American Indians.* 2 vols. New York: Harper & Brothers, 1839.

—— ed. *Historical and Statistical Information Respecting the History, Condition, and Prospects of the Indian Tribes of the United States.* 6 vols. Philadelphia: Lippincott, Grambo, 1851–57.
——. *Personal Memoir of a Residence of Thirty Years with the Indian Tribes on the American Frontiers* . . . Philadelphia: Lippincott, Grambo & Co., 1851.
——. *Summary Narrative of an Exploratory Expedition to the Sources of the Mississippi River, in 1820* . . . Philadelphia: Lippincott, Grambo & Co., 1855.
Scofield, Carl S. *The Salt Water Limits of Wild Rice.* U.S. Department of Agriculture, Bureau of Plant Industry Bulletin 72, pt. 2. Washington, D.C., 1905.
Seymour, Ephraim S. *Sketches of Minnesota, the New England of the West* . . . New York: Harper, 1850.
Siebert, Frank, Jr. "Resurrecting Virginia Algonquian from the Dead: The Reconstituted and Historical Phonology of Powhatan." In *Studies in Southeastern Indian Languages,* ed. James M. Crawford. Athens: University of Georgia Press, 1975.
Skinner, Alanson. *Material Culture of the Menomini.* Museum of the American Indian, Heye Foundation, Indian Notes and Monographs, Miscellaneous, no. 20 (1921).
——. "Plains Ojibwa Tales." *Journal of American Folk-Lore* 32 (1919): 280–305.
——. Social Life and Ceremonial Bundles of the Menomini Indians. Anthropological Papers of the American Museum of Natural History, vol. 13, pt. 1 (1913): 1–165.
——, and John V. Satterlee. "Mänäbus Visits his Little Brother, Red Squirrel." In *Folklore of the Menomini Indians,* Anthropological Papers of the American Museum of Natural History, vol. 13, pt. 3 (1915): 282–84.
Smith, Charlene L., and Howard J. Vogel. "The Wild Rice Mystique: Resource Management and American Indians' Rights as a Problem of Law and Culture." *William Mitchell Law Review* 10 (1984): 743–804.
Smith, Huron H. *Ethnobotany of the Ojibwe Indians.* Bulletin of the Public Museum of the City of Milwaukee, 4 (May 1932): 327–525.
Smith, Norma. "What Ricing Means to Me." *Wisconsin Trails* 24 (September–October 1983): 25.
Speth, John D., and Katherine A. Spielmann. "Energy Source, Protein Metabolism, and Hunter-Gatherer Subsistence Strategies." *Journal of Anthropological Archaeology* 2 (March 1983): 1–31.
Stanchfield, Daniel. "History of Pioneer Lumbering on the Upper Mississippi and Its Tributaries, with Biographic Sketches." *Collections of the Minnesota Historical Society* 9 (1901): 325–62.
Steeves, Taylor A. "Wild Rice—Indian Food and a Modern Delicacy." *Economic Botany* 6 (1952): 107–42.
Stickney, Gardner P. "Indian Use of Wild Rice." *American Anthropologist* 9 (April 1896): 115–21.
Taube, Edward. "Wild Rice." *Scientific Monthly* 73 (December 1951): 369–75.
Thwaites, Reuben G., ed. "Dickson and Grignon Papers—1812–1815." *Collections of the State Historical Society of Wisconsin* 11 (1888): 271–315.
——, ed. "The Fur-Trade in Wisconsin, 1812–25." *Collections of the State Historical Society of Wisconsin* 20 (1911): 1–395.

——. *Historic Waterways: Six Hundred Miles of Canoeing down the Rock, Fox and Wisconsin Rivers.* Chicago: A. C. McClurg and Co., 1888.

——, ed. *The Jesuit Relations and Allied Documents: Travels and Explorations of the Jesuit Missionaries in New France, 1610–1791.* 73 vols. Cleveland: The Burrows Brothers Co., 1896–1901.

——, ed. "A Wisconsin Fur-Trader's Journal, 1804–05." *Collections of the State Historical Society of Wisconsin* 19 (1910): 163–233.

——, ed. "A Wisconsin Fur-Trader's Journal, 1803–04." *Collections of the State Historical Society of Wisconsin* 20 (1911): 396–471.

Titford, W. J. *Sketches Towards a Hortus Botanicus Americanus* . . . London: Printed for the author by C. Stower, pub. by Sherwood, Neely, and Jones, 1811–12.

Titus, Claude E. "Wild Rice Paddies Aid Waterfowl." *Jim Peterson's Outdoor News* (Golden Valley, Minn.), June 6, 1986, p. 1.

Traill, Catherine Parr. *The Backwoods of Canada: Being Letters from the Wife of an Emigrant Officer.* London: Charles Knight, 1836.

——. *The Canadian Crusoes. A Tale of the Rice Lake Plains,* ed. Agnes Stickland. 2d ed. Boston: Crosby and Nichols, 1862.

Trelease, William. *Preliminary List of Wisconsin Parasitic Fungi.* In Wisconsin Academy of Sciences, Arts and Letters; Transactions 6 (1885): 106–44.

Tyrrell, J. B., ed. *David Thompson's Narrative of His Explorations in Western America 1784*–1812. Toronto: The Champlain Society, 1916.

Umfreville, Edward. *Nipigon to Winnipeg. A Canoe Voyage through Western Ontario by Edward Umfreville in 1784* . . . Ottawa: R. Douglas, 1929.

U.S. Congress. *Message of the President of the United States, Transmitting A Treaty between the United States and Chiefs, Headmen, and Warriors of Red Lake and Pembina Bands of Chippewa Indians, Concluded on the 2nd of October, 1863.* 38th Cong., 1st sess. Executive, P; confidential.

——. *Message of the President of the United States, Transmitting Articles of Agreement Concluded at the City of Washington, the 7th of May, 1864, between William P. Dole, Commissioner of Indian Affairs, and Clark W. Thompson, Superintendent of Indian Affairs for the Northern Superintendency, on the Part of the United States and the Chippewa Chief, Hole-in-the-day, and Mis-qua-dace, of the Mississippi, and Pillager and Lake Winnebagoshish Bands of Chippewa Indians in Minnesota.* 38th Cong., 1st sess. Executive, Y; confidential.

——. House. *Annual Report of the Commissioner of Indian Affairs.* 25th Cong., 3d sess., 1839, H. Doc. 2, Serial 344; 31st Cong., 1st sess., 1849–50, H. Doc. 5, Serial 570; 31st Cong., 2d sess., 1850, H. Doc. 1, Serial 595; 34th Cong., 1st sess., 1855, H. Doc. 1, Serial 840; 38th Cong., 1st sess., 1863, H. Doc. 1, Serial 1182; 41st Cong., 3d sess., 1870, H. Doc. 1, Serial 1449.

——. House. *Chippewa Indians in Minnesota* . . . 51st Cong., 1st sess., 1889–90. H. Ex. Doc. 247. Serial 2747.

——. House. *Petition of the Head Chiefs of the Chippewa Tribe of Indians on Lake Superior.* 30th Cong., 2d sess., 1849. H. Doc. 36. Serial 544.

——. House. *Report of Major [Samuel] Wood.* 31st Cong., 1st sess., 1850. H. Doc. 51. Serial 577.

——. Senate. *Report of the Secretary of War, Communicating The Report of an Exploration of the Territory of Minnesota, by Brevet Captain Pope.* 31st Cong., 1st sess., 1850. S. Ex. Doc. 42. Serial 558.

U.S. Department of Agriculture, Technical Bulletin 634, "Ranges of Zizania aquatica."

U.S. Office of Indian Affairs. *Constitution and Bylaws of the Minnesota Chippewa Tribe Minnesota: Approved July 24, 1936.* Washington, D.C.: GPO, 1936.

Upham, Warren. *Catalogue of the Flora of Minnesota.* In Geological and Natural History Survey of Minnesota, Annual Report of Progress for the Year 1883. Minneapolis, 1884.

Vaughan, Alden T., and Edward W. Clark, eds. *Puritans Among the Indians: Accounts of Captivity and Redemption, 1676–1724.* Cambridge, Mass.: Harvard University Press, 1981.

Vecsey, Christopher. *Traditional Ojibwa Religion and Its Historical Changes.* Memoirs of the American Philosophical Society, vol. 152. Philadelphia: The Society, 1983.

——, and John F. Fisher. "The Ojibwa Creation Myth: An Analysis of its Structure and Content." *Temenos: Studies in Comparative Religion* 20 (1984): 66–100.

Vennum, Thomas, Jr. "The Ojibwa Begging Dance." In *Music and Context: Essays for John M. Ward,* ed. Anne D. Shapiro, 54–78. Cambridge, Mass.: Department of Music, Harvard University, 1985.

——. *The Ojibwa Dance Drum: Its History and Construction.* Smithsonian Folklife Studies 2. Washington, D.C.: Smithsonian Institution Press, 1982.

——. "Ojibwa Origin-Migration Songs of the *mitewiwin.*" *Journal of American Folklore* 91 (July–September 1978): 753–91.

Verwyst, Chrysostom. "Geographical Names in Wisconsin, Minnesota, and Michigan, Having a Chippewa Origin." *Collections of the State Historical Society of Wisconsin* 12 (1892): 390–98.

——. "A Glossary of Chippewa Indian Names of Rivers, Lakes and Villages." *Acta et Dicta* 4 (July 1916): 253–74.

——. "Historic Sites on Chequamegon Bay." *Collections of the State Historical Society of Wisconsin* 13 (1895): 426–40.

——. *Missionary Labors of Fathers Marquette, Menard and Allouez, in the Lake Superior Region.* Milwaukee: Hoffmann Brothers, 1886.

Vizenor, Gerald. *The People Named the Chippewa.* Minneapolis: University of Minnesota Press, 1984.

Wahlberg, Hazel H. *The North Land: A History of Roseau County.* Roseau: Roseau County Historical Society, 1975.

Waisberg, Leo G. "An Ethnographic and Historical Outline of the Rainy River Ojibway." In *Historical Synthesis,* vol. 1, *Archaeological and Ethnographic Evidence,* ed. Noble, 118–326.

——. "Ojibway Commercial Production." In *Historical Synthesis,* ed. Noble, 108–18.

Warren, William W. *History of the Ojibway People.* 1885. Reprint. St. Paul: Minnesota Historical Society Press, Borealis Books, 1984.

Warwick, Suzanne I., and Susan G. Aiken. "Electrophoretic Evidence for the Recognition of Two Species in Annual Wild Rice (*Zizania,* Poaceae)." *Systematic Botany* 11 (July–September 1986): 464–73.

Whittlesey, Charles. "Among the Otchipwees." *Magazine of Western History* 1 (1884/1885): 86–91, 177–92, 335–42.

——. "Recollections of a Tour through Wisconsin in 1832." *First Annual Report and Collections of the State Historical Society of Wisconsin* 1 (1855): 64–85.

Wilkes, Charles. *Narrative of the United States Exploring Expedition. During the Years 1838, 1839, 1840, 1841, 1842.* 5 vols. Philadelphia: Lea and Blanchard, 1845.

Williams, Mentor L., ed. *Narrative Journal of Travels Through the Northwestern Regions of the United States . . . in the Year 1820.* Lansing: Michigan State College Press, 1953.

Wilson, Edward F. *The Ojebway language . . .* Toronto: Printed by Rowsell and Hutchinson for the Society for Promoting Christian Knowledge, 1874.

Wilson, H. Clyde. "A New Interpretation of the Wild Rice District of Wisconsin." *American Anthropologist* 58 (1956): 1059–64.

Winchell, Elizabeth H., and Reynold P. Dahl. *Wild Rice: Production, Prices, and Marketing.* University of Minnesota, Agricultural Experiment Station, Miscellaneous Publication 29. St. Paul, 1984.

Winchell, Newton H. *The Aborigines of Minnesota . . .* St. Paul: Minnesota Historical Society, 1911.

Yarrow, H. C. *Introduction to the Study of Mortuary Customs among the North American Indians.* Bureau of Ethnology, Smithsonian Institution. Washington, D.C.: GPO, 1880.

DISSERTATIONS AND THESES

Borgelt, Kathren J. "Wild Rice in the Cultural Landscape of Nett Lake Indian Reservation." Master's thesis, Mankato State College, 1970.

Rohrl, Vivian J. "The People of Mille Lacs: A Study of Social Organization and Value Orientations." Ph.D. diss., University of Minnesota, 1967.

Van de Vorst, Edward. "The Changing Ecology of Indian Wildrice Use." Master's thesis, University of Manitoba, 1987.

Index

Picture Credits

The following photographs appear through the courtesy of the institutions and individuals listed below. The names of the photographers, when known, are given in parentheses.

Frontispiece (James P. Leary); pages 97 bottom, 121 (Thomas Vennum, Jr.)—Office of Folklife Programs, Smithsonian Institution

Pages 10, 37—Library of Congress, Geography and Map Division

Pages 16 left; 79; 84 top, 85, 106, 111, 147, 190 (Frances Densmore); 92; 94; 98, 173 top, 189 top, 214 (Kenneth M. Wright); 102, 103; 105; 114 bottom, 120, 124, 168, 173 bottom, 189 bottom, 222 bottom, 252 (Monroe Killy); 115, 131 (Gordon R. Sommers); 119; 126; 128; 129 bottom; 135 top; 163, 170 top, 174 top (Carl Gustaf Linde); 167 (A. F. Raymond); 174 bottom; 230, 241 (Bill Burnson)—Minnesota Historical Society

Page 16 right—Minnesota Extension Service, University of Minnesota

Pages 19, 97 top, 114 top (Frances Densmore)—Bureau of American Ethnology, Smithsonian Institution

Pages 21, 135 bottom, 221 (Charles Brill)— © Charles Brill

Pages 84 bottom, 87, 96, 100, 129 top, 172, 196, 220, 222 top (Robert E. Ritzenthaler)—Milwaukee Public Museum

Page 93 (Clifton Adams, © 1937)—National Geographic Society

Pages 101, 112, 159, 176, 192, 195 (David Noble)—David Noble, photographer

Pages 117, 125, 136, 216 (Albert E. Jenks); 142 (Frances Densmore)—National Anthropological Archives, Smithsonian Institution

Page 139—Edward E. Ayer Collection, The Newberry Library

Page 144—Cranbrook Institute of Science

Pages 155 (Gordon R. Sommers), 258—National Archives and Records Administration, Still Pictures Section and Diplomatic Branch, respectively

Page 161—James Mustache, Sr.

Page 170 bottom—Earl Nyholm Collection

Pages 225, 226 (Dave Bonner)—Supply and Services Canada-Photo Center-ASC

Page 238—Office of Horticulture Branch, Smithsonian Institution Libraries

Page 257—Archives Division, State Historical Society of Wisconsin